Not all at sea

Not all at sea
A memoir

Alastair Hannay

'... the nautical phrase "at sea" ... dates from the days of sail when land was in an uncertain position and in danger of becoming lost.'
   Sir William Blackstone's Commentaries on the laws of England, 1768.

Kennedy & Boyd,
an imprint of
Zeticula Ltd,
Unit 13,
196 Rose Street,
Edinburgh,
EH2 4AT,
Scotland.

http://www.kennedyandboyd.co.uk
admin@kennedyandboyd.co.uk

First published in 2020
Copyright © Robert Alastair Hannay 2020
Front Cover photograph © Robert Alastair Hannay 2020
Back Cover photograph © Brit Berggreen 2020

All photographs © by the author except where otherwise noted.

Paperback ISBN 978-1-84921-208-3

Remembering Mariot, Ian, and Jane

Acknowledgements

The co-passengers whose lives have touched mine for varying stretches on the journey, and mine theirs for good or bad, are too many to mention and in some cases even recall.

They include the famous composers for sustaining the inner spirit, but also co-members in its early days of Edinburgh's Climax Jazz Band for tolerating my participation when vital energy was needed.

There are colleagues in the philosophy business whose correspondence sustained an at times flagging enthusiasm for that trade.

They and a host of others, sailing friends, companions, relatives, partners and their families, have made possible the quite long story told here.

In so far as Lady Luck may have a hand in its course, as well as length, she too should be thanked.

More to the present, I am grateful to my publisher for being so bold as to allow the telling.

Contents

Dedication	v
Acknowledgements	vii
Illustrations	xi
Pro-log: 'Down to the seas again'	1
Part One: Fathoming	7
Chapter One: Keel laying	9
Chapter Two: Homeport Carlisle	28
Chapter Three: In irons	48
Chapter Four: Unshackled	64
Chaper Five: Shipshape	95
Chapter Six: Ticketed	114
Chapter Seven: Lightening ship	138
Chapter Eight: Clearing the decks	158
Part Two: Surfacing	163
Chapter Nine: In commission	165
Chapter Ten: Ghosting	190
Chapter Eleven: A good deal	204
Chapter Twelve: On the beach	211
Chapter Thirteen: Long shots	221
Part Three: By and large	231
Chapter Fourteen: Higher latitudes	233
Chapter Fifteen: Top of the tide	246
Chapter Sixteen: Off and on	267
Chapter Seventeen: With the flow	285
Chapter Eighteen: Coming adrift	295
Chapter Nineteen: Taken aback	308
Chapter Twenty: Squared away	321
Chapter Twenty-one: Signing off	335
Epi-log: 'When the long trick's over'	342
Below deck recovery	348
References	351
Father's and Mother's Genealogies	352

Illustrations

My sister Mariot, myself and Nanny, Carlisle, 1933 *Photo source unknown*	10
My parent's wedding at St. Giles Cathedral, Edinburgh, July 26, 1930 *Photo source unknown*	24
Down the Little Minch in a good northerly breeze	122
Gathering heather. A sprig on the bow	123
At Norwegian Maritime Museum, June 1992	291
Building *Amaryllis*, Risør Trebåtbyggeri, 2005. *Photo Ole-Jacob Broch*.	332
Amaryllis's maiden voyage, Risør, July 2005. *Photo Ole-Jacob Broch*	333
La Lydia, since 1967	341
Hvitsten today, our former house now painted white	342
Barrow	348
Hamburg, Jo with his cousin Tessa Wulff Lothian	349
… and with his uncle, Jens Wiebel	349
With Jane, Banchory, 1996 *Photo source unknown*	354
… and with Ian, Gatehouse-of-Fleet, 2011 *Photo Brit Berggreen*	355

Pro-log: 'Down to the seas again'

'to the vagrant gypsy life, to the gull's way and the whale's way where the wind's like a whetted knife ...'

Sea Fever, John Masefield

The forecast for small craft was for waves at most a half-metre high with wind moderate westerly turning northwest then north. It does that when a low pressure to the north passes on its way east. I have to sail the boat back to its lay-up before the days get too short and the weather less benign, so this may be a last opportunity. Up at seven, off at ten past nine with one thermos of pork and beans and another with coffee as well as a bottle of coke and some chocolate and nuts. The port of departure is Sandefjord, once the centre of a whaling industry and ten kilometres up a narrow fjord on the southern coast of Norway just outside the fifty-mile long Oslo Fjord.

I hesitate to hoist the mainsail in case it has to be lowered again, a desperate business in a high wind when sailing alone. I am solo this time because on the last trip from the winter lay-up my crew cracked a vertebra. A diabetic neighbour with sailing experience up to forty years ago offered to help but the responsibility would weigh heavily.

I motored the ten kilometres down the fjord out into the Skagerrak and called home on the mobile to say things looked all right. It was blowing a fresh breeze but the forecast promised it would lighten. Relying on this, and with the gusts up to something more than fresh, I turned southwest on course for the destination seventy kilometres further on. Keeping at first to the jib and a bit of motor, but with the wind proving still too close on the bow for the jib, I decided to furl it until the wind moved further north. The furling went badly, leaving a large balloon of sail at the top flapping and thrashing in the wind. I turned downwind to try to unfurl it under less pressure prior to another attempt and even considered going back. But the thought of having to start all over again the next day put that out of my mind.

Downwind the jib furled nicely. Turning again I set course under motor, past Svenner light on the port side with its archipelago of islands and reefs, and on the starboard just past Larvik, notorious Rakkebåene, an extensive area of just submerged offshore reefs over which, in a wind, large waves crash in a frightening foam. The chart says, in red and in English: 'Dangerous Waves'. Coasters have capsized there, and in a gale, rather than linger, yachtsmen turn for home. Avoiding the area means heading further out to sea; only those familiar with the underwater details dare the inside passage. The new course being further off the wind, I unfurl the jib. Happily the fresh breeze soon turns more north, as predicted, and we are galloping along in fine style straight for Risør.

I look for the next lighthouse, Tvistein, also on its island a kilometre or so offshore, about two hours away. Although some of it is still under the horizon I can just make out its characteristic profile and set course accordingly to a point well off its southeast side, to escape the very visible reefs it is there to warn us off. The seas are jumbled and now well over two metres high but the boat is still in charge and the helmsman hangs on, one hand to the tiller and the other clasping the outside of the cockpit coaming. Two hours later, just off Tvistein light, he tries to phone progress and give a possible time of arrival, the plan being to be met and driven home. But the mobile has succumbed to the spray. A pity, the crew may conclude he has drowned. Besides it was his only means of seeking assistance.

A helicopter in the colours of the air-ambulance service flies by resolutely but indifferently. Would they have noticed this small dot of white sail in the wind-lashed sea? The only other company was a container ship whose stolid indifference to the surrounding commotion was enviable. Up there they were all dry. I was not. My right arm acted as a scoop for the water gushing along the outside of the cockpit coaming, so that in spite of waterproof gear I was soon drenched from the right shoulder down. Apart from full frontal spray there was that wave, familiar to small-boat people, which licks against the hull unexpectedly and sends a bucketful right in the helmsman's face. All in the day's work.

By now I was on the next and worst stage, Langesundbukta, a broad bay, according to Google the most exposed part of the Norwegian coast. In the summer the lifeboat service provides escort for convoys of cabin cruisers heading for the idyllic skerry-protected coastlines to the south. Halfway across this mini-Biscay you are about ten kilometres from any land, and a north-westerly has the space to whip up waves impressive enough to do battle with a constant south-westerly swell from the North Sea. On top of that, or underneath, is a continuous torrent of freshwater debouched into the bay from the navigable river that passes Ibsen's native town, once Norway's most trafficked seaport. Its current meets another that flows constantly, in a southwest direction, at about two nautical miles an hour down the southern coast of Norway, making the southwest swell even steeper than the uneven coastal seabed already manages.

The result today is a surface lacking both pattern and direction, with towering masses of water hitting out in all directions. Now, in the even stronger gusts of an already fresh breeze, usually heralded by a series of even larger waves, the hull drops as into a hole, heeling even further over, straining the drenched helmsman's arm and shoulder muscles still more. About one hour into the bay, ten kilometres from land there is the silhouette of a hill to the left of which is our destination, itself still below the horizon and four hours away. Instead of heading for it, I tighten the jib sheet and head closer to the wind to seek the lee of a long, low island, Jomfruland, the '[is]land of the virgin', allegedly named after a cloister to the Holy Virgin Mary. It is now a popular holiday location with long beaches, a grassy and wooded area founded on rubble left by the ice age. Here, with some respite from the battle, there is a chance at last to pour some coffee more or less into a cup and to eat some chocolate and almonds. The helmsman begins to ponder: why was he here?

I was here in my student days exactly fifty years ago, that time from Edinburgh with four friends for a three-week summer holiday. The boat was quite a lot larger than the one I sailed three days ago to its birthplace. I don't recall the seas in July 1957 making such an impression, but then I was younger and with some recent practice. Now, at seventy-five and after at least four decades of land-lubberly existence, I find the sea a test as well as a source of nostalgia. This was the sixth time I had made this voyage, the second time solo. In spite of moments when, half way over the bay and land appearing to come no nearer while the seas increased, and as doubts as to my fate entertained ashore came vividly to mind, for at least five seconds the chill of fear gripped me, it ended well —- more or less. After Jomfruland the course took me under the lee of the land and more settled conditions. I even got some diesel into the tank (though a lot of it onto my clothes too) just in case we ran out before reaching the tricky entrance to the fjord at the end of which the builder's yard lies.

Arriving there two hours on I found the yard deserted; it was late Saturday afternoon. How to contact headquarters and put its worries to rest? A man hosing down his car apologized for not having a mobile phone, for which I nevertheless felt impelled to congratulate him. Along the quay I found a pair of legs sticking out from under a car repair and asked them if they had a mobile phone A head appeared, a phone was produced and though my land-bound crew had been wondering what hymns should be played at my funeral, all was now well.

The day's maritime adventure brought vividly to mind how my actually being on it was the outcome of many unexpected twists of fate, most of them lucky. Its setting made me think of the way in which any account of why I was there might resemble the details of an unplanned voyage; or rather as here, the unplanned details of a planned voyage. Such, in either of those two ways, is the story of many a life. The typical logbook of a life's voyage would present not one long narrative but very many stories strung together. My less than rash guess is that in our times and culture, and mainly for the better, lives resemble more the vagrant gypsy life of the tramp steamer than the premeditated route of a freight-liner.

My own erratic course in the element of life had now straightened out considerably. I had in a way reached home port, though it was far from where I had set out both geographically and, if one can call it that, vocationally. I first saw the light of day in the south of England and here I am at a latitude roughly that of the Orkneys except I am in Norway. There have been sorties into music, sport, literature, commerce, and, yes, sailing — quite a lot of the latter. There have also been trips abroad, some with definite destinations connected with work, some not, and others 'merely' exploratory, though exploration and looking abroad have somehow been instilled in me from the start. Without having to dig too deep into memory I can count twenty-seven so-called permanent addresses and dozens that were temporary, many of them lost in the confusion of memory.

But here I am, now, literally at sea. Today's short voyage has been something like a microcosm of the longer one. I had named my boat '*Amaryllis*'. Why she should have that name is something I don't remember. Maybe the aggressive but beautiful flower, or was it simply the music of the word, or an echo of a time past studying classics and literature? *Amaryllis*, as I need hardly remind anyone, was the girl of whom Milton spoke as one to whom sporting with her in the shade might be an appreciable way of spending time, better than just watching sheep. Bucolic goings-on in Arcadia were the medium through which Milton's Roman heroes constantly prettified their own personal present. The fact that he was lamenting a friend lost in the Irish Sea is easily missed. But any unseasoned hand that dallies with the waves can end up 'clos'd o're' by the 'remorseless deep'. Perhaps safe enough in the shade of a fjord, but less so on that perennial reminder of life's unpredictability as well as its ups and downs, the open briny.

Actual lives are no more poetic than those transfigured in poems and Arcadian innocence never lingers. More than one friend has accused me of lacking morals and even principles. For my casuistic ways one friend once called me a 'prostitute'. But then he was trying to live a life that he had designed or re-designed by himself. With no course pre-set for my own, I have made my way as the choices and opportunities or challenges to engage in what I might be good at arose. My *Amaryllis*, in design a Nordic Folkboat from 1942, is no aristocrat. Built of wood in 2004-5 with such skill as to earn from neighbours verbal accolades of 'furniture' and 'swan', she nevertheless has the historical aura it takes to make the Miltonian connection. Unlike whatever has borne her skipper through life, this lady is no tramp, although a fond-eyed mariner knowing the ropes might find some humour in priding her with the title of 'hooker'.

But where were we? Yes, calm if not here, at least in my life. Like *Amaryllis* of legend, I had risen not quite to her poetic heights but at least to the surface. I was at one with the waves, occasionally above them and only at bad moments submerged again. Yet surfaces too can be rough. Today's for instance, rough and unpleasant enough to make me shout to everything and with no one to listen: Why in God's name here?

September 2007

Part One: Fathoming

Fathom:
From Middle English fathome, fadome,
from Old English fæþm, fæþme,
Dano-Norwegian favn ('outstretched or encircling arms, embrace, grasp').
Embracing the past can bring light to the present.
Getting to the bottom of things.

Chapter One: Keel laying

Keel laying is one of the four specially-celebrated events in the life of a ship; the others are launching, commissioning, and decommissioning. In earlier times, the event recognized as the keel laying was the initial placement of the central timber making up the backbone of a vessel ...

Wikipedia

Yes, why? After sixty years in Norway I am a pensioner. No longer contributing to the economy, I feel less integrated into its social and cultural life than I once pretended. Less an integrated immigrant, more a disintegrating emigrant. Not that, in general, shelving some Scottishness might not be a good thing. But with me it began too early, in fact even before acquiring some could begin. Born in Plymouth, after some unremembered residence in Edinburgh and baptism in St. Giles Cathedral, I was transported at less than two years old to a town ten miles south of the border. At school there I felt English and thought of fellow pupils from across the border as foreigners. Carlisle was where I began. But then its castle, according to one legend, was the gaol from which after the '45 rising a condemned Jacobite Highlander wrote the lyrics of 'The Bonnie Banks of Loch Lomond'. That is some kind of beginning. There is also consolation in a fact I discovered only lately. Our home on Cavendish Terrace in Carlisle straddled Hadrian's Wall. Most of it lay on the 'barbarian' side but the front door would have opened conveniently onto the Roman Empire.

One and a half thousand years after the Romans had left, that front door was the location of my first still-remembered happening. At the age when experience becomes memory, around two years old in my case, we were living in this large house in Carlisle. Up to then with no remaining memory of it I had been lodged even more grandly in a mansion near Edinburgh. What I still remember is being photographed with my one-year-older sister and a nanny on the steps of a house that the family had recently moved into in an upper-middle-class residential area high on the north side of the meandering river Eden. It was and still is 'Eden Hey', 'hey' meaning 'height' or 'rise'. It has a short 'drive' shaded by a purple beach, the memory of whose rambling branches and deep red leaves also remains, as does on the testimony of a recent photograph the tree itself and the double wooden teak gate, thinly covered now as then in green mould. That drive was the backdrop of my first recollected nightmare. Human figures with long beaks on bird's heads threatened to destroy me in some way not made explicit. It was shortly after the refuse collectors had playfully suggested they dispose of me too.

Beneath that tree's widely spreading branches were two horizons, the furthest formed by the outline of the Lake District hills. The dark profile of Carlisle Castle, home to the Border Regiment framed the nearer horizon with its brooding keep. Bugle calls rang over the river, the most frequent answering to the words 'Come to the cookhouse door boys'. On the left stood the Cathedral, second smallest in England but imposing in silhouette, and behind the castle, visible from all angles, that Carlisle icon the tall and famous Dixon's chimney. They said the rim near the top was wide enough to drive a horse and cart around it, which set me wondering for some years how they got them up there to find out. I was and perhaps still am in some ways fairly naïve.

Somewhere in the industrial area marked by that chimney was my father's office. Below the open terrace, on which our house was one of a distinguished row just out of sight of which lay the Edenside Cricket Ground. Intervening vegetation meant that you had to be there actually to hear 'shot!' and 'well put away, sir!' But the thwack of willow on leather was audible enough and the fielders' concerted 'how'zat!' on a batsman suspected of being 'leg-before-wicket' could still reach our ears.

My sister Mariot, myself and Nanny, Carlisle, 1933

There are many motives for writing memoirs. Last-minute excuses, retrospective discovery, self-wonderment, grabbing a last chance of fame. For fading celebrity, it might be a final puff into the dying embers, or even the chance of a quick valedictory buck or perhaps just a way of still being there. With, in my case, no blaze to rekindle I must look among my antecedents and early life to find anything that might explain what became of me.

As, by any statistical calculation my own life is nearing its end, its essence seems to have been a mixture of happenstance and fate with these merging so frequently that it is hard to determine which is which. Still, I have a strong sense of having been the same all along, not just abstractly as the same peg on which to hang the same name with whatever deeds attach to it, but as having always been the same basic tool kit and set of attitudes. Possibly that is because I haven't come far except perhaps in coping with life's up and downs. The perceptive person with whom I now share my later life says that character-wise I am about thirteen years old. That's fine by me, although I'd like to think of myself as slightly ahead of some of these dedicatedly puerile entertainers playing with automobiles on television.

I confess that I am less than happy with what has become of me. Under the accumulated dust lie many causes for regret and some for remorse. Soon it will be too late for me to retrieve them from oblivion and, for good or ill, put my side of the matter.

Then again, I am not looking for excuses; it is just that having good recall and there being a lot to pluck out of the gathering mist, I feel a need not just to come clean about myself but also to make some sense of it all if only with the aid of creative memory. If I were to be totally honest, a human impossibility, I might have to add that I like writing. Having now late in life run out of topics of the kind my mind seems designed to make some sense of, I need to look elsewhere. But then having a mind like that is also something whose background and origin I would like to look into, not for your sake but mine.

Some years ago, to my bewilderment, I scraped onto a list contrived by the *Daily Telegraph* of the first hundred living geniuses. My position at ninety-one was just ahead of Dolly Parton though quite far behind Osama bin Laden. Astounded at seeing my name there, I searched the Internet for doubles. Finding none with a background in philosophy I reflected on the most obvious explanations: 'joke' or 'mistake'. Alas, on checking the evidence I could only conclude it was I. Even if on the Internet initially under a portrait of Osama himself, I was listed correctly as 'philosopher, British', with a few breaks my working life has been spent entirely in Norway and as for being a philosopher, these days that is either just having a university degree with that name or being some kind of media guru or crank. What seemed doubtful, to say the least, were the credentials of the consultants composing the list and the methods by which they had arrived at this result. Better than anyone, I know I am no genius. If nothing else, the sweat of the brow and the stoop in my shoulders tell as much. Still, however suspect the unexpected accolade, it did set me thinking about thinking, my own included, and what there might be about it that ended in me becoming what the academic trade calls a philosopher. I am certain that is not what I am, at least not in the way of those who are famous for being so; nor is it anything that I ever became but no longer am. I am quite obviously not a crank either, even too obviously. If anything, it is something that became of me, perhaps a kind of personal malfunction, even a disease.

If so, what I am writing here can be treated in the more obvious sense as just another symptom. And the malady's name? It has too many. What of the generic condition? Could it be trying to make more sense than there is to make? As in Tristram Shandy the beginning is not the start. Since parents have quite a lot to do with outcomes, I begin with them and also with their own antecedents and lives, though with Tristram's highways and byways in mind, only in thumbnail.

My parents' marriage was a meeting of cultures. My father was an only child of respected but not affluent academics. My mother was one of a family of six whose wealthy parents treated them as one. Where my father suffered from parental neglect, it may be said that my mother and her siblings suffered the suffocation of too little. For several reasons not wholly clear to me even now but which may become clearer as I go along, I grew up in a space of my own that from an early age gave room for anxiety and scope for solitary reflection. At the age of perhaps seven I recall clearly thinking I might with luck reach seventy-two (just now I am a few days short of eighty-eight). Why seventy-two? The year may have been 1938. My father's mother died that year and she was seventy. To his friends it was obvious the loss was great and his father died two years later at seventy-two. To me that seemed a kind of fixed maximum, two more than the Bible's three score and ten.

My paternal grandfather visited us soon after his wife died. While he watched us being bathed I asked him, with I hope no cheeky motive, since I already knew, if 'Granny' was dead. Perhaps it was to get first-hand confirmation since no one had mentioned it since he came. He looked at me with a sorrow I still remember and said 'Yes'. I also recall thinking that, long before reaching that age myself, I would have to go through the time-consuming process of becoming an adult. This, for some reason, I associated with being thickset, of medium height and given to hearty laughter. Adults also seemed to have either intractably curly hair or else straight with a centre parting, if otherwise little or none. Being myself quite sparely built, I wondered what metamorphoses I would have to endure before becoming like that. The prospect was unattractive.

It never occurred to me that I might follow in the pattern of my father. At over six feet six inches he was as far as you could imagine from the mesomorph model that first came to mind. It could be that to me he was of another world.

One reason for this blindness may have been that my parents were an unobtrusive framework for their children's lives, its implicit point of view, so to speak. Rather than being part of the world itself they were its unseen gods. It was not they but whatever appeared within their frame that gave us our first glimpses of life, the kind that stick in the mind as its lasting stereotypes.

Those existential reflections occurred in the spacious back garden of our upper middle-class home. I recall the setting in detail, a brownish-red but paint-worn pavilion in a corner of a high wall up which grew cultivated plants. The equally secluded garden of a neighbour gave signs of what might happen out there. At the cinema, to which our uniformed nanny frequently took us, and before or after Bugs Bunny, Shirley Temple, or *The Wizard of Oz*, my elder sister and I sat watching Movietone News coverage of marching troops against a background of bombed buildings. When I approached the kitchen staff about these troubling pictures — they being my most accessible informants on world affairs — and wondering if this was going to happen in Carlisle, the answers were veiled enough to arouse further anxiety. Over the wall from the pavilion, our neighbour Mrs Stead was having a shelter built in re-enforced concrete. Soon after, our parents had heavy wooden railway sleepers or cross-ties placed over the low roof of our cloakroom.

It was our mother's family that provided our amenities as well as the more extensive backcloth to our lives. Its lifestyle was the product of two generations of industry and enterprise, a case of rags to riches or in this case riches from rags, the 'rag trade' itself being the source of the family's wealth. That was due first to my great-grandfather's industry, imagination and enterprise, and secondly to the special abilities of his second son, my grandfather, who although leaving school at thirteen became the first recipient of the Faraday Medal and later an honorary LLD and a knighted industrialist. His wife, born Beatrice Emily Fagan of Anglo-Irish landed gentry and daughter and granddaughter of successive Major-Generals in the Indian Army, was a woman of independent mind but not means. She had been among the small group of first-year students at a newly established career-oriented 'House of Education', at Ambleside in the Lake District, an educationally innovative college dedicated to literature and nature. In the latter respect the Lake District formed a setting to which she remained strongly attached throughout her life. On leaving college she had become governess to the family of the headmaster of Uppingham, a prestigious public school, and afterwards a schoolteacher herself at a preparatory school.

An invitation from some progressively minded Scots in the small Ayrshire town of Darvel in the Irvine Valley took my grandmother over the border on something of a missionary journey, inspired, it is said, by a recent unhappy love affair. There she held classes explaining and demonstrating the new educational ideas. My grandfather, the now thirty-one-year old James Morton, second son of the local hero, Alexander Morton (1844-1923), was one of her 'pupils'.

Beyond the age of nine, Alexander Morton, my great-grandfather, had no formal education. After a brief period as a herdsman, his widowed mother introduced him to the weaver's trade and he became a weaver in a district where lace was produced in weavers' homes and their earnings consequently subject to the vagaries of the established centres of Lancashire and Nottingham. To allow them to sell their products at fixed prices and thus stabilize their economies, Alexander founded Alexander Morton & Co., which once established increased its range, producing chenille, woollen fabrics and also carpeting. Not long after, another operation was added across the border in Carlisle. With a high-minded desire to ease a desperate unemployment situation, though coupled to a promise of local subsidies and perhaps cheap labour, Alexander later moved on to Ireland, establishing yet another industrial setting, this time in Donegal and focused solely on carpet-weaving. That too prospered. A previously cultivated interest in hackney horses, which by the time he had moved to Ireland had made him already a much-sought-after breeder with customers in the USA and Canada, and also an international horse-show judge, no doubt helped the marketing. Having handed over his business to his second son James, Alexander Morton spent the last twenty years of his life in Donegal farming and raising horses. Back in Darvel on the roadside beside the grounds of the large villa that he and his family once occupied, his life is commemorated to this day by a monument designed by the acclaimed architect Robert Lorimer and 'erected by public subscription' to the man 'who led this valley to industrial fame and prosperity'.

In the town-centre itself there is a monument to another and more widely known Alexander, surnamed Fleming, the discoverer in 1928 of penicillin. Few knowing his achievement could name his native town, while to textile retailers this small country town in the back of beyond, little more than a village, was known already in the 1880s, and by 1898 its wares were available in all of Europe as well as North America. Alexander Morton's Donegal carpets, made also in Carlisle, were sold in 1906 to the tune of 30,000 square yards a year. Some found their way to Buckingham Palace and Windsor Castle, others to maharajas.

Forging these connections was the work of my grandfather. On his father's death, James inherited a firm with over two thousand employees and a world-wide reputation extending from Irvine Valley lace to woven cloth, tapestries, and prints, as well as carpets. In 1914 most of what had been Alexander Morton & Co. became Morton Sundour Fabrics Ltd.

To the results of his father's creative energies, and supported now by his intellectually progressive wife, James brought not only an artistic sensibility to his business sense but also creative scientific instincts. Early on, while passing the display in Liberty's windows on London's Regent Street, he had noted that his own handiwork had been rendered virtually unrecognizable by exposure to the sun. He set up a subsidiary to supervise research into fast dyestuffs, the brand name 'Sundour' signalling a resolve to produce textiles resistant to sunlight. Under his supervision a body of chemists and chemical engineers drawn from many universities discovered the industrially important Caledon dyes, and in 1919 James Morton founded Scottish Dyes at Grangemouth, which in 1928 was acquired by Imperial Chemicals Incorporated, onto to whose board James was co-opted. It was in July 1930 that in recognition of these achievements he received the Faraday Medal.

As an eager disciple of William Morris's back-to-roots activist Arts & Crafts movement, James also gave practical support to its campaign to raise craft to the status of art, thus encouraging the democratizing of art itself. Not at all a matter of blinkered nostalgia, this was the gateway to new beginnings. Sundour Fabrics along with its avant-garde subsidiary Edinburgh Weavers would in the years to come be renowned for its transfers to furnishings of designs by members of the Arts & Crafts movement as well as many of the most eminent modern artists. The director of Edinburgh Weavers, my uncle and James Morton's elder son Alastair, head of Edinburgh Weavers, himself an innovative craftsman of the loom, became a significant and respected abstract artist. Under his direction Edinburgh Weavers was launched as a high-profile Modernist design company, its brand identity kept distinct from that of the more traditional 'MSF'.

It goes without saying that my mother with her three sisters and two brothers grew up in circumstances quite unlike those of the people upon whose labour and enterprise their wealth depended. Living in large houses within spacious grounds, they received what were then considered the best of educations in schools chosen for their progressive educational ideas. But rather than becoming unlicensed spendthrifts in the time-honoured manner of children of the nouveaux riches, they appear to have formed a culturally and even somewhat self-consciously morally superior community apart. Brought up on principles of thrift and decorum, they appear never to have sought or begged for opportunities to venture out into the wild and wicked world.

A need to cultivate a protective belt against that world can be traced back to the venturesome but moral Alexander. A man of abstemious habits, he was, besides being a teetotaller, a social ascetic. Customers in the hackney trade who had travelled from Canada or the USA to strike deals with him were reputedly disconcerted at not being offered the conventional welcoming cup. As for my grandparents, they never touched a drop, nor was consumption, conspicuous or otherwise, their style. My mother later told me that she and her sisters were constantly begged by the firm's accountant to spend more money. As for the large houses, these 'homes' too were factored into the cause of arts and crafts. Rented or leased rather than bought, in order to ensure the mobility required for new developments in the business, they were filled with specially commissioned furniture and paintings. In that mansion where I spent my first year, Craigiehall at Dalmeny near Edinburgh, leased by James Morton from 1926 to 1935 from Lord Rosebery, my mother's parents also provided accommodation as well as cash support for artists and composers.

There was something of enlightened humanism in all this and little trace of dour Scottish Presbyterianism. In fact, rather than being a legacy of its small-town origins, the family's morality had in almost mafia-fashion an inner organization based on itself. No doubt Alexander's public-spirited energies had owed more than a little to a prevailing work ethic, but even he was no prude. Like that of his son, his own correspondence, although betraying a settled belief in the existence of Providence, indicates that deeds rather than devotion were what counted. Alexander's wife, Jeanie Wiseman, was from all accounts of Jewish origin and the fact that their son James was not a church-goer may have had something to do with my grandmother's investigative open-mindedness in these matters. As early as October 1899 James had noted a theosophical title, *The Way the Truth the Life*, lent to him by Beatrice 'for perusal'. Its author, John Hamlin Dewey, a doctor of medicine, spoke for an occult reading of the New Testament. My grandmother's own leanings later strayed in an easterly direction. At her funeral service in 1958, officiated over by her friend the Bishop of Carlisle, the latter apologized in case some of what he was about to say was inconsistent with her disbeliefs.

In a setting so conspicuously high-minded and progressive, it must have been hard for my mother's generation to make any personal mark. What could they offer to the world? Brought up to be good but with no clear direction in which to exercise their goodness, they were easy prey to a quick moral fix from the 'right' quarter. It came in the large and amiable shape of Loudon Hamilton. A young ex-army officer and survivor of the trenches, he was a leader of the newly established Oxford Group Movement, later named Moral Rearmament and now calling itself Initiatives for Change. It was in Loudon Hamilton's student rooms in Oxford that the movement began and he remained its second-in-command for life. The Group's message spread through the family like wildfire and extended even to my grandmother. As for her offspring, to the tinder of a philanthropic urge unclear in what direction to go, the Group brought the spark necessary to ignite the flame. To that fire was added the messianic message of its founder, the American evangelist Frank Buchman: in joining the movement they would be preventing the downfall of civilization, its descending trajectory owing to communism, the cynical hedonism of the Jazz-age, and not least homosexuality, but also plain moral sloth. As for the capitalism that kept Buchman's ship afloat, the latter's pronouncement that God is a millionaire would offer the best of reasons for believing that wealth is no obstacle to being good. But to James Morton, whose own mission had been clear to him practically from birth, the Oxford Group was a 'salvation army for the rich'. When in June 1930 a Group 'house-party' in Oxford kept four of his children away from St. Andrews on the occasion of his receiving (along with John Masefield and Dean Inge) an honorary doctorate (LLD), James, accustomed by his Scottish background to a sense of family solidarity, felt deserted by his own.

Among those attending the house-party was my mother's identical twin sister Beatrice (Bea) later to marry Loudon Hamilton. Helen, my mother, having found a way out of the Morton mafia in the shape of a tall young naval officer had not been at the party. Just a month later she married Lieutenant Commander Robert Stewart Erskine Hannay at St. Giles Cathedral in Edinburgh. The captain and officers of HMS *Renown* provided a naval guard of honour. There was a lavish reception at Craigiehall with a send-off by the Dalmeny Pipers.

My parent's families had become acquainted in Edinburgh. At their first encounter my father was seventeen and my mother ten. Whatever contact they kept if any in the meantime, it was in the late 1920s that they met again as adults in London. Bea and Helen were at the time student nurses at the Truby King Mothercraft Hospital in Highgate (Cromwell House, now the Ghanaian Embassy). Although the choice of vocation may not speak highly for her parents' conception of how she might best have developed her talents, it was the latest evidence of their assiduous devotion to providing what they saw as the best for their children. (Sir) Frederic Truby King, a New Zealander with Edinburgh degrees in medicine and public health, is mainly remembered as the Dr Spock of his time, and for his role in the 'mothercraft' and child-care movements that gained wide support among women's organizations. There was, in a way, something progressive in having a rich young girl learn to take care of babies including her own, but I am almost certain that had she been given the chance to test herself in a less confined environment, with her independent mind my mother would have been better prepared to follow her own children down their own chosen paths. As I see it, she was corralled into a family setting isolated from its own time and ill prepared for ours. Both her brothers went 'up' to universities but with no thought of this being offered to the girls. As if nothing more was to be added, for my mother and her twin their preparation for life ended at a 'finishing' school in Lausanne. The two elder sisters were sent on improving travels abroad.

Prior to that, all six children had been pupils at the co-educational St. George's School at Harpenden. Designed to foster community on a Christian basis, this school emphasized a sense of family togetherness. But the cult of exclusivity already implicit in this family was exaggerated by the fact that, in spite of their age differences, the Morton siblings sat together at meals and ate a special diet. My mother remarked on this as being a matter of acute embarrassment, and the idea of a family within the family does indeed seem less than consistent with the Christian ideal of a universal fellowship. However, the education provided was of a high standard and the school produced an impressively inclusive array of alumni. Recalling her school-mates, my mother asked me later if I'd heard of a clever ex-pupil called Michael Oakeshott, and when the name of Kenneth Horne came up on the BBC ('Much Binding in the Marsh'), she could well remember the comedian as among her fellow pupils.

Our father's origins were quite different. Where our mother's grandfather was wed at nineteen in a marriage producing seven children, while his son James, waiting until he was thirty-four, became father of six, my own father was an only child. Nor were his parents at all equipped or concerned to nurture a family. Intellectuals with strong Church backgrounds, their focus on good works was outside the home. My father's mother, born Jane Ewing Wilson, was the daughter of the Rev. James Stewart Wilson, DD, minister of the parish of New Abbey in Dumfriesshire. Through generations of United Church ministers her own mother, born Jane Ewing Brown, was a direct descendant of the Rev. John Brown of Haddington, another notable Scot who refused to let the absence of a formal education stand in the way of ambition. A shepherd boy at twelve, his later mastery (after Christian conversion) not only of Latin but also of Greek and Hebrew, were such as to expose him to charges of having consorted with the devil. However, a reputation as minister, theologian and author won the day and 'John Brown of Haddington' received lasting fame for *The Dictionary of the Bible*, from 1769, but also and especially for his commentary from 1778 on the Old and New Testaments, *The Self-Interpreting Bible*. The latter is still to be found in Antiquarian bookshops and even, as I lately discovered, on the internet. This self-educating John Brown, the son of a self-educated weaver and river-fisherman later became a professor of the Church Synod.

His descendants had more conventional educations. Not uncommonly among the Scottish clergy at the time, my paternal grandmother's family had a German governess take care of their children's schooling. Jane, my grandmother, was the family's second daughter and as an eager letter-writer she was described in a letter to her mother from the latter's half-brother as 'that most epistolary Jane'. The uncle was Dr John Brown, physician, noted literary figure and accomplished letter-writer himself who kept up a correspondence with his many friends, these including Gladstone, Thackeray, Ruskin and S. L. Clemens (Mark Twain). Jane went to Girton College, Cambridge, passing the Classical Tripos in 1889 and later travelled with a sketchbook in the North of England and Germany. She taught Classics and German and became House Mistress at St. Leonard's School for Girls in St. Andrews and later a Governor of the school.

It was at St. Andrews that she met Robert Kerr Hannay, then lecturer in Classics and Ancient History at University College in Dundee, later to become a part of St. Andrews University. In 1901, a year after my father was born in Newport, Fife, at the southern end of the Tay Bridge, my grandfather became Lecturer in Ancient History and Archaeology at St. Andrews. I remember him as an imposing but kindly man with a keen sense of humour tending to the boyish. Staying with my grandparents when I was five or six, I recall him detaining me at the door of the dining room to show me how to fill a salad leaf with sugar and wrap it into a parcel to pop into your mouth. 'Don't tell Grannie', he said. A Memoir prefacing a collection of letters that he had researched and published after his death, tells of someone who enjoyed company especially when at its centre. A personal memory, quoted there, speaks of 'the time of the 1905-06 election', when he was 'persuaded to join a group of four University teachers at St. Andrews to go "crusading on behalf of Free Trade among the fishermen and farmers of East Fife and St. Andrews Burghs" '. Some of these, it is said 'to the delight of their students did not show to advantage in the rough and tumble of heckling and impromptu debate.' But Hannay was different and '[r]equests for his services came from neighbouring constituencies'. Someone hearing him preside at a Liberal rally in East Perthshire records an evening 'memorable and exhilarating in the highest degree'.

> He first gave a rattling party-speech with all the arguments for Free Trade —
> we thought it had come to stay! — tellingly put, which the old Liberal stalwarts

of that hard-headed and argumentative community, born hecklers every man of them, snuffed up with infinite relish. These points he illustrated and reinforced with one or two exceedingly funny and unhackneyed stories, which bowled everybody over, and were, no doubt, retailed next day at the factory to those who had not the good fortune to be present. Then he sang—accompanying himself, as he always did, with consummate artistry—one or two songs which his audience all knew by heart, but had never heard rendered in such a fashion before. Finally, in response to insistent demands for an encore, he gave that *tour de force* of his, "The Eelephant," and then the meeting—nine-tenths Liberal and the minority Tory, dispersed in the gayest of humours, leaving a committee overflowing with delight and gratitude to the "Purfessor," as they insisted on dubbing him, long before he won that title.'[1]

On my future grandfather's appointment in 1911 to the Curatorship of the Historical Department at HM Register House, the family moved to Edinburgh, where in 1919 he became Fraser Professor of Scottish History and Palaeography at the University and was later appointed Historiographer Royal for Scotland.

The move suited my grandmother, it being reported in *The Scotsman* on her death in 1938 to have offered 'wide scope for her activities'. These were social. Mrs Hannay was instrumental in the introduction in Scotland of 'Women's Patrols', a first step towards introducing women police which began in measures taken to deal with social and personal problems connected with prostitution. She was an official of the National Council of Women and served on several Trade Boards as well as being a Justice of the Peace. In 1933, for her work on the Scottish Savings Committee, and with a reputation as a gifted public speaker on its behalf, she was awarded a CBE. A member of the Church of Scotland, she also attended its General Assembly, using her gifts as a speaker to address it from the floor. She is described as 'a remarkably gifted woman with abilities far beyond the common' and for whose 'judgment and scholarship, and gifts as an administrator and speaker' her husband had 'the most profound admiration and respect'. I remember her as a kindly figure with a readily smiling face.

As for her husband, many of whose days were to be spent in the still, dry atmosphere of the Register House, just off the East end of Princes Street, the move may in one way have been confining. A man of much physical energy, able to stimulate his surroundings outside university circles, now gave himself to the task of patiently bringing a vast resource of hitherto unexplored documents to the attention of academic historians. It was a calendaring and indexing task that he considered vital for a sober account of Scotland's development, one that didn't fall foul of the sentimentalists or 'greetin' patriots'. A similar attitude lay behind his view that fine writing had no place in the presentation of the nation's history. One colleague was surprised at how someone with a 'Herodotean relish for a racy anecdote' could 'write in such a desiccated style', but then thought that this and Hannay's suspicion of colourful language and fine writing were a deliberate antidote to an early collaborator John Herkless's penchant for eloquence. Prior to Hannay's move to Edinburgh, that pair had assembled and edited several volumes of *The Archbishops of St. Andrews*. The style adopted there by my grandfather reads as though his English had been translated from Latin of which he was a master. But recently, through the internet, I bought a used copy of my grandfather's *The Early History of the Scottish Signet*, signed by him in 1936. Here there is a clarity and economy that today one seeks in vain in much academic writing and can give aesthetic pleasure even to someone little interested in the privy seal and the use of sealed writs from the twelfth century.

According to his students no inspiring teacher, 'R. K.'s gifts as accomplished raconteur and singer were shared with students invited to his home. Earlier an active sportsman he remained a keen golfer, a recreation he handed on to my father. His own mother was the daughter of a minister of the United Presbyterian Church and although reported to be of 'deeply pious and even puritanical and prudish leanings', and with 'more than a tinge of anxious melancholy', she was also 'blessed with a deeply innate sense of humour'. She seemed to have passed it on to her son and he to my father. I recall as a seven-year-old some surprise and embarrassment when both of these large gentlemen, one on either side of me, tumbled from their seats with laughter at a pantomime at the King's Theatre in Edinburgh, an entertainment designed primarily for children. On his more serious side, and in the family tradition, my grandfather was an Elder of St. Giles Cathedral as well as organist there and choirmaster in the University Chapel.

His grandfather had been an iron-master with interests in Barrow-on-Furness, once a small fishing village but due to its convenient location the later centre for smelting and the export of steel for the growing ship-building industry on the Clyde. Once the Barrow Shipbuilding Company had been taken over by the acquisitive Vickers, Sons and Co., it became known as 'The Naval Construction Yard'. My great-great-grandfather lived in nearby Ulverston, a market town with several famous sons to come, including Stan Laurel of Laurel and Hardy. Vicarious fame came to a local daughter as the mother of the rock pioneer Bill Haley. Back in the mid-eighties a financial crash deprived my great-great-grandfather, also Robert Kerr Hannay, of a considerable fortune of which he is reported to have been locally generous. It is said that enforced poverty hastened his end. He died in 1874.

His second son, Thomas, who inherited the family estate of Rusko in Galloway, built with the profits from slave-grown sugar in the West Indies, found it necessary to sell the property to pay off several debts. When he married some years later there was little to spend on the educations of his seven children. The eldest, my grandfather, born in 1867, was sent to live with his aunts in Alloa. He attended Albany Academy and later studied classics first at Glasgow University and then University College, Oxford. His second sister, Mary Baird Hannay, the oldest sister having married and thus forfeited her chance of an education, attended the University of Glasgow to become one of the first women physicians to graduate there. While the married sister left for India, lacking funds for their further education the remaining male members moved to California. One, after an unsuccessful attempt to grow oranges at Riverside, settled in La Jolla and began another farm close to the fledgling Scripps Oceanographic Institute, while his wife built an inn on the shore. The farm has been replaced by a magnificent aquarium while the Spindrift inn, often rebuilt after winter storms, survives today as a de-luxe weather-resistant Marine Room of the same name. Another brother became secretary of the Los Angeles tennis club, while the youngest living brother, a mining engineer, became a lay preacher in the mining community in Northern California. He died comparatively young of a tropical fever soon after arriving in West Africa as a missionary. A still younger brother died at the age of four.

As a family we knew little of these relatives. Apart from visiting the retired Dr Mary Baird Hannay in Honiton, Devon, just before D-Day, the street lined with relaxing GIs who stood up in series to salute my father then in uniform (who, as we passed, said to me and my sister, 'they don't have to do that'), they remained unknown. For reasons still unclear they were not spoken of either. The simple but unpalatable truth may be that their becoming American citizens placed them in the position of deserters from the family or even from the national cause. In later years, while teaching at the University of California in San Diego, a development of the Scripps Institute and also at La Jolla, I was able to get in touch with the family that had settled there, these apparently the only recoverable vestiges. That I suspected their existence was due to a receipt my mother had made of wedding gifts with 'La Jolla' noted in the margin.

Born in 1900, my father was baptized Robert Stewart Erskine. The latter name, by which he was known, was the surname of two eighteenth-century ministers responsible for the secession that led in the mid-eighteenth century to Scotland's United Free Church. That church's early traditions had deep inroads in both sides of my father's family. Among the inheritance is a miniportrait of Ralph Erskine bizarrely enclosing locks of his eighteenth-century hair. 'Stewart' is derived from my father's maternal grandfather, the Rev. James Stewart Wilson. 'Robert' is a traditional Hannay prefix, my own included.

Although my father's genealogical coordinates were nominally fixed for him from infancy, as an only child with parents devoted to the betterment of others he had to find his own ways of filling time. Lacking access to the topics that bound his parents together Erskine ('Eckety') sought his own friends and hobbies.

I found he had written 'Nil desperandum' over a rather cool assessment on a preserved school reports — perhaps it was a wry dig at his classically minded parents. As a riposte to their habit of speaking German when they didn't want him to overhear, he and his friends invented a code that rendered their own conversation unintelligible to the parents. We were given its key and could use it ourselves. In spite of being inventive in the areas of his own interests, my father did poorly at school in subjects where his parents excelled and perhaps believed they expected him to do likewise. Their home was on Inverleith Terrace, not far from the Edinburgh Academy, and he could tell me how good it was to hear the bell sounding while he lay in bed with some usual ailment. Much later he found a taste and talent for mathematics and engineering. It became his mantra and thematic advice for everyone that they be allowed to find and develop what they are good at.

Summer vacations were with school friends whose parents owned a large house at Glenuig, a small village on the west coast, west of Fort William.. There he met other guests, including Janet Grierson, one of the four daughters of his father' s colleague Sir Herbert Grierson, Chair of English Literature. The intrepid twelve-year-old Janet (later Teissier du Cros), failing to catch the eye of another guest, recalls asking my father to teach her how to acquire abilities that would attract the opposite sex, such as bowling overarm, throwing from the shoulder, catching balls thrown straight at one, and 'above all' appearing fearless in the face of 'whatever challenge'. Seventeen at the time, my father had 'the glamour about him of being on the point of joining the navy'. [2] He had then chosen the sea as his career, while as hers Janet found the piano and became a pupil of Sir Donald Tovey.

It was only after trying first and unsuccessfully to follow the example of a neighbour and senior school colleague, Kenneth McLean that my father tried the Navy. McLean had joined the Royal Engineers and would rise to the rank of Lieutenant General. My father failed the army entrance examination but succeeded in enlisting in the Royal Navy as a cadet with engineering in sight. At the time his experience of the sea had been limited to a canoe. He and his school friends had made their own and due to its instability named it 'The Bloody Mackenzie', a Lord Advocate infamous for his persecution of the Covenanters during the reign of Charles II.

Erskine was to spend sixteen years in the service as an engineer and by the age of thirty, at the time of his marriage, was chief engineer on board the battle cruiser HMS *Repulse*. Of his naval career I have found only scattered details, although he could show us films of early attempts to land planes on HMS *Furious*, a cruiser converted to an aircraft carrier. Recently I read his name as winner in 1922 of the Royal Malta Golf Club Challenge Cup. By then, at twenty-two, he had risen from Midshipman to Sub-Lieutenant with HMS *Iron Duke*, flagship of the Home Fleet during World War I, at that time serving the same role in the Mediterranean. He was on-board during the ship's support of the White Russians in the Black Sea during the Russian Civil War. When, now in Edinburgh in the 'fifties he recognized the Royal Field Ambulance Ship *Maine*, docked at Granton Harbour, he recalled swimming parties diving from her decks in the Grand Harbour at Malta. By the time of my mother's training in London he was lecturing in engineer-related mathematics to officers at the Royal Naval College in Greenwich. After serving for three years on HMS *Renown* then part of the Atlantic Fleet, knowing he would otherwise have to spend much of his life in foreign stations, and with a growing distaste for the social side of a serving officer's life, he resigned his commission and joined his father-in-law's textile concern. This he did in spite of selection for a two-year course in advanced engineering at the Royal Naval College at Greenwich with promise of rapid promotion.

My parent's wedding at St. Giles Cathedral, Edinburgh, July 26, 1930, with officers of HMS *Renown forming a sabre arch.*

It is clear that, acquired as they were from long training and experience, my father's perspective and strengths differed sharply from my mother's. Accompanied nearly always by her twin sister, Helen had been under permanent family protection, while Erskine found his feet entirely outside family life. Those same feet that kept him balanced on swaying decks and down in the engine room were firmly on the ground. He knew the ropes and also his way among people. He was fond of women, apparently more widely so than his mother thought appropriate. According to my mother, when she and my father's mother met, the latter expressed relief as well as delight at the forthcoming marriage: it would 'save Erskine from the gutter'. Whatever unworldly fears lay behind that remark, they convey something of the atmosphere in his home or perhaps lack of it. Erskine's mother was no doubt relieved that her wayward son, for whom she must once have held hopes for a future with one of Professor Grierson's lively daughters, was now about to be taken into the embrace of a family as well-ordered and high-minded as anyone could wish.

Yet there was something not quite right about the atmosphere within a family on whom the more immediate effects of the Oxford Group had been considerable and proved lasting. While studying at Oxford, my mother's younger brother Jocelyn, about to be my father's business partner and later boss, suffered a nervous breakdown that propelled him into an unassailable and lifelong faith in God and the Church. On an autumn cruise as a guest onboard HMS *Renown* after my parents' marriage, he had tried to involve my father in the Group. Jocelyn's elder brother Alastair, who suffered severely from rheumatic fever and was, like my mother, more independent in spirit, although first smitten was able to keep the Group at arm's length by declaring a commitment to the Quakers.

The two brothers were diametrical opposites, the one a creative artist, the other almost a control freak. Alastair would become a leading figure in modernist textile and interior design, as well as a noted abstract artist now represented in many collections. He had studied mathematics at Edinburgh but decided to lend his creative abilities to the family firm, bringing about the visionary fabrics produced by Edinburgh Weavers in the pre- and early post World War II years. Unafraid of spending his inheritance on visual luxury, in 1938 he had a house built near Carlisle, designed by the later 'Sir' Leslie Martin, the architect later responsible for the Royal Festival Hall, and Sady Speight (Lady Martin). A description in the *Daily Telegraph* from 2002 headed 'Masterpiece or Monstrosity' opts for the former describing it as an early example of function determining form. I remember visiting the new-built house on the crest of a hill with a view to the Lake District hills when I was aged six. I must have marvelled openly at the abstract paintings since on waking one morning I found a colour sketch of a man playing golf pinned over the example on my bedroom wall. I appreciated my uncle's concern but perhaps didn't then see the humour so clearly. After the war, in another but old house near the Solway, my uncle bought a herd of Belted Galloway cows so that his eyes could rest on them from his studio window. Jocelyn, on the other hand, remained ever the obedient nose-to-the-grindstone son, his life spent in thrifty and dutiful though finally vain custodianship of his father's achievement.

The sisters, of whom less was expected in these terms, found their own solutions. The eldest in the family, Guenevere, in wiser times quite possibly an effective business leader, devoted her life to the Group and settled in Rhodesia, keeping open house to its members. Jean, moved to New Zealand with her Welsh husband and in between fostering three daughters wrote uplifting novels under the name Jean O. Hill. As already noted, my mother's twin sister Bea was to marry Loudon Hamilton.

My father had in many ways more in common with his new father-in-law than with his new brothers and sisters-in-law. Both their educations came in practice, took time and came late. They shared an early enthusiasm for the Scottish fiddle and my father had been able to regale his fellow officers and crew with the bagpipes. True enough, my mother's generation was musically accomplished; it included an excellent violinist (Guenevere), a near professional cellist (Jean), and a flautist (Jocelyn). All were adept pianists. I clearly (and audibly) remember Uncle Jocelyn's incessant 'Jesu, Joy of Man's Desiring' during the early war years when for a while we lived with our grandparents. A fainter memory is of Uncle Jocelyn with his flute in the orchestra pit at the pantomime. I think it was 'Jack and the Beanstalk' or it could have been 'Aladdin' or 'Dick Whittington and his Cat'. The truly artistic instincts and attendant individualism of Uncle Alastair set him apart, so much so that an infringement of family ethics would lead to his excommunication.

Deprived in childhood of a real home, our father admitted a deep dependence on his new one. He once said to us that he would be quite lost should our mother die before him. As for the home that was ours, he seems to have thought that being numerous (four children all born before the outbreak of World War Two) we would escape the loneliness that marked his own childhood. He had a natural authority, and both his enthusiasm and openness made for a strong but always friendly presence. From his Navy upbringing in Devon he had acquired the local habit of addressing people, but not indiscriminately, as 'M'dear'. He could share our humour at his own expense and enjoyed as much as we did the Popeye and Mutt and Jeff films he hired for our entertainment. When Kodak went into colour he shot films of us playing.

To balance Carlisle's infamously wet weather we were exposed to a sun-ray lamp, whose warmth over a naked body brought early intimations of corporeal pleasures that no one spoke of. Alarmed by the tendency of my penis to stiffen when bathing and fearing the same might happen to other body parts, I asked my mother, now putting her training to use in the bathroom, whether this was normal. She said she knew it happened and I shouldn't worry.

Our father formed a bulwark behind which our mother protected herself and her children from the encroachments of her omnipresent relatives; so much so that to his disappointment she showed no interest in his work on behalf of the family business. It was only half-jokingly that he remarked how nice it would have been on coming home in the evening to be asked what happened at the office. Consequently, we too knew nothing of what went on there, though occasionally small devices that were parts of inventions he was developing for the firm were brought home (for instance teaspoons that melted in tea!). I recall a Sunday visit to a new packing shed where we took rides on the conveyor belt. It was as though our father simply had some job in the town while our mother, the cook, a maid and a gardener managed the home. We were left on our own but in the charge of yet another minion, Nurse Chalmers, known to us as 'green' nanny due to her uniform. When not 'helping' Chandler, we dug endlessly in a sandpit that I still recall being concreted. When one-year older sister Mariot began nursery school I went with my mother on her rounds in the role expected of the wife in a well-to-do family, selling flags for the Royal Life Boat Institution to those whose houses looked quite a lot more modestly financed than our own.

Chapter Two: Homeport Carlisle

Home port: the port where the company's head office was situated.

Realizing that our parents' unobtrusiveness had something to do with a deliberate hands-off policy took time. It was only when life had already begun to present its account that my father once remarked to me that this liberal attitude to upbringing might make it look as if we were being let off lightly, but we would pay for it later. In the style of pre-war, well-off middle-class families there was little scope in any case for close family involvement. Having a trained nanny as well as a cook, a maid and a gardener, these were the daily contacts and sources of news or gossip, as well as my own models for real people. With his well-developed sense of right and wrong our gardener, Tommy Chandler, provided what my parents seem deliberately to have left to chance. For us, his word was gospel: not only could he do no wrong, there was nothing he could not do. On my sister waking to find the garden covered in snow one morning, she saw this as further proof of Chandler's omnipotence. 'Clever Chandler', she said, although not yet mastering the word's phonetics, 'clever' came nearer to 'cuvvy'. Later, Tommy fixed our bicycles and in the garden sheds we met his friends. We visited his home and his wife Grace, where he kept canaries and we listened to his advice. Our devoted nanny on the other hand, an intruder in the family rather than part of it, or perhaps a poor substitute for a parent, was held in less esteem. Her attempts to induce polite table manners encouraged a lasting tendency to obstinacy and cheekiness.

In the course of twelve years there were three nannies. Their first names were never known to us or, if known, used. They were Nanny Hale, Nanny Chalmers, Nanny Marriott. Since 'Green Nanny', as we called the second of these because of her uniform, was there all the time while our parents led their own lives except for Sunday tours in my father's latest car or to watch him playing golf, we inevitably grew attached to her. There were daily afternoon walks through Carlisle's Bitt's Park, below the Castle, with Ian, my three-year-younger brother, in a pram, to watch the non-stop Glasgow to London *Coronation Scot* thunder by. This latest in streamlined steam-driven trains, custom white strips down its whole length, had been inaugurated with the coronation of George VI in 1937 and it ran every day until the war. Probably this daily experience was at my request, fraught as it was with confused images of rushing power and of places in either direction where things really happened. The closed level-crossing gates were a kind of allegiance to this fleeting symbol of urgency and strength. I was given a book written by its most famous driver and, like many young boys at the time, thought of the glamour of becoming an 'engine driver'. The walk also took us conveniently past a tobacconist where our nanny bought her daily packet of Gold Flake. On the way home one day we passed a man lying on the pavement with something glutinous exuding from his mouth and a woman bending over him. I was shocked at such disharmony, but our nanny could tell us it was something called epilepsy. That 'shit happens' came to us rather late. It was the off-putting sight, rather than the sad reality, that first made an impact.

Although seemingly ever-present, our nanny must have had a regular holiday; perhaps it was when we had ours. In the pre-war autumns our parents left us, with the nanny, for a week of golf at Dornoch. Three July months were spent *en famille* in a rented house, 'Langhills West', at Gullane, our father visiting at weekends, as at times did his grieving father from nearby Edinburgh and occasionally an old school friend Charlie Mackintosh and his wife Marion. On the long sloping garden, my father and his school friend tested a model plane we had built, and we also flew it on one of the nearby hills. Looking down on to the main road below on arrival we would look out for the firm's lorry bringing our belongings in a large hamper. There was a beach hut whose warm damp air I can still smell, the irritating sand on the floor, and the reed-like grass that stuck into our feet or between our toes as we made our way to the beach. We spent days building sandcastles or paddling and searching for small crabs in the rock pools, though never, so far as I recall, swimming. Compared to Carlisle's constant clouds, these sunny days were for me memorable. We had a radio and music was in the air. 'Don't Fence Me In', 'Down Mexico Way', 'Roll Out the Barrel.' The air was filled with small yellow real planes on training flights from nearby Drem aerodrome.

When the declaration of war came, typically it was in the Carlisle kitchen that we listened to Prime Minister Neville Chamberlain's announcement just as it was in the nursery that two years earlier we had listened to King Edward VIII declaring that he was unable to reign without the support of the woman he loved. I was then in bed with pneumonia and with long spells of bronchial problems I became a regular listener to Children's Hour and, when war broke out, the 'Garrison Theatre' with Jack Warner.

In the summer just prior to the declaration, we holidayed at North Berwick, a little further east from Gullane and opposite the Bass Rock. I recall little of that holiday except for a climb to the top of Berwick Law, and a close-hand view of the famous whale's jawbones at its summit, and long walks on the beach alone, about which more later. That autumn we gave refuge in Carlisle to David Robson, the son of a family my own had met on the beach at Troon, when my father had begun working for his father-in-law and was stationed temporarily at Darvel. Chandler drove David and me daily to the nursery school at Wetheral, some ten miles out of town. The middle of the road being marked in the usual way with white strips, continuous on corners and staccato in straights, David and I sat watching out of the back window and chorusing 'drip, drop, drip drop, big monster, big monster ...'. For some reason I can still remember it with a smile. David shared my bedroom for the few months he was with us and we got along well before he returned to Glasgow when regarded as safe from bombing. The last I heard of David was that he had emigrated to Canada. I have often wondered why I have more successfully found friends outside the family. It may have something to do with that 'enlightened' hands-off approach to upbringing, leaving us to our own separate devices.

A policy of encouraging us to go our own ways may have defeated the purpose of providing a home of the kind he felt that he himself had never enjoyed. An each-for-his-or-her-own policy meant that the places our parents provided for a home seldom served as such. Their faith in the boarding school system and disruption due to war put paid to that plan in any case. Both of these magnified the volatilizing effect of their liberal attitude to upbringing. Beyond our nanny's remonstrations and the gardener's homespun wisdom, there was little guidance to be had or walls to bang your head against and few models to follow in life's detail. Arrival at boarding school was a rude awakening. It was apparently meant to be so.

Mariot and I went to separate nursery schools from the start. After finishing hers ahead of me, she was packed off to Calder's Girls School at Seascale on the Cumbrian coast, now a hotel but described in a historical note as having been patronized by the day's well-to-do. She later graduated seamlessly to another boarding school, St. Leonard's, the school for young ladies at St. Andrews where our grandmother had been house-mistress. A consequence was that we hardly met until she left school, while even then her interests in animals kept her apart from her boat-preoccupied brothers. With co-education a rarity, such infra-generational separation was natural at the time, as was the thought that boarding schools were better for personal development than attendance at day schools. As a result, we grew up as virtual strangers unable to share experiences between ourselves let alone with our parents. An extreme symptom of this dislocation, concealed under a cloak of easy familiarity and shared jokes, occurred much later when, as part of her own education at agricultural college, Mariot spent a summer as assistant to a sheep farmer. One day she returned to find the farmer, a woman, had hanged herself. The only intimation I ever received of this was as a confidence at a later date from my mother, who perhaps thought I then had the psychological stomach to digest it. Between the rest of us it was never mentioned let alone discussed. I suppose we all, similarly, kept our deeper secrets from each other.

Boarding schools flourished under the notion that its supposed community life, its cultivation of the sporting spirit and leadership offered a fast lane to maturity and to the mix of responsible attitudes needed to keep the nation rolling. The founding headmaster of the 'preparatory' school for which I was destined had said its aim was to 'lay foundations from which boys should develop into citizens of the world with a natural desire to take an intelligent and active interest in human welfare'.

What alternative could a good-hearted parent with the means propose? Many were prepared to sacrifice their own living standards to be able to send their children to 'public school'. A golfing companion of my father chose a settled job as a bank clerk to be able to send his three sons to St. Bees, a public school on the Cumbrian coast. The Scotter family of two parents and four children lived in a modest terrace house on the main road through Stanwix, just opposite the stationer where I bought my weekly *Beano*. One son, enlisting in the ranks of the Scots Guards, a Lance-Corporal in 1942, became C-in-C of the British Army of the Rhine. Knighted, he died at sixty-nine just prior to assuming the post of Deputy Supreme Commander of Allied Forces in Europe. I recall him vividly on two occasions, both in the presence of my father and regarding women. There was mention of an attractive young lady just down the road, of whom more later. The other, in Edinburgh before a Calcutta Cup Rugby match, involved a brief discussion of the merits of Indian brides. Bill had served with the Gurkha Rifles; although conceding their beauty he regretted its transience. I didn't mention these occasions to his widow when, very many years later, she attended my uncle Jocelyn's funeral.

My mother's faith in the public school was brought in upon me by her oft-repeated respect for its exemplary products. The many tales of woe that have been told, the miseries and suicides, most of them no doubt still untold, have left high-minded notions of it if not in tatters, at least up for major revision, as also the belief that a British public-school education qualifies for an active interest in the nation's welfare or, now incredibly, world citizenship.

The views, now rife, that these schools are parking areas for parents who want to live their lives undisturbed by their progeny, or perhaps to conceal marital disharmony, or else heighten their children's prospects in prestigious positions, may be exaggerated but have no doubt always held some truth. I have no reason to suppose that any of these latter suspicions apply in our case. I feel sure my parents would have sent us to boarding school with the best of motives even if the war had not made it their only rational expedient. At that time, for me too, there was simply no inkling of an alternative; it was how things were. Nor, indeed, was there any alternative, not at least in England. In Scotland a tradition of day schools that were also 'public' in the paradoxical sense that they were private, was the order of the day. But I knew nothing of that. We were ten miles south of the border.

As it turned out, except for the occasional item of knowledge that my mind seemed to have a special place for, I found it hard to take in what teachers taught us. My mind was a reservoir of impressions and recent memories; it wandered and dwelt on something that had been said, losing track of what came later. If I could fill it with anything, it had to appeal to my own imagination. My first steps as an autodidact took the form of avidly reading the children's comics that had begun publication in the late 'thirties: *Beano*, I've mentioned, but also the *Dandy*, *Knockout*, and *Radio Fun*. Every week I followed the exploits of Judy Garland and Mickey Rooney, Deed a Day Danny, Oor Wullie, Lord Snooty and the Gasworks Gang, Keyhole Kate, Billy Bunter, Desperate Dan, Pansy Potter (the Strong Man's Daughter), Sexton Blake, Joe E. Brown, Abbott and Costello, and Tommy Trinder. The shadow of war produced a new series: Musso the Wop. I also read *The Boys' Own Paper* though with no recollection now of its contents; it was no doubt more serious and with fewer cartoons. Our parents had provided books, these including Arthur Mee's ten-volume *Children's Encyclopædia* and the *Geographical Magazine*, which had begun as a huge success in 1935. Both could feed the imagination and inspire thoughts of elsewhere, while the World-War-I-traumatized A. A. Milne's therapeutic narrowing of the world to exploits by the lovable occupants of the Hundred Acre Wood kept us entertainingly at home with Christopher Robin, an accessible role model for those being taught to fix the world's problems. There were also outside intimations of elsewhere. Those days just prior to war were filled with the droning of yellow-painted De Havilland Tiger Moths doing circuits and bumps at nearby Kingstown, an RAF station until 1996 but now a business and retail park. Watching them from the back garden I became fascinated by flying. At an air display we were allowed to climb into the pilot's seat of the centrepiece, a De Havilland Dragon Rapide that flew a regular route to the Isle of Man. I collected copies of *Flight Magazine*, or was it *Aeroplane*? The exciting smell of the newly printed pages is still with me and my dismay was great when they were removed and burned while I underwent a bout of chicken pox. It felt as if a life had been taken away, but the fascination with aircraft never disappeared. The first German bombing raid of the war was directed at naval vessels anchored off the naval base at Rosyth, just east of the Forth Bridge. That was on 19 October 1939. I had just had my tonsils removed at a private nursing home in Edinburgh and the sirens sent us down into the basement. The experience rubber-stamped an impression of Edinburgh as a place of excitement and danger. On an earlier visit, perhaps for prior consultation, I had stayed with my grandparents at 5 Royal Terrace. The early morning sound of trams hurtling up and down London Road as I lay in bed remains with me to this day, as does the memory of a roller-skating ruffian who swept daringly past us around the corner of Leith Walk while I accompanied my grandmother on a shopping tour. To one brought up on protective bourgeois comforts that both denied and probably feared the triumphant freedom of sweeping defiantly and serenely among staid shoppers, it was a complex experience.

The war years put those comforts behind us. For my younger sister Jane, born less than a year before war broke out, there would be no period of stability of the kind we others enjoyed in those safe years at Eden Hey, and once war broke out she would be a victim of the disruptions that followed. Until then Jane was in the kindly care of a trained infant nurse from Edinburgh, Nurse Conley, who three years earlier had also attended the birth of my brother. When the official envelope calling my father back into service was read to us at breakfast, she broke into tears. It was the first time I had seen a weeping adult and the novelty shook me. At the time I thought it must be at the thought of disruption due to my father being called up. In our smaller than Hundred Acre Wood world we were all that mattered. That she might have her own personal fears didn't occur to me. Soon after, we heard that our home was to be requisitioned by the army. My father, promoted to Commander, went south to a job at the Admiralty while the rest of us, along with our 'green' nanny and now without the kindly Nurse Conley, were housed along with three sets of cousins in my grandparents' latest rented accommodation. This was Dalston Hall, part of it the restored remains of a medieval castle just outside Carlisle. From there I started at preparatory school as a day boy, setting out early down the long driveway to the bus stop to be picked up in town along with several other day boys in an ancient car driven by a Mr. French for delivery on time at school.

Anxiety at beginning school knew no bounds. The world beyond the garden gates was full of strangers; the idea of having to consort with boys I had never met struck terror into me. I was also consumed by the intimidating thought that they would all know far more than I did. Spending our first war-time summer holiday in North Berwick, I would whenever possible slip out of the house to walk up and down the shore rehearsing the multiplication tables up to twelve.

I assumed that if I didn't I would be the only pupil unable to recite them. There was no thought of being superior, simply of not being the odd one out. On arriving at the bus station to board Mr. French's car on the first day of school I found that things were of course not as bad as I'd feared. Soon I suspected that I was the only one able to multiply up to twelve time twelve by rote. Perhaps I had acquired a sense of superiority; things can tend to go from one extreme to the other. But if so, it was a fragile sense that would have to remain private, since it would cut no ice with my fellow pupils. On the other hand, it would give my life at school something that held it together in the form of a constant challenge to prove, at least to myself, that I had something going for me.

Moving into her parents' home was for my mother a return into captivity. The housekeeping was no longer in her hands and in our father's absence the large family from which her marriage had been an escape was breathing down her neck once more. Although curtailment of the infant nurse's appointment left her with more to attend to, with my elder sister at boarding school and me at school all day her sole responsibility was to my brother and infant sister, both still under the care of our permanent nanny. There was little else for my mother to do but help in the large garden, which except with my occasional assistance, she did alone. When helping her I could witness her irritation and when the shears broke hear her for the first time swear. Unused to my parents showing any sign of anger, or any indication that the framework provided for our lives was not iron-cast, this upset me. A further glimpse of my fragility or their fatigue came a year or two later when on school vacation in far off Buckinghamshire, where they now lived. My father, who commuted to the Admiralty, came home one day and, out of character, unexpectedly complained about the dinner, saying he'd have to find somewhere else if it didn't improve. So foreign was this to everything I was led to expect that I openly wept at the table, whereupon my father remarked to my mother that this was something of a kind I didn't like.

That was not so surprising. Thirty-three of the year's fifty-two weeks were spent four hundred miles away in an environment that offered few comforts and no escape. After counting the days at school until I could return home, then to feel that my mental refuge should be falling apart was the last thing I could endure. What our parents failed to realize was that by offering us no glimpses of the conflicts that must have been there, if only expressions of their tiredness and even at times despair, they were offering a false picture of what homes are made of. In a family better able to express its tantrums and used to its tiffs and general bickering, blended with humour such momentary episodes would have passed off as a piece of normal everyday drama, the kind of thing now fed to us on popular television as the meaning of everyday life. In a home where there was no such drama, except for the occasional childish outburst of anger and contrariness on our part, mainly mine, and where humour was sanitized in the form of private jokes, such moments assumed apocalyptic proportions. If only I had been able to say, 'There you go again!'

At times I wonder whether this *laissez-faire* thing was due partly to my parents wanting to spend more time recapturing together what the workload of everyday life had taken from them. When my father was settled in London and my mother had finally moved south to join him, she later said it was a time she especially enjoyed. With an apartment in Kensington Square they must have relived some of the closeness of their meeting in London and first years together. The joy was short-lived. Up north my grandmother sacked our nanny for some misdemeanour undisclosed even to our parents, and five-year-old Ian and two-year old Jane had to go south too. A house with a garden and trees ('Tall Timbers') was rented in Stoke Poges, just a short walk from the churchyard of Thomas Gray's 'Elegy' and, on his commute to the Admiralty, my father cycled the three miles or so to Slough station, later by motorcycle. Up north, all the cousins who had been lodged with my grandparents had disappeared over the Atlantic for the duration and others left to New Zealand forever.

How, you might ask, can a regime designed to make useful citizens help pupils to forge their own futures? Traditionally, for all the talk of cultivating responsibility, the tendency in a public school has been to produce conformity and even uniformity. My own experience was confined to a preparatory school, the purpose of which was to prepare the ground for budding citizenship and world membership. Most of my fellows bore clear marks of the social niches to which their parents belonged. A varied bunch, there were sons of shopkeepers, merchants, farmers, general practitioners, two had an army general as their father and there were two refugees, from France and Belgium. Having acquired no sense of a niche of my own I didn't really know where I belonged. These boys were all in their different ways mannered as I was not. They were almost young men no doubt aping their fathers while the only language I knew was a shared family argot that was childish in the extreme. I was glaringly naïve in my speech and behaviour, a social dunce without a vestige of a code of behaviour, in fact an unwitting social savage.

Our headmaster must already have suspected as much. Before enrolling in the school, I was taken by my parents to visit him and his wife at their home for approval. He shared at that time the headship with a stay-in colleague and lived not far from our own home. While they were speaking of my future, my eye caught an ashtray surrounded by an attractively realistic motor tyre, Dunlop or was it Goodyear? It was in any case irresistible. I took it out of the room and placed it on the side-table in the hall to pick up on departure. My doing the latter was naturally remarked, and with surprisingly little said I was made to hand it back.

With the trauma of actually beginning school, to which I was nevertheless admitted, I had forgotten the whole episode. But several things suggest that the headmaster had not. One day when discussing politics he mentioned that my parents were 'liberals'. He was strongly conservative and although I can't imagine them having discussed politics, I can well imagine that a *laissez-faire* explanation of my bad behaviour on that inauspicious occasion was subsequently offered afterwards perhaps on the telephone. Secondly, much in the headmaster's subsequent attitude to me can be read as directed at someone suspected of moral fragility. One episode stands out. The head found out that a group of pupils were playing at experimental sex in the wooded area of the school grounds. He called us all in and asked those responsible to raise their hands, which after some hesitation they duly did. But he said there was still one who hadn't owned up, and looking I believed firmly in my direction, he said he hoped that person would one day learn to be honest, admit to his sins and mend his ways. Having had nothing to do with these shenanigans but not being directly accused, I couldn't defend myself either. I never ascended to the rank of 'house leader', though on returning briefly to the school to say farewell after a year of absence due to illness, I was assured by Mr Richardson ('Ritchie' to us) in the presence of my mother that I would have been elevated had I stayed on.

Having a good ear, I had little difficulty affecting the various social accents of my schoolfellows. Defence mechanisms sharpened my awareness of where I was about to put a foot wrong so that for the most part I managed to conceal my naïveté under cover of an imitative smartness, something I seem to have been born with. But it kept me in a constant state of alert. Most of my spare time was spent either watching my step or wisecracking on cue — bad habits that may have lingered, I was, after all, practising them for five of life's most formative years. I notice even now that when I have to speak and not having anything immediately to say to the issue, I hear myself speaking in quotes simply to fill a silence, in which I always feel awkward. I am indeed over-conscious of the actual words of my utterances even when sincere, and easily lose track of the conversation itself. It generates a kind of autism in which what I say loses touch with the thread of a conversation and can therefore appear abrupt and even impolite, sometimes being misinterpreted as deep irony, although in certain circles that can be quite convenient. I have even been accused in some of my more naïve utterances of triple bluff. But it can go the other way too, complying too readily with what others are saying. It is a habit now well recognized among children who are able with the help of lively imaginations to conjure up rumours of, for instance, widespread paedophilia. I remember at about the age of six a plain-clothes police officer arriving at our door to investigate a burglary in a neighbour's house. I was there when my mother opened the door and, since I sometimes played out on the road, the officer asked me if I'd seen anything suspicious, at the same time imitating someone loitering hands in pocket in a typically suspicious manner. I hadn't seen anything like that, but the idea seemed a good one and I felt an instinctive desire to help, which usually means saying yes. I said yes but don't think for a second he believed me. But this habit too, as I have discovered, can linger on well beyond childhood. It is an admirable defence mechanism for those stuck with a belief that what they would normally say, and with truth in mind, is so extraordinarily dull as not to capture interest or to book a place in a current conversation. And it is of course a habit that professional writers carry on into their work, if that isn't also where it tends to carry them. Only journalists, historians, and biographers — especially auto-biographers be it noted — do so at a real risk to their integrity.

There may be something of the Asperger's disorder syndrome in this, the distance that makes social behaviour a problem and compensates by hyper-focusing on interests over which one can gain total and independent control. It is said that boys and girls differ in their Aspergerian strategies: the latter learn to observe people from a distance, aiming to appease, to imitate them, while boys simply grow frustrated and explode. I see myself as being forced through terror to adopt the girl's way out, part of which is also to live in a world of fiction, whether in books or soap operas or vicariously following the lives of celebrities. In this light, Asperger's may seem more like the tendency of our age than the comparatively rare condition it was only recently thought to be. Could its diagnosis perhaps reveal something of the fragile structure of human existence itself?

However little or much my prep school experience may support this hypothesis, the features attributed to the syndrome certainly provide a frame into which much of it can be fitted. The behaviour as well as speech I picked up at school was a script that I internalized not by making it my own, meeting it as it were with my person, but as the means for warding off attack and thus leaving the actual position of the constant defender dangerously vacant. Typically, the Asperger begins with the latter and develops the asocial or falsely appeasing behaviour patterns afterwards; here it was the behaviour that disclosed the space this side of it, waiting for some private mission or, if you like, saving obsession to fill its emptiness. But who knows how much of what is diagnosed as Asperger may not have its origin in this reversal? At my school the compensatory space-filling could be done in two ways, the first in sport, still in some ways a form of defensive appeasement, especially since to begin with I was so bad at it, but later as an opportune and acceptable outlet for the explosive energy and aggression said to be the way in which the male Aspergian typically manifests himself in society.

The other way was that of the supposedly typical female response, an escape into imitation, pretence or fantasy. A great and for me saving virtue of the school was a library well stocked with adventure tales. On winter evenings I would rush to grab an armchair by the glowing library fire and devour Percy F. Westerman, Captain Marryat, G. A. Henty, Henry Rider Haggard, and Edgar Rice-Burroughs. These authors, unlike both Richmal Crompton and even W. E. Johns whose stories seemed then too close to normal life to lift me out of the world, offered pure escape to a reader able and disposed to be absorbed. Their worlds were quite remote from the one I was in and, in retrospect, I realize quite different from my first immersion in children's literature. While I was still enjoying the comfort of my grandparents' large house outside Carlisle I would wake well before breakfast to read Arthur Ransome, whose books were to me totally enthralling though in quite another way. They were about a family whose adventures were their own way of bringing imagination and fantasy into otherwise normal holidays. Instead of an escape from by own life they offered it enlargements and I remember the excitement when it finally dawned on me that events in Ransome's stories were set in the very Lake District whose hills I could see as I walked to the bus. I could also learn practicalities from these books, which could hardly be said of the exotic tales of Tarzan, King Solomon's Mines or the more realistic but hardly captivating Just William, Mister Midshipman Easy or Biggles. The practical pay-off of my Arthur Ransome reading came with my first sailing experience, when I found that I knew already how to hoist a sail, trim it and keep from capsizing.

Rickerby House School lay a short distance from the River Eden, which yearly flooded the outer perimeter of the school grounds. The property itself provided scope for a variety of activities including sports, hut-building and even gardening. Recently I read from the 1873 Cumberland Post Office Directory that our school had been built on what had once housed the Reformatory for Juvenile Criminals, opened by the owner of Rickerby House 'for the reception of boys of the criminal class in October, 1854'. In our day Rickerby House was the school building itself. It is interesting that the high walls enclosing the large garden in which we played cricket were designed to keep members of the 'criminal class' inside, and that the building on one side of it, from whose windows we tore bits of valuable lead tracery to weight arrows for bows fashioned from branches in the surrounding woods, included workshops where class members up to forty in numbers were 'daily instructed' and 'taught some useful trade, as that of a tailor, carpenter, or agriculturalist'.

Others look back at their school days as a period of horror. To do so in my case would be to dramatize the past. I cannot say I was unhappy at school. The probable truth is that I refused to be so because the result would have been too disastrous. I can see in retrospect that I did in fact suffer, for instance from the cold. In the winter I frequently sneaked up to the bathroom and filled a basin with hot water to warm my hands and wrists. And I was beaten at least once by the headmaster for disorderly conduct, having been the last to escape back to my bed when he interrupted a pillow fight ('Come to my room after breakfast'). There was some compensation in being able to tell my mates that the rod had snapped with the tip hitting one of the room's large windows. I was also set upon one morning by a group of older pupils who, under the leadership of one who later spent a spell behind bars, picked out juniors who were to be given a 'scare'. Somehow, even though there was plenty to complain about, I kept in good heart. I may have wept at this treatment by my fellows, but it was more from surprise and much to his surprise when I struck back at the ringleader. It was supposed to be just a lark, but what prevented me from treating it as such was the constant tension and also the wishful thought that these were my friends. As I have said, I am quite naïve or perhaps wishfully over trustful. At the same time there was an unquestioning belief that life's trials were part of life itself and to be endured. The school was a mini-Sparta where we were to be hardened for further trials ahead. At a deeper level there was, again, the hidden thought that once you begin looking life's miseries in the eye, the whole world collapses. Where else is there to go? Who to complain to? Your fellow-pupils will punish you if you tell on them. Complaints to the headmaster, when relayed to the parents, will either reach them encoded as reports of bad behaviour or, if serious enough, lead to removal and the need to start over again somewhere else. Complaining to parents was impossible anyway since, under the pretence of checking our spelling, the headmaster censored our letters home.

The truth, however, is that the image of home itself grew dim. Parents became a remote almost otherworldly ideal of temporary release and rest. Contact was lost but, if lucky, new compensatory relationships were formed at school. I was lucky. The second head, a recent arrival ignorant of my early misdemeanour, treated me with kindness as well as firmness, as indeed he treated us all. He and the head were polar opposites. The latter, I would guess a historian, was keen on cricket and knew a lot about the empire. It was no doubt he who had stocked the library with books of ennobling adventure at the expense of the Zulus and Matabele. Apsley Cherry-Garrard, a member of Scott's last expedition and author of *The Worst Journey in the World*, was invited to speak to us of heroism and endurance. Cherry-Garrard had been in the group that found the tent where Scott and his remaining companions had died. We were told of the scoundrelly Roald Amundsen but there was no mention of the heroic Fridtjof Nansen. News of brave deeds by our fighting forces was continuously fed to us; famous last words were written on the blackboard, including Nurse Edith Cavell's 'Patriotism is not enough' before a German firing-squad in World War I, and Commodore Warburton-Lee's 'Well done Number One Gun!' pronounced when mortally wounded on HMS *Hardy* at Narvik in April 1940. Inspired by this when we were made to give fifteen-minute talks on chosen topics, I picked on the World War I Battle of Jutland. I had an illustrated book on that epic from my father from which it was impossible to see the outcome as other than a decisive victory, which it was not. The latest Victoria Cross awards were relayed to us, and on hearing that Field Marshall Montgomery took his troops out for a morning run before breakfast, even though he had lost a lung from tuberculosis, Maurice Richardson decided we could do the same.

As for cricket, then the quintessentially English sport and a preparation for life itself, word reached our head that the Lancashire and England 'fast-medium' bowler and now Sergeant Dick Pollard was stationed at a nearby army camp. He was invited over to bowl at us, an alarming experience although I imagine the famous cricketer didn't let fly at his medium-fastest. Richardson himself was no mean bowler and we players became quite competitive. I enjoyed cricket: focusing attention on a small ball liable to hit either you or the stumps puts everything else out of your mind. We tended our bats with linseed oil and were proud of them when the pale blades turned darker with seasoning. My bat had the signature of the famous Walter Hammond inscribed on it, and great was the occasion when we were allowed to attend a match at Edenside with Hammond himself playing along with West Indian celebrities who included Manny Martindale and Learie (later Lord) Constantine. I got Martindale to sign my autograph book.

The head's colleague was a quite different character. He gave no thoughts to empire and I never saw him lift a cricket bat, though he did play soccer with us. He taught us English and staged plays attended by local parents, in two of which I was given roles. One of these was the one-act 'Campbell of Kilmhor'. I was the redcoat Captain Sandeman chasing a renegade Scot after the '45 rising. My still remembered opening lines were 'Open, in the King's name' followed by 'Ha, the bird has flown'. I didn't realize that, on uttering the latter, the three-cornered cardboard brim of my headgear had touched the doorpost and fallen off. Nor was I particularly put out by being cast as part of a brutal clearing-up operation. This head teacher also wrote a long poem in Scots dialect in my autograph book called 'Alasdair MacAlasdair'. He had the popular task of buying playthings for us with money our parents had deposited with him for that purpose, in my case thirty shillings a term. I collected model warships. He would tell us stories before 'lights out'. I remember especially the many instalments of *The Prisoner of Zenda*, *The Lost World* and *The Count of Monte Cristo*. When I was leaving and he heard that I was to begin Greek at my next school, he gave me his own Ritchie and Moore Practical Greek Method for Beginners from 1908. I have it still. It contains his first attempts to transcribe his own name in Greek together with those of his own one-time classmates, to which I then added mine. Norman Hammand is a man I remember with respect and affection.

Five years are a long time in the life of a child turning teenager. This school experience coincided almost exactly with that of the European war. It was a time of excitement as well as anxiety. At night we heard German bombers on the way to Clydeside. Some of us rigged up crystal radio receivers, very simple devices also known as cat's whisker radios that need no battery and with a crystalline mineral doing the work of a diode. The energy source is its antenna, for which we used our bedsprings. Listening was of course 'illegal' in the sense that we were supposed to be sleeping. But there was a sense of wonder that voices and music could be conjured out of such a simple assembly of things so readily at hand. In a way it epitomizes a benefit of being part of a school community, where the pool of interests is so much wider than at home and imaginative possibilities for experimentation thus multiplied.

To combine the two, school and home, can be hazardous. For a while my brother Ian was transplanted from Stoke Poges to join me. For him the move proved disastrous. In the complicated and pitiless hierarchy that comes so naturally to schoolchildren, the three-year age gap meant we were more apart than at home. During holidays the greater distance may also have continued at home; these were after all only brief episodes in a life mainly spent outside the family. Nor, due to undetected dyslexia, did Ian thrive when both he and my six-year-younger sister Jane later attended the Steiner School in Edinburgh. It was only later in school life that he found his form amid the rigours and challenges of Gordonstoun in Moray.

Two other brother pairs at the school seemed not to come off too badly. The reason may lie in their backgrounds. There were two sons of a general later described by Field Marshall Montgomery as 'the best artilleryman in the British Army'. Our headmaster was not slow to tell us that their father, Brigadier Kirkman, had been chief gunnery officer at El Alamein. The two boys, though several years apart, seemed cut from the same cloth, a more ordered and clear-cut fabric than the loosely woven textile from which Ian and I were still struggling to emerge. The other pair appeared to have an equally unambiguous background at the other end of the social scale. Getting wind of the wealth of my grandparents, the elder of the two lost no opportunity to mock me as well as everything he could associate with me. After my mother had attended a sports meeting, he remarked with no provocation that she didn't have good legs. My mother's legs were as elegant as the rest of her. Why he should say anything so provocative and cruel, as well as far-fetched, I couldn't imagine unless it was because besides being beautiful she came from a wealthy family. I wished Dobson Major a sticky end, though without saying so. My show of indifference he no doubt attributed to upper-class superiority. When Mr. Hammand was trying to introduce us to an appreciation of classical music by playing a record of Beethoven's Moonlight Sonata, the same Dobson said to us, not without some musical perception but in an obvious attempt to sabotage the occasion, that it sounded just like 'In the Mood'.

Summer holidays, ten or eleven weeks long, were a welcome respite and memorable as such. The first war summer took us to Dunbar, further down the coast, but before that our parents had rented a cottage on the seafront at Southerness, a small village on the Solway coast not far from Dumfries. It was during the later stages of the Battle of Britain, but here the only visible evidence of war was a Fairey Battle single-engined bomber that aimed dummy bombs on a target floating some hundreds of yards offshore from the historic lighthouse. At low tide we found bombs in the sand and kept one. On our father's arrival we went shrimping round the rocks with a wide net. This was a place where he had spent summer holidays as a child, his mother's home having been at nearby New Abbey. When quite young, used to his parents' comments on England and its inhabitants, my father had taken up a pair of binoculars to look at the coast opposite, expecting to see people with black skins. Whether, with its nasty association, his parents had put that idea into his mind, he didn't say. The family had its slave-owner past, but such ideas would be rife anyway among his school friends. The more significant thought is that his parents should speak so badly of England.

For myself, Southerness provided a first sense of femininity. Playing with other children, one day sheltering from the rain we sat huddled in a porch. From Susan, a girl sitting opposite and perhaps a year older than the rest, there exuded a sense of wholeness and warmth. Perhaps it was projection due to want; no doubt years exclusively in the company of boys helped it either way. The two following summers we stayed south. It was not until the late summer of 1943 that some summer weeks were spent again in Scotland, this time at Lawers on Loch Tay. We were booked in at a farm where we could lend a hand with the harvest. My father and I climbed Ben Lawers, the highest mountain in the Southern Highlands, though on a ridge near the summit vertigo brought me to a stop, a lasting problem. We rowed and fished. Once idly twisting my foot around what I thought was twig, I broke off the end of my father's valuable fishing rod. Typically, he took it without any sign of anger and we repaired the section with tightly bound fishing line. After attending the local very 'free' church, Spartan in the extreme and with a piano instead of an organ, I foolishly, though I am afraid not uncharacteristically, imitated the minister's rather quavering voice. For this my father ticked me off, I was making fun of what was serious enough in times when bombs were still falling on London. One had already destroyed part of the Admiralty where he worked. On rainy days when harvesting had to stop I walked down the road alone, which is how I have always preferred to walk, letting the surroundings sink so that they could lend me thoughts of my own. On occasion I had to stop and turn back due to asthma.

It became a problem. By the time the war ended the strain of school life had begun to tell. On Sundays we had at first been led like a regiment by the headmaster past the cenotaph in Rickerby Park and into the city centre to attend the Sunday service in the cathedral. It was a welcome change of scenery and atmosphere. But after a while the journey took its toll and several boys fainted during the service. To shorten the Sunday outing we later attended the service in the nearby St. Michael's Church in Stanwix, where I remember the vicar as a tall man with wiry grey hair who gave down to earth sermons, the gist of which one might remember on the walk back to school where a special Sunday lunch would be waiting. On Sunday we even had teatime cakes.

My own condition had worsened, with recurring styes in my eyes. These are usually associated with dietary causes. Large scabs formed periodically on my knees and neck. There was occasional bed-wetting, something my parents had tried to cure me of long before. A perpetually dripping nose and bronchitis, both of which dogged my pre-school days, returned. At night I began to suffer regular attacks of asthma, doubtless aggravated by covering myself with the bedspread as a kind of tent to prevent my wheezing from reaching the ears of my fellows in the dormitory. If at all, I slept badly. As a result I couldn't last the running tours that the head insisted would strengthen mind as well as body, and usually returned walking along with 'Fatty' Hall, an overweight pharmacist's son, whose normal lungs simply wouldn't let him keep up. As for my own lack of breath, out of embarrassment and because the problem tended to subside during the day I refrained from telling the matron. Relief only came later when my parents returned to Carlisle.

When the war ended they bought a house in the street behind the one that was still requisitioned. Before moving in we spent an Easter vacation at Auchencairn, a small village on the Solway Firth with a view of Hestan Island, made famous for its history of smuggling and intrigue in S. R. Crockett's historical novel *The Raiders*. For us, having spent our earliest years on the other side of the Solway Firth and having had our parents recently based in the south, this was our first proper introduction to the Scottish region to which the family name belonged. Now, however, with both of them back in Carlisle and myself still at school there, I could stay at home during the weekends. There was, so far as I know, no thought of my descending again to that lesser breed, the dayboy.

Late one Saturday night I suffered a serious attack of asthma, managing to gasp out, in a voice loud enough to carry to my parents' bedroom, that I could scarcely breathe. They sent for the school doctor and a shot of adrenalin produced the bliss of relief that is every asthmatic's joy on recovering the ability to breathe freely. Shortly afterwards I was moved to Broadgreen, a hospital in Liverpool, for examination and suspected tuberculosis. I lay there for several weeks, during which I had my first confrontation with the thoughtlessness medical people sometimes show in the presence of patients and especially children. I had just undergone a nasty examination involving a pipe being pierced into my throat and some glutinous liquid poured down it to provide illumination for X-ray. While they were standing there examining the plates, a nurse remarked on how small my heart was. God, I thought, having grown so quickly the last year and now quite tall though very thin, am I outpacing my heart? Next morning a bustling 'now let's get some life back into you' lady physiotherapist got me out of bed to join in some gymnastics. I fell to the floor in a faint almost as soon as we began. It all went too quickly for me to think this must be the end and it helped that my mother had just come down from Carlisle. She brought me a guitar. Prior to hospitalization I had spent quite some time at home in bed listening to the radio and fell for the twanging sounds of an orchestra that presented itself as 'Felix Mendelssohn and his Hawaiian Serenaders'. Back home I planned to learn the fingering and adapt it later with whatever was needed to achieve the sliding effect. But apart from the usual three grips it came to little. Like many others, I kept the guitar as a kind of forlorn hope, finally selling it in London many years later to a budding Norwegian businessman for five pounds.

That bedridden year in a period of rapid growth and a deficient wartime diet left me with a bent, stiff and twisted lower spine, and a stoop that I never got rid of. It didn't worry me unduly at the time, but as I grew older I became increasingly conscious of it and did what I could by way of clothes to hide it. The extra effort of breathing caused by asthma also enlarged my chest beyond natural proportions and tended, if I went with the stoop, to accentuate the crookedness. I was later diagnosed as a victim of *morbus Scheuermann*, a largely unexplained deformity to which young adolescents are prone. Fellow pupils at my next school were not backward in remarking the abnormality although generally my height enabled me to conceal it. A doctor once calculated that if they could straighten out my spine I would be two inches taller, which would have brought me up to my father's six foot and six inches.

Such setbacks pale pitifully compared with what we learned from those who came back from the war. One day, not long after VJ Day in August 1945, Tommy Chandler, thin and pale, walked quite unexpectedly up the street to our new house to greet us. His experiences had been unimaginably worse than any we could conceive at the time. The last we had heard of him was on returning from Dunkirk as one of the three hundred and thirty thousand members of the British Expeditionary Force saved by the 'small ships'. He had sent me a postcard from France inscribed 'All Quiet on the Western Front'. He was then shipped to Malaya, only to be captured in 1942 at the fall of Singapore. Tommy spent the rest of the war in a prisoner-of-war camp in Japan, where he owed his life to his skills as a barber, fairly simple skills that he had once practised on me with the traditional bowl and cutting round the edges. Tommy had no wish to talk about what happened in captivity and mentioned the war to me only once. He told me of the many soldiers who broke their necks at Dunkirk by leaping into the sea with their brimmed helmets on when the rescue ship they had boarded was bombed by the Luftwaffe.

That year, though still only thirteen, I received my first driving lessons. Mary Tyson, our cook from before the war, was now married with a small daughter, named Mariot after my elder sister. They lived in our house. Jack Armstrong, her husband, drove Italian prisoners of war to and from their place of work every day in a Ford V-8 army truck. In the afternoons I went to the end of the road to meet him and he would let me drive to the other end and then back to the house. The clutch was heavily sprung and we once ended up in contact with a tree. But Jack was wonderfully patient and after several jerky rides I managed at thirteen to get a general grip on the art of driving. I also entered into poetry competitions with Jack. I would leave one on his door and he would leave a rejoinder there the next day. One of them recounted in ironic tones the fact

I had related to him that the day before I had cycled out to Crosby to see the military airfield, now Carlisle's airport and five miles from the city. It was then full of DC-3s and Lockheed Hudsons. Finding the headwind too strong on the way back, I was forced to wave down a delivery van, which took me with my bike back to Carlisle. Of Jack's poem I recall only the last line: 'and couldn't face it back.'

There was a second cycle incident. I had cycled to the town centre to buy a book and on coming out again climbed onto the wrong bicycle just as its owner was returning. I had begun peddling way but he grasped hold of it and we stopped. I tried to explain that my own bike was as large as his and I had made a mistake and was not trying to steal it. He gave no sign of accepting this explanation and I suppose he went off complimenting himself for his charity in not summoning the police.

Although for about a year we sustained a form of family life, it began to unwind almost as soon as it was resumed. My elder sister acquired a horse, tended by Tommy Chandler, while my brother and I joined our father in his newly found interest in sailing. The three of us took to the sea, in our case the widely sand-banked Solway Firth, which forms part of the boundary between England and Scotland. The boat was *Molita*, or 'Little Molly', named I discovered later after the designer's daughter. Part of my father's job during the war, for which he received an OBE, was to organize hundreds of small firms working with metal and flotation systems to produce and deliver the chain links and other gear used to form the underwater barriers known as Boom Defence. These nets closed off harbours from enemy submarines around the whole British coast. One such firm was located at Sandbank on the Holy Loch and it was there that this fine old ketch, formerly a gaff cutter and built at Birkenhead in 1898, caught his eye. The war over, he bought the yacht. He and a local Carlisle business man, Ivan Carr, a seasoned sailor, sailed *Molita* to Kirkcudbright on an arduous voyage during which my father spent most of the time trying to locate and stop a dangerous leak. For the next two hears *Molita* was moored there next to Ivan Carr's much newer Fife-designed sloop *Solway Maid*, completed during the war and now itself at the time of writing classified as a classic yacht. Both yachts, *Molita* now back to her magnificent original rig but renamed *Marigan* (to preserve a tradition, a combination of the names of the new owner's three daughters) are presently regulars on the 'Mediterranean circuit'.

It was on Kirkcudbright's river Dee that, with the details provided by Arthur Ransome still in my head, I managed for the first time to rig a sailing dinghy and hoist and trim the sail. The less technical feat of preventing capsize had to be learned there and then. The boat itself, eleven feet long and rather narrow, had been amateur-built in mahogany in West Africa by a merchant marine officer, who then transported it to Britain on the deck of his freighter. With no lateral stability, and effectively little more than a surfboard with sides, it was a death trap and indeed looked not unlike a coffin. Had I read *Moby Dick*, it might have been named 'Queequeg' after Ishmael's Polynesian shipmate. As readers know, the coffin that Queequeg fashioned on board for himself when caught by a fever was what saved Ishmael's life when the *Pequod* sank.

Chapter Three: In irons

In irons: a sailing ship headed directly into the wind without steerage-way. Being 'put in irons' is having chains fastened to your ankles.

Due to the rapid changes in family life that schooling entails, *Molita* was not kept for long. But the following year (1946) we sailed in her to Larne in Northern Ireland. We lived in a rented cottage called 'Northwesters' where, sheltering under its roof, we spent one of the wettest summers on record. Twice a week, rain or shine, Ian and I were able to learn some small-boat seamanship by crewing for members of the local sailing club in their eighteen-foot 'Highland' dinghies. Under the guidance of Alec Niblock, a recently demobilized naval officer who had worked closely with my father in the Department of Boom Defence, we also fished effectively for red mullet, a coastal fish asking for trouble by swimming in the warm waters of the nearby power station. My mother and I played golf on the shoreline course at Larne but gave up after I had sent all the golf balls I had with me into the sea. It would be fifty years before I lifted another golf club, not through dismay at this unprofessional profligacy, but because the occasion to resume just didn't occur.

Shortage of accommodation aboard *Molita* the previous summer had meant that some of us spent nights in a Kirkcudbright hotel. There my father ran into a teacher at his old school, the Edinburgh Academy. Without consulting me and thinking, as was explained to me later, that my lungs would benefit from the Edinburgh air — and one must admit there is plenty of it — an entrance test was arranged. If accepted, I would board at this same teacher's home until the family moved to Edinburgh as was now planned. On this rain-soaked summer in Larne I had taken with me the Greek primer given to me by my thoughtful prep-school teacher, it having also been determined without consultation that I should begin with classical studies that autumn. A trip to Edinburgh and a brief session with the mathematics master Mr. Lockhart ('Fushie' to his pupils) satisfied the latter that I could count. Sometime before Christmas 1945 I was driven to Barnton on the western outskirts of Edinburgh to join the teacher's family. Little more than a mile from the spacious mansion where I lived my first years, in term time I was now to spend the next two sharing with another pupil a small, narrow and unheated room in the home of Mr and Mrs Philip ('Bill') R. L. Heath together with their children and nanny.

My parents no doubt thought that living with a family was a gentler option than one of the school's 'houses' where stresses of the kind I'd endured the last seven years would only be continued. But living with a family on sufferance, and to whose activities one was admitted only at set times, was worse. The proximity gave a sense of exile rather than belonging. The two children, one born while I was there, were the household's main focus. A boarder in one of the school's houses has at least a society to mix with, or disappear into, or within which some kindred spirits might be found. Here I was stuck in a cell with a slightly older boy with whom I had little in common. Physically more mature and struggling with the tortures of puberty, he was led once to propose sharing his company with me in my bed. Maybe it showed a positive side to my lack of upbringing that this led to curiosity more than shame. He was also if not inconsistently a scout leader and encouraged me on Sundays to accompany him to the nearby Cramond Church where we listened to the sermons of the Rev. Leonard Small, later Moderator of the Church of Scotland. Necessarily we got along. No doubt it was a trial for him too.

The first day at Edinburgh Academy was traumatic. Members of IV Classical all knew each other. Not only had they already started in the autumn, during the war many had been pupils in the junior school. I was placed in the front row and Mr Atkinson, our class-master, a well-known cricketer who had played for Middlesex and now for Scotland, whether to hide his own shyness or because he thought I looked as if I needed putting in place, made me feel foolish as he asked me publicly for particulars of my age and home address. The latter was still the district in Carlisle north of the river known as Stanwix, which is pronounced 'Stannicks'. I suppose that was what he wrote down, but when I spelled it out he exclaimed 'What?', so that I had to repeat the spelling with the class listening as if they were his audience and I part of his act. He made no welcoming remarks and I hated him instantly. On the way to the tram after school I saw him walking in the same direction on the other side of the road and reflected that if I had a pistol I would have shot him. Bernard G. W. Atkinson, known among us as 'Bagwash', was no doubt an amiable man as Mr. Heath later insisted, and the drama was probably in my own mind.

I found myself at ease in the company of pleasant, and in many cases extremely intelligent, classmates who — except for the following year when I was placed with a rougher crowd — were my companions until I left the Academy four and a half years later. They were a mixed bunch. Two were to become law lords, another a London publisher and a third a well-known novelist under the name 'J. K. Mayo'. Much later described by John Calder as 'one of the finest minds and wittiest personalities on the Scottish Arts scene', I warmed to Bill Watson, as to his studied indifference to cosmology and outer space and for his quick wit, examples of which I still recall. Bill's favourite author at the time was Dornford Yates (also a pen name), a writer I too preferred at the time to the likes of Sir Walter Scott, one of the school's founding fathers from 1823. Another class companion became a lawyer; in his younger days he was a great rugby player. For reasons I never fathomed, he used to taunt me in a friendly way. He died too early of drink, something that appeared to be an occupational hazard for those choosing the law profession. Another fellow pupil became a minister of the church and for a time a missionary in Pakistan. Yet another, referred to once as 'the peer of contracts experts, Lord Clark of Copyright', and famous for his championship of authors' rights, was Charles (to us 'Chick') Clark. He became editor of Penguin's Pelican list and managing director of Allen Lane, which could be a reason for his remembering me at a school reunion some years ago — he may have seen my name as a translator for Penguin Classics. He died in 2006 aged seventy-three. At a later reunion I met several septuagenarian classroom survivors. They included Iain 'Kay' Stiven and the now Lords Cameron and Clyde. Today Stiven, ex-missionary, and James Clyde, both then in apparent good health, are no longer with us, as too more recently Norman Laurie. Clyde played cello, and with Laurie an excellent pianist and myself a budding clarinettist, we formed a trio that played for the school.

    Only a week after arriving at the Heath family home, perhaps still smarting under the embarrassment of the class master's approach to my arrival, I had written to my mother expressing my unhappiness over this new arrangement. She didn't reply and later said she'd hoped my 'homesickness' would go over. I was not really homesick since I had no sense of home being a better alternative, and my mother's silence led me to conclude that there was no point in seeking advice or help in personal matters from my parents. Previously I had merely been unwilling to admit that I needed help, a matter of juvenile pride; but now although some of that remained, I felt they simply lacked the resources even to grasp what was needed. As for that, I felt I lacked the resources they hoped my schooling would cultivate. On what these were I already knew they were divided. Whatever other future my mother had in mind for me, entering the family business was to be no part of it. I feel sure that in vindication of the sacrifice of his own naval career, my father would have been relieved had I shown an interest in his work and some aptitude in that direction. Other eyes in the family would be looking towards me too. I was the eldest son of the Managing Director, but was also the eldest great grandson of the firm's founder. If anything was becoming clear to me, it was my lack of leadership qualities as of any interest in acquiring them.

    The distance to those who gave every impression of being leader material became greater as I grew more familiar with the school. On Friday evenings

Mr. Heath ran a poetry-reading club at his home for certain senior boys who, on arrival, trooped through the main door just beside our narrow cell, which was situated appropriately enough by the entrance hall. They talked in deep adult tones and were here on equal social terms with our host. As scions of solid Edinburgh families they were already lining up for positions in society as lawyers and judges. If destined first for military service, they would certainly be commissioned.

That indeed was a future for which we were all being prepared through compulsory enrolment as members in the Combined Cadet Force. It too assembled on Fridays in the afternoon. Mr. Heath was sometimes put in charge of raw recruits like myself and on one occasion he took it upon himself to bark at me in a military fashion for not keeping time. Lacking the alacrity or focused attention of most of my colleagues, I was indeed sometimes slower to respond. But I was pained that he should make such a song and dance about it. As I cycled 'home' I dwelt on this, resentment boring itself deep into my soul. It felt like actual pain and laid the basis both for rejection of these theatrical goings-on and a desire for a space of my own where I could develop whatever I had it in me to become. I began even then to reflect in ways that, with the years, increasingly became a habit. Did Heath behave like this because he wanted to show me that living in his home didn't affect matters of discipline? Or, if it was a show, was he putting it on for the benefit of my companions because he knew my fellow marchers were aware that I was his lodger and he wished to assure them there could be no favouritism on that account? Was that, then, because he actually liked me and it was for military reasons that he felt he had to resist an impulse to turn a blind eye on my clumsiness? Or did he dislike me, using the cover of military necessity to give vent to his true feelings? If it is usual for doubters to choose the least comforting interpretation, this was at least one respect in which I was normal.

Towards the end of that first year my 'cell-mate' and I spent Easter on a cycle-and-tent tour of the Southern Highlands, which was something of a busman's holiday since we now cycled to and from school every weekday and often on Saturdays too, that being set aside for matches with other schools. I recall one Saturday cycling across Edinburgh from Barnton to Musselburgh and back, a total of twenty-eight miles, to play rugby with Loretto School, a game in which my nose was broken.

A curiously symbolic event occurred on that Easter cycle tour. It was a time that I might have been spending with my family, but just after we'd left North Queensferry and were climbing up the fairly gentle hill on the way to Kinross, a car drove by and stopped. It was my father on his way to a newly started farming project in Aberdeenshire. There was something grotesque about this brief encounter. He seemed like an emissary from another world, almost a stranger. My family appeared even more remote, although I think I may have actively made it so –consciously and with lasting effect.

There had been more to the planned move to Edinburgh than the air and my health. Before the war, perhaps bolstering their intellectual defences against the infectious simplicities of Moral Rearmament, my parents had explored the kind of literature that appealed to a post-World War I readership disillusioned with the world and searching for ways of renewal in Christian thought. On first noticing such things, I saw on the drawing room table titles like *Experiment with Time* and the *Screwtape Letters*. J. W. Dunne, C. S. Lewis, and also J. B. Priestley were the kind of authors people read, writers who although well on this side of revolution, held out hopes for better things to come. Underlying this hope lay the possibility of a world beyond the familiar and unsatisfactory but still in the here and now rather than a beyond. At some time just before or after the First World War, the Edinburgh family, whose son's military example my father had tried unsuccessfully to follow in 1917, introduced them to Anthroposophy. From their separate perspectives my parents took to it with enthusiasm.

Founded on an allegedly scientific approach to matters spiritual and purportedly accepting normal science as far as it goes, the Gnosticism of this movement appealed to my father's sense of the close relation between good practice and knowledge. For my mother, on the other hand, apart from providing a substitute for a university education, it answered to her need for faith in a religious order. I still have her teenage copy of the Dent Library collection of *Verba Christi*. This development was offered through contact with Evelyn Francis, a priest in the devotional wing of the Steiner movement calling itself the Christian Community. It had been established in Stuttgart in 1922 by a German evangelical minister, Friedrich Rittelmeyer, as a movement for Christian renewal with its priesthood open also to women. In 1939 Evelyn became the first English woman ordained to celebrate the sacraments. In the post-war Allied Control Commission, and with the rank of colonel, she had been helping in the rebuilding of Christian groups of all denominations in Germany. A well-known writer and lecturer, she also travelled a great deal at home and abroad. My parents met and befriended her on one of her visits to local Communities. I suspect that in my mother's case this connection also served in the way of all such dedication, as a prophylactic against fundamental anxiety and a sense of not feeling at home in a world in the way that her upbringing had tried to assure her she should.

Even here, there was no attempt on our parents' part to indoctrinate us. If this absence was also part of the authentic Steiner educational philosophy, then it has to be said that my parents understood this philosophy better than its more vocal adherents, among whom I later sensed varying degrees of bigotry, delusion and even fanaticism. From the distance of time, however, I now sense the protective and cautious arm of my father. From listening to the message of these immigrant intellectuals and artists from the ravaged Continent, my mother's inclinations were to save us along with the rest of the world. As with Moral Rearmament, though perhaps in the shadow of recent events in Germany more cogently, here too there was a messianic sense of the world needing to be saved by something radically other.

In the event, my parents' dedication to Anthroposophy, apart from the occasional meeting, proved to confine itself to financial support and sending two of their children, my brother Ian and younger sister Jane, to the Edinburgh Steiner School. They funded refugee Steiner School teachers and the proceeds of the sale of my father's parents' Edinburgh home in Royal Terrace went to the purchase of a house for the family of my brother's class teacher. When I met my father on the road that Easter holiday, he was on his way to a biodynamic farm to be driven on Steiner principles. He, together with Derek Duffy, a pioneer in biodynamic farming in South Africa, had recently established it in Aberdeenshire, this in spite of his already demanding business affairs centred in the south. By now chairman of Standfast Dyers and Printers Ltd, a subsidiary of Morton Sundour Fabrics established in Lancaster by James Morton in 1921, he was also involved further south, at Stoke-on-Trent, in a collaborative enterprise with Courtaulds that had started before the war. There he was helping to perfect a high-speed, high-volume knitting machine that could also knit carpets. On top of that he was completing the development of a successful dying process that, instead of rollers, used molten metal in a specially designed bath to impress dyestuffs evenly into cloth. Commuting in addition, as need arose, to the newly established biodynamic farm in Aberdeenshire left him little time for Anthroposophy itself.

Or for us, but then in coping with school life we had enough to keep us busy. The one to suffer was our mother who had to keep pace with all this change. Her children spread to the winds, she herself was perpetually in motion, with new houses and homes her own responsibility. After moving back to Carlisle at the end of the war my parents had sought a suitable home base in the Annan district just north of the border, a kind of compromise with the thought of us all still attending boarding schools, the focal points bringing us together being horses and sailing. For reasons given, Edinburgh had been chosen instead.

After two years thankfully escaping from the cramped and shared lodgings at Barnton, but still waiting to move into our new home in Edinburgh, I lived with my parents in a boarding house down the same road and close to Newhaven. In Edinburgh my brother and younger sister were still boarders, as too my elder sister in St. Andrews. Our mother was by now tired and on edge. I remember her rushing back upstairs after some unfortunate remark my father and I had come up with during breakfast. Driving me to school he tried to explain that my mother's mood had gynaecological causes. While in that area, he also took the opportunity to ask me, at what seemed to me rather late in the day, whether I knew about such things. I did and had done so since prep school and was slightly surprised that he seemed so out of tune with our younger times as to think that I might not. By now I had sealed myself off from parents and their problems. They were an aspect of life to be negotiated and where necessary avoided although in some abstract sense still identified as 'home' with myself a dependent. That my mother sensed this alienation might have been one element in her discontent, but always having to keep up with my father's new projects was obviously a factor even if she would never admit to it. The more secretive I became in their company, to them the less predictable became my behaviour. My mother had always observed that I had a habit of creeping around silently. She called it 'lurking'. I continued to be a lurker, watching out, waiting to surprise rather than be surprised by whatever lay round the corner.

The new house on Trinity Road, into which we all now moved, was in fact quite old. As 'Trinity Grove' it was built sometime around 1790 by the father of a later partner of Sir Walter Scott's publisher, Archibald Constable. It later belonged to Lord Provost Creech, publisher of the second edition of Robert Burns's poems. He in turn sold it to John Ballantyne, younger brother of James Ballantyne, Scott's editor and friend from their time together at Kelso Grammar School. It was the venue of 'entertainments' mentioned in J. G. Lockhart's famous biography of Walter Scott. Contrasting these with the staid gatherings to which guests were accustomed in the 'substantial citizen-like snugness' of his elder brother's 'domestic appointments' in St. John Street ('a row of good, old-fashioned, and spacious houses, adjoining the Canongate and Holyrood, and at no great distance from his printing establishment'), Lockhart exclaims: 'What a different affair was a dinner, although probably including many of the same guests, at the junior partner's!' It was at this villa ('near to the Frith of Forth, by Trinity') renamed 'Harmony Hall' by the 'little man', that Walter Scott himself used to 'partake' of their entertainments. This was clearly hallowed ground.

At that time, it had been a genuine retreat with the surrounding area open enough for the 'frolicsome' Johnny to have a 'well-furnished stable' so that he could follow the foxhounds 'whenever the cover was within easy distance'. His horses were named after heroes in Scott's poems and novels, and Lockhart tells that 'he usually rode up to his auction on a tall milk-white hunter, yclept Old Mortality, attended by a leash or two of greyhounds, kept horses and hounds'. The house itself was

> ... surrounded by gardens so contrived as to seem of considerable extent, having many a shady tuft, trellised alley, and mysterious alcove, interspersed among their bright parterres. It was a fairy-like labyrinth, and there was no want of pretty Armidas, such as they might be, to glide half-seen among its mazes. The sitting-rooms opened upon gay and perfumed conservatories, and John's professional excursions to Paris and Brussels in quest of objects of *virtu*, had supplied both the temptation and the means to set forth the interior in a fashion that might have satisfied the most fastidious *petite maîtresse* of Norwood or St. Denis. John, too, was a married man: he had, however, erected for himself a private wing, the accesses to which, whether from the main building or the *bosquet*, were so narrow that it was physically impossible for the handsome and portly lady who bore his name to force her person through any one of them. His dinners were in all respects Parisian, for his wasted palate disdained such John Bull luxuries as were all in all with James. The piquant pasty of Strasburg or Perigord was never to seek; and even the *pièce de résistance* was probably a boar's head from Coblentz, or a turkey ready stuffed with truffles from the Palais Royal. The pictures scattered among John's innumerable mirrors were chiefly of theatrical subjects — many of them portraits of beautiful actresses — the same Peg Woffingtons, Bellamys, Kitty Clives, and so forth, that found their way in the sequel to Charles Mathews's gallery at Highgate. Here that exquisite comedian's own mimicries and parodies were the life and soul of many a festival, and here, too, he gathered from his facetious host not a few of the richest materials for his *at homes* and *monopolylogues*. But, indeed, whatever actor or singer of eminence visited Edinburgh, of the evenings when he did not perform several were sure to be reserved for Trinity. Here Braham quavered, and here Liston drolled his best — here Johnstone, and Murray, and Yates mixed jest and stav — here Kean revelled and rioted — and here the Roman Kemble often played the Greek from sunset to dawn. Nor did the popular *cantatrice* or *danseuse* of the time disdain to freshen her roses, after a laborious week, amidst these Paphian arbors of Harmony Hall.

The property in our time was a retreat only in the war chronicler's sense. It was the site of the old estate's last stand against the encroachment of advancing ranks of small two-storey dwellings, the new norm for the district. The villa itself had been divided into three, the part with a four-storey balustraded tower visible from the top of Hanover Street belonged to an architect. But the bay-windowed accommodations and garden with its lawns, large beech tree and a cedar, together with the usual dark Victorian undergrowth of rhododendrons, was ours and there was a conservatory with adjoining billiard room, panelled and with a full-sized table. From the eaves overlooking the neighbour's more modest allotment were two leaden herons — remnants of former glory — gazing bleakly upon that shrunken garden. Out of the corner of their eyes the herons would see the ranks of modest post-World War I back-gardens that had now taken over much of the space that once boasted a trellised alley, a mysterious cove and even a labyrinth. Behind its still impressively high walls, our shaded garden was a refuge but also an anomalous leftover that harboured memories of less democratic times.

It was not a place where one could easily forget the causes of our less optimistic or carefree age. Tommy Chandler, our gardener from pre-war Carlisle, was offered a job and came to live with his wife Grace in an annex. What psychological blind spot on the part of my parents encouraged them to offer Tommy this post I cannot imagine. From the fall of Singapore in February 1942 to the Japanese surrender in September 1945, Tommy had suffered the endless inhumanity of a prisoner-of-war camp in Japan itself. In this 'respectable' part of Edinburgh he would neither find friends nor have the opportunity to make any. Grace told me as much on my visiting them many years later not long before Tommy finally succumbed to the wear and tear of his experiences. They soon returned to Carlisle.

There were other reminders of the real world. The interior decoration was in the care of an architect friend, Robert Scott Morton, who had spent the war in Burma with Wingate's 'special force', the so-called Chindits. He had just married the doctor who attended to my asthma, Elspeth Hardie. She was a sister of Robert Hardie, also a physician, whose 'Secret Diary' records his unutterable and otherwise untold experiences on the Siam railway. From these memories, for these people, there was no retreat.

A later entertainment at the villa, after we had moved to another home, would leave its mark on my own life. Meanwhile the few gatherings offered by my parents while we lived there were focused on a network quite other than John Ballantyne's. The catchment area was now largely anthroposophical. A visiting pianist and Jewish refugee from Holland provided real entertainment in the shape of Schubert's A Flat Major Impromptu (Op. 90), which he performed on the Blüthner baby grand my father had bought for my mother with his first pay cheque on joining the family firm. That had been in the year Hitler came to power. The pianist's son and wife were teachers at the Steiner school, both supported by my parents. We had visits from Adam Bittleston, once a close friend of William Golding and since 1935 an ordained priest in the Christian Community. There was also Alfred Heidenreich, a World-War I German prisoner-of war who, after meeting Rudolf Steiner and as a step towards spreading the work of religious renewal beyond the German-speaking countries, had chosen to live in Britain. Elly Wilkie, an Austrian lady, also teaching at the Steiner school, and author of a work entitled *Music: Its Occult Basis and Healing Value*, gave me my first genuinely helpful lesson in piano playing. Instead of parade ground finger exercises and scales, she showed me the chord progressions and encouraged me to improvise. I still do.

In the ordinary course of events the house functioned as a headquarters for our daily attendance at Edinburgh schools and for my father's weekend visits from his work in the south as well as his new agricultural hobby in the north. During the winter the garden also provided winter lay-up for several boats, a small plywood pram dinghy with a gaff rig, a fourteen-foot gunter-rigged *Swallow* and now also *Mazoe*, a Dragon class yacht named after the Mazoe Dam Sailing Club, north of what was then Salisbury, now Harare, capital city of Zimbabwe. Ian Forsyth, the previous owner, also of a large department store on Princes Street, had served there in the R.A.F. during the war. For my brother and myself it was the beginning of a life devoted to boats and regattas. My younger sister, Jane, with other interests, found the garden to be a place to experiment with a worm farm. She had plans to keep pigeons. There were also parts where one could do acrobatics without being seen by neighbours.

My own experiments extended beyond the wall's perimeter. It was the time of puberty. Standing in the cockpit of the Dragon gave me a view over several back-gardens and in one of them I caught sight of a young girl whose dark-haired aspect caught my immature fancy. I can't recall how, but we met and walked around in the evenings chatting and gradually becoming engaged in some experimental groping under the shadow of trees. Some neighbours were more advanced. A Royal High School footballer had befriended the exotic foreign-born adopted daughter of an elderly couple down the same side road where my new friend lived. I caught them on their nocturnal rendezvous in a garage neighbouring ours at the back of our garden. Maybe it was where James Ballantyne had once stabled Old Mortality.

I was crossing several social frontiers. My friend, in spite of her smaller home, was the daughter of a prosperous trawler owner who named one of his boats after her. A tennis-playing girl friend of hers turned out to be the daughter of the chauffeur and handyman of our wheelchair confined family lawyer. Several nearby school friends had quite different backgrounds from my own. Although we formed something like an informal gang, I was never properly inducted so that the house and the garden continued to play the role of sanctuary. I would leave the 'gang' to go and listen to the BBC Scottish Orchestra playing the Beethoven symphonies under Ian Whyte. They gripped me deeply and filled a void by giving a sense of something more gripping and lasting. The girl and I parted on the understanding we might meet again when both were more independent and mature. She later wrote to me suggesting the time had come but by then it was too late. In the meantime, for my brother and myself Granton Harbour, closely shared by the coal-consuming trawlers with their rough-tongued working force and Edinburgh's very variously heeled sailing community, became our social centre.

Ian aged now eleven displayed his coming interest in nautical aero-and hydrodynamics through experimenting in the harbour with sail configurations on the aforementioned tiny diagonal-ply pram dinghy. It so happened that a retired major-general was doing exactly the same in an identical dinghy, with a sail stiffened like a wing on an aeroplane. The two of them, the young future Olympic crewman and the retired senior army officer, who in the 'thirties had bought himself an autogiro and later came to promote the use of aerial observation for concentrating artillery fire, tacked to and fro in the harbour together in their little dinghies. General 'Jack' Parham had also brought back a portable wind tunnel from Germany and could demonstrate to the yacht club members the principles of airflow over sails and the benefits of such things as getting rid of twist. I learned later that he became deeply involved in the development of land yachts and the now super-speed catamarans. My brother, for his part, became a recognized expert in the same field. Just a few years later he built his first experimental boat in plywood at Gordonstoun.

Due to a recurrence of asthma, back problems and a below-par state of health in general, I was now excused from school sports. This reduced my self-image at least as reflected in what I took to be my shortcomings in respect of the ideals to which my fellow-pupils and I were being constantly exposed. A growing reputation as a physical weakling rankled. In the school gym-hour one day I tried to change it. I leaped onto the back of a burly opponent, one J. D. Grant, who was to become a military man and whose possession of the ball inevitably meant that he would score. Since no one dared stop him, I decided to try bringing him to a halt, so I clung to his back and he simply carried me all the way to the goal. 'I wouldn't do that', I heard someone say. It was a kind of vindication. Sailing became another.

It began as an extra-curricular diversion. Freedom from other sports gave me time instead to prepare for mid-week and Saturday afternoon regattas. I felt less like a deserter when I noted one of our masters also joining the dinghy racing. With the Dragon, a thirty-foot racing design from the board of the celebrated Norwegian boat-designer Johan Anker, we graduated to keelboat racing. Still an international regatta boat, the Dragon first saw the light of day in 1927. Ours was from the first batch to be built in Britain, in 1938, in fact the third, and before receiving the name 'Mazoe' had been variously called 'Achtung', 'Eleanora', and 'Taiping'. At Granton there was a class of six gradually increasing to a dozen and with plenty of time to become used to these boats, mastering some basic tactics in addition to seamanship, learning about the wind and so on, we became contenders, winning the usual range of small silver-plate toast-racks, sugar jars, and the occasional cup.

I was persuaded to enter a crew from my school for the annual national championships on the Clyde, also held in Dragons kindly loaned by their owners. Knowing no one at school with any sailing experience, I managed to recruit two total novices. One was Harry Woodward, a violinist in the school orchestra where I had begun playing clarinet. The fact that he had accompanied his Yorkshire industrialist father on his luxury motor yacht meant at least he knew the sea from reasonably close quarters, and it was no drawback that his father kindly offered to accommodate us on board during the week of the races, which took place on the Gareloch, where his yacht was in any case moored. The other crew member was a Canadian, Lindsay Nicolson. He had an optimistic nature that boded well for our team spirit and a prowess at throwing balls to immense heights in the school yard that indicated great strength in arms and wrists, an asset that from us earned him the nickname 'Winch'. After, if I recall, just one short training spell outside Granton Harbour, where we concentrated on short tacking, and another the day before the first race on the Gareloch, we were ready in spirit to try our luck.

With some experience of starts, in which timing is of the essence but placing just as important, we managed in the first race to squeeze in close to the race commodore ship at the leeward end of the line, that being the position that would give us the cleanest wind but only if we were as close to it as possible. As we crossed the line the breeze sharpened slightly and the top of the mast all but grazed the commodore ship's bow. The race organizer leaped to the bow with his megaphone and bellowed so all could hear, '*Tass*, don't you dare do that again!'. Either from discretion or because he hadn't memorized the boat assignments, he didn't bring ignominy down upon the school by revealing who we were. To our surprise, and possibly his, we won the heat. Afterwards, I was ferried to the commodore ship and brought before the commodore himself, who gave me a sharp dressing down, softened somewhat by his saying that he understood that I'd had some experience with sailing. We also did well in subsequent heats, winning some more, and finally, surprising most of all ourselves, the

Clark Challenge Cup itself, which we shared with Glasgow Academy. The final run-off race had to be abandoned after an hour due to total lack of wind; we lit a candle behind the cockpit to see if we could detect where any wind was coming from. Winning the cup, even if shared, was almost unbelievable. So impressed were my parents when I phoned the good news that they came over from Edinburgh to drive us home. Shortly after, the rector of the Academy sent a congratulatory postcard saying he had heard 'rumours' of our success on the Clyde. I felt I had become more equal.

Sailing is an absorbing pastime. A sea of troubles that may afflict you on dry land vanishes once you are literally at sea, rather like video games but healthier and still real — often very much so. It is also social, bringing together people from many walks of life. By providing a common theme and range of experience, it gives one plenty to talk about without having to choose between baring souls and shutting up. But, like video games, it can also become an obsession. It began so in my case at the age of seven when, as mentioned earlier, reading Arthur Ransome before breakfast in the first year of the war. In our grandparents' home I had been given my own bedroom situated on a corridor opposite theirs. My grandfather had respiratory problems and coughed a lot during the night and was to die just a year later. I generally woke up early and ate several digestive biscuits generously placed every night in a tin on the bedside table, and would read until seven. The adventures of the Walker and Blackett families with Captain Flint became increasingly exotic and by the time I left them they had been captured by Chinese pirates under the rule of the Cambridge educated Missee Lee, an opinionated lady who admitted that when it came to marmalades Oxford was superior. This kind of fiction appealed directly and when my father showed an interest in boats, I had been quick to show mine.

The watery world itself was of course something else. To me it was as though a door had been opened on something elemental and fresh. Until three years ago and after many misspent land-locked years. I once more had a boat, a wooden one with sails. I have sailed enough to know that at times it can be hell and possibly even worse, but somehow it kept its attraction. Not, for me, the clubhouse, though in those early days its cheerful sociality was a saving grace. Now it had become the perfection of being alone with something natural and working both with and against the elements. Anyone with experience of how a boat with well-cut and properly trimmed sails can point almost into the eye of the wind, make good speed with the wind feeling even stronger, will know what that means. It is like a coming to life.

Regattas are something else. A second's lapse can lose you the race and five seconds can mean a hundred yards. The following year I entered the championship for the second time but with another crew. 'Winch' Nicolson had now left school. Tragically, he was to die three years later in a motorcycle accident near his home. Turning into a road on his first trial run, he couldn't brake in time in the face of an oncoming lorry. On top of that, the machine had been a birthday present from his parents. Sadly, three out of the only eight crew in the five years that I took part in those competitions — subsequently for Edinburgh University — died young. That second year we achieved fourth place, but the following year we won the Clark Cup outright.

By that time, under the guidance of Lewis Bilton, an Edinburgh lawyer and leading dinghy helmsman with Olympic experience, the Royal Forth Yacht Club had instituted a cadet section offering training in two club dinghies, 'Eildon' and 'Royston', and encouraging junior members to build their own boats. My crews on these later occasions, Sandy Shackles and the Darling brothers, James and David, were recruited from the club itself. When, on the fourth year of competing, it came to representing the university, the strain was beginning to tell. There was a record to maintain and the competition was improving. At home my brother and I continued to collect first prizes in our father's Dragon. Recently I came across a cup with my name carved under the initials ANUS., which at a guess stands for Association of Northern Universities Sailing Club. The lettering is indistinct and the cup has never been polished, a sign indicating, together with this unusual lapse of my otherwise quite efficient memory, that competitive sailing was not something I was cut out for.

Wanting to provide his sea-going sons with a less strenuous style afloat, my father had bought an old ex-gaff-cutter, now ketch. Like *Molita*, this too had been designed and built just before the turn of the previous century, this time in the Isle of Wight by the innovative Charles Sibbick. She was named *Sayonara* and was a slim boat built for speed rather than responding gracefully to heavy seas. On the second occasion of our winning the challenge cup we managed to sail the cup back to Edinburgh on board *Sayonara* via the Caledonian Canal, Loch Ness and the Moray Firth. As an inexperienced deep-water sailor, shortly after rounding the northeast tip of the Aberdeenshire coast by night and just outside Peterhead, I committed the elementary blunder of consulting the chart in the cockpit instead of below. As I tried with a torch to coordinate the lights leading to the harbour entrance with the markings on the chart, a wave took me off-balance, and the wind whisked the chart out of my hands and into the waves. Somehow, we made port by reading the sailing directions and stayed there for two days amid the seagulls and the stench of rotting fish, while my father left us briefly to attend a family funeral.

At school I had been slowly making the grade but without dedication, scraping through by virtue of last-minute 'swotting'. My mind was generally elsewhere. Besides sailing there were other activities that invited or demanded some dedication. Having mastered the basics of clarinet playing, I had joined the school orchestra. There were also those military matters to attend to and camps to endure in the summer. On Thursday nights I pressed my uniform for the Friday afternoon parade. There too I wasn't quite at home. Three memories stand out as clues to prospects in the military. We had to pass a test called Certificate A at Dreghorn barracks. By then I had acquired a liking for rhythmic music and was inclined to step slightly behind the beat. It gave the momentum needed to stay interested in the next step. The hesitation was visible to our sergeant, Magnus Magnusson, the later BBC and Mastermind celebrity who, in drilling us, was also undergoing some higher test of his own military proficiency. He said to me, affably rather than barkingly, that if I wanted to pass I'd better keep step. I did pass. On another occasion, by now myself a sergeant, I was told off by our teacher officer for not barking but asking individual marchers to smarten up, rather than in the expected manner screaming hoarsely at the lot of them. I have never found an easy way of speaking to more than one person at a time. Much later in life while booking a flight on the phone I was asked by my mother who I was trying to get off with. But then, with her background, she knew what 'service' meant. My inability to merge with the military finally came home to me when our commanding officer confronted me with the annual photo of the assembled company. My beret was conspicuous for its rakish angle. He said it spoiled the whole thing. I had to agree.

Bicycling to school one day, my knee hit the brief case dangling irresponsibly on the handlebars. I fell off, breaking my left elbow. I didn't realize this until the gym hour when it became obvious. Our sergeant instructor, the same who had instructed my father in his time at the Academy and said he recognized him in me, sent me off to the infirmary. I took the tram there and they put me in a ward. Sergeant ('The Bud') Atkinson was reprimanded for failing to inform either teachers or my parents, who came to my bedside after, I think, the operation of sewing the pieces together had been performed. By a strange coincidence, the head surgeon Dr Hartley had been a neighbour in Carlisle. Recognizing me and looking at the repair he asked the junior doctor who was responsible for the job. It turned out to be a rough one carried out by a student, but it has held since. I remember also, before the operation, without warning being unceremoniously wheeled into an auditorium where arrays of students were given a look at the break and the x-rays. Not the best advertisement for a famous centre of medical science and care.

During these years my father became so heavily engaged in the farm in Aberdeenshire that my parents decided to move there. An added factor was that my older sister Mariot had chosen a farming career and might join them. The 'farm' in this case was yet another castle, a sixteenth-century tower with seventeenth and nineteenth century additions and a farm steading in more than fifty acres. Westhall was now an experimental farm and school run by the aforementioned Derek Duffy, an Irishman with a South-African background and an aristocratic Russian wife. As his partner and financial supporter, my father became actively engaged in its running. In Edinburgh the once Harmony Hall was exchanged for a modest terrace house on nearby Netherby Road, serving as a posting station for my father on his way to and from Lancaster and as a base for those of us still attending school and, subsequently, in my case, the university, and for my sister, agricultural college. A housekeeper from Edinburgh, who had briefly helped out in Carlisle, came to keep order. We were within convenient walking distance of the Royal Forth Yacht Club, then on Boswall Road above Granton harbour. For the next six years the sea became a seasonal obsession, a quite un-relaxing 'relaxation' in which my father too occasionally shared, though mostly as a spectator of our efforts in the local regattas.

Chapter Four: Unshackled

Unshackled: To be freed from metal links used to secure a chain or rope to something.

Fortunately, these activities did not prevent me from passing what was then called School Certificate and later the Oxford and Cambridge School Leaving Certificate. Ahead enough to spend two years in the upper seven class, I passed the latter twice. The first year was a continuation of classics with Mr. Longson, who to my puzzlement told me that I looked like Goethe — poor Goethe, I thought. Checking pictures of Goethe didn't help either. He looked at me with wide-eyed unhappiness. It chanced that Mr. Longson was now lodged with one of the Steiner staff assisted by my parents and the table in his room was one that had stood in the hallway in Carlisle. Later I would retrieve it as the centrepiece of a basement flat in Edinburgh where much would change.

The second year, my last at school, was a high point thanks to our teacher Wilfred Hook's enthusiastic grip on English literature. My acting career reached new heights in the role of the fourth knight in Mr. Hook's staging of *King Lear* ('He says, my Lord, your daughter is not well'). In the Easter vacation of the last year at the Academy he took a group of the Sixth and Seventh for a fortnight in France. It was my introduction to Paris. 'You can sense the champagne in the air,' he said on our first morning in Paris. At least it was at a different air. There were inexpensive wines to be won at a local shooting booth near the school where we were quartered. Among our numbers were members of the school's Bisley shooting team, so there were prizes. I don't think that was the reason why I fell asleep while attending a light opera with a famous tenor whose Polish name I don't recall; the performance was just too long. The second week was spent based on a chateau in the Dordogne, near Domme — the so-called Acropolis of the Périgord and a favourite haunt of painters, among them A. C. Dodds ('Doddy'), for more than forty years our school's art master. Looking for possible talent in that field I had recently attended his class. A linocut was even printed in the school magazine. We visited cave paintings more than 17,000 years old, and while others played table tennis and cards indoors, I went into the surrounding woodlands and lay on the previous autumn's leaves listening to the wind in the trees. It was a defining experience. Edinburgh might be more than Carlisle, but it was not everywhere and Paris had been exciting.

On leaving school several of my classmates made the quantum leap to Oxford. I simply took a longer morning tram-ride to Chambers Street and the

Old Quad. While most were on course to a career in law, I like many young people qualifying for university entry had no particular ambition or well-defined academic interest. For those like me the University was a kind of waiting room in which one met others equally at a loss but interested in finding something to absorb them behind one or another of those lecture room doors, and just as much so meeting others to exchange pasts, hopes for the future and some diversion in the present. Among those we met were those older and vastly more experienced, recently back from the war and keen to make up for lost time, people whose greater maturity gave the likes of me a sense of what little distance we had covered. Without any rigid timetable I was at first quite disoriented. Free to come and go as I pleased, I went more rarely than I should or felt inspired to by any particular academic aim that might substitute for the enforced regime of school attendance. No longer bottled up in a school uniform (on my last day, while walking back from a girl-friend's house, I had thrown my cap into the Water of Leith), I became acutely self-conscious about what to wear. Sometimes having tried on a few jackets, I simply gave up and stayed at home.

For want of anything more attractive, and still infected with Mr Hook's enthusiasm, I settled for English Literature and also Language, with (British) History as my other main subject. I quickly discovered I could get to grips with neither, nor they with me. I did, however, enjoy my first taste of coffee house talk in the company of some fellow students who met after the English Literature lectures in the coffee bar of a nearby department store at the corner of Chambers Street and South Bridge. Although the discussion being far above my head I was largely silent, the group suffered my presence with friendly equanimity. The burden of discussion was borne mainly by Andrew (Drew) Hook, who in spite of the literature connection was not a relative of my previous teacher. Then hardly twenty years old, and now Emeritus Bradley Professor of English Literature at the University of Glasgow with a Centre for American Studies named after him, Andrew had even then what seemed to me a precocious a grasp of the subject, one that struck me as well beyond what we were being told by Professor Renwick and not least Dr Melville Clark. There was also Iain Walker, who after graduation followed the path of journalism to Australia, returning before his early death to work for *The Scotsman*. David Reid was also there, he too to die early having held positions in English departments in Amsterdam and Utrecht. Another was the Orcadian, Rognvald Scott. After becoming an Education Officer in the RAF, he was later organizer of studies abroad programmes for American students. I owe these facts to recent correspondence with Andrew Hook, whose name I recently came across on the Internet as a regular contributor to that constant reminder of complacency in my homeland, the *Scottish Review*.

During this time, I had an acute experience of the kind that at one time would possibly have been called a vision, but with none of the now discredited revelatory connotations. No, Jesus didn't speak to me, nor did God give me a mission. On the contrary, what I 'saw' was quite negative. I felt myself pressed up as close as could be against the wall of nothing. Anything 'beyond' that I could envisage was just another though fake version of what we have in the here and now. I was on an introspective tack and easily captivated by the romantic mysticism of tales like that of Somerset Maugham's hero Larry in *The Razor's Edge*. But where Larry gained the wisdom of the East only after detours and a long apprenticeship (of which the book tells us next to nothing), I was looking for something more direct, some form of awareness that gave me a direct fix on the way things really are. I had tried my parents' Steiner books, but to me they were incomprehensible, as I suspect they also were to them; maybe they bought the books to boost sales. At night I made efforts to confront Being itself by emptying my mind of the world I knew. But all scenarios simply pushed the problem ahead. It was my positivist moment. I realized that all I could talk about meaningfully was what I could already in some way describe to myself in the language I used every day. The only alternative would be to dispose of the describer, and I could see that the sense of panic was due to the realization that any wisdom that might come in this way would require a reduction rather than an access of self-consciousness. But I was unprepared to let go of what little I had. Looking back, I can see why people generally stick closely and even blindly to the world they know and understand the fear that arises when, for one reason or other, it is impossible to get a lasting grip on it.

Fortunately, the course requirements for the very ordinary degree that I hoped to pocket before facing real life included 'First Ordinary Moral Philosophy'. If my memory serves me, this was in 1951, my second year. The course was given by a slightly built, elderly (as I thought then, though he was considerably younger than I am today), grey-haired man. He had a beard, some thought it pretentious in a philosopher, others said it was to cover a wound received in World War I. Dressed impeccably in a dark-blue, rather too spacious suit and with white collar and tie, his head held at a slight angle, he spoke in a thin but incisive voice to a hushed audience for an hour, twice, or was it three times, a week. In my then general state of youthful ignorance, it was unsurprising that I had never heard of John Macmurray. Today it would be excusable. Apart from a few enclaves in the USA, where his work is still discussed, or here at home among the elderly who heard him, or because he has been praised by Tony Blair, Macmurray has disappeared from the philosophical landscape.

He may not have belonged there anyway; as a thinker he was more like those who caught the interest of non-academics like my parents in the inter-war years, although it was only later, on reading the prefaces to re-editions of his books, that it became clear to me that in pre-World War II years Macmurray had been a household name. This, although owed partly to pamphlets and books with a strong political reference, was due mainly to a controversy caused by a series of talks broadcast by the BBC in the summer of 1930 and later published in a book with the title *Freedom in the Modern World*. What I did see from the start was that the themes that Macmurray was lecturing on were of the kind in which I could become absorbed. That he was no ordinary professor of moral philosophy became evident to me only when I discovered that not everyone approved. There was no arduous introduction to the history of the subject, no account of its later developments, and no attempt by Macmurray to place what he said about freedom, reason, emotion, agency and the person in relation to what other philosophers had said or were now saying on these self-same topics. Some American scholarship students assigned to Edinburgh asked for immediate transfers to Cambridge or Oxford. I can understand them, for Macmurray was in effect using his post-war appointment to the Chair of Moral Philosophy in Edinburgh to continue the campaigning of his broadcasting career. Nevertheless, for a receptive majority of his captive audience, Macmurray's message of cultural crisis and his appeal to our lives and environments, delivered with charisma and engagement, was just what many including myself wanted. Years later, with wider experience of the intricacies of the philosophy game, I came to realize that if Macmurray failed to introduce us to the subject in the way now familiar to most students, he was that rare phenomenon, a thinker who without unnecessary preliminaries brought religion and philosophy together in a way that allowed students to make some sense of the modern world and of their place in it. We were plunged into an integrative vision that we could later digest and criticize if we could and wished.

No other lectures similarly inspired me. I followed a basic course in English History without absorbing a single sentence of the complex matters monotonously intoned from a wheelchair by the distinguished but ailing Richard Pares. To my embarrassment, but even more so to teachers in the Scottish History Department, all former students of my grandfather (his portrait beamed down from the office wall), I failed twice (or was it three times?) in that subject before scraping a pass. I resumed my study of Latin begun at the age of eight, but found no source of renewal there either.

Refreshment if not renewal was nevertheless available. To complete the programme for the 'ordinary' MA degree there was a scientific requirement. For no other reason than that it had something to do with language, I chose phonetics. This was lucky, since the Department of Phonetics at Edinburgh was special then in at once having its feet in a prestigious past and a colourful future. Its head and founder, David Abercrombie, had been a student of Daniel Jones, the original of *Pygmalion* and *My Fair Lady*'s 'Professor Higgins' while Peter Ladefoged, who later founded and directed the world-famous Phonetics Laboratory in UCLA Department of Linguistics, taught us how to use the departmental machinery. With a background in physics, Ladefoged, according to his own description a poet who had become interested in acoustic phonetics and later became an expert in African languages through teaching in Africa, inspired us all. His breezy website (he died fourteen years ago) informs us that he was married for fifty years to Jenny Ladefoged, 'a notorious Episcopal Church Woman,' while he himself was a 'member of Atheists for Jesus'. Here, in the phonetics department, I gained in Ladefoged a glimpse of a form of inventive enthusiasm and intelligent playfulness all too rare in academic life. I think it was the otherwise general lack of it that made it seem obvious to me that my future was elsewhere.

Where that might be was less obvious. But life had opened up in several directions. In the last term at school I had come across an advertisement for army surplus motorcycles. Knowing my father had once been an enthusiast and even raced on motorbikes, I asked him if I might have one. He said, having had one himself, he supposed he couldn't say no. A green-painted Ariel 350 W/NG was duly delivered to me while on holiday at the farm in Aberdeenshire. After some practise runs on the grounds, with L-plates mounted my first tour was to Edinburgh, scary to begin with but without mishap although a near thing; vibration from the motor had worked the main bolt holding the engine to the frame to its last two threads. A friend observed the situation on my arrival and I was able to avoid disaster. The machine was noisy and I didn't keep it for long, but at school I could park it proudly by the gates alongside two brand new MG sports cars eased from some even more generous parents' pockets — in unfeeling contrast to the antiquated vehicles in which some of our poorly paid teachers themselves arrived in the morning. There was a kind of freedom in arriving at the school gates under my own steam rather than by courtesy of Edinburgh's public transport. There was symbolism in the machine, a taste of a greater freedom still, to be enjoyed once those gates had been left behind.

That taste was sharpened at a party. The invitation was given only because the house in which it was held — and borrowed for the occasion due to its ample accommodations — was that once Harmony Hall from which we had quite recently moved. There were other reasons. The brother of the girl whose birthday was being celebrated played violin in the school orchestra where I played clarinet and their father and mine had been pupils together at the Academy. Looking for likely males, the girl's family may have thought of me in connection with that house where, being neighbours, they knew we had recently lived.

Back in my once spacious home, amid the music and the flowers now decorating the conservatory, I was gripped to the depths by the sight of a lively and beautiful girl. When I asked her where she was from, she said Greece. I thought of Arcadia, the land of classic beauty so enthused over by my teachers, and of course eternal sunshine. But that was not where Maria came from. She was a temporary refugee from the brutal civil war then raging around her home. Under the guardianship of a Scotsman, with whom her mother had some Red Cross dealings but who, according to Maria's later admission, had a more than custodial interest in her, she was presently boarding at the school attended by the girl whose birthday we were celebrating.

The occasion was an excuse for a weekend escape from the school. I had no idea where her guardian lived, but when the Easter vacation arrived and with the memory of Maria still vivid, I asked the school friend. She could tell me only that Maria spent her weekends at Denny, a small and somewhat dismal place near Falkirk. One morning I drove the family two-cylinder Bradford van out to Denny with no idea where precisely to look, but as luck would have it I caught sight of her walking past a local cinema close to her temporary home. She seemed happy as well as surprised at this second encounter and we agreed to meet again.

Some days later I returned to Denny on my noisy Ariel. Maria riding pillion we drove to Stirling, with its castle's grey ramparts the visible relics of Scotland's warring past along with monuments and famous locations visible from there: Wallace and Stirling Bridge to say nothing of Bannockburn. When we kissed that day in the spring of 1951, it was the first time lips were like a door to another a world, one that was not grey at all, a land far from Falkirk, far from this land once epitomized for me by a paterfamilias who confided in me that in Scotland 'sex' (which as a better Scot than myself was also his way of pronouncing 'six') was the time for 'high tea'. Within its own category a poor excuse for a decent meal, the intended parallel is indeed perfect. But that the luscious in life should first be reduced to a cheap word and then dissolved in the thought of pale sausages and overcooked cabbage with dry potatoes, whatever its local phonetics, it all made 'somewhere else' a pretty sound.

The ways in which such encounters are fated owe nothing to fortune and everything to circumstance. Maria too ached to get out of school and into the swim of life. She told me of her older sister and their parents in Chalcis, or Chalkida, the main town on Evvia, or as our teachers named it, Euboea. Zena had just married Theo, her father's business partner but Maria wanted out of that narrow circle. She succeeded. After leaving the Edinburgh school, she took a secretarial course and became the centre of many young men's interests. The Greek community in Edinburgh welcomed her with open arms. I don't know if I was the first to whom she had unburdened herself about her family and a left-behind boy-friend George with some prior claim on her, no doubt adduced as a kind of insurance policy; but I did feel that at the core of an obsession that made Maria a symbol of where I would rather be, there was trust and understanding in our exchanges of mutual confidences. On my side there was the disturbing but sobering realization that I had nothing to offer her anyway, and that my future, if anything could be called that, was still in the blue or, in the worst case, this continuing grey. I survived the anguish that shaped itself at one time in infantile but nevertheless painful thoughts of driving my motorcycle into the nearest tree, and I laughed off rather hysterically the sight of her on Princes Street with a young Norwegian. In the long run Maria and I became firm friends until her death and she a friend of my family. The young Norwegian, who died four years ago, also became a friend.

Maria was to make a rapid ascent, her first job after leaving Edinburgh being secretary to the C-in-C of the NATO Fleet in Malta. There she married, not George but the Greek naval attaché, and after his spell of duty there they returned to Athens, had two children and a restless marriage. In his early 'fifties her husband Nasos was to have a fatal heart attack and her second husband also pre-deceased her. Maria was seventeen when I first met her now nearly seventy years ago. Ten years or so ago, at Christmas and worried that I hadn't heard from her for a while, I sent a letter asking how she was. The unopened envelope was returned three weeks later with the message 'deceased'. From her son I learned that since we last met in Athens she had contracted cancer but refused treatment. There had been many years sorrowing over the suicide of her artistically gifted daughter. Maria had borne her pain stoically, admitting she had made mistakes, but whenever we met she remained still her open, humorous, chiding and forthright self. A woman of character, she perhaps had more of it than she could handle.

On first meeting her, I was still lost in a sea of possibility, something that also separated our youthful expectations. She hankered after a context of solidity that her home in Greece lacked and which she thought she might find in the grey Scotland from which I longed to escape. For me she was a defining moment, a breath of fresh air and promise of a lighter and sunnier somewhere else.

But a dream hard to be rid of. That summer, when Maria said she was flying home for the vacation and stopping at Rome on the way, the sunnier elsewhere became an ephemeral somewhere. Whether just an excuse to get abroad again or the lunatic consequence of an obsession, I told Maria I would meet her in Rome. She said she would only be changing planes. I said I'd be there anyway.

Without informing David, my travelling companion and former crew member of our winning team, of the absurd peg on which our journey hung, he and I set off south for the continent in the above-mentioned two-cylinder van with all its twenty-five horsepower. We booked in at a primitive hotel in Paris not far from Chatelet on the now rehabilitated but then quite dilapidated rue St. Germain-l'Auxerrois. Later nights were spent in the van or camping in fields by the roadside, making our own makeshift meals. A camping British family had recently been murdered in the south where we had pitched our tent some days later, and although there were rumours that it was connected with unresolved enmities from resistance days, we were wary of unexpected sounds. The campsites were not all well chosen. One early morning we woke to see large shadows moving across the walls of the tent. They were cows in whose path we had pitched it. We decamped and left before the farmer could put in his word. A never-to-be-forgotten first glimpse of the legendary Mediterranean came as we drove down to Nice, where on the Promenade des Anglais we tested native ice-cream. Struggling on to Rome and its airport we briefly met the amazed Maria. My own insane mission accomplished, we headed home.

New horizons opened on our journey home. In Pisa the motor was disassembled by an opera-singing mechanic who, after we had spent a stifling night sleeping in the insect infested van, perfumed by over-ripe melons, could tell us that the oil loss was due to excessive heat. We struggled on with our limited horsepower but were still able to tow a tired student from Freiberg on his cycle to the top of the Furka pass. We then headed for Lausanne and found a spot to pitch our tent on the shore at nearby Préverenges. The patch we chose happened to be adjacent to the summer property of a family whose head, Dr Jeanneret, was a retired physician. We met his nephew and were invited in. They were extremely hospitable and I kept contact with the nephew Henri and Georgette, his girl-friend, over several years, I with the nickname 'Golly' or Goliath due to being taller than the more normally proportioned David. We stayed several days swimming and played table tennis in their garden but, time and cash getting short, we soon headed back to Edinburgh. David was, I think, bemused and disappointed by my not having shown as much interest in the traditional goal of travel abroad for earthy young males of our background. That David's and my mutual colleagues suspected I was gay occurred to me some years later from the muttered expressions of surprise with which they greeted me on my arrival at a party with the particularly attractive Barbara, a girl whose reputation they respected.

There was another attraction. One day walking down Lothian Road, I saw a motorcycle displayed in the window of the car dealer MacAndrews. That, I said to myself, has to be mine. Surprisingly soon, with my father's help, it was. The raucous single-cylinder army surplus Ariel was exchanged for a smoothly throbbing two-cylinder 500 cc Norton 'Dominator'. When we moved in 1954 from Edinburgh to a country house in the Borders, it became my means of commuting and later of escape.

Why the Borders? The manager of the Aberdeenshire farm and my father, men of equal character but unequal temperament, had by that time agreed to resolve their growing differences by dissolving the partnership. My parents found a new home near Melrose. Although a county residence rather than farmhouse, there was a steading attached and acres enough to make farming possible with some subsidy from our father's income. Mariot would take care of the farm and for the next seven years 'Sunnyside' became our idyllic home and headquarters.

Meanwhile I found 'digs' in Edinburgh, joined the university ski club and took part in its regular Sunday search for snow in Perthshire, making little progress on skis myself, yet full of wonder at the extraordinary agility and balance of the Norwegian students, of whom there were many in Edinburgh. One Easter, I think it was in 1954, a group of us spent two weeks at Donnersbach in Styria. I progressed a little, receiving a diploma for sliding down a gentle slope between poles guided by Carlo, a bronzed Baywatch-type ski-trainer.

By then I had through complex motives befriended the Norwegian sighted walking out with Maria that day in Edinburgh. He was now about to be engaged to the ski club's English secretary, this being part of his plan in joining us in Austria. To get there he and I chose to ride my new motorcycle as far as Paris. Looking back, I think my own motive was less to save money than to try out the bike. Starting in Melrose and spending the night in Grantham, we reached the outskirts of Paris two days later, parked the bike in a fashionable Paris suburb with a family, where a fellow girl student was spending a more leisurely holiday, and found a night train to Bischofshofen, the wooden seats prohibiting anything close to sleep. After inspecting the huge ski-jump there we spent a night in a spotless and fresh-smelling Gasthof under warm and feather-weight quilts, continuing the next day on a smaller train to Schladming. From there we took the long walk up to Steinach-Irdning and the ski slopes to join our group of ten or so. We slept on a broad platform covered in hard mattresses. It was an exotic as well as energetic and also convivial experience. By the time we left, Susan and Leif were more or less engaged. They went on to Salzburg, but since he and I were to ride back together we met again at Bischofshofen on a train to

Paris and rode thence not too perilously back to Melrose. My passenger's only complaint was that, being shorter, his only view had been my back, although he did remark, when I could point proudly to the nearby Eildon Hills, that in Norway they would be holes.

An interest in an activity more physically demanding than sailing began while we were still living in Edinburgh. Despairing of any future in matters of intellect or art, and tired of considering myself a physical weakling, I tried on my old school rugby kit and took a look at myself in the mirror. It seemed to fit better and what I saw looked reasonably athletic. I joined the Edinburgh Academical (Rugby) Football Club, of which several more energetic and less scholarly of my former fellow-pupils were already members. I began training with them two evenings a week and maybe because I drank less beer soon found myself outrunning them at distance and also competing with the fastest. To my mixed amazement and horror, I was chosen to play as a second-row forward in the junior fifteen, composed of recent school leavers several of whom had played in the first team. It began fairly well. Our first match was against the school's present first team. I believe we beat them to the consternation of their trainer, Mr Bevan, who was heard to berate his protégés for losing against people who had never played before.

Bevan had arrived after I had stopped playing rugby football at school, so that was an exaggeration and I never came near to excelling in that sport. Asthma had destroyed the lung tissue that allows the air sacs to stay in shape, the same effect as emphysema, so I had neither the lungs nor the legs to keep charging about in ever-new directions, which is what second-row forwards are for. In reality our team was playing one man short. My father came to watch us one day playing Heriot's and afterwards commented that not everyone was suited to just any form of sport or activity. He knew that himself. My performance at training and dedication had fooled the selectors. On finally graduating and when the time had come for me to move to England, the head selector said that next season they would try me out as a three-quarter. Running like the wind or as near as possible was something to which I was much better suited, mentally and physically. Serious or not, the remark made me wish they'd thought of it sooner.

So little attention to my studies, or focus on my intellectual development generally, made me a stranger to the heady conversations of some of my fellow students. Among them were budding and even *au fait* intellectuals whose elevated conversations and casual name-dropping left me speechless. At times I even dozed off and not only because my energies had been spent on the playing field; my vocabulary and name index were simply too limited for the conversation to keep me awake or rouse me to any noteworthy contribution.

Although I studied enough to pass the mix of courses required of my Ordinary Master of Art's Degree, the particular blend was itself not such as to lay foundations for some serious study that I might find personally edifying. On the other hand, I did make many lasting friends, friends I like to remind myself of to this day with a good feeling tempered by the fact that I have not seen them for a long time and the knowledge that many are now dead.

It must have been sometime in 1952 or thereabouts. I had become a member of Edinburgh's International House on the corner of Castle Street and Princes Street. Its cosmopolitan clientele helped to dispel the enclosing fog infecting the little I knew of Edinburgh's social life. It also had a wide frontage on Princes Street with a fine view of the castle as well as of pedestrians on the other side of the street. From it, an American friend, later and even now quite famous, then stationed at a NATO base on the nearby Pentland Hills, used to spy out likely lady companions to help him escape the loneliness of a Scottish weekend. It also had a centrally placed bar. Leaning on it one day, I noticed at the other end a serious looking and seemingly not very approachable man sucking away at a pipe. He stared at the wall and seemed to prefer ruminating to talking to anyone. I discovered that he too was in pursuit of a Greek girl — happily not the same one. His, small and neat with a nice rather than beautiful face, and dressed usually in olive green, was from Cyprus. The pipe-smoker was from Norway. He was introduced to me as Peter Frøstrup. Although several Norwegians frequented International House, this Frøstrup didn't mix with these, nor with the large Norwegian colony who, as at the time he did, studied engineering and kept largely to themselves. As if engaged in some independent existential project, this man seemed intent on appropriating his own private space. It was one that he took around with him wherever he went and admittance was selective. Amid the flirtation and chatter of the expatriates and their local *aficionados*, the impression he gave was of an oasis of calm reflection, possibly even a source of important truths about how one should go about one's life. The pipe strengthened the impression; it demanded its own silence and spoke earnest. With their aura of quiet authority, both he and the pipe were very attractive to women, as I am sure he was aware. A portrait by a mutual lady acquaintance at the Art College included the pipe. He also dressed differently — if not exactly in homespun, plainly and certainly less modishly than the other members. There was this air of naturalness, a quality Norwegians I was quick to learn pride themselves on, and which when abroad they sometimes try, a little self-consciously and to that extent self-contradictorily and so less convincingly, to export in their own persons. Mainly, however, Peter Frøstrup presented at that time an air of resolute cool. If he expressed enthusiasm, it was to friends and in private and on matters of principle. His conversation was thoughtful and to the point. Often ironic, and when addressing you directly and in my case often critically, his manner was such as to convey the impression of nevertheless having your best interests at heart. If you know your Ibsen, there was something of Gregers Werle about him; he tended to probe you for your life-lies as if the truth if only faced would make you free. Whether quiet or animated, Peter exuded presence though with no hint of showiness or extravagance in manner any more than dress. In the urbane and cosmopolitan surroundings of International House he was conspicuously and no doubt to himself agreeably out of place. Were it not for the Cypriot girl he might never have become a member; there were many other places to enjoy a beer and Peter had many Scottish friends who would consider International House foreign territory. Although officially studying engineering at the Heriot-Watt College (now University) with a view to supporting his half-brother's engineering firm, his interests were in literature, especially poetry, subjects of which, due to the way academics treated them, I myself had quickly grown tired. But unlike my literary contacts at the university, Peter's were with the living (and drinking) literati resident in the equally history-soaked hostelries of Rose Street which lay just a few yards from International House yet a world apart. I mention these details because it is due to Peter Frøstrup that I am now writing this in his native land and not my own. He left it long ago. The script for that follows later.

Other lasting friends included a bright quartet of visiting Vassar students, Lee, Margot, Phoebe and Georgia ('Georgie'), who had come to spend a year (or was it two?) at the University. Their good humour and American optimism, intelligence and style, and not least their ability, in spite of unaccustomed rigours dictated by Edinburgh landladies, to see Edinburgh as a destination rather than a point of departure, added spice to many lives including my own, as well as lasting memories to all those lucky enough to have enjoyed their company. Having lost touch with them over the years, the sadness of reading of later deaths of two and their bereavements brings these memories now into bold relief. But, by some repeated strokes of fate, Margot (Schutt, later Backas) re-appeared periodically in my own life through the decades through her quite coincidental professional involvement in my own work.

As recorded, I made friends abroad as well. Although memory is not altogether secure on this point, and the order and detail of events may be confused, I have good independent evidence in the form of photos as well as some flashes of what strike me as memories rather then dreams, that make the following a reasonably accurate account of a journey that did actually occur in 1953.

The silver cup commemorating victory at a regatta of the Association of Northern Universities is dated 28 June 1953. My recollection is that I rode south immediately afterwards on my motorcycle. For someone living in Melrose and sold on a sunnier south, the extra hour in that direction can give a sense of being already on the way. With no particular mission in mind, but recalling the kindness shown to David and myself when we happened upon them on our return trip from Rome, I chose to head in the direction of Lake Geneva and Dr Jeanneret. I was armed with a new camera, a twenty-first birthday present from my brother and younger sister, the celebration itself in style at Peebles Hydro with friends and boosted by revellers celebrating Queen Elizabeth's coronation that same day, the 2nd of June 1953. It was also the day on which news broke of Hillary and Tenzing's ascent of Everest.

It was in July that I rode from Melrose to Grantham as once before, reaching the Silver City Airways car ferry at Lympne the next mid-morning. The bike was the only vehicle on board a Bristol Freighter, and I the only passenger, in a plane big enough to freight at least four Rolls Royces. This was long-delayed excitement for someone fascinated by planes since early childhood but who had never taken to the air. Landing safely at Le Touquet, and deciding to avoid Paris, I rode through Troyes and down through the Jura mountains. There, the back tyre punctured and after driving slowly to a petrol station, with the skilful help of the daughter of the absent owner managed the quite complicated repair. Due to bad weather the visit to Préverenges was shorter than anticipated. On arrival, Dr Jeanneret and his wife were no less hospitable but he much reduced compared to his form two years previously, so I chose not to stay long. Heavy rain began to fall and I wondered where to go next.

As the rain began to seep into the tent I had begun considering a hotel when it occurred to me that not far away I had an aunt and an uncle and several cousins. Two thoughts were uppermost. At the exclusive Moral Rearmament headquarters at nearby Caux, high up on the mountainside above Montreux just a short distance away, I would find drier accommodation. Not having met the family at all since they returned from Canada and the USA, where they spent the war summers in the Buchmanite lair at Mackinac Island on Lake Huron, not only had I a genuine wish to see them, there was the thought that they would be hurt if they learned I had been nearby without calling.

Only later did I appreciate the polite but questioning look Dr Jeanneret gave me when I said that I planned to visit relatives at Caux. Later, in December, I received a *Bonne Année* from Henri, Georgette and Mrs Jeanneret saying that Dr Jeanneret had died. At the time I had only a vague notion that Maurice Jeanneret had been a notable figure, not only in his canton, but also in the nation. Born in 1886, the son of a watchmaker and active Christian, on marrying his first wife, a Russian student, he changed his name to Jeanneret-Minkine and later put his medical qualifications to active use as a volunteer in the Balkans. It was there that World War I had been triggered by the Austro-Hungarian Empire's peremptory declaration of war on Russia for supporting Serbia's defiance of impossible demands following the assassination of Archduke Franz-Ferdinand, the heir to the Austro-Hungarian throne. Maurice's medical interests had been inspired by his experiences there, but they also shaped his radical political views. In 1917 he became co-founder of a young radical party and joined the Labour Party which as typically in the 'twenties and 'thirties took a pro-Soviet line. In 1934 he was expelled for clandestine communist activities and in November 1932 had been briefly imprisoned for defamation of the national flag during riots — yes in Switzerland — between conservative and socialist supporters that had left thirteen dead and sixty injured. He later became co-founder of the Swiss Socialist Federation, which would break the deadlock in which, in World War II, the Communist Party had been declared illegal. When I last met him, Dr Jeanneret was still president of the Vaud branch of the Swiss Labour Party, known as 'Parti Ouvrier et Populaire' and its members 'Popistes'. He was also, at the time, a Lausanne town councillor and had been a member of the two-hundred strong national council. I knew nothing of this, only that Henri was his nephew and, as I later discovered, the son of a brother of Dr Jeanneret's second wife. She, like Jeanneret himself, had been a medical student. I seem to recall a brief comment in passing that Dr Jeanneret was a communist, but he never said so himself; to us he was an energetic old man dressed in a shirt, white shorts and sandals, and offering friendly hospitality. He was, above all, and from all I have later learned of him, an exemplary human being.

I drove up to Moral Rearmament's otherworldly eyrie and stayed there a week or ten days. In his uncomplicated faith, my uncle, too, was a good man. He treated my arrival at Caux as an act of God and felt called upon to convert me to the cause. When I suggested that the rain had driven me to Caux, he said this could be God's work too. I could see that Loudon Hamilton had humour as well as, in every respect, largeness. He did his best. I refrained from saying the rain had also driven me from some communists, since for him that would have clinched it. The next day he took me to the top of a mountain where I tried to defend the spirituality of poetry, while he quite rightly pointed to the condition of the real world.

When exposed, thus unexpectedly, to the heady circus of Moral Rearmament, I was lucky to have some protective reflection up my sleeve. Clearly, in my despair at not having marked out a course of my own at the mature age of twenty-one, and open to whatever hope that something worth doing might turn up, I was a prime candidate for enrolment. In a reversal of the actual geographical coordinates, I was an empty lot waiting for the circus to roll in. The atmosphere up there on the mountainside was in some ways indeed bizarre and circus-like. Overlooking the East end of Lake Geneva and with Les Dents de Midi silhouetted on the horizon and Mont Blanc in the distance, we seemed enveloped in a veil of exclusivity and importance, to say nothing of goodness, a world apart, and yet the internal affairs were conducted at a level of simplicity and even banality that appeared to owe little to an understanding of the world below and its devious operations. The arrival of a Kentucky Bluegrass group injected a lighter touch into meetings with suitably value-laden numbers like 'Morgan Poisoned the Water Hole'. We were warned not to idolize them or to let their giddy rhythms distract us from the moral everyday. The latter began with 'quiet times' in which 'guidance' was sought from God on what the day was to bring. Just as no swallow falls to the ground but that God sees it, so no problem, however small, escapes God's advice. It only needs to be asked to be given — in the form of compliance with the 'absolutes' of honesty, purity, unselfishness and love.

These, so I discovered later, had reached Moral Rearmament by way of a professor at Yale, Henry B. Wright, whose *The Will of God and a Man's Lifework*, published in 1909, taught surrender to God as the only path to goodness, or indeed the only way of knowing what goodness is. His work was in turn based on a distillation of Christ's teaching presented in 1902 by a Presbyterian missionary leader, Robert Elliott Speer, in *The Principles of Jesus: Applied to Some Questions of Today*. It was due to Wright, by whom Frank Buchman was clearly influenced, that these principles became 'absolutes' and, as practised at Caux, the standards by which any step taken in our lives, however great or small, was to be measured. Having no firm principles of my own on which to stand, or any ready intellectual arguments good enough simply to dismiss the whole thing as puerile, it was impossible in that atmosphere not to feel that my reservations might really be weaknesses. Nor could I seriously admit to an indifference to the ideals they were promoting. It was, after all, the state of the world they were concerned with, or so went the message. It all had the appearance of being a happily functioning self-help community in which everyone played a part. I had to admit, even if only for self-protection, to feeling something quite new in being briefly a part of it. It was something like intoxication. Only later was I able to put words to that sense or intuition, if that is what it was.

Whether or not by design, the atmosphere was of a kind to create a self-induced addiction and a form of low-key but non-stop hysteria. This is both odd and significant: odd since the four 'absolutes' are also part of the programme adopted by Alcoholics Anonymous, which is designed specifically as a cure for addiction; and significant because as some insightful Californian colleagues (Bert Dreyfus and Jane Rubin) have indicated, part of the twelve-step programme for recovery requires those who take part actually to define themselves as addicts, thus making the programme for them the proper form of recovery. Calling yourself an alcoholic is a simplifying act. It diverts attention from the social or psychological contexts in which you are actually embedded and provides a simple description that frees you from responsibility for what you are. In this way it makes you eligible for a ready-made form of recovery, calling for a commitment on your part that can make it feel as if you were at last making room for your real self. The commitment has then to be sustained, which makes active membership of the group an essential part of the programme, while a continual fear of backsliding or the tendency to do so, or even just the perpetual reminder implied by the programme, means that you now have something to keep you busy for the rest of your life. Essentially, it means substituting one form of addiction for another, a way of life called 'abstinence' motivated by fear of reversal and loss of this 'new' or 'real' self. The group helps to prevent such loss, but only by opening up another source of fear, that of the group's disapproval and one's own manifest failure.

To measure daily life against ideals that are absolute is asking for trouble. It makes support of the group even more crucial and 'failure' inevitable when the support is not forthcoming. I read somewhere of an erstwhile supporter of the Oxford Group who actually applied its principles to recovery from alcoholic addiction. He had said that putting the word 'absolute' in front of these ideals either kept people out altogether or, more to the point, gave a short fix that led inevitably to collapse. As for Caux, the true picture was probably that there was a mixed population here, composed for the most part by those who came for a moral boost, something like an annual injection that made them on average better the rest of the year, and also a targeted minority of key public figures in politics and commerce, the part of the movement that my grandfather had called 'the salvation army for the rich' and on which the movement relied for money and prestige. To call the boost 'spiritual' would be highly misleading; the level of communication and its content, a mixture of 'humour, piety and crassness' as someone has described it, had about as much relation to real life as a television commercial and with the same insensitivity to any personal depths out of which anything truly meriting the title of spirituality can grow.

I confess that in the poverty of my own real possibilities I had recently thought briefly of becoming a priest. It was much as one thinks of becoming an architect or a physician, or an engine-driver for that matter, in short anything that 'helps' but also offers some self-confirming and necessarily conspicuous if specialized status as an 'authority'. What better than God's mouthpiece? The idea had stirred ephemerally in my mind during the autumn term at the university while sharing lodgings with three American theology students. They were worldly enough to beat me at poker and one of them had shaken hands with Marlon Brando, recalling his surprise at the limpness of the famed actor's handclasp. More than good-looking enough to make a career for himself in films, that same theology student had sung with the pre-Hollywood Doris Day. All three had moved to our shared accommodation on the daughter of their previous lodgings showing too active an interest in our ex-singer's less visible parts. Their company, as so often with intelligent Americans, was refreshing and I reflected that a career in the church would at least be in the family tradition. Their casual approach to ritual also appealed to me, even if it meant that having already fleeced me at poker, when I was invited to accompany them to St Giles one Sunday the one next to me needed a hand-out for the collection. It seemed to be an aspect of devotion for which they were unprepared; not for a moment did I suspect they might not be theology students. However, what I did quickly realize was that without their worldly background, any fast-track project for entering the priesthood would be like buying a commission in a modern army.

On the day before my departure, my large-hearted uncle compèred the morning meeting so that he could direct remarks especially at me. He wanted to impart in me thoughts of soon returning, or perhaps even staying. I could see that Buchman himself knew better, or was it my bad conscience that made his beady eyes seem to stare at me with suspicion? But situations like that are exceedingly labile and hard to decipher. He appeared at every meeting to glare at me as at one not wholly, or at all, present in the gathering. I felt he had a gift of that kind, and he was indeed no ordinary person. As for the rest, I had dug in with them, taking my turn at washing dishes for the two thousand, along with my aunt, my mother's twin but so unlike her, and also attending morning gatherings in the groups into which we were arranged. Mine included my cousin David, this being the first time we had been able to meet as more than just kids. He seemed less gone on 'guidance' than the hard-core of Groupers in the family and appeared to be holidaying with his family rather than finding himself. He, too, had taken up the clarinet. He came further than I and even formed his life around music.

But this was no holiday resort, no place for tourists or visitors: anyone involved had to take part. My own role became less that of an intruder interrupting their games than of an infiltrator gathering information but then, typically, also exposing myself to the forces that kept the show going. At the time I had little opportunity to reflect on the significance of their approach, but the philosophical ballast I had acquired in my last year at university had made questioning a habit and gave me some power to judge and resist.

It was clear to me from the start that I would have to keep any questions to myself. Raising them would be to have them read as weaknesses to be confessed in ways reminiscent of Marxist culture-revolutions. The afternoon sessions were paradigms of 'self-criticism' in which happy sinners, content to abandon their previously irresponsible selves, sought applause. To me they appeared to be willing to stoop to bathetic depths in seeking out moral peccadilloes so as to present them proudly to an applauding public. I began to suspect that my uncle's opening remarks about the weather were not just a joke. Any attempt to criticize their principles or practice would be treated as an evasion on my part, an excuse for not surrendering to Buchman's God.

On our enjoyable climb to the nearest summit at the outset I had told my uncle I'd been studying philosophy. At that last meeting, the only one he chaired with Buchman looking on in the background, he tried that old chestnut now widely attributed by an increasingly ignorant public to Leonard Cohen. It was the famous Dr Johnson's long-lost school colleague who, having tried to study philosophy, found that 'cheerfulness kept breaking through'. I can appreciate the point; studying philosophy, as opposed to finding something of value to yourself in someone else's thoughts, will get you nowhere, and an ability to laugh should never be sacrificed for trying. But I do have a weakness to confess. One of many, it is that cheerfulness was never my forte, and as far as jollity is concerned, I prefer Mark Twain's remark that 'laughter without philosophy is but a sneeze of humour'.

I tried later to analyze this experience. Where did my uncle and I differ? Was his overt goodness so much better than my secretive hold on a self that I still had to come to grips with? In his account of how the Moral Rearmament Movement began, my uncle stressed a mood of cynicism that had prevailed among his generation of World War I survivors. His story bears repeating.

It began with the Indian Army in France and him being awarded the Military Cross. After the war he took a two-year philosophy course at Oxford. There he played rugby and with like-minded veterans formed the Beef and Beer Club, one of several debating societies where they 'solved the world's problems by drinking long beers, smoking long pipes and having long philosophical arguments'. At the suggestion of an American member, Buchman then visiting Oxford was invited along. As my uncle records, 'Luckily for me I did not then know who Frank Buchman was. Had I known I would certainly not have asked him to the Beef and Beer Club. We used the name of God often enough — but not quite in the way

Frank Buchman did.' At the meeting of mainly 'ex-officer undergraduates from majors downward, veterans of twenty-three or twenty-four, with decorations never seen or referred to', Buchman sat modestly at the back.

When, after the general discussion, he was asked what he thought, he surprised them by saying that he agreed with everything they had said: 'Of course there has to be a change in the world, but that change might begin with people.' He then told them of two students he had met in Cambridge who had 'decided to change their ways'. My uncle duly notes, 'Naturally it aroused our interest in Oxford that Cambridge men were changing'. He and his roommate subsequently invited Buchman to a breakfast at Christ Church served by their scout. The meal proceeded somewhat stonily until, the usual topics of conversation having been exhausted, Buchman told how while in India he had been asked by the principal of a school how to deal with a pupil who had stolen money. Instead of offering advice he had asked the principal when it was that he himself had last stolen money. The principal recalled that he had done so as a child. Buchman asked if he would tell that to the child. He had done so with, as my uncle put it, 'happy results all round'. This triggered off a spate of suppressed or even long-forgotten admissions of minor guilt, first between my uncle and his roommate, but then, on Buchman producing the two Cambridge men in person, with a group my uncle had invited to his rooms.

> News of what was happening spread rapidly. An air of expectancy was abroad, in the college, and beyond. Men I hardly knew would come to my rooms to ask what it was all about. Underneath a carefully assumed air of neutrality, or even of un-assumed hostility, there lurked more than idle curiosity. All of us had been compelled to think, even to face things we would have preferred to forget. After all, no one likes to be made to think, least of all in a university where you have to learn what other people have thought. We prided ourselves that as would-be philosophers we made no assumptions. In actual fact we assumed much: that there was no God, that human nature could not be changed, and that it was impossible to live moral standards anyway. How did we know? We had never tried.

These young upper-class survivors of the front-line in the worst war in history had become 'men' precociously. But their maturity had come at a cost. Apart from the radical disorientation normal to those returning from the comradeship and focused ideals of the battlefield, the world that it was their birthright to keep rolling had shown itself capable of grotesque inhumanity and, above all, stupidity. To repeat the ideals that led them to fight was to invite hollow laughter. Not surprisingly, some with time on their hands searched in philosophy for ways of rethinking the world; nor was it surprising that they should fail to find in it anything that might restore to them a sense of their own place in the world. After a while, they found that for too long they had been 'caught up in the clouds of philosophic abstraction and intellectual finesse'. Their 'fundamental questions remained unanswered.

> What really mattered? What to live for bigger than self-interest? Had we really to let go all the high hopes and comradeship of wartime and admit that victory must be left unfinished after all? It seemed a sad prospect. Having no answer to it all, we took refuge in cynicism and flippancy. By habit and training you learn to maintain a 'front' and hope your friends will not see through it.

What struck me when I came to think of my own first reaction to these later manifestations of the Oxford Group, now some thirty years on, was the pettiness of the 'sins' confessed in public and the one-dimensional way in which every misdemeanour was treated. One effect was to suggest that no cranny was hidden from the stern gaze of God; but the reverse of that was that the tritest of sins acquired the same importance as any others. To 'change' in Moral Rearmament's parlance seemed less a matter of growing into a moral outlook born of experience than re-entry into inherited values from which one had taken a holiday. Any question of whether these sins, typically the partying peccadilloes of the 'bright young things', and of their generation's political disengagement, really mattered, or that there might be others that mattered more, dropped out of sight.

On later reflection, I sensed something seriously pernicious in Moral Rearmament's one-dimensional approach to morality. It encouraged an unnecessarily premature belief in one's own lack of moral health, disabling the inner mechanisms whereby one takes hold of oneself as a whole, with a past and a future, and learns to appreciate rights and wrongs livingly, confessing them to oneself. This is something a person does in the pursuit of truth and honesty, but it is done in private or in context and not in set-piece public confessions. Holding on to oneself is not the same as just putting on a front, and getting hold of oneself is not just making peace with your neighbours. To me it seemed in retrospect that these precociously mature young men had chosen to lock themselves into a state of permanent moral and therefore personal immaturity. Their personal goodness was not in question, but their gospel was vapid and as abstract as those philosophies in which my uncle looked in vain for answers to his fundamental questions.

So, no, after this short exposure to the movement I myself had not 'changed'. Yet I was not the same. For a week I had been in a strangely remote world-in-itself where people had no thought for my kind of reflections. These seemed no longer to matter. I had entered a community life where everyone smoothly interacted with everyone else. If there was a surge of relief at being out of their clutches, this feeling was soon overtaken by a loneliness I had not felt before. I had been on an open-ended journey trying to get the feel of what it is to be a freely wandering soul and now I had become suddenly enmeshed in a well-functioning society dedicated to goodness but in a way that left no room for wandering souls. Their well-articulated mission had upstaged my unscripted project and left it looking puny and selfish.

But obstinacy is a life-saving virtue. I directed my thoughts towards what those people at Caux had no thought for, or if they had, then only as something either to push out of sight or to which to confess as a moral blip. This was the self that you disown responsibility for as soon as you demand that everything you do from now on should be unselfish. One thought was that it might well be those who find no trace of a self in themselves that turn to solution-suited self-definitions of the kind that Moral Rearmament and Alcoholics Anonymous rely on, and which keep their memberships on a tether. A second and connected thought was that it is only out of the depths in which an actual experience of having no self can arise that there can be any talk at all of a self emerging with knowledge of what unselfishness truly means and, if there is a God and he has a will, of what his willing our unselfishness amounts to.

I packed my panniers and rode downhill to ordinary life. For over a week I had been indoctrinated into thinking it was a cesspit of sin. Where now? Straight home? No, I needed time to let this thought and my experiences find their proper perspective. In the glow of now uninterrupted sunshine, and with a sense of recovered freedom and normality, I drove up the Rhone valley in the direction of the river's source and booked in after an hour or so at the delightful Hotel de Londres in Brig, then a comparatively small hotel where I had a room looking on to a back-garden through a window framed in flowers. I thought, how nice it would be to stay there for a time, even live there and write down my thoughts. I did write some and may have spent two nights, I don't really remember, but afterwards I rode part of the way up the Simplon to take some pictures before heading anticlockwise round the Bernese Oberland for Zürich where, after a spectacular ride through sunlit landscapes and outrageously idyllic scenery, I arrived well after dark.

On approaching Zürich, having ridden the bike all day in blistering heat, I saw in the gathering darkness what looked like a fairground surrounded by coloured lights. Well, I thought, here in the cool of the evening they must be having a good time. I had no wish to join in; it was just the idea of the world being one where people gathered in joy and warmth, a warming enough idea in itself. On passing it I saw it was a deserted lot from which, if there had been any revellers, all had gone home and taken their instruments of joy with them. The desolate scene sat like a gravestone in my heart; it seemed to say that even if cheerfulness breaks through now and then, there is too little vital energy to keep it going. The moment passed, but not the memory. The following day, thinking vaguely of Wagner but also of a more restful site for reflection, I decided to visit Lucerne. There I took in at the best hotel I could find, the Schweizerhof, the uniformed doormen diplomatically treating my Norton as though it were a Rolls and ignoring my travel-stained and generally unkempt appearance. I luxuriated in a deep old-fashioned bathtub with surprisingly blue water, ate grandly and the following day did some sightseeing before setting off for home.

Having followed the Rhone to its source, the journey North was given shape by following its opposite partner the Rhine downstream. I stopped off at a small town in Alsace whose name I forget, staying at a very uncomplicated and apart from myself un-guested hotel and the next morning headed for Le Touquet. The short flight completed, just south of London I was stopped for speeding by a motorcycling policeman: 'You're not on the continent now, young man.' What better affirmation that I was on home ground again. Let off with this avuncular warning, I rode up through London and along the Edgware Road to the A1 and was in Melrose the next evening.

I stopped off at our former Carlisle home, now taken on by an uncle after it had been released by the military. His meeting with the Oxford Group in the late 'twenties had contributed. to a nervous breakdown. I mentioned my visit to the Swiss headquarters but tried, without disparaging the organization, to make it clear that my visit was not due to my being 'guided' and was driven by purely selfish motives to see them. I think I said something banal to the effect that it takes all sorts to make a world, to which he responded with a non-committal smile.

The degree I was signed up for at Edinburgh should have taken three years. These now over, I still hadn't completed the requirements. If this continued, I would soon be called up for military service. This led me to think that my sea-experience might inject some meaning into these ominously approaching years out of time. Enlisting as an Ordinary Seaman in the Royal Naval Volunteer Reserve meant no real interference in normal life, but to qualify I had to spend the winter vacation together with a group of young and equally ordinary seamen on a three-week training spell aboard the Fleet Aircraft Carrier HMS Indefatigable, anchored all the while in the middle of Portland Harbour. We drilled on the spacious deck of this vessel, raced each other rowing in whalers, got out of our hammocks at seven in the morning, had breakfast and then went down on our knees and polished linoleum while snotty young officers walked past without looking down. I knew immediately this was not for me. Not so much the snotty young officers, perhaps I might become one, but one reason was just physical. Pulling the seaman's jersey over my enlarged chest and rounded back every morning took up to twenty minutes. The Chief Petty Officer, specially brought in from the dreaded Whale Island training establishment to pull us into shape, kept shouting at me to stand straight. I failed miserably also at the lie test, which is the principle established in Naval training that you never admit to not knowing the answer to any question posed. When our commanding officer, also a reservist and schoolmaster, a very decent man, asked me if I knew where to find the 'boom boats', I should have said something like 'hanging from the main brace on the yardarm, sir', or just 'of course, sir,' rather than admit that I had no idea. I have a feeling this officer thought the practice ridiculous too, but for the moment he was an officer and had to abide by the rules of maritime behaviour. I felt a little better when after giving a lecture and being asked by one of our number how he had earned his DSO, he answered the unthinking idiot who posed the question by saying it was as improper one.

As for me, I had the horrible feeling that this was all just another script to be learned while whatever I amounted to simply cowered behind a show of confidence, or even worse, actually became that show of confidence. The only thing I remember, with amusement and even affection, is being hoisted from a lighter alongside onto the flight deck in a huge basket of cabbages. No, there was one other thing: the Chief Petty Officer with whom we established a good relationship. This fiery but big-hearted little man seemed genuinely saddened at our mutual farewell. I think he and his life depended on the likes of us.

Having now registered for National Service, I braced myself for the medical, rather hoping to prove a disgrace. If I failed for the Navy, I'd be put into the Army. When it came, the doctor asked me about sports and I said, yes, I played rugby for Edinburgh Academicals. Any ailments? Yes, asthma, now and then but not as often or as much as before. He looked at my back. Rugby? he said with a hint of surprise. Yes, but I go to a chiropractor. A few weeks later, on 16 October 1953, I received a card saying that 'under present arrangements' I was not regarded as available for call-up for military service.

Great was my relief. It might have made a man of me, who knows, though on the other hand, God forbid — or in any case not the kind I felt I wanted to become, although I had still little idea of what kind I had it in me to become. Either I would be a colossal military failure or else absorb all too easily its limited scripts as a *modus vivendi*. But now, wonder of wonders, I had time to think again. Not that the way forward was anything like clear. Marking time at the university would have to stop. Should I follow the path of least resistance and prepare myself for a job in the family firm? Where could I turn to seek some more original alternative? With no autonomous leanings towards a life in industry, nor any marked talents or absorbing interests, all I could think of with some despondency was the life of a schoolteacher, a Mr. Chips in fading tweeds. Again, God forbid.

Ideally, I would have preferred a life in music, and if it were possible a life from music. Unhappily, whatever musical gifts I have are mainly of the listening sort. By dint of sheer effort and from a genuine desire to be able to play, I had practised the piano, self-learnt the clarinet and was eventually allowed by the music teacher to play on the organ in St. Andrews Church in Edinburgh. I could also practise on the smaller instrument in the Academy's school hall. I took part in lunchtime performances put on by the music teacher, offering the captive audience a tortured rendering of Saint Saëns's 'The Swan' from *The Carnival of Animals*, which I had to play in a key well-nigh impossible on the B-flat clarinet. As already mentioned, three of us even tackled a Beethoven trio for clarinet, cello and piano. The cellist, the later and now unhappily late advocate Lord Clyde, later composed a trio for us to perform at yet another concert, this time in front of parents and a judge from the Reid School of Music. She referred to my effort too kindly as that of a promising clarinettist.

I knew better. A band-musician advertising clarinet instruction had been invited home to give me lessons. We had one session in which he got me going but after that I decided to proceed on my own, thinking I'd get all the practice I was good for in the school orchestra. That proved to be true, but the level of ambition was low. In terms of actually playing music my first greatest breakthrough came when, as I have mentioned earlier, my mother called on Elly Wilkie. She was a eurythmy teacher who also taught improvisation. In one session I could grasp the interrelationships between the chords and play what came to my fingers instead of translating written music to sound, an accomplishment my brain seemed constitutionally unable to cultivate sufficiently to have it connect my eyes directly to my fingers. After ten years of plodding through the usual beginner's repertoire, I was free to make my own. Ideally, of course, I would have liked to become a famous conductor allowed to choose my own limited repertoire.

I had seen many conductors. The year we had settled in Edinburgh, 1947, coincided with the beginning of the Edinburgh Festival. Watching Furtwängler *en face* from the Usher Hall's organ gallery, I had been fascinated by his pulsating frame and shaking arms, even some spitting, all apparently disconnected from the actual bars of the glorious music he elicited from the orchestra. Some similarity struck me, later on, with Charlton Heston urging on his horses in the famous chariot race in Ben Hur. At the other extreme there was Adrian Boult, with the demeanour of an authoritative butler suavely waving a long stick over his subservient staff. The result was more pedestrian and less charged but still convincing. I watched Bruno Walter eliciting emanations of spirituality from his Viennese players. Sir Thomas Beecham produced ravishing music without undue display, although after the interval he ostentatiously peered at the programme notes on his podium as if to refresh his memory about what he was to conduct next. I happened to pass his hotel one day when, I am almost certain, he deliberately dropped something on the way to his waiting taxi just so that the footman could pick it up. There were Victor da Sabata and Dimitri Mitropoulos, both neat and fit, rather like Putin, and the earnest Eduard van Beinum coercing the Concertgebouw orchestra to its excellent best. The idea of conducting became a distant dream of my own. John Barbirolli seemed to smile encouragingly at me from a portrait on the wall of the soundproof cabin in Rae Mac's where one listened to records before buying them. My mother once caught me in the sitting room conducting the final bars of Ravel's *La Valse*.

Typically, she quietly withdrew without saying a word. Mutual embarrassment? Not long afterwards the BBC's Scottish Director of Music was invited to tea. Herbert Wiseman, well known for his 'Music for Schools' broadcasts, knew my father's parents well. If the plan was to test the ground for any promise in the direction of a musical future, nothing came of it. I was unprepared and therefore unable and therefore unwilling to demonstrate any performing ability, compared with which my addiction to music was totally out of proportion.

Musical parents are a godsend for any child. That mine had musical taste and some performing ability was a fact I woke up to quite early. On the piano my mother had the three-volume Tovey Beethoven Sonatas. My father was a Sibelius fan with several albums of the Sibelius Society recordings under Thomas Beecham. His favourites were the second and fourth symphonies. The parental record collection, largely neglected as time passed, included two gripping overtures, *William Tell* and *Rienzi*, the 'Ingemisco' from Verdi's *Requiem*, sung in cool clear tones by what must have been a Russian tenor, sundry lighter works such as the Boccherini Minuet, an abbreviated version of Ravel's climactic *Bolero* (having to flip a 78 rpm of that piece would be out of the question), and the early Stravinsky's strangely haunting *Pastorale*. There was Felix Weingartner Beethoven with the seventh symphony in particular making an early impression, and later the Toscanini Beethoven symphonies with the BBC Symphony Orchestra, and as a matter of course the back-to-back Schumann and Grieg piano concertos, which it took me some time to tell apart. Schubert's fifth was played quite often. After the war I remember a Sunday when I sat beside my father listening to Beethoven's ninth while we both read it from a miniature score, of which he had many. In another vein I also recall my parents after the war ordering 'Red Sails in the Sunset' from a Carlisle record shop on the corner of Lowther Street. It spoke of nostalgia and a taste for music of a more informal kind that they must have enjoyed when first meeting. When asked what I'd like for my thirteenth birthday, I suggested the beginnings of a record collection of my own. He chose Moritz Rosenthal, a pupil of Liszt as well as of one of Chopin's, playing the latter, the Third Bach Suite performed by the Busch Chamber Players, Elisabeth Schumann singing 'Horch! Horch! die Lerch' and (I think) 'Sandmännchen', accompanied by Gerald Moore.

For those with an ear for it, there are as many ways of relating to music as there are kinds. In some forms, it provides a kind of habitation. Church music, for instance, provides a home for the soul seeking comfort on the day God rested. There is participation but the home is open only on Sundays and to a small and even vanishing part of your being. Heavy Metal is captivating and participatory but escapist and self-indulgent, an assault on sensibility as well as the ears, at least mine. It doesn't take you anywhere. Most classical music is not at all participatory and by no means all of it is good, more like art-work in the home — nice sounds offering a consoling glimpse of harmony unlike anything in the here and now. If much of it expresses sorrow, the genius of art has turned it into something pleasurable. 'What is a poet?' one writer asks, and answers: 'an unhappy man who hides deep anguish in his heart, but whose lips are so formed that when the sigh and cry pass through them, it sounds like lovely music.' A music critic, glowing over a Toscanini performance of Beethoven's *Missa Solemnis*, praised it as though it was a direct revelation of the divine spirit. To me it seemed more like one man's last-ditch attempt to retrieve a vision of human fulfilment in the face of mankind's folly. Romantic music properly defined, speaks more narrowly to the unhappy man. The Blues bring this closer to home for the hard-done-by: the banal lyrics record harrowing personal experiences of loss and jealousy, even hate, never love. A few simple rhythmic formulas distance singer and audience from the reality in a kind of cathartic irony that also serves as participatory musical entertainment. The uncomplicated nature of this music makes it easy for an audience to feel it is taking part, not sitting in astonishment at the skills of composers and performers. While classically inclined, I had been gripped by the blues element that the gifted Ferdinand La Menthe (Jelly Roll Morton) had woven into those polished versions of New Orleans Jazz recorded by his Red Hot Peppers. A 78 disc with 'Sidewalk Blues' and 'Dead Man Blues' had accompanied David and myself with a wind-up turntable on our trip to Rome in 1950, and I had already sensed the melancholic strain in composers like Brahms, more encrypted than in Schubert but, recalling the words of the poet, all the more expressive for that. I even heard plaint unending in such apparent pastoral jollities as those perpetrated by the splendidly garrulous oboe in Richard Strauss's late concerto, but that may be because I first heard it on the radio while recovering from pneumonia.

As the otherwise fruitless limbo of university existence neared its end, I had become a Mahler addict and a jazz fan, the latter largely with the help of Mike Pollett, a fellow-yachtsman who played revival New Orleans trombone. At a student party I had heard the passionate and adventurous clarinettist Sandy Brown, then still studying architecture at the Art College. I was bowled over and for months afterwards and tried vainly to produce a similar Johnny Dodds sound from my clarinet. A group of Chicago musicians, the Eddie Condon All-Stars with Wild Bill Davison, Bud Freeman, Cutty Cutshall and George Wettling, came to the Usher Hall. When I mentioned to my parents that I was going to the concert, no doubt searching their anthroposophical consciences they looked at each other questioningly. Their worry, recalling Virgil's famous line, 'Easy is the decent to hell', may have been a reflection on their own experiences of the roaring 'twenties. Or perhaps, having reason to be uneasy about the future of a son who seemed to be going nowhere, they may have had doubts about my ability to resist the intoxicant of rhythm; it might prevent me from rising to the level of spirituality they aspired to themselves. Something they could feel easier about was the recently acquired addiction to Mahler, originating in a shared enthusiasm for Kathleen Ferrier. The famous singer had worked for a while as a telephone operator in Carlisle and we may even have heard her contralto voice saying 'number please'. I heard her first as a singer in 1952 at the Edinburgh Festival, where she sang Brahms' Liebesleider-Walzer with Irmgard Seefried, Julius Patzak, and Horst Günther, accompanied by either Clifford Curzon or Hans Gál. Her recording with Patzak of *Das Lied von der Erde*, conducted by Bruno Walter, appeared a year later and if ever there was a composition in which the sigh and cry of the composer's anguish sounded like lovely music, this was it, even if in Mahler the sighs and even shrieks can at times become audible. I bought the symphonies as they gradually became available, the pioneering recordings of the first, seventh and ninth, as well as of the Adagio of the unfinished tenth, by Hermann Scherchen, from whose book *Music for Everyone* I took many notes, and then Rafael Kubelik's less Nietzschean readings. The addiction grew and became a kind of home from home, where feelings formed by the lips of music could be safely vented and at the same time enjoyed. But since, although an emotional home, or a foster home of sorts, music was not going to offer a livelihood, I planned to accept my father's invitation to be suitably 'brainwashed', as he put it, into the world of textiles. I would undergo a two-year's trainee programme with Courtaulds, the firm which had interests in our family business.

Before this revamping of my brain was to begin, I chose to try filling it with some thoughts of its own. For my final year, freed from military service, I revisited philosophy, a typical resort for the wayward and wandering. I had taken a course on social philosophy from Frederick (Freddie) Broadie. The topic for the half-term essay had been 'You Can't Call Your Soul Your Own', which in a way was a comforting thought since it put some of the blame for its condition on others. For the last spring and summer terms, beginning in January 1954, I attended a course on Modern Ethical Thinking, spanning Bradley's idealism and Stevenson's emotivism. It was given by Erroll Bedford, whose own thinking as I only later realized was heavily influenced by Wittgenstein. In the summer I attended a series on political philosophy given by Peter Heath, an Oxford philosopher with a war-time army career, and also a course in Italian. In the autumn, however, I had already begun Junior Honours Moral Philosophy, a course designed to stretch over the whole year and given by John Macmurray. He began with Greek philosophy and moved along via Kant and Hamann in the spring and summer to 'Present Day Philosophy'.

This included several lectures on a writer with a name quite new to me. On January 15th, 1954, in the copious and almost verbatim notes I took on Macmurray's lectures, beside the name 'Kierkegaard' I wrote in brackets 'a Dane'. It took more than a decade before I came across that passage in his *Either/Or* about the poet's lips being formed to make anguish into lovely sounds. I hardly set eyes on Macmurray since I was feverishly writing down almost everything he said; nor did I meet him face-to face at that time. Professors didn't tutor and although Macmurray was often to be seen on campus, he was always unstoppably going somewhere. There was also a certain aloofness or perhaps just shyness. He once admitted to us that when invited on to a television panel, his participation had been a total failure. Indirectly, in his lectures he told us quite a lot about himself, illustrating one point by describing himself running in panic from the German trenches in World War I (in which he was decorated with the Military Cross, something he did not tell us).

I discovered later that in his earlier years Macmurray had a considerable sympathy for Marxism. Now he was focussing on a principle that he called the primacy of the personal, 'person' being for him an irreducible concept with which philosophy should begin, as against reflection or thought, which traditionally seemed either never to get as far as the person or to skip over it. Within that concept, action became basic, replacing as he says, the Kantian 'I think' with the 'I do' — thinking backing up action already in progress rather than preceding action itself. In political terms, Macmurray had been at one time, and for all I know became perpetually, a member of a group called the Christian Left. But he had formulated a position that reformed the group's views. Its own conception of the relation of religion to politics had been to make religion the source of values in terms of doctrine, creed and ritual, with these translated into conventional political goals to be pursued by the usual political means within the appropriate parties, as currently in German politics and, I may add, Norwegian. The Macmurray twist was that cultural and political goals must themselves be issues of a religious nature under the category of 'community'. In the end it was whatever supports community as cooperative activity that determined economic affairs, wealth distribution and other social, and even state boundaries. In a *world* fellowship, if ever there should be such a thing, there would be 'no national boundaries', though Macmurray doubted that this could ever be achieved. In arguing for the indispensability of the notion of God, he claimed that the theological question of God's existence is wrongly put in the form 'Does God exist?' It should be expressed by asking 'Is what exists personal?' If you say Yes, then you must ask whether the Other to which the totality of fellowship relations itself relates is *impersonal or is itself personal*. If personal, then God is this Other, but now only and exclusively with reference to action. There was a touch of Hegel in this, though also, as I was to realize much later, much more than just a touch of Kierkegaard.

Macmurray's lectures in the spring of 1954, first on Kant, Hamann and Herder, took us in easy stages to Hegel, Marx and Kierkegaard. He described all three as 'dialectical thinkers'. The description stuck in my mind and left me with Kierkegaard not as a poet or literary innovator with philosophy and theology as his vehicle, but a thinker, a dialectical thinker at that, a kind of philosopher. With crammed notebooks to be perused in an indefinite future and something of a personal kind for my mind to chew over, I felt I had done what I could in the academic sphere. With the embarrassment of graduation over and before venturing into the satanic mills, I mounted my motorcycle and headed once more for the sun.

The previous December I had received a Christmas card from my friends in Switzerland saying that Henri's uncle, Dr Jeanneret, had died. I thought I should visit but, first of all, take this opportunity for a last sortie into the great outside. Macmurray had talked of the nothingness of human personality, a notion common to atheism and existentialism, and which he told us had its origin in Kierkegaard. In the latter, however, it had a positive ring. It was the narrow pass you need to go through to retrieve the world as the place you then choose as the right one to be in. But that is a very abstract thought and leaves you as much a wanderer without a base as someone living on a potato patch. I had read *The Razor's Edge* with enthusiasm and thought the life of a wanderer owing his soul only to himself, equally at home in any context, would be a better one than total spiritual isolation. But any reflections I had arrived at in my half-term essay on not being able to call my soul my own were now forgotten. I had even delved into my parents' Steiner literature looking for some spiritual training programme that might answer to the physical regime of my foray into rugby football. But most of what was intelligible to me spoke of how to get out of oneself into something more ethereal that would carry us beyond the threshold of death; I was looking for something on this side of the hereafter. But I may have been wrong in thinking they were not the same thing.

This time I rode to Paris and booked into the previously visited hotel on the rue St. Germain-l'Auxerrois. The street being narrow I decided not to park my Norton there and asked advice of a gendarme. He looked admiringly at the machine and said they'd be happy to look after it at the local police station. I stayed for two days, much of it in the company of two Swedish girls and a young Pakistani. They were about to move on to Geneva and we said we'd try to meet, which we did but briefly. I pitched my tent again on the shore of the lake at Préverenges, but this time the visit was clouded by Dr Jeanneret's absence. In spite of my indifferent wardrobe, Henri and Georgette took me to a nightclub, but being eyed menacingly by the patron after I had twice danced with a girl without offering her a drink, I realized this was not my kind of place. Henri, too, seemed to mistake the meaning of my visit, his suspicions perhaps aroused by the fact that I was travelling alone. I tried placing a friendly arm round Georgette's shoulder as he took our photo, but he frowned and waved it away with a 'Non!' I had no designs on Georgette and it was their friendship that I valued with a wish to renew happy memories. We kept in contact and I met them again several years later in London.

There was little time to spare before the new life in commerce began. As I drove north again, glancing back on the way from Rheims to the coast ferry, I saw my new Burberry had fallen off. Having nothing like leathers or even a crash helmet, and fearing the weather might change for the worse, I decided to ride as far north as possible. By nightfall I had crossed the channel, traversed London, and reached Scotch Corner in North Yorkshire, a trip of well over five-hundred miles.

I was lucky. On the way from Dover to London I had been all but wiped off the road by a careering green Bentley of early 'thirties Le Mans vintage. Its driver, a long-haired, silk-scarfed young man of aristocratic mien, was so convivially engaged with his load of gaily dressed young lady passengers, their hair and scarves flying in the wind, that he clearly had difficulty taking corners at speed. It was a close thing, so close that his image stuck in my mind.

Chapter Five: Shipshape

Shipshape: orderly, neat, trim, and well-kept in way that a ship should be.

The new life began in August 1954. Groomed and charcoal-greyed, white shirted and tied, I arrived at 16 St Martins-le-Grand under the shadow of St Paul's Cathedral to make myself known to the personnel department of Courtaulds Ltd. I was introduced to Mr Gratwick, the director who was my father's closest contact. They put me up in a good hotel near Russell Square and I was sent to a general practitioner for a medical. It was just after lunch. Probing my abdominal regions with his stethoscope he hastily pulled it away saying it sounded like the traffic at Piccadilly Circus. It seemed not to matter; things were at least moving. I was introduced to two other trainees and then given my marching orders. To get some idea of how trees were turned into yarn and then yarn into fabrics, I was to visit all the main production plants. I would then spend longer periods at various locations in order to acquire a deeper understanding of the administrative and organizational aspects of complex chemical and textile processes. Finally, I would be tried for size in one of the firm's district sales offices. The firm was a large one and controlled a major part of the artificial fibre market. Some history is needed.

In 1810 Samuel Courtauld opened a silk mill in Braintree, Essex. He had been born in America, where his father George had emigrated out of sympathy for the American Revolutionaries. George returned briefly to England with his family before returning again to America in 1818, leaving Samuel behind to be the virtual founder of the firm. To the Braintree mill others were added at Halstead and Bocking. In 1850 the three mills employed two thousand workers, mainly women drawn from London's workhouses. 1861 was a pivotal year. Bad plumbing at Windsor Castle caused Prince Albert to die of typhus. The queen's prolonged mourning made black silk a fashion and, with it, a high and lasting demand for silk crepe. Samuel died an extremely wealthy man and, at the time of my own brief engagement with the firm, Courtaulds was now an industrial giant with two main divisions, a chemical and a textile. Their factories were spread over England and North Wales with rayon-producing plants in Coventry, Derby, Preston, Wolverhampton, and Greenfield in Flintshire, and textile processing plants at Nuneaton and Braintree as well as another in Flintshire. Weaving of various kinds continued in Essex at Halstead.

At this time of writing it is history. The name 'Courtauld' survives only in the Institute of Art, now part of the University of London and endowed by Samuel's great nephew, also Samuel, who became chairman of the company in 1921. The chemical and fibre manufacturing and the clothing divisions were split in 1991, each later bought by other conglomerates keyed into a new world situation. For textiles it meant cheaper labour in the East. The factories are now vacant or have been demolished. *Sic transit* ...

My start was with viscose production at Wolverhampton. I was put up grandly at the *Star and Garter Hotel*, a half-timbered building with connections back to Charles I, later replaced by a shopping centre with a Pizza Hut in place of the facade. I spent most my time observing and, in canteen breaks, joining in conversation with 'staff', among them people my father had known in his early years. This made me think that, whatever else came of *these* years, at least they would fill in a gap in our family's, and particularly my own, knowledge of the world in which our over-working father moved. But there was little to do other than get the hang of what was being done and how. For whatever reason this day-long inactivity left me hungry. On returning to the hotel in the late afternoon I chose liberally from the dinner menu. This caused the personnel department in London to remind me that they didn't cover the cost of guests. After I wrote saying that sheer hunger drove me to adding a steak to the mixed grill, they made no further fuss.

I was transferred briefly to Coventry to learn about acetate production, again accommodated in comfort but beginning to find my solitary journey with no real goal disconcerting. I experienced the first of many nervous attacks that took the form of a sense of heart stoppage. The sensation triggers an immediate impulse to jump into action as though to kick-start the pump again. They say that a quick and decent cough can re-start a stopped heart. I still have no idea what this really is and, for lack of a better diagnosis I treat it as a navigational warning that I am not on course. It came as I sat eating alone at a table in the middle of the dining room, feeling uneasily conspicuous. In a second, I found myself outside in the parking lot. The next day I bought a cheap Philips radio to have something to listen to other than my own thoughts.

That helped. Distractions do. Soon after, I was sent to Deeside in Flintshire. The Coleshill Guest House was a nice enough place surrounded by trees but consequently humid. My clothes, which I hung on a chair during the night, were sodden by morning. Several weeks were spent finding out how yarn was processed. It involved spinning, then winding and coning. The machinery made a terrific noise and, in the winding shed, produced complex harmonics based on a steady key against which I found I could shout the blues without anyone hearing me, a way of both relieving and expressing the boredom of just watching things happen. For all I know this was the birth of Heavy Metal but it was of the ear-buzz that has increasingly plagued me through the years. Ear protection was still in the future. The staff at Deeside Mill and the Aber Works were kindness itself, the assistant manager even offering to ask his wife to take care of my laundry.

Again, weekends posed a problem. Except for the hospital where I had once spent some time, Liverpool was unfamiliar. On one weekend I visited home to enjoy one more motorcycle trip before selling the machine the next weekend for that 'ton', also the term for its official maximum speed, which I achieved only once. Another weekend, I took a bus to Widnes to watch a Saturday afternoon rugby league game. I felt alien, or just lonely, and the same heart-stopping occurred as I got off the bus. The game and the enthusiastic crowd helped recovery.

The whole operation from spinning to warping could be followed in Nuneaton, the end product being large rollers ready for delivery to weavers. For several months I lived at the Castlemere Guest House on the Old Hinckley Road, together with a mixed but gregarious band of secretaries, schoolteachers, shop assistants and an ex-army man on the same trainee course. We were a disparate group that any dramatist from Coward to Pinter with an ear for the possibilities of self-revelation in a context of shared board and lodging could exploit. The determined friendliness of one co-lodger could be caught by his insistence on calling me 'Haggis'. Friendly disrespect is a typically British way of cementing relations, banter an effective way of avoiding the embarrassment of too much closeness. Going to the cinema offered an opportunity for joint activity. *On the Waterfront* had just been released and we went to see it together, discussing its merits and slightly heavy symbolism afterwards. A girl lodger approached me with a headache problem and I wrote to my parents' physician in Glasgow for advice. I began to see myself as a kind of travelling social curator, but this was a closeness I wanted to avoid. I found it easier to talk to the workers on the shop floor. I even spent evenings walking some country lanes with a young lady who worked in the warping shed. In Nuneaton I met another trainee, Oliver Tetley, an Etonian to say the least. He seemed to have his own living arrangements.

Oliver was a breath of fresh air, or rather a wind that swept through the whole establishment, though it was hard to say from where or in what direction. Rather than making people turn up their collars, his supreme self-confidence worked more as a social solvent, drawing all levels of management together in a spirit of conviviality that fudged the distinction between working hours and time off. Within a week he had persuaded the dispatch department to place products ready for delivery in a new geometrical pattern that speeded up access. When the works manager had a birthday, all management were invited, and myself, to a party arranged at a local pub. Oliver was the essence of good cheer and danced with the manager's wife. Trade union regulations, as well as concern for quality, prohibited trainees from taking part in production and we had a lot of time on our hands. An empty office provided an opportunity to read and discuss life. I spoke of Macmurray and he of Bertrand Russell. He had been in Scotland and we had several common acquaintances. He spoke of girls and charity queens enthroned during the Edinburgh students' charity week. I'd known them too, but he spoke as though his relations with them were of another order. He spoke of Tanya and their son, Jonathan. He visited them, I think in Essex, at weekends, weekends that also involved parties in London given by Lady this or Lady that, who would be sure to make 'short work' of me had I been invited. So he said, but I never was. He probably saw I'd be a misfit; he remarked jokingly on my Scottishness, the way people in England do, but perhaps correctly concluded that I was insufficiently free-spirited to negotiate in safety the life of the landed and London élite. I was a trifle disappointed not to be invited to a dinner at which Gregory Peck was also to be a guest. Oliver said he had forgotten. It is quite likely that he did, he also drank quite liberally and his memory was taxed by serial enthusiasms. He was a sort of multi-purpose Don Giovanni, a force of human nature. I felt rather like a Leporello *in absentia*.

One weekend he did take me to London. We visited Tanya's father, Igor Vinogradoff, then married to his second wife, Julian, daughter of Lady Ottoline Morrell. It occurred to me afterwards that the house in Gower Street where I was introduced to the couple was the more modest abode to which the Morrells resorted when no longer able to afford their grander premises on Bedford Square. It was at this latter residence that Lady Ottoline helped herself to the male members of the Bloomsbury Group. I was also introduced to Tanya herself, a striking blonde with humour and a mind of her own, suggesting sparks might fly in private. Oliver had told me of how, when unable to find parking space in the Strand, she simply abandoned her car in the middle of the street. I could see why he was fond of her, as he obviously was.

I didn't meet Oliver again until over a year later when finally stationed in Bradford as an apprentice sales representative. I don't know what he was doing in the area, but one late evening he drove past me as I was walking home. It was a side street, so it looked as though he was in fact trying to find me. I wondered a bit at that. But there was a lonely streak in him and we got on well. I invited him in and we drank the half bottle of whisky he was carrying. Unfortunately,

I was to catch an early train in the morning to attend a conference with worker representatives of several trade unions. I managed in spite of a terrible headache and hangover.

That was the last I saw of Oliver Tetley though my memory of him remains fresh. Searching recently on the Internet, I found he had been married previously and that Tanya had married again and died already in 1988. By then Oliver had married and divorced again twice, most recently to a niece of the Queen Mother. In the 1960s, as I also read, he had been politically active in South Africa. One of his daughter's wrote that he had been 'instrumental in the Sharpeville airlift that got most of the ANC out of South Africa after Nelson Mandela's arrest'. Banned from South Africa, he lived for a while in Swaziland. This daughter, who appeared to have no living memory of him, gathered that he was a 'colourful and passionate personality'. In 1974 for whatever sad reason, at the age of forty-five Oliver took his own life. It became clear, from a conversation we once had, that on the Dover to London road in 1954, driving his green Bentley with friends for a weekend in Paris, he had very nearly taken mine. Leporello lives on.

The fact of my lucky escape emerged while we reminisced in our commandeered office in Nuneaton. There, shocked that I had no knowledge of the processes whereby trees became blouses, Oliver gave me a short course in basic chemistry. We talked cars and Oliver told of a Bentley he had recently sold. The thought striking me, I asked if he had ever driven to France in it. Yes, a visit to Paris a year or so ago. No, he didn't recall any particular motorcyclist. The Bentley had fixed itself more firmly in my own mind, along with a fleeting and peripheral glimpse of its energized driver. I am quite certain it was Oliver Tetley at the wheel.

Two further 'officer material' trainees I met in the course of these two years suffered unusual fates, one of them fatally. Angus MacDonald, turned journalist, died on Nicosia's 'murder mile' in 1956, the last EOKA victim before Cyprus gained independence. The third, whose name I forget, became engaged while sharing my stay in Wolverhampton. There, as in his enthusiasm he felt impelled to inform me, he bought several products from a chemist to facilitate what at the time he took to be the most rewarding aspect of his coming status. Later, by then a male model, he went missing in Spain. I don't know if he was found, but I did wonder whether this had something to do with his marriage.

Weekends in Nuneaton being for non-residents to be avoided at all costs, on Friday evenings I took the train to London, returning late on Sundays. I stayed first at the Bonnington Hotel by Russell Square but later secured membership of the RNVR Club. It gave me a Mayfair address though only a dormitory bunk to lie down on. In London I walked a great deal, had meals mainly in Soho and went to concerts at the Festival Hall, as well as the occasional cinema, sometimes both on the same day. I saw *The Student Prince* with Mario Lanza's voice emanating from the unlikely mouth of Edmund Purdom, and in the evening Hans Hotter singing with inspired gloom Schubert's *Winterreise*.

I was alone in London but managed to ward off loneliness by so to speak cultivating it. The unhappy wanderer of the *Winterreise* was confirmation, not a threat. It brought to mind my experience on the way to Zürich, the festive fairground that turned out to be deserted. It might have provided another verse. I once sat long at lunch in a Greek restaurant reading something I found totally absorbing that only some years later I realized was by *the* Samuel Beckett. The author's name meant nothing to me then. In Charing Cross Road I came across a copy of *Merlin*, a literary journal edited in Paris by Alexander Trocchi, an expatriate Glaswegian into culture and drugs in Paris. It was its second number. Surviving on a shoestring, the journal ran for only a short time, but before it folded Merlin had included the work of Genet and Ionesco as well as Beckett, and regular writers such as Richard Seaver, who translated Beckett's French, and Trocchi himself. What I read was 'The End', a bleak, close-to-earth narrative of a man who ends by taking himself out on a boat and stage-setting his own suicide by drowning. It was as though the itinerary of a *Winterreise* could be told without being refracted through the protective forms of poetry and music. These were not lips formed to make anguish sound like lovely music. There was in fact no anguish, just a deadpan narrative from point zero. I have often wondered whether that is where spiritual life begins rather than ends.

Either way, in retrospect I can see that this was where I was myself homing in. My actions were those of someone protecting himself from the actual prospect of acute loneliness. Cultivating it was one way of doing this and certainly not uncreative. But lack of confidants can weaken contact with reality. In my travels, apart from Tetley, I had met no one with whom I could be entirely at ease. On my London weekends I walked the streets incessantly and never entered a coffee shop or bar to mingle with others. I chose the informality of Greek restaurants in Soho for my meals, and on several occasions recall standing around at the exit of the Piccadilly Circus underground just to feel part of the whirl. Anywhere else I might well have been picked up for loitering; as it was, after several nights there, a man sidled up to me and said I must be an undercover cop. A person alone can easily be suspected of this or that.

One evening in the South Bank Festival Hall I happened to catch the eye of a man who sat down a few seats away, just a polite smile. At the interval he asked me if I'd care to join him at the Strand Hotel afterwards. Happy to have someone to talk to and a concert to talk about, I agreed. Walking over Waterloo Bridge he told me he taught at a boarding school in Berkshire. At the hotel, instead of going for the bar, he led me to the lift and we went to his room. The extent of my naïveté can be judged by the fact that not for a second did occur to me that we were destined for the bed rather than the mini-bar. But if I was unsuspecting, once in the room he himself grasped the situation immediately and said, 'We'd better go down to the bar'. With no suspicion of my host's expectations at the time, our conversation there continued uninhibited by any sense of my having disappointed them. When later I cottoned on, I tried to imagine the situation if it had been a woman; would I have followed her to the room, if invited? Would a thought of the possible expense put me off? Why should that thought arise in the case of a woman but not with this man? Does eye-catching in the Festival Hall, as against knowing looks in a bar, offer something for the soul if also by extension for the body? What if the man had possessed Grecian beauty and was full of grace? Some aspects of one's self remain inscrutable, but I have never found a man that attractive or attractive in that way. As for women, the only girl I met in London then was, a receptionist at the Bonnington, a Yorkshire lass I think and equally lonely. I asked her out to dinner, walked her home and we parted with a kiss which put a little more, or quite a lot, between me and point zero.

In the spring and until the following autumn I was transferred to Essex, the original Courtauld country. I was introduced at Halstead to the seeming miracle of textile weaving in all its forms. At Braintree they let me try my hand at dying considerable lengths of fabric designed for parachutes. Due to the quality demands of customers who placed large orders, cloth destined for the likes of Marks & Spencer called for more seasoned hands. The oil patches I left on several hundred yards of parachute fabric were not enough to have me seen off the premises.

I shared digs for several months with another young man who was a dinghy racer. Our hosts were an elderly couple along Coggeshall Road on the eastern outskirts of Braintree. Mrs Furbeck was a Quaker, or perhaps they both were, so I was either 'thou' or 'thee'. For some reason my fellow lodger, when in their presence, referred to me as 'his lordship'. Perhaps it was because I never got around to saying 'just call me Alastair'. I never have. For some reason all such talk sounds to me pretentious and, besides, my name not being as common then as it is now, I was embarrassed by it. At the time, 'Just call me Al' didn't suit my self-image. To my host and hostess, I was 'Mr Hannay' while if my memory is correct my fellow-lodger was 'Michael'.

I had no such problems on the shop floor when they allowed me to take a hand. The workers treated me as one of their own, and even, doubtless because

I was an outsider, took me into their confidence. I was made privy to their illnesses and handicaps. When Mr Nankivell, the division director and a colleague of my father came looking for me one day, at first he didn't recognize me in my shirt-sleeves and dye-flecked trousers. Things were otherwise at the Halstead weaving mill, where the manager, a lay preacher, had sent in a complaint about me to main office for challenging him when he brusquely told me to close a newspaper during a coffee break. Mr Nankivell wrote to my father of the incident but fortunately only after seeing me cleaning out a dye vat. His lasting impression was positive, or so I gathered from my father's possibly diplomatic way of putting it. He may even have been encouraged to see in my recalcitrance some indication that the brainwashing process was meeting healthy resistance.

During the sailing season, my co-lodger and I spent Saturdays and Sundays at Burnham-on-Crouch racing. The boats were Hornets, and with a trapeze and a spinnaker there was plenty for the crew to do. Only once did I fall into the river. Otherwise, being so near London, I spent most weekends at the RNVR Club and walked immense distances alone. It was bracing and I continued my creative dedication to solitude and even desolation. In May 1955 I heard Mahler's first symphony with Bruno Walter, conducting the BBC Symphony Orchestra at its twenty-fifth anniversary concert, attended by the Harewoods and other musical grandees. With a Decca portable player in my room at Braintree, I often played music during the night, listening to Scherchen's recording of the Adagio of Mahler's unfinished tenth symphony over and over again. I listened often to Kathleen Ferrier, two years after her death, singing the contralto movements of *Das Lied von der Erde*. The night focused the grotesque contrast between the disembodied voice in its heart-rending presence and the body's irredeemable return to the dust, the bitterness made marginally sweeter in the *Abschied*'s words of an eternally returning spring.

Those I met in the factories, in ordinary positions and roles, with whom I felt far more at ease than with the well-suited gentlemen that ran the firm, helped to keep me on an even keel. There are advantages and disadvantages with the cultivation of solitude. On the one hand, I felt less and less able or inclined to adopt the styles and vocabulary of those I was supposed to be on the way to joining; while, on the other hand, the world experienced from a solitary point of view became more intense and interesting. There were also heroes to be cultivated, the world's odd-balls. I found myself reading the lives of the supposedly similarly solitary, but since they were written about also extraordinary people. I read avidly of Lawrence of Arabia, studied Kennington's head in the crypt of St. Paul's, was upset by Richard Aldington's critical biography, which revealed homosexuality and the creator of his own legend. In the long run, however, these claims enriched my view of the national hero, adding a human dimension that I felt I could easily relate to. I remember turning such thoughts over in my mind as I read the Sunday papers while lazing on the bottom-boards of a rowing boat one sunny afternoon on the Serpentine.

That spring my father and I met several times in London. He was negotiating changes in the family business, forging connections outside that would keep it competitive in the changing world. These, against the inclinations of his brother-in-law, the nominal head, would dent the image of the firm as a purveyor of exclusive textiles. My father had been diagnosed with a heart problem and was supposed to take things easy. In one meeting with him in London he told me not to tell my mother he had flown the previous day to an exhibition in Brussels. In my own quasi-neurasthenic condition, I felt his problem keenly and probably more than he did. I was livid when a fellow-member of the Liberal Club chided my father and myself for taking the lift up just one floor. That he himself had no immediate fears seemed proved when he opened an envelope to show me the photograph of a schooner based near Southampton that a business contact intended to sell, and which my father was clearly bent on buying — which he subsequently did. These dinner occasions brought us into a closer contact than had been possible before. I was, after all, seeing my father in the context of his working life and could make out the world that had been his ever since we lived in Carlisle with its castle separating us from its industry. I was given time off to accompany him to Burton-on-Trent, where Courtaulds and Morton Sundour collaborated on the development of a high-speed knitting machine, called FNF (Fly Needle Frame), and was introduced to the boss Andy Bowron, the managing director, who was obviously much attached to my father. At Wolverhampton I had met people who knew him from early times. Arnold Smith recalled him in the 'thirties sitting pipe in mouth absorbing quietly what was being said and done. One afternoon, after I had finally arrived in Bradford, I was eating crumpets with tea, as I usually did after leaving the office at five. There being no unoccupied tables, a stranger asked if he could join me. We got talking. He ran a firm making textile machinery and it turned out he knew my father well. Here, as everywhere I went, I heard him spoken of with respect.

To me, my father confided things I found saddening. His current negotiations and ensuing struggles with his brother-in-law left him sighing at times for the cut-and-dried life of the Navy. Problems there were practical and as an engineer he had been trained how to solve them. More than once he said he sometimes wished he'd never left. What possible implications these thoughts had for my own future, or my father's hopes for it, was not something that occurred to me at the time, though soon the question would become a burning one. At the time my guess would have been that I was better off in Courtaulds than with Morton Sundour Fabrics. The latter was on the slide and would probably be bought up by Courtaulds anyway, the prestigious name and textile experience saving it from disappearing entirely down its maw. Perhaps I might lead the bit that remained? Or work my way up in Courtaulds and make a name for myself there, a minor take-over in reverse?

In the autumn I spent a new but again brief period at Coventry where I was interviewed for placement in one of the firm's regional sales offices. When offered a choice between Belfast and Bradford, I said Belfast, citing my interest in sailing. I was posted instead to York House, the company's Yorkshire base in Bradford, possibly because one of their representatives, Austin Boyd, himself from Belfast and connected through his family with the Northern Irish office, was under treatment for testicular cancer. It was Austin's rounds that I was to take over.

After lodging briefly in Shipley with an Austrian couple, whose son it turned out to some embarrassment was due to be interviewed for a job with my family's firm, I found myself an apartment in Mornington Villas, not far from the town centre. This was I think the first time I had ever cooked for myself. Hitherto, since leaving home, I had been provided for by landladies and hotel kitchens. I was totally inexperienced and under-equipped for house management, let alone meal preparation, but couldn't afford to eat out except at weekends. Office hours began at eight, when we assembled around a table while Mr Davenport, our golf-playing boss, reviewed our efforts and detailed our tasks for the day. Whereupon we went to the firm's garage to pick up a car to be returned at the end of the working day. As luck would have it, lunch was on the firm and since my customers enjoyed their lunches, I could spend some time on them too, coming to familiarize myself with several excellent hostelries and their car parks, where I could sleep it off before making the afternoon calls. I acquired a taste for jugged hare and Wensleydale cheese. After a month or two, the Ulsterman returned, ostensibly recovered from an operation. But it became clear to us all, and particularly to me as we both called on his customers, that in making introductions on my behalf he was also taking his farewell. He excused his recent failure to keep contact as due to 'a touch of cancer', and although he never suggested to me that it might be more than that, there was at that time a sense of doom in the word 'cancer', something his wry humour also expressed. It cast its shadow over our travels as we trudged through the rain-wet cobbled streets of Halifax and Huddersfield, and spoke with mill managers in Brighouse, Bingley, Cleckheaton, Sowerby Bridge and several other more isolated locations. Austin was a young man of silent fortitude as well as wry humour. He died in the early summer.

Although Bradford's weekends were little better than Nuneaton's, having a flat made them more tolerable. The colleagues I got on with had families to keep them busy. One of them, Harry, invited me to his farm at Holmfirth, and I twice visited York to visit my uncle Alastair's divorced wife Flavia, who was very welcoming and good for a chat. I had an easy-going relationship with Gwyneth, our tough-minded and amusing office girl, but never contemplated asking her out at the weekend, not because she was an office girl but because with a sense of just passing through I had no thought of establishing relations that would have to be severed. London being too far, but my own home all that closer, through the good offices of Harry I presently bought a means of transport, not quite a car but a Land Rover. It had been used for milk rounds at Holmfirth and was going for an appreciably modest sum. I bought it without much further thought, something anyone compiling a dossier on my business competence would immediately take note of. However, with the freedom of motorcycling still a vivid memory, the idea of something that could be open appealed to me. I reasoned that if I was about to be a business man, I'd soon be getting something better anyway. I drove it to Melrose and my father, who was home for the weekend, was not only unimpressed but also directly disappointed. A bad sign, he must have thought — not exactly what successful indoctrination into the world of business would lead one to expect. In the end he relented and even agreed, after a while, to have it overhauled as a possible contribution to the farm, as in fact it became. As someone always on the lookout for interesting cars, he was at the time driving a second-hand Jowett Javelin, a wonderful car with a flat-four engine. Now regarded as a classic, it was built near Bradford but had already, for three years, been out of production.

Now with a job at Courtaulds, I faced a major decision. Was I to go on as now, gain more experience, deepening my involvement, and earn some kind of position in the firm; or should I deliver myself half-trained to the family business? The latter seemed a perilous option, not least for a business already in decline. I had neither administrative qualifications nor any background in economics. As James Morton's eldest grandson, I might be expected to uphold a tradition that great changes in the textile industry had made increasingly difficult to sustain. I was not the one to stem the tide to which my own father was doing his best to adjust. I sensed that he foresaw the collapse of Morton Sundour Fabrics as an independent entity, his hope being that his own strenuous efforts would leave enough for Courtaulds to consider worth taking over at a price that would leave something to keep the family shareholders intact. That still left my own position in the dark. If he saw me in the role of a family survivor on the side of the purchaser, was that because he was truly interested in the firm's nominal survival under quite different management, or was it because he thought it was a viable option for my personal future? To me his remarks about sometimes wishing he had never joined the firm suggested that the former consideration was not high on his agenda. On the other hand, like any father, he would have been pleased if I could have found my own destiny in something to which he had devoted twenty-five years of his life, years in terms of which he seemed increasingly inclined to think of in terms of personal sacrifice. But during my now close-on two years in Courtaulds, there had been nothing to show that I had any talent in this direction let alone burning interest. There was certainly no sign that any of James Morton's exceptional abilities had rubbed off on his eldest grandson.

In the near future these thoughts were to acquire great moment. At the time, now that I had stopped wandering from place to place, they coincided with a renewed interest in philosophical writing. There wasn't much to fill my mind in Bradford. The Hallé visited with John Barbirolli, but that was during the week. One weekend I found a bookshop and bought two works by Karl Jaspers. One was *Man in the Modern Age*, written just before the Nazi era, and the other, *Tragedy is Not Enough*, written after that time. I also found a slim volume by the Italian philosopher Norberto Bobbio, entitled *The Philosophy of Decadentism: A Study in Existentialism*. I copied passages and made notes, without really deepening myself in what they said. It would require a lot of concentration and more background than the little I had acquired. Maybe I could again delay decisions about my future, this time to improve my grasp of the world of experience itself and my place in it.

With this in mind, in mid-January, the sump of the year, and not telling anyone, I wrote to two well-known philosophers, the only ones whose names came readily to mind, Gilbert Ryle and A. J. Ayer. The latter was constantly to he heard on the BBC Brains Trust. In that combination of curiosity and fascination in which celebrity returns the rational mind to a childish excitement, on a weekend visit to London I even sneak-viewed his name in typically neat and small writing at the door leading up to his bachelor flat in Mayfair. I already felt some engagement with Ayer due to the challenge of his dismissal as nonsense of most of what I found interesting. Likewise, with Ryle who I later discovered had been Ayer's tutor at Oxford. In Edinburgh I had heard Ryle's *Concept of Mind* discussed and with all too little reflection found his view that a mind is linguistically open to view similarly challenging. Knowing no other suitable addresses in Oxford, and having nothing to lose by aiming high, I decided to try him too.

To my excitement and surprise both replied. Ryle's letter dated 25 January began by saying: 'Sorry to be damping, but I'm afraid your qualifications as they stand don't suffice for admission to graduate work in Philosophy of any kind'. He was of course right and the advice entirely sound; all I had to show on my record at the time was two courses in Moral Philosophy. After mentioning what it would require, a B. Phil. or a First from Edinburgh with strong support from some professor, Ryle concluded by saying that, considering the time this would take, 'I suspect that the right advice for me to give to you is to abandon the whole scheme'. Fair enough, I thought, though regretful at having to abandon a one- or two-year pause before resuming my present course. But then, although dated a day earlier, came Ayer's letter. Having brought my case before the Board of Philosophical Studies, he said they'd accept me as a Ph.D. student at University College London on condition of taking a qualifying examination.

Looking back, I see something typical in both replies. Ryle's was obviously the more prudent. It was cautionary but not altogether off-putting since he also suggested that, if I wanted to pursue philosophy, I might take an Honours course at Edinburgh. Oxford was of course out of the question. Ayer, however, who had put together his own department at UCL, with no inhibiting traditions to prevent him, was renowned for his willingness to take on students from regions beyond Oxford's usual catchment area. The Bradford address may have helped.

If I were to follow Ayer's proposal, the qualifying examination would consist of Logic, Epistemology and Metaphysics, Ancient Greek Philosophy and History of Modern Philosophy from Kant to Descartes. Assuming apparently that this would offer no great obstacle, Ayer's letter ended by asking what subject I had in mind for my thesis. With no sense of vengeance in mind, but having noted that in his attack on the notion of mind as something 'inner' Ryle seemed to be asserting the transparent falsehood that mental images didn't exist, I decided that I would write a thesis on 'Images and Imagining'. I wrote back confirming my intention and accepting the conditions. A letter from Ayer came together with a form that I was to send to the Deputy Registrar, and a month later came another dated 7 March from the senior tutor saying I was formally accepted.

Still not clear in what I still considered my own quite private mind that this is what I should do, even though it was clear to me that I wanted to do it, and not having leaked this new possibility to anyone, I took the train home to Melrose on the 24th of March for the weekend, planning to tell my parents of this development. My father, too, had arrived there from Lancaster. Being more than usually tired, on Sunday morning he was resting in bed. I don't recall his comments when I told him I thought that just now a period at university pursuing philosophy was what I felt I needed, but he made no objection that I remember. Since I had given no hint of this previously, it must nevertheless have come as quite a surprise. Nor did he raise the matter when he came down to join my mother and two sisters at lunch. Ian, my brother, was doing his national service on-board HMS *Vanguard* in the south. I do recall we ate ham sandwiches and salad. Just afterwards I was looking for something in his study when I heard him calling to my mother by the pet name he often used for her. Not thinking, I called to her in the kitchen. Instantly she knew something was wrong; he would never have called her if he had been able to go to her himself. A split-second later I realized the same since we all feared this might happen. I was the first to find him slumped forward on the seat of the toilet in the cloakroom with visible signs of a heart attack. Impulsively and quite by instinct I found myself kissing his head, I who had, so far as I recalled, never had physical contact with him in my life, nor he with me except when I was a helpless child. My mother arrived fearing the worst and in her matter-of-fact way that says so much more, proclaimed 'He's a goner'. We did what was necessary and my brother was called home.

My father was fifty-five. There was a funeral in Edinburgh. The noise and chatter of friends and family at the reception in the George Hotel, I found appalling. As did 'Andy' Bowron, my father's close friend and managing director of FNF, when he came to shake hands. Waving towards the multitudinous and chattering family he said he'd retire to be able to think. I felt the same and drove back to the chapel to recover the sense of my father's presence. It was quite close to where he had lived as a schoolboy. The moment I recall best on that day, and still vividly, is my grandmother's taxi stopping just where my uncle Alastair happened to be standing before we entered the chapel. When she stepped out of her taxi, he went forward and they shook hands with obvious pleasure. Alastair Morton, defying the family code, had established a relationship with his former physiotherapist while his own family were refugees in the United States. On remarrying he had given his mother another granddaughter of whom, until that day, she knew nothing. Our own mother later recounted how pleased Lady Morton was to be able to add another to her list of eighteen. She also pointed out how delighted our father would have been to be the occasion for this reunion. At the time I thought it happily symbolic that the length of the coffin defied the mechanism designed to lower it from our sight.

Strangely or perhaps not, it was difficult for us to speak of 'Daddy' when he was no longer there. It took several years before it became natural for the family to do so, my mother later remarking or even complaining that he would have liked to be talked about. He was a modest man who appreciated being appreciated and would have been genuinely surprised at having an obituary in the *Times*. We certainly thought about him and for many years after I dreamt of him practically every night. Usually it was as though he had recently recovered from a heart attack and having to take things easy.

The attack was clearly brought on by my disclosure. If I'd broached the matter during one of our get-togethers in London he would have had time to reflect on it himself and discuss it with me. Or would it have had just the same effect with the added pain of being away from home? At the funeral, Dr Ross said he had refrained from telling my mother that it could happen at any moment, the main reason being my father's refusal to let up on his work. Was my silence then a blessing in disguise? What if he had died alone in his Morecombe hotel. It was just as well that it happened at home. Later I heard that a week earlier he had been visiting old friends in London, among them the married daughter of his father's colleague, now married to a Frenchman, the Janet he had shown how to throw like a boy when she was twelve and he seventeen. He may have sensed the end was near. But then there poured down on me all the questions about what his thoughts were in those moments after I told him my plans. Disappointment that I was not motivated enough to tread the path he himself had been paving if, in recent years, with some regret? That I would not be a colleague on the other side of an eventual takeover, as he struggled to make it worth being taken over? That his elder son had again shown himself incapable of sticking to and working with something? That a *laissez-faire* in childhood had been a policy that failed?

A consoling thought was my father's firm belief that people should give up activities in which they proved unable to give of their best. He believed that all or most had abilities, in cultivating which and giving of their best they would in fact find self-confirmation. It was indeed the backbone of his liberal thinking. A chapter of a book written by his brother-in-law on the history of the family firm concluded its account of my father's part in it by quoting the Directors' Minute recording his death:

> Those who worked with him knew that he was at one and the same time passionately devoted to the job in hand and also equally concerned that they as individuals should get the maximum out of life, by realizing and exercising to the full their abilities and potentialities; this, surely, is the essence of true leadership, which he so fully provided.

My father's boss during the war, Captain Gerald Bannister, director of Boom Defence, wrote to my mother on the 2nd of April from his home near Fort William, addressing her as 'Dear Helen' and saying he 'admired' my father as 'an exceptional officer and a man of outstanding character'.

His kindly nature & modesty [were] as outstanding as his zeal & ability & I was never in doubt as to the value of his work for the department & the country. The country has lost a great man, for all those who came into contact with him were the better for knowing him. By virtue of this fact he was in my opinion also a great Christian. It was always my hope that he found the work in the department gave him scope & satisfaction in the war. I feel his going very much indeed & hope you will be sustained in this hour of trial & sorrow.'...

Yours with great sympathy,
Gerald Bannister

I remember our mother, after his death, remarking that our father had no pride. It could be an ambiguous remark, and in her circles perhaps not unequivocally a compliment. Used to members of a self-confident upper class, those 'Well, here I am' people who before putting an appearance make sure of their own, it might be a source of embarrassment. My father was fairly casual about his. He was entirely informal and could joke about it, and also take jokes at his own expense from us children without it in any way denting a benevolent authority that seemed to come quite naturally to him. He had an innocent self-confidence that cut through the variable niceties of convention. On several occasions he said to me that he had no special gifts but used what he had to their limit. Talents are of course nothing to be proud of; they are givens and what counts is that and how you put them to use.

The Courtaulds directors and others I had met on my travels sent me letters of condolence. The 'others' included Joe Barke, the textile engineer who had so adventitiously joined me for muffins at the teashop in Bradford. One month after my father died, sensing this was the time to excuse myself from burdening Courtaulds further, I wrote my letters of resignation. These were received with grace and understanding, though I had dishonestly added something I did not fully mean, that their hospitality would be repaid. I think I discovered in myself an eerie talent to produce in words thoughts that I did not have but nevertheless expressed because not perfectly sure that I did not have them. Bowron wrote to say that if ever I came to Wolverhampton or Coventry, he would send a car for me so that I could visit him in Burton-on-Trent. If he could help with any 'advice or action', I was to be sure just to ask. They all took it for granted I would now transfer to the family business and might soon see me again.

No longer feeling any call to do so, I told my uncle I needed a rest and had decided to spend two years doing philosophy. It didn't seem to disturb him. He knew philosophy himself, having secured a first in PPE at Oxford in the 'thirties. When he said that he had thought of sending me to Japan to sell my father's patented molten-metal dying machine, the prospect of travel, a house, a settled life made me briefly pause. However, in my low state of morale I felt I lacked the substance to carry out such a life. In fact, preoccupation with my father's fragile heart over the last two years had given me an unhealthy concern for my own. I began thinking of it as an engine that due to failure of some essential part, might at any moment stop. It was like returning to the Aristotelian theory of motion from the Galilean, to the thought that motion and speed are the constantly achieved result of many contributory impulses, any of which might fail, like those that keep an aircraft in flight, instead of the less strenuous idea that motion and speed are a constant until impeded by factors outside. I had already experienced enough of what felt like actual stoppage when taking the dog for a walk round the fields at Melrose. I had several times seriously wondered whether both would make it back home. I even postponed dentist appointments because the money would be wasted if I were to die soon. Philosophy, in retrospect, may have been a rescue attempt, whether just something to absorb my mind or a search for some substitute for religion. It may also have been an attempt to find some hard ground to stand on, or simply to justify delay.

When I returned to Bradford to work out my time there, a brief visit to the Manchester sales office gave me another glimpse into my father's own life. I met there for the first time 'Jumbo' Wilson, as my father had referred to him, a former Naval colleague now working for Courtaulds. I met him on the stairs and he expressed profound shock at my father's death, saying it was only yesterday he had been playing the bagpipes for them all on board HMS *Renown*. With this last reminder, I said good-bye in early May to colleagues and friends, including several customers, and drove the Land Rover home with accumulated belongings and a sense of relief and renewal. In May, Gwyneth, our spirited office girl, wrote in answer to my farewell letter, telling me how things in York House were, including some acute observations on its remaining denizens. She wondered if she might call on me on a bicycle tour she had planned over the border.

Nothing came of that, but there was another farewell letter. In Bradford I had spoken very briefly to my neighbour in the flat below, a rather eye-catching and elegantly dressed, intense and good-looking lady, not yet middle-aged. Once home it occurred to me I should have gone down to say goodbye. Instead I wrote, and she replied.

> Dear Mr. Hannay
> Thank you so much for your little 'signing off' note — it was much appreciated 'tho I didn't need your confirmation that you had gone! How I missed your heavy policeman beat on the floor above!! Said I to myself: "No more music in the wee

small hours ... no more sounds of someone doing a hasty 'clean up' because things were getting too bad — no more intimations that the master is at home round about 6: pm each evening (save Friday) no more sounds of toilet strings being pulled, & water heaters on —---- no more anything." Oh dear! Alastair — you have been missed .... I think perhaps we have a female taking your place — I heard someone in this morning, and it didn't sound at all like manly feet. The Pearsons are leaving, and Group Capt. Beaman is 'looking round' — ah well! That's life! Thank you for being an equally good neighbour. I shall frame your testimonial & show it to the owners of the next flat I occupy!! They'll say: "Pass Friend, you're just the tenant we've been looking for." Keep your chin up, & be kind to your mother. She may not show grief very much, but it will be deeper than you think. I'm quite certain your Father knows how well you're going to take his place. Go to it. And all the best.

God Bless!
Lily Langley

I must have been a noisy neighbour or the insulation was paper-thin. The last sentence reminded me of something she once said that suggested spiritualism. The letter brought two regrets, first that I had been so inconsiderate a neighbour, my only excuse being that I was a newcomer to flat-living and unaware of the way sounds travel in old houses, but also that we hadn't become more fully acquainted. She was a stylish and attractive woman with a depth of spirit, however one wishes to unpack that notion.

I later found the name Lily Langley-Bateson listed as a speaker at the Bradford Theosophical Society, where she spoke on 'Holism and Identity'. The Society, based in Shipley, defined the spirit of theosophy as a willingness to 'promote understanding and respect for spiritual lifestyles', to encourage 'true friendliness and open-mindedness to other people's religions', to seek reconciliation between natural science and teachings about the 'soul of things', and to contribute to the 'welfare of mankind by developing the potentials innate in each one of us'. The Society's aim was to 'form a nucleus of the Universal Brotherhood of Humanity without distinction of race, creed, caste and colour', to 'encourage the study of comparative religion, philosophy and science', and to 'investigate unexplained laws of nature and the powers latent in man'.

Out of context, the way ahead could have seemed refreshingly clear of the uncertainties of a chequered past. No longer constrained by others' expectations, it was now possible to get down to what really mattered. But then, hold on, what was it that mattered and why? Was it just because a couple of years wandering in a wilderness had generated a megalomaniacal desire to find out how I and the world might fit together — in thought, even someone else's thought? Madness. And the immediate past would cast shadows on the way forward in any case: my father's disappointment, my letting him down, having brought about his abrupt death, and not least its abruptness scuppering any chance to let him see their point from my side and perhaps his too.

There was also the new uncertainty of what it could lead to. I was now twenty-two. Visiting Melrose, a sensibly clad and distinctly aristocratic lady of some years, an old friend of the family, asked me in her upper-crust way, 'What do you plan doing with your philosopher's ticket?' I found no answer beyond 'Perhaps teaching'. At the time, acquisition seemed enough to be going on with. Such worries would in the two years following be upstaged by the sheer effort of getting to grips with others' world-collecting thoughts. You might call it a kind of blessing even if worries of what to do afterwards never went away. The worries may even have provided some impetus through a subconscious desire to show that the unwitting sacrifice could be worthwhile.

Chapter Six: Ticketed

Ticket: v. to furnish with a ticket; n. informal term for the certificate of competence issued to a ship's captain, hence any document certifying a competence gained through training and a test.

To prepare the way forward I paid three visits. The first was an appointment with the Student Adviser. Appropriately enough, on my asking to be admitted to an Honours course in Philosophy, he said 'Are you mad?' He was Peter Heath, himself a philosopher, the one whose course on political philosophy I had followed two years before. 'Probably', I replied. 'Then it shouldn't do you much harm.' I was signed in for 'Honours in Mental Philosophy after Graduation'.

Next was Fiona Mouat. She had sent a letter of condolence on behalf of 'all the Failures'. These were members of an informal club founded the previous autumn by Fiona, its self-appointed president. A tall and ethereally beautiful girl, a potential world model if ever there was one, and gifted with intuition and intelligence as well as an upper-class serenity, Fiona was also (one might almost say therefore) beset by demons that gave her a merely fragile hold on everyday life. Severely agoraphobic, any sortie beyond the familiar bounds of her world produced panic. She had studied art and still painted, but the demons led her to doubt her own ability here too. In a letter appointing me an honorary member, she had written saying the world was 'too full of clubs for the great big, good-at-everything, sociable successful, well-adjusted types'. Non-achievers should also have theirs, a place where demerit didn't matter and even counted. Fiona's grasp of other people's anxieties was profound and her innate warmth and humour made her a natural centre-point for socially homeless colleagues and acquaintances. Affording them a refuge solved the problem of social deprivation that agoraphobia can easily give rise to.

I had met Fiona in my first university days on a double date with lasting implications. She had caught the eye of an architect student, a mature man-of-the-world with experience in the merchant navy. I had tutored him in the smaller scale art of dinghy sailing. Since Fiona shunned all forms of social exposure, Andy, that was his name, had asked me to make up a foursome for dinner at the then fashionable *Aperitif* restaurant on Frederick Street, at that time Edinburgh's only serious attempt at gourmet serving. Fiona would bring along Norma, a close friend and fellow art student. When Norma appeared I instantly recognized an elegant fine-featured West-Endy young woman my own eye had chanced on just a week earlier on Princes Street. For some reason her image had stuck in my mind and here she was — and would be again. That is another story.

Andy, due to the disqualifying assumption that his pride might be hurt, since it implied that he had some, had not been invited to join the Failures. The rules of membership were strict: one should neither be a success nor behave as if success became one, or was sought, or could occur naturally. A man of the world approaching a beautiful woman with evident self-confidence would not qualify. Just now, I had no such qualms on my own behalf. I was in any case already enrolled as an honorary member, my credentials those of a 'low pressure' salesman. Beyond thanking Fiona now for her condolences, to this qualification I was able, when we now met, to add a debacle in the world of commerce.

When escape from that world had seemed increasingly possible, the example of Peter Frøstrup crossed my mind. It was to him I paid my third visit. A private man oozing dedication and principle, he seemed a role model for what I sought to become. I told him of my plans. These he took up warmly, instructing me straight away on how to set about them. In sum, I was to break with all my local contacts, school friends, possibly even family, give up rugby playing and yachting, indeed disconnect myself from my whole past. It sounded as though membership of a one-member sect was to be my lot, Scientology would demand no less. In Peter's view the sacrifice was needed if I was to focus on my project and not lapse into the usual personal disarray that befalls all who stay at home, letting familiar surroundings dictate their fate. Seeing the point, but not immediately attracted to it, I later realized that Peter was in fact telling me to repeat in my hometown a situation he himself had been able to achieve quite easily, if less dramatically, by boarding ship for another country.

Not unnaturally, I failed to make a clean break with a past that was all around me. Through Peter's own new connections, I was nevertheless able to establish a headquarters from where I could control its influence. It was a large basement, part of a first-floor apartment inside the New Town but at its very edge. The continuation of the lane, containing garages and what used to be servants' housing, led immediately down to Stockbridge, once a village to the north of Edinburgh but brought nearer as the New Town gradually encroached on it from the south and later incorporated in the city. The apartment's owner was Dr Mariella Fischer-Williams. Her partner, Dr Erich Geiringer, a Faustian verging on Mephistophelian physician from Vienna, had used the basement for his medical studies. Before I took over the flat, the walk-in closet at the end of the main room contained body parts and also a foetus in formaldehyde.

Mariella and Erich lived elsewhere, the first floor now rented to a Latvian lady refugee. Forced by the outbreak of war to interrupt his medical studies in Vienna, Erich had hitch-hiked from Austria to England, only to be interned on the Isle of Man along with the greater part of Vienna's intelligentsia. With peace, he had to start his studies over again at the Edinburgh Medical School. When I met Erich, he was an established researcher working on gerontology. His personal history had offered him the missionary role of undermining bourgeois complacency. Any opportunity for furthering this campaign he seized with open arms. His indifference to conventional morals could take a humorously provocative turn. To put what he sensed was my stiff-upper-lip British psyche to the test, or perhaps to show his innate superiority to my kind, he wrote a cheque on a 'dirty' postcard for an amount I had overpaid him. On my presenting the cheque to the bank, the teller, seeing a lunatic before him, backed off in alarm and called the manager. He, however, on seeing the payer's signature knew straight away what was up.

Erich reminded me of Oliver Tetley. Both of them surfed with effortless superiority on a life-wave that rode over all the inhibitions and petty anxieties that impede those confined to the daily trough. The difference was that Tetley's indifference was a case of upper-class self-confidence that simply ignored the moral niceties of social inferiors, while Erich's was born of a vision of death that had given him a freer association with everyday life. The son of a Jewish Left-Wing radical, he brought his cultural background with him and had accumulated vast learning in almost anything you cared to mention.

I met him seldom during those two years in the basement, but for those two years the flat itself provided a headquarters from where I could focus on catching up. I was packing a three-year course into two. Could it have been otherwise? When I wrote to my grandmother to tell her of my plans, thinking she at least might understand, she thought I was biting off more than any normal person could chew. The Anglo-Irish once Beatrice Fagan who had braved the Scottish border and found herself a worthy husband, now Lady Morton and a widow of ten years, had in her old age returned from London to Carlisle, there to live out her life with Theodora, her younger and unmarried sister. In response to her thoughtful remembrance of my birthday, just one among nineteen grandchildren all of whose birthdays she may, as far as I know, have remembered, I kept up a yearly correspondence. Thanking her for the usual birthday reminder, a fairly modest banknote, I had sent her a list of philosophers I was supposed to read. Her response was to say that, if I was to absorb as well as read them, it seemed 'pretty overwhelming', even enough 'to put you off' though no doubt (I could sense the light irony) I was 'of sterner stuff'. As for herself, she was 'tottering downhill' and found it 'increasingly hard to concentrate', adding 'Drat' with several exclamation marks. Her idea was that philosophy should allow me to 'walk safely and fruitfully in many fields of thought', that it should illuminate me enough to make me 'glow for others' too. When I mentioned that I found those philosophers easier to grasp whose thoughts were not transmitted in the medium of abstract reasoning, she replied:

> Personally, I think Reason is a trifle stodgy (what an awful way to talk!) but what I mean is it somehow lacks sparkle. Being a woman, I naturally have great faith in intuition, & trust to that as a criterion of what is true (even in such a subject as spiritualism: don't jeer!). *Life* would be almost a prison to me if I hadn't learnt to look forward to what *Death* leads to & this written by men whom I dare say your professors would not allow (?) you to spend your time on just now. However, the lovely thing is that we are responsible for ourselves and free to read all that helps and feeds us. I hope the University will not take this freedom from you.

Not many of my colleagues, either then or in the future, began philosophy to find answers to what death leads to. Some saw it simply as a career opportunity that allowed them to flex their minds on conceptual puzzles for money, but my guess is that the majority see it as a chance to gain some perspective on a multifaceted and, let's face it, perplexing reality. Few, however, go to universities to gain a life perspective that is large enough to encompass their own death. My grandmother, then eighty-five, and whose death came before my three years in Edinburgh were over, had reflected on it from her youth. Profoundly deaf from the age of thirty-five, she had ample opportunity to think and reflect, and above all read. Her mind was in fact more in tune with Montaigne who, following a tradition traceable to Socrates and continued through Cicero, saw philosophizing as a preparation for death. Showing rather greater confidence in my prospects than I felt justified at the time, she wrote: 'I shall be greatly interested to see what other University you choose to move to. Perhaps Göttingen — or some other famous German place (if there is no war on by then!) — or America?' But she was aware of the diversions too. She said plunging into philosophy would be 'quite a cheery business' with 'a number of pals of both sexes' but trusted I could keep 'steadily on' and not be 'drawn aside too constantly by all the attractive humans with whom you must be surrounded'. As for philosophy, I was to let her know if I found 'any decided views on the matter'. She would 'just love to know what *branch* of philosophy' I found most congenial 'and perhaps even uplifting, and which writer I found expressed my own 'feelings & ideas best'. Since, for her, philosophy meant finding the light, it worried her that I planned to live in a basement. I was fated to do so for the next five years until light beckoned in, of all places, the North.

Yes, I did come to meet many people of different interests, found 'pals of both sexes', and life became at times 'quite a cheery business'. The second-floor apartment above belonged to a hard-drinking piano-playing advocate, to whom Erich had introduced three of his former fellow Isle of Man internees. These were members of the Amadeus String Quartet. During the Edinburgh Festival the Quartet gave private recitals in the Fischer-Williams drawing room. There was more music. On viewing the basement apartment for the first time, I had found, bathed in surprising sunshine on the washing bench by the window, two American Music LP recordings of Bunk Johnson, the resurrected New Orleans trumpet player. I had recently been introduced to his vintage jazz and found in the unaffected perfection and maturity of this kind of music a quality that jazz in its later guises was never to possess. Who had left the records there I never found out, but this being the only kind of music at which I had any chance of becoming good enough actually to play along in, I was in a mood to take up the clarinet again. Mike Pollett, the sailing friend who played trombone, had already introduced me to this early 'forties' music. Soon after, when there was a temporary need for a clarinettist, he urged me to join his band. With no practice I launched into my undistinguished career as an amateur jazz clarinettist in the Climax Jazz Band, playing at the Stud Club and various other locations during the rest of my two years in Edinburgh. My tottering career reached its highpoint one evening after a traumatic moment when, while soloing in Tiger Rag, my eye fell with horror on the unmistakable figure of the incomparable Sandy Brown himself walking past the platform just in front of me. Mr Brown was by then recognized as perhaps the greatest living Jazz clarinettist. I paused in mid-flight but managed to squeak a few phrases to finish off my contribution. When time came for the break I decided not to re-join them, the contrast would be too awful. But, to my added horror, as he unpacked his clarinet Sandy turned to me and insisted we first play something together. I said I couldn't possibly, but he wouldn't listen, proposing a blues, 'B-flattish' he suggested, this being the simplest key on a B-flat clarinet. Sandy announced it as 'Alastair Blues'. Somehow, by virtue of imitation or osmosis, I didn't do too badly; at least my colleagues told me afterwards, however little it says, that it was the best they'd heard me play. Myself, I was touched by this show of kindness from such an outsize and allegedly difficult and outspoken personality.

Although I never mastered the New Orleans idiom of my musical colleagues, the jazz experience was a needed palliative to the strain of trying to absorb so much philosophy in such a short time. It also introduced me to a new circle of friends for whom the study of philosophy would seem a fruitless occupation suited only to the idle rich. To avoid making specious explanations I remained to them simply a student. There were interesting social collisions. At Paddy's Bar on Rose Street, musicians met and were occasionally approached to provide music for parties. I was once in a group hired at short notice for an upper-class binge in the West End. One guest, Nicholas Fairbairn, a lawyer and socialite, later a member of parliament and knighted, perhaps in the belief that it was how we were to be paid, plied us generously with cognac. He returned several times to the stand with a new bottle before the old one was finished. So frequently did he return that our drummer began storing bottles in his big drum, which was conveniently provided with a small trapdoor. When we left, there were several unopened bottles inside. Some days later the good Nicholas, destined for celebrity to say nothing of scandal, knocked on my door and asked if we would kindly return them.

It was a dilemma. My mates would immediately take his approaching me to imply I belonged to his kind; any attempt on my part to retrieve a bottle or two would be treachery. After some pleading with them, they or we managed to come up with an unopened bottle or two and the matter was settled amicably, at least as far as we were concerned. Nicholas himself had no doubt been accused of excessive liberality by his peers or even with consorting with the riff-raff. In the company I kept, the usually well oiled because segregated class structure of Edinburgh revealed itself in all its nakedness. Inevitably, I came into situations where old school friends were bemused or even shocked to see me in such 'low-life' company. To me, with their own codes and models of behaviour, these dedicated amateur musicians with real jobs were helpful and comradely. I came in contact with the living life of Jazz at that time, an enthusiasm that remains with me to this day.

It also enabled me to provide a cultural addition to the music making at 1 Doune Terrace. When that dedicated cultivator of the New Orleans style, the trumpeter and cornetist Ken Colyer arrived in Edinburgh with his band for a concert, my musical colleagues suggested they be invited to the basement for an after-concert party. They were. They played well into the night until a neighbour came to the door asking us, almost apologetically, to let people have some sleep. The location itself was ideal for practising music, which I did together with a student colleague, the musically gifted Vincent Hope. Captivated by the great Sidney Bechet's playing, I even bought a second-hand soprano saxophone but soon found the clarinet more to my taste as well as more neighbourly. Vincent and I played clarinet duets both in Doune Terrace and at his home. On leaving Edinburgh I sold the saxophone to a dealer, but Vincent told me later that he bought it back.

Vincent and his wife-soon-to-be, Annette, were among new acquaintances introduced to me by Peter Frøstrup. Vincent was studying philosophy. So too was Ben Lassers. Ben came to occupy the least attractive of the rooms in the basement and as a Californian used to a generally acceptable level of sunshine, he kept a supply of oranges to compensate for its lack. Neil Ross, a sailing friend of many years, generally sceptical of students and their time-wasting, troublemaking ways, occupied the other spare room before finding less gloomy quarters elsewhere. The neighbouring address housed a reclusive New Yorker on a scholarship to write a novel. Thin and pale, Norman Seifert was constantly to be seen bearing a small container of paraffin as, like us, he tried to keep warm in a part of a New Town house on which a largely symbolic sun shone only sparingly. Another American visitor, familiar first on campus as a monk-like figure wrapped in a dark-blue duffle-coat, was James A. Haynes. He was studying comparative religion while off-duty from a NATO communications base located on the nearby Pentland Hills. Jim Haynes, a man with a talent for persuasive communication, could already in the following spring open 'The Paperback' coffee shop and library. That would be the first step on his way to becoming the founding father of the Edinburgh Fringe Festival, the Traverse Theatre, and much else that quickly obliterated any suggestion of the monastery.

Peter Frøstrup, too, was by now a neighbour with his wife to be. When I first called on Peter on that day in March, he had invited me to a party to be held the same evening by two classy literary ladies, one of whom I was led to believe was a fan of Peter. But Peter had brought with him another girl, a very young art student, small and lively, and just a little lost among these sophisticates though far from visibly or audibly 'at' a loss for all that. The fresh young Joan may even have been an intended provocation to the hosts and also, in contrast to them, an emblem of the pure creative spirit that Peter so much admired and which, I suspect, he craved in himself. Joan, who Peter with his good command of colloquial English frequently spoke to fondly as 'Titch', was soon to become his wife, his 'child wife' as everyone said. And so it looked. A Pygmalion situation too but with complexities and ramifications I will not enter into here, except to say that for Peter, if he had ambitions to be a creative artist of the kind he was so skilled in discussing and criticizing, breaking all ties with the past was not the way to cultivate the talents he required. These develop over time within a cultural setting and in its language.

In general, I would guess that looking for something special in oneself that cannot be nurtured in normal channels but has its real future down the lonely path of self-cultivation, is a dangerous game. In his lively, streetwise and sharp-witted as well as sharp-tongued child-wife, Peter had a substitute upon whom he could bestow his ambitions, now that he had abandoned the career of civil engineer that had ostensibly taken him to Edinburgh. After trying out a succession of increasingly dismal quarters, the couple finally established themselves in better style at the top of the New Town address next to my own. Lacking working space there, Peter sought to exploit, in our flat, a portion of the lower staircase that had been left unused. The Latvian lady occupying the first floor seldom used the stair down to the basement and the space was a widening of the stair just before the back door into the garden, almost a room. Peter decided to paint it. It was already dark but he chose to daub it a deep green. Was this some subterranean urge on his part to be exposed to the cosmic forces out of which the Norwegian soul was forged in all its self-declared natural purity?

Later, hearing of King Ludwig II's artificial grotto in Bavaria, I wondered whether there was some general trait in human behaviour to be uncovered here. By emulating the scene in Tannhäuser's first act, Ludwig's grotto formed a private theatre of whose disco-type illumination with fountain and waves he liked to be the sole witness. Later, having enjoyed some Peer Gynt performances, Peter's green cavern put me in mind of some typical stage designs for Dovregubben's Hall. I don't think he ever used it. It may simply have been a case of the creative urge itself.

From that first autumn, Peter and I took over as sub-editors of *Gambit*, a university review recently established by two medical students, Peter McMullin and Fereydoun Ala. Given a free hand, and living close to each other, Peter and I managed to produce some reasonably good issues without consuming too much study time. We persuaded friends to contribute, among them Vincent Hope. Later, after I had left Edinburgh, Peter became for a short while the journal's editor. We both contributed material. I wrote short reviews of Isaiah Berlin's *Two Concepts of Liberty*, which had appeared in the autumn of 1958, and a new edition of Croce's *Aesthetic*, as well as an article on jazz prompted by a visit by Humphrey Lyttleton's band at the Usher Hall. Peter had a piece on the uprising in Hungary that same autumn in connection with which the students had collected money for an ambulance. The journal survived until 1965, publishing articles, short stories and poems by Scotland's leading poets.

Against the letter of Peter's strict advice to abandon the past, I kept up with sailing. My brother and I had inherited from our father the fifty-three-foot schooner a photo of which he had shown me just a year earlier at the Liberal Club in London. We decided not to sell her as long as we could afford the upkeep. In the summer of 1956, the year of the Dragon Gold Cup on the Clyde, a delivery crew brought *Charm III* to the Gareloch on the Clyde. A group of friends attended the regatta at Rothesay on the Isle of Bute, and we took on whatever crew or skippering jobs were available. The two-week regatta was an exhilarating occasion with the extra if specious glamour of royal presence. Not only was the Duke of Edinburgh's *Bluebottle* in contention, the sailing fraternity was joined at breakfast at the Glenburn Hotel by the entire Greek monarchy, the two princesses closely protected by a forbidding Greek version of the duenna.

Down the Little Minch in a good northerly breeze

The fortnight over, we cruised to Oban via the Crinan Canal, on to Tobermory and then round Ardnamurchan to Kyle of Lochalsh, where we rested at the hotel with welcome bathtubs of peat-coloured water, which worked as well as any other. After that it was the Outer Hebrides, down the Little Minch to Barra, and then east to the south coast of the Isle of Skye, where we anchored in the bay at Soay. This small island off the coast of Skye was where ex-SOE (Special Operations Executive, a British covert operations unit in WW II designed to carry out espionage and sabotage as well reconnaissance and the support of resistance movements) agent and writer Gavin Maxwell began his short-lived venture in basking shark oil, a messy business in which the island's small population was also involved. When it failed, most of the residents left for the larger island of Mull where usable land was provided. When the island went into receivership, Joseph 'Tex' Geddes, Maxwell's former harpoon gunner and former special-forces instructor, bought it and settled there. He had, according to some accounts, a directly communicated antipathy to intruders. With no idea that there was anyone there at all, we anchored in the bay, a group of derelict houses the first signs of what had been life. Out of one of the less derelict came 'Tex' who immediately invited us in for refreshments and anecdotes with his very English-spoken wife Jan. We would have agreed more with another account of this man that I read recently and which described Tex Geddes as 'immensely kind' and the kind of person with a hunger for life that the Hebrides needed, 'and also the world'.

Gathering heather. A sprig on the bow signals we had rounded Ardnamurchan.

Heading south again we anchored at Iona on the southwest corner of Mull. There we met another ex-soldier, George McLeod, founder of the international ecumenical Iona Community, centred on the rebuilt Iona Abbey, scholastic centre for three centuries and burial place for kings of Scotland, Ireland and Norway. His welcome was also friendly but more formal, though it impressed him that first-time visitors had found the Bull Hole, the best, and not to everyone obvious, place to drop anchor. I forget the exact composition of our crew, but it was at the time of the Suez crisis in 1956 and there were on-board discussions of the related stupidities.

I had my own internal discussions. Not wanting to lose sight of the longer-term enterprise, Bishop Berkeley's *Principles of Human Understanding* was packed away in my 'dunnage'. It argues for a form of idealism which says that even physical objects are known only in the experience of them getting in the way. Samuel Johnson's rebuttal of Berkeleyan idealism was to kick a stone. If that didn't quite get to the crux of the view, it made a point. At sea idealism has to accommodate those incontrovertibly 'hard' if sodden facts that face anyone testing wind and waves. How can stones and sodden facts as we experience them in some way be in the mind? If they are, the mind can't be in the head, since that too is a combination of hard and sodden facts. I have wondered all my thinking life what 'in the mind' can mean and what it includes.

Back in the Clyde, the boat was laid up in Dumbarton, where in the following spring I drove on Sundays with helping hands to scrape and paint after Saturday night clarinet playing.

Going to sea in a boat is a venture under any circumstances. An occasional sea voyage offers hazards enough to drive all normal worries out of your mind. The old joke has it that sailing is like standing in a cold shower tearing up banknotes. We had few of the latter and did most of the work ourselves. It has also been said that sailing the seas reduces morality to survival, though there are also principles of good conduct when in need. Philosophers can't keep their bureaucratic hands off even here. Given the dreadful choice, they ask, 'Is it right to save your wife rather than the drowning child of someone you don't know?'

Happily we escaped that dilemma. However, to make the most of our boat while we could, it was decided that in the following summer we would 'discover' Norway. I had no difficulty co-opting a willing Peter into this enterprise. Before leaving for Norway by other means that summer he and Joan helped myself and two friends to bring *Charm III* from Oban through the Caledonian Canal and round the east coast to Granton Harbour. From there, soon after — it was a Friday evening in July 1957 — a crew of four, with myself as nominal skipper, left Granton and headed out over the North Sea towards Norway. We were all reasonably skilled at handling boats, and one of us a mariner with convoy experience from the war. But setting sail from Granton towards the open horizon on that Friday evening was something new. Two similar ventures from Granton had recently ended in the crews having to be rescued by North Sea fishermen.

We did fairly well until the Sunday afternoon when a fierce headwind arose with heavy cloud and rain, forcing us to choose between tacking southeast towards the Danish coast and northeast towards Norway. Due to the shallows off Jutland, and some mention on our old charts of un-cleared minefields, we chose the latter. With two of us on watch and in a confusion of wind and spray, we lowered the mainsail and hoisted the heavy trysail. A brave soul below, in fact my trombone friend Mike, kept handing up sandwiches through the slot in the otherwise closed hatchway. Having no appetite for food, we threw them overboard one by one without informing our hardy supplier. The weather lightened as we made a landfall with unidentified cliffs suddenly appearing three miles straight ahead. The compass, which we had failed to swing, was quite unreliable and it was only after hailing a fishing boat that we discovered our position well north of the lower tip of Norway. I slept all night, and when I awoke on a sunny Monday morning the crew had already brought *Charm III* safely into the harbour at Kristiansand. We stayed there to dry out and collect some duty-free liquor due to arrive from Newcastle on the Fred Olsen boat. This secured, we spent the next ten days or so coasting up the Skagerrak to Hankø at the foot of the Oslofjord. This was the fashionable venue for that year's Dragon Gold Cup, once more in the presence of marine-minded monarchy. Fifty miles further up the Oslofjord we arrived at Oslo itself. There we met several friends from Edinburgh, among them Peter and Joan, and did a little tourism. Since the crew were on three weeks vacation, our stay was necessarily short. For me it was a first glimpse of a land where, though with not the slightest intimation of it at the time, I was to spend the larger part of my life.

The return voyage with one extra hand was without hazard. We could even row the dinghy off to take photos of the yacht ghosting in a gentle breeze on a North Sea covered only in ripples. We headed for Inverness, attended a pub where, resplendent in heavy Norwegian jerseys, certain shipmates affected Norwegian accents without inviting any violent repercussions. The Caledonian Canal once more behind us, the crew signed off at Oban. To help cover the costs, *Charm III* was chartered for the rest of the season.

You would think such activities left little time for the main project in hand, or that here at least we might understand the point of Peter's stern line about cutting out ties that get in the way of renewal. This was not so. The adventure was itself something quite new, yet it would have been impossible without the particular abilities and equipment I had hauled along with me from this part of my past.

More than that, activity of this kind, like the music, formed an indispensable accompaniment to the arid intellectual grind. For that, from the nature of the curriculum required of Honours after Graduation, is just what it was.

When you enter philosophy on personal grounds, as I did, unless distracted by the sheer cleverness of much of it — something that can occupy your mind in the way my grandmother occupied hers by spending two hours a day on the *Daily Telegraph* crossword puzzle — you will be looking to see what sense can be made of your world, the world as you meet whatever it gives you in its confrontation with your own range of responses. For those colleagues who take philosophy as a career, what gives shape to their lives is the academic world with its own ready-made curriculum. What might have provided an interesting pastime can become either an obsession or an unstoppable treadmill. In the circumstances of survival and safe entry into that career, the important thing is then not how to make sense of your world, but how to get along in this one upon which your survival depends.

Looking back, I can see that my own long-term view of philosophy remained closer to my grandmother's vision than to that prevailing in the citadels of learning to which my private search had led me. I have never felt at ease in an academic environment, and its philosophy made special demands that I found increasingly to be beyond my native capacity. Although I have a superficial quickness that gets me by if not tested over time, and an imitative ability aided by a good auditory memory that helps me to produce some more or less state-of-the-art essays and even a book or two, I am not quick or 'smart' in the way in which, in the United States in particular, it is mandatory to refer to one's more successful colleagues. My analytical powers are at the mercy of an unruly if on occasion helpful imagination. I am quite unable to keep track of double negatives and the like, and even when the topic is abstract I think visually, not by rule. That is to say, my mind, at least as I experience it, is very unlike my computer.

At the beginning this was not obvious. Philosophy in Edinburgh was still something with which an ordinary mind could grapple. I had, after all, understood Macmurray, though perhaps not enough to be able to criticize what he was saying as some of my colleagues did, either his whole manner of thinking or by picking holes in the details. I had simply been 'absorbing' what I could take on-board in the manner my grandmother assumed one should, leaving difficulties and any obscurities aside. Now, with the screw tightening, and as I was introduced to the rival thoughts of a whole series of philosophers from ancient times to the present, I would have to become more discerning. Even here, though, and thankfully, the task being less in the detail than in grasping differences in whole views of the world, I found myself still within my capacity.

It didn't take long to realize that my project was the opposite of the one my grandmother envisaged. Rather than finding a thinker whose thoughts I could absorb and make my own, my instinct led me by a *via negativa* to get to grips with philosophers whose views my intuitions told me were seriously mistaken. This, as I have already remarked, was why Ryle and Ayer were the names that first came to mind when I was seeking access to the academic world. In my apprenticeship so far, the only philosopher who came near to giving elbowroom to questions of life and death had been Spinoza. The proposition, seemingly in sharp contrast to Montaigne, that a wise man 'thinks of nothing less than of death' while his wisdom 'is a meditation not on death but on life' (4, prop. lxvii), had a depth that seemed to warrant its implied optimism. I liked what I had heard about existentialism from Macmurray, but it was Ayer's dismissal of existentialism as nothing but an exercise in the art of 'misusing the verb *to be*' that made me the more eager to find out why he should feel entitled to say such a thing, just as his dismissal of Plato on a BBC Brains Trust programme and of the rationalist metaphysics represented by Spinoza, made me want to find out what these philosophers' thoughts actually amounted to, and what might conceivably be wrong or even 'nonsensical' about them.

That of course implied that I had some preconceived and possibly false notions of my own concerning what was not nonsensical, and also a sense of what kind of philosophy I would be able to take on board. I found reassuring a remark made by John Macmurray in class. He said that the difference between positivism and existentialism was that the former retained the traditional methods of philosophy but abandoned its topics, while the latter retained the topics but abandoned the methods. The question for me was which of these could be regarded as the more progressive.

A continuing attachment to a bright-spirited Indian girl taking the same course leavened my otherwise strenuous and mostly lonely intellectual pursuit. She visited us at Melrose and we climbed the Eildon Hills. I joined her occasionally in her small Bristo Street flat, her closest neighbours a professional thief and an American girl on a post-graduate grant from Harvard. On the occasions when the thief periodically lodged elsewhere the two girls watched over his flat. Bristo Street has long since disappeared in the Potterrow re- or deconstruction. But there, in what is now an undefined empty space in the air between new buildings, I enjoyed her sharp-witted, optimistic and good-natured presence. I was introduced to Indian food and music. It was the most engaging companionship good fortune has ever brought me. Alas, plunging into philosophy in the headlong fashion that I had forced upon myself was no way in which to acquire the confidence and forward perspective demanded of a lasting relationship. After keeping up some contact subsequent to Edinburgh, we chose to go our separate ways, something that realism made it impossible to regret but left in me a sense of unworthiness and impotence. A few years later she sent me a friendly letter with photos of her wedding ceremony in New Delhi.

It seems that, rather than my philosophy studies causing a light to glow in me that might shine on others as my grandmother hoped, by their sheer intensity they had driven me into a variety of extraneous activities designed to relieve the strain. Quite apart from the confusing confrontation with so many different thinkers, I had been propelled into quite separate circles in diverse walks of life, and consorted with people with such differing interests, that the light that should shine from the centre on all of them became a kind of stroboscope flashing intermittently on rotating segments of a circle.

Yet all this extramural activity was needed to prevent the strain of taking on board such a heavy cargo of mind-blowing ideas. I wrote acceptable essays and received various certificates of merit, and when honours were bestowed I received a modest scholarship. Both inside the university and outside I had the 'cheery time' with friends 'of both sexes' that my grandmother may have wished me but may also have been gently warning me against, my mind increasingly clogged with the nuts and bolts of philosophy in general, I was quite incapable of complying with her request to tell her of any decided views I might have of my own, or what branch I found most congenial 'and perhaps even uplifting,' or to say which writer I found expressed my own feelings and ideas best. My mind was indeed still confined to its own basement.

It was a strain as well as an education. In the early stages I re-experienced that sense of heart stoppage, finding myself in the middle of the night in the corridor just to keep things going — nerves no doubt, but real enough in the dark. A sailing friend who worked at a jeweller's on George Street said he had seen me one morning walking to the university looking 'quite dreadful'. I began to suspect that this was not an activity that was going to be good for my health. Perhaps, following my father's principle that people should look to their strengths, I ought to have been trying something else. But at twenty-four my bridges had been well and properly burnt. There was no way back to the mainland of ordinary life. For as long as it could support me, philosophy would have to be my future.

John Macmurray, the one philosopher who had given me some sense of where philosophy might be educative and even edifying, had retired the summer I returned to Edinburgh. My further philosophical instruction was in the hands of A. D. Ritchie, successor to the Kantian scholar Norman Kemp-Smith's as Professor of Logic and Metaphysics, together with W. F. M. ('Willie') Stewart,

Errol Bedford, Frederick Broadie, Alan Fairweather and also Peter Heath, the man who had questioned my sanity. What I learnt from these informed people made Macmurray seem far more problematic, and the job of making sense of things harder than it may seem to one who picks up a book and happens to find some philosopher's thoughts congenial. But I couldn't complain. Willie Stewart's lectures were the best prepared in all my experience. Today I can still read with advantage the copious notes I took from them. As I realized after my sharp-witted Indian girl friend had pointed it out to me, Willie was a positivist though with religious leanings in the background, a combination that I later found made quite good sense, not least in connection with Kierkegaard who at that time was not a contender for my favourite philosopher, or even to be considered a philosopher at all — in my view at that time a defect. Bedford, as the same source also made me realize, was a Wittgensteinian, which accounted for his less than clear-cut though always thought-provoking and piece-meal approach to ethics. Freddie Broadie took us (just myself and one other in this case) into Spinoza, with whose systematic way with all things was something I had looked forward to familiarizing myself. Broadie (he died in 2009 at the age of ninety-five) gave me credit for at least asking the right questions.

A remarkable lecturer and man, his parents were from Odessa and although born in Manchester with Yiddish as his first language, he made money as a violinist before joining the RAF Bomber Command as a wireless operator. Although he left school at fourteen, his interest in philosophy led him to write to Oxford, just as I had done, though in his case from an airfield and knowing no names. He addressed his application 'to whom it may concern at the University of Oxford' and enclosed a piece he had written on Spinoza. He was admitted to Balliol on a War Memorial Scholarship and arrived at Edinburgh on John Macmurray's bidding. Broadie's questioning style was captivating, and especially the feeling he transmitted of philosophy as the unearthing of thoughts that were unfamiliar but vital. It was like a voyage to Treasure Island without any close inspection of sea charts beforehand.

With Alan Fairweather, a former student of Norman Kemp-Smith, the famous Kantian scholar, it was just the opposite and I was all at sea. He taught us Kant obscurely from well inside Kant's world of thought, more or less in the form of a commentary on a text he knew by heart but which was quite new to me. It wasn't until I got hold of Stefan Körner's Pelican introduction that, after no more than half an hour, it was possible to see what Immanuel Kant was driving at.

My appointed tutor was a Canadian, Bob McGowan. With him I could speak unashamedly for myself however ignorantly, unlike the departmental seminars where the assembled 'brass' led high-level debates that reduced us to silent gaping. Brave the soul who dared to mumble a question, let alone an objection. On one occasion, displaying a naïve grasp of the psychology appropriate to these occasions, the staff said nothing at all, not even as a start. The silence continued for ten minutes until they admitted that they were trying to give us a chance to say something. Imagine what our words would sound like in such a falsely dramatic silence. Their own discussions were instructive enough, not least about the nature of philosophical discussion itself, something for which only a few, and not necessarily the sanest, are born with the necessary skills. Our teachers were nevertheless kind and helpful and invited us home. In fact I owe my doctorate and first book to one such visit. When, at a party given to his class by the hospitable Willie Stewart, I told him I was thinking of writing a dissertation on Ryle's chapter on imagination in *The Concept of Mind*, he fetched and handed me a short hand-written paper that he had given at some seminar raising an important question about Ryle's form of argument. I pocketed it for later perusal. It would stand me in good stead. I may even owe my career to it, although that would be a long time coming. By then Willie Stewart had moved to New Brunswick where his reputation as a lecturer is enshrined in a 'Willie Stewart Prize in Arts' established by a former Edinburgh student who he had persuaded to join him there. At Edinburgh the students and other tutors, including the Icelandic Pál Árdal and his wife Harpa, became friends, evenings with them enlivened by some later all-too-familiar Scandinavian drinking songs.

The letter informing me of my results told me I had achieved a 'second'. Shortly afterwards a letter came from Professor A. D. Ritchie saying that 'in the circumstances of only 2 years and an overcrowded programme' the results were 'very satisfactory'. My aggregate marks were 'well into the upper half of 2nd Class' while my worst paper, Ancient Philosophy, was 'not below the middle'. He said he would like to have a talk with me about my plans. But by then I had written to University College London re-seeking admission and had been told by the Senior Tutor there that, on condition of obtaining 'at least' Second Class Honours in my M.A., I had been accepted as a 'full-time postgraduate student reading for the Ph.D. Degree in Philosophy'.

It was time to say goodbye to 1 Doune Terrace. The basement flat soon became a noted address among the younger cultural circles and the home of Jim Haynes who was to give it even wider repute. To help Peter prepare for his own finals in English literature, he and Joan took up quarters in our farm in Melrose, which meant I could still meet them on visits home over the next years. As for Peter himself, ostensibly due to back problems, he kept postponing his finals. Except for George Mackay Brown, whose studies were not his sole focus, Peter's literary friends were not students at the Old Quad. As Mackay Brown says in his autobiography (*For the Islands I Sing*), the cream of Scotland's poets were to be found in Milne's Bar (the 'Poets' Pub') or in the Abbotsford in Rose Street: George Mackay Brown himself, Sydney Goodsir Smith, Norman MacCaig, Tom Scott and Hugh MacDiarmid. Peter's literary insights were as profound as his knowledge and appreciation of those parts of literature that appealed to him. That his responsive spine should shun exposure to the examination of academic inspectors with their endemically teetotal approach to literature was easy to understand. Six years earlier I had abandoned academic literature studies because it seemed to me to be a *post-mortem* environment run by the literary equivalent of coroners. At that time and place philosophy had seemed closer to the street. Just now it ceased to seem so.

Yes, the ticket. What to do with it? When asked, I had no alternative to teaching. But teaching what? Philosophy? How absurd when studying philosophy had been such a personal matter. Just now the answer was 'just to be able to continue', which left the question open. Maybe Peter was right thinking of me, in contrast to himself, as a 'prostitute'. My studies were tailored according to rules that lead to a degree while his own aversion to examinations meant he could be 'true to himself', freeing his personal progress from dependence on a diploma. You don't need a degree to be an accredited member of a cultural or any other circle. A talent above the ordinary tends not to be susceptible to academic tests anyway, while the free spirits lucky to have such talents will look down on those who had to toe the academic line in order to 'qualify'.

There is also that other side to it: a fear of putting one's skills to a public test lest failure dents a self-esteem dependent on the judgement of the extra-mural circles to which one has been admitted. Such circles might indeed respect someone who could descend from the academic skies and speak knowledgeably to their shared interests in ways they all understood and even help them into those rarefied regions. But failure in academia might show that one lacked talent and belonged only as a bystander. I speak not only of Peter, who did finally sit for his finals; I speak also of myself and of others I have met since. Success and failure are diffuse notions when applied to so complex a matter as a person's achievement. Through various twists of fortune, Peter was to become a highly successful and thoroughly professional foreign editor of the *Irish Times*, something to which a degree in literature would have helped but little and, if good enough, might have drawn him into a life quite unsuited to his then undiscovered wider talents and interests.

Getting my diploma was most of all a matter of self-confirmation. I doubt that my motives were of a sort that, if encouraged, would bring out whatever the best might be in me. Under the grand title of 'philosophy', I was pursuing a vague self-centred goal that had little to do with life around me. The light that should glow within became a lamp focused down a never-ending road, even a tunnel. Not only shining little light on others, philosophy provided little illumination in myself.

In others it even seemed to have produced the reverse effect. Although contact with the Failures had lapsed, a club member not averse to passing on confidences told me that it was after a visit to Doune Terrace that the club's president succumbed to a severe depression. Her eye fell on a piece of nihilistic prose poetry written in a moment of creative gloom. Perhaps having thought of me in some better light, it sent her into a spin. Fiona left for the South to stay in quiet surroundings with her sister's family in Penn. She wrote to me describing her life down there and of her later restoration to her normal fragile state at a psychiatric hospital near Edinburgh. That, thankfully, she had recovered was confirmed by a letter I received after moving to London. Having arranged with the remaining occupants of Doune Terrace for Fiona to store some canvases there while she was away, that autumn she had contacted Mariella Fischer-Williams to retrieve them. She herself being occupied, her companion Erich Geiringer had been more than happy to step in. In a pass she thought so unusual that she rather liked it, Erich had called her a 'Greek goddess' and chased her round the kitchen table, so she said.

If things were normal in at least that respect, Fiona had begun to lose faith in me. In another letter she was to say that I had become 'all abstract and inhuman'. 'Philosophy I suppose', she said, 'I do wish there were human philosophers'. However fragile her own mental condition, Fiona had a mercilessly sharp eye and was not one to mince words. I took hers to heart and bore them in mind. As for Erich, my last direct contact was a Christmas card from Dunedin. I later learned that, having moved to New Zealand, he wrought havoc in its medical profession. His uninhibited ways, his wicked wit and endless energy had enabled him, so I read recently in an obituary, to drag the country's medicine single-handedly into the twentieth century.

On learning this, I was reminded of some remarks my freethinking grandmother had made in connection with Moral Rearmament. I wondered how she would have reacted to Erich and to some other friends of mine. I had told her of my reluctance to revisit Moral Rearmament on that last of motorcycle trip, assuring her it was not an intended slight on the family. She quite understood my reservations: 'one can't bear having one's inmost convictions hawked out for public examination, but if they have to be, for any good reason, one wants to be allowed to justify them in discussion & argument.' I agreed, and although she thought this a weak point, she gave them credit for 'setting people going on new & better paths for themselves and the world around them'. Discerningly she asked, 'Do we reserved (mind-your-own-business) people have any success in this way?'

Realizing I was one of these, I kept that loaded question on hold. Erich had also set things in motion, yet it was impossible to imagine him in any guise other than the devil's. Seemingly programmed to test conventional moral conventions to destruction, he was unashamedly open about everything he did or felt. He was a man to whom Moral Rearmament's sins were painful banalities and their confessions expressions of a misdirected concern for souls they still lacked. As for the world around him, it has to be said of Erich that he devoted his own energies to it on a larger scale and over a wider range than most. Not only did he become a leading member of International Physicians for the Prevention of Nuclear Weapons, he was party to the presentation to the International Court of Justice of the case for the illegality of such weapons. Radical though he was, true to the Viennese type Erich retained vestiges of a strongly conservative sense of propriety. When his son took to dying his hair, Erich showed his disapproval by dying his beard orange and also, if less correctly, the legs of the family cat.

Beatrice Emily Fagan, who had written to me eighteen months earlier of learning to 'look forward to what *Death* leads to', died just before my studies in Edinburgh ended. For me she was the most inspiring of my older-generation relatives. When, as children, we all stayed in her home prior to dispersion at the beginning of the war, at only eight or nine years old I was allowed to join her at tea, which she took regularly at three in the afternoon after a nap. I remember her taking my cap off when I omitted to do so myself on returning from school. She put it in the waste paper basket. There was some mixed symbolism and considerable humour in that. I defended myself by saying the house was so big that it was hard to tell inside from outside. She may have liked that. Profoundly deaf, she made her moods known by the changing modes of her constant humming.

While she was bedridden Carlisle I had visited her and was allowed, after her death, to take over a good selection of her favourite books. These included a comprehensive and informative one-volume Oxford English Dictionary ('A New English Dictionary on Historical Principles') from 1943, its unusual range especially suited to crossword solving. I still have it although the pages are now mostly loose and several are missing with the fabric of a cloth cover from the once family firm in tatters. I have treasured the books as evidence of her free-ranging investigative mind. She had works by Tolstoy and about the French poet and aviator Antoine de Saint-Exupéry. She was interested in the Danish playwright and Lutheran pastor Kaj Munk, assassinated by the Gestapo for anti-Nazi activity during the occupation of Denmark in spite of once admiring Hitler's ability to unify a nation. Of one book she had shown me when I last visited her, she said she had been disappointed at the author 'finishing up by taking shelter in the R.C. Church after all … *most* unsatisfactory from my point of view'.

Perhaps it was because she, too, would have liked to attend a university that she showed such interest in my own experience there. Still, some of her comments held some latent admonition, or a realization that a university education of the kind I was committed to would not have suited her. When I told her of the topics for my ordinary MA degree four years previously, she had responded: 'What a terrible lot of things I *don't* know and (in the history papers, at least) I never *shall* know — so, no 'MA Edin. for me'. She had also followed my progress among the satanic mills and in a letter to me at Nuneaton expressed concern at my father's health. I was to enjoy myself wherever I was, and be 'busy over something interesting and useful', to which she added: '*what a lot of instructions.*' She was alone in our family in following my philosophical interests with sympathy, anxiety and understanding.

Although by giving life a new sense of urgency, as well as making many new friendships, these two years had without any effort on my part brought about a break with the past, there was still sporadic contact with home. A week before my grandmother died there had been the wedding of my elder sister Mariot and Morrison Lothian. They had met at agricultural college and I had come to know Morrison quite well on my visits to Melrose, that being part of his sales territory. We were close enough for Morrison to visit me once in the Edinburgh basement to report that Mariot had not accepted his offer of marriage — so far. I can't recall what I said concerning his prospects but we listened to some jazz records. Musical himself, and formerly Pipe-Major at George Watson's School, we had similar tastes. With his dark, handsome looks Morrison must have been descended from Armada ancestors shipwrecked in the Hebrides. He died twenty-eight years later after he and Mariot with their so far three children had moved from Melrose to Aberdeenshire.

As a form of recovery but also to make good on a promise I had made to myself, on the invitation of Maria and her husband Nasos I travelled that last summer in 1958 to Greece. Memories of those exotic weeks are a confusion of excessive heat, sunburn, and overwhelming hospitality. On the way to Bari to catch the boat to Athens, I stopped off in Milan, a furnace in which too much of my ready cash went on cool lemon drinks. Travelling alone was once again a rich experience and in more ways than one. Approaching Bari by train, I was unlucky enough to poke my face out of the window for air just as a mother a few compartments upwind emptied her young child's pot. My own compartment reeked of garlic. A cool and fresh interlude was provided by the voyage to Piraeus through the Corinth Canal. The rest of the upper deck being occupied by what must have been first-generation back-packers, I slept behind a lifeboat. When the backpackers started singing I was inspired to play 'Over the Waves' for them on my clarinet, which for some reason I had taken along — I must have been rather attached to it at the time. As we berthed in Piraeus, I saw Maria and Nasos waiting on the quayside. I was too caught up in thoughts of the past to show myself and wave, for which Maria characteristically chided me. My crash course in philosophy had done me little good in the sphere of human relations.

In Athens and also Chalcis, Maria's hometown, and on trips to Epidavros, Mycenae, Navplion and Poros, we all got on well and, in some ways, too well. Maria's marriage was in a tired state and my presence became an opportunity for comfort. Zena, her older sister, not knowing the extent of our former friendship, also chose to devote herself to my welfare, taking me around most mornings in a car with her driver while Maria was at work. Nasos being a naval officer, we had access to the officers' beach on Salamis. We all spent several mornings there swimming and enjoying a late lunch before driving home for a siesta. In the comparative cool of the late evening we would gather again for dinner in town, always a relaxed and recreational gathering. All the sounds and smells were fascinatingly 'eastern'. Athens was then still far from Europe and with the sound of street criers waking one in the morning its mid-Eastern orientation was seductively ambiguous. So seductive was it that I wondered if I could perhaps move and settle down there. Through Maria, who seemed also to favour that idea, a meeting was arranged with the head of the local English school. He said that if I was interested they could probably find something for me. For that I would have to change course, not so easy at this stage, but what if philosophy proved a dead-end?

When the time came for me to leave, Zena startled everyone by announcing that she would accompany me. And so it was. Zena and I sailed from Piraeus to Bari though in different classes. We took a train to Paris and then later to London. In both places I insisted we book in at different hotels. Her husband, on a business trip, met us in London and I joined them for breakfast at the Cumberland Hotel. Theo rose and greeted me with the exculpatory words 'I like Alastair too'. Zena's relationship with her husband was uneven, to say the least. Like Burton and Taylor, they later divorced and re-married. At the time I had the feeling he was happy to have me take her off his hands for a while, probably sensing that mine were safe. He, too, had after all been generous with his hospitality. While Zena continued her travels as far as Edinburgh, I took a train back to Melrose. For reasons she understood I refrained from inviting her home.

At Melrose, Peter and Joan had moved into the rooms behind the farm kitchen and settled there for the next year. They led a country life. To Morrison, now my farming brother-in-law, Peter became 'Pete the lad'. On a break from London there was a visit from Uncle Edward, my mother's elder sister Jean's husband. Once shipping firm director, later army officer, then Anglican clergyman and recently mayor of New Plymouth in New Zealand, Edward Owen Eustace Hill was another member of the family who owed that membership to a background in the Moral Rearmament Movement. He joined enthusiastically in our activities. One of these was the only 'sport' we as a family all played: a card game, a form of Patience better named 'Impatience' due to its high-tempo very competitive nature. Uncle Edward seemed to revel in rivalry with a boyish eagerness. There was a fishing expedition on, or rather in, the Tweed, where knee-deep Peter and Uncle Edward vied with each other over the best fly to use, the one eager to look at the other's whenever a fish appeared.

On these home visits I would be initiated into Peter's current gods, Knut Hamsun and Axel Sandemose. The latter was a Danish author who had settled in Southern Norway in the early 'thirties, beginning life anew as Peter had tried. Both authors, as I subsequently discovered, were authoritarian in private — quite awful people but sublime writers. Hamsun was on the wrong side during the war but had the temerity to visit the Eagle's Nest and tick Hitler off for the execution of Norwegians. Sandemose, according to a biography by his son, was a child molester and worse. Peter had Sandemose's famous journal (*Årstidene: Brev fra Kjørkelvik* [The Seasons: Letters from Kjørkelvik] (1951-55), which I was then unable to read. Hamsun I could read in translation: *Pan, Hunger* and the Nobel-prize-winning *The Growth of the Soil*, the latter a favourite among Hamsun's appreciative pre-war German public. Izak, its hero, also Peter's, is a roughly clad 'barge of a man' who steers his simple plough over the uneven land to eke out a living for his family. He epitomized a characteristically mystic attachment to the soil.

I must admit that this solitary sodbuster was far from anything I could imagine myself wanting to be. But then, according to a Norwegian ethnologist who I read recently, this 'Isak Sellanrå has never existed'. The reason is not the platitude that he is fictional: it is simply that no normal Norwegian would expose his wife and young children to an existence outside the reach of neighbours.

Paradoxically, it was exactly such a back-to-pure-basics ideal that inspired Peter's flight *from* Norway. His favourite records were the guitar-playing blues singer Big Bill Broonzy and Pablo Casals playing Bach's unaccompanied cello suites. You can't get much less adulterated than that. These went well with a taste for very strong Greek coffee, the secret of whose brewing he learnt from his Cypriot girl-friend. A lingering memory from our first days in Doune Terrace was the long Sunday walk to a Polish bakery somewhere near the Cowgate to buy rye bread. the Frøstrups conjured up a kind of ghetto existence. In our relatively threadbare isolation we formed a precious cell at odds with the world, yet superior in our simplicity. Peter's path was a lone trail where people were met one by one: crowds were anathema. I saw him standing, ashen faced, on the balcony surrounding the Old Quad as students threw old fish and tomatoes at one another in a typically puerile 'celebration' of the 1956 Hungary uprising.

Chapter Seven: Lightening ship

Lightening ship: '*After they had satisfied their hunger, they lightened the ship by throwing the wheat into the sea*'

(Acts 27:38).

In October I was in London ready to submit my quickly ingested yet still undigested feast of philosophical learning to the inspection of England's celebrated, and by some reviled, high priest of positivism. Not unprepared to have my half-absorbed learning dismissed as utter nonsense, it occurred to me that for a cluttered mind this might even be balm — no more over-exertion of mental enzymes down a seemingly endless path of subtle reasoning. Logical Positivism, by clearing away confusion, might even promise my fresh start. Its puritanical tenets would be hard to accept but the case against metaphysics would in itself be an interesting intellectual challenge. There was also religion, which as Ted Honderich, who was soon to be a colleague, remarks in his pungent autobiography, Ayer was 'known for removing from the agenda of thinking persons'. [3]

There was irony in the situation. Under Ayer, the University College department had become something of a philosophical Mecca. It offered the best discussion, it was said, not just in town but anywhere. Ayer himself was a celebrity and his Monday evening seminars were visited by the currently and future famous. Ayer was recognized as having rescued the department from the parlous condition (or 'impoverished slumbers' as one writer put it) [4] in which his predecessor had left it, or so the story goes. The previous Grote Professor of Mind and Logic had been none other then John Macmurray, the only philosopher I had so far met with anything to say of personal interest, and the real reason I was still in the business at all. On accepting an offer of the chair of Moral Philosophy in Edinburgh in 1944, after fifteen years at UCL, Macmurray had been asked by the Provost to consider the candidates for the Grote chair. Of Ayer he wrote: 'Narrowly logical — though a leading light of the new logical school. I should think most unsuitable for you.' [5] That Ayer got the job and made the department a legend must have rankled. An already well-known broadcaster in his time, understandably Macmurray had no such aim. Ayer, in his inaugural lecture, notoriously made no mention of his predecessor, although in his autobiography he would pillory him by name. Conversely, when attending a Gifford Lecture given by Ayer in St. Andrews, John Macmurray sat in the front row conspicuously shaking his head in disbelief.

Before venturing into these lists, I had to find somewhere to stay. The first address was yet another basement, this time much smaller, a wall-to-wall carpeted and immaculate room, confining, though maybe appropriately so in view of the now more focused approach to my chosen subject. It was in Chelsea's Markham Square off King's Road. My hostess was a refined Scottish aristocrat living with her military son, their willingness to house me owing to Evelyn Francis, that long-term friend of my parents who formed their principal *liaison* with the world of anthroposophy. I discovered later that, after reading history at Somerville College, Evelyn too had given up a lucrative career in the interest of renewal. A non-conformist family background meant that her renewal could embrace the intended renewal of others. In its anthroposophical guise, religion depended on forms of knowledge that were not accessible to me, and in my limited acquaintance with its followers neither had it been made available to them except on the messianic word of Rudolf Steiner himself. I was sufficiently positivistic by nature to require first-hand evidence of these truths, even if it meant a paradigm shift away from the methods of current science, though as Steiner kept insisting, without loss of its standards. Faith in this case, where knowledge was at stake but not one's own, was not enough.

Among English intellectuals, with their native aversion to 'impenetrable' German concept-mongering dismissed by some as sophistry,[6] the twenty-four-year-old Ayer's *Language, Truth and Logic* published in 1936 had caused a frisson touched with glee. It also caused revulsion among those who found the supports of their habitual religious leanings knocked from under them. When I told my former church organ-playing Latin teacher, Ayer's colleague at both Eton and Oxford, that I intended to study under Ayer, he went so far as to refer to my about-to-be tutor as a 'reptile'. Yet the mature Ayer was not insensitive to religion. When asked for his thoughts on the subject in a *Guardian* interview in 1979 (30th August), he said that 'if we could be socially conditioned to acquire veneration for life and respect for one another's rights and feelings, we should be better off without religion'. Deploring its quiescence and pessimism, he admitted there was nevertheless much to be said for Buddhism, but that if the climate of opinion which made Buddhism the prevalent religion ever existed, religion too would be unnecessary. As for Christianity, it was 'not the only religion nor evidently the best'. But then, as he pointed out, no moral system at all could be founded on authority, since for that there has to be 'the independent assumption that what the authority commands is right'.

If the radicalism of Ayer the *enfant terrible* had softened with the years, it was still this that drew people to him. The truth of the matter was not as Peter Heath had it in one of our Edinburgh seminars when remarking that *Language, Truth and Logic* hung like a millstone round the mature A. J. Ayer's neck. It was more like a medal that bore witness to its possessor's enthusiasm for the fray and a prospect of more closely considered thoughts to come, some on matters too cavalierly dismissed in that earlier work. Ayer's later remarks on religion post-dated my own contact with him, but when I read them I found myself largely in agreement, with the proviso that human nature even at its best will always get in the way of the conditions that Ayer said could make religion redundant.

The Vienna positivists who had inspired him were intent mainly on freeing serious thinking, including science, from the imperious grip of German idealist metaphysics. Like the French encyclopaedists, the new positivists saw a bright new path opening once the dangerous metaphysical clobber was out of the way, and allowing our true relation to the world to be revealed. This path, once lit, would be the one that the better of us would find it natural to follow.

The existentialists had come to something like the same conclusion, except that for them objective study of our actual relations to the world was not the way to free ourselves from prejudices and to make us human; rather it was a subjective renewal in the individual who must take over responsibility for the tasks that metaphysics had treated inappropriately in an objective and therefore self-distancing spirit, ultimately leaving no room for the individual's real-life situation. To me it was an added attraction that Ayer evidently had a feeling for existential questions, whether or not he would go so far as to discuss them in public.

In spite of his conventional upper-class English upbringing, Alfred Jules Ayer retained the slightly prickly presence and un-English vigour of his Dutch-Swiss Jewish origins. Anyone further from the stereotype of the unworldly but likeably tweedy English academic is hard to imagine. A rather short, dapper, quick-moving, man with lively eyes, self-conscious to the point of vanity, Ayer was all-present. 'Likeable' was not the first word that came to mind, at least to a student given access only to those aspects that Ayer chose to reveal in a context such as ours. There was indeed something vaguely though fascinatingly reptilian about his features, but no more so than those of several colleagues subjected to Steve Pyke's wrinkle-enhancing camera. Behind whatever protective measures he took to conceal a certain social shyness, in his glance, his engagement and quick attention to what was said, to me Ayer expressed a concern that felt very like friendliness and which belied all suspicion of arrogance.

My first meeting with 'Freddie' Ayer was as he descended the stairs from his room in Gordon Square to talk to his protective and fear-inspiring departmental secretary Lyndsay Darling, who then introduced me to him. In my awe and zealous wish to be both civil and respectful, but still in the spirit of one who had sought out the doorbell to his bachelor pad in Whitehorse Street, I addressed him as 'sir'. Batting not one eyelid he cordially invited me to his room where he asked me about my teachers in Edinburgh and what I wanted to work on. The names of Errol Bedford and Peter Heath were familiar to him. I rightly didn't expect him to have heard of Willie Stewart, Freddie Broadie or Alan Fairweather. It was no doubt fortunate that it didn't occur to me to mention Macmurray. When I said that I planned to write a thesis on images and imagining, Ayer grew interested and, to my more than slight surprise, recommended that I read Sartre. Why surprise? In declining a suggested meeting with Ayer some years earlier, the famous French existentialist is said to have called him 'un con'. This was no doubt due to Ayer's directly post-war essays on existentialism in *Horizon*. These not only made their differences abundantly clear, they also dismissed what Sartre had to say on the second of the two seminal notions in his celebrated *Being and Nothingness* as 'literally nonsensical'.

Even if temperamentally as well as intellectually opposed to the existentialist's doting on the meaninglessness of life as we find it, as much as to the heroics of defiance that defined their ethics, Ayer had some respect for the acumen of a writer who he may well have considered his main continental rival. At any rate, he told me I should have a look at Sartre's *L'imagination* from 1936 as well as the lengthier *L'imaginaire: Psychologie phénoménologique de l' imagination*, published four years later. Perhaps in my interest in the topic he saw an opportunity to look again at Sartre, this time in the latter's less grandiose and more empirical or phenomenological vein.

Once we began and I had assembled enough thoughts to be able to offer them to him for consideration, Ayer acted as though he was just as interested as myself. Accepting my obvious incompetence and lack of experience in philosophical discussion, he did what he could to put my badly framed thoughts into manageable form. Letting me sit in one of the comfortable armchairs reserved for the main voices at his Monday seminar, Ayer himself strode about the room, clutching the curtains as he stared out of the window, only occasionally taking to the chair behind his desk. Sitting on the desk itself would have been wholly uncharacteristic of his un-casual and self-possessed nature.

These first efforts with Sartre were followed up with Husserl, the philosopher Sartre takes issue with particularly in the first of those two books. Here too Ayer showed an interest equal to my own, and by the end of the first term I had amassed an impressive collection of notes on both, their number and formulation made possible only through this interaction with a mind quicker and much less cluttered than my own. Preparing for the fortnightly tutorial was always a strain on my nerves. It kept me busy at 33b Earls Court Square, my latest and larger basement. There, with intervals spent wallowing in music, mainly Mahler and New Orleans Jazz, but also Schoenberg who I listened to while lying on the floor looking at the ceiling to be able to focus on the unfamiliar combination of sounds, I struggled with the not always pellucid connections these philosophers were making between their separate sentences. I was grateful on one occasion when influenza intervened so that the next meeting could be put off. Walking home from each tutorial I called in at Dobell's Jazz Record shop on Charing Cross Road and bought myself a record by way of reward.

In the spring term the topics we raised and the texts discussed included Peter Geach's *Mental Acts* and others lost to memory. I came to realize how much I had to learn and account for before ever thinking of committing my own thoughts on images and imagining to paper. In the summer, to my utter disappointment, we were told that Ayer was moving to Oxford.

The Monday evening seminars until then although they were to continue after his move, saw an Ayer quite other than the one who helped me in private. Here the celebrity in action presided from behind his desk, twirling his golden chain and with the familiar cigarette holder placed before him, the orb and sceptre that marked the special occasion. Attending the seminars were the teaching staff and guests, some distinguished, some less so, some to be so, and also the postgraduate students for whose further instruction and practice in philosophy they were officially intended. There were postgraduates from other colleges as well as visiting scholars. We sat in serried rows, myself usually against the wall, daring ourselves to say something and feeling defeated when, as was typically the case, we did not. The first seminar I attended took on Peter Strawson's just published *Individuals*. To me, its Kantian-flavoured argument for the necessity of the conceptual scheme implied by our normal thoughts on identity and habits of reference at least made some immediate kind of sense. We had hardly got into the book before, to my horror, Ayer assigned me the task of introducing its complex chapter on 'Persons'. For a week I struggled to locate the architecture of the argument and typed out a paper that might take no more than twenty minutes. So nervous was I on the dreaded occasion that it felt like reciting someone else's words. I hardly noticed what they said and inadvertently skipped a page. Luckily, the grammar of the half sentence at the end of the one page happened to be tailored to that of the half sentence at the beginning of the next but one, so no one seemed to notice, a fact that bears several interpretations. I recall my eye being continually drawn down to the floor on the left, where the immaculately suited Richard Wollheim's light beige socks competed for attention. Having finished, I waited miserably for Ayer's reaction. To my relief he refrained from direct comment or criticism and, showing great constraint and even consideration, spoke these words: 'Heroic effort, but it isn't absolutely certain that the argument is crystal clear.' He thereupon counted off on his fingers the steps in the argument as he himself had deciphered it, though leaving it open to others to believe that he had done this from my introduction, and the discussion proceeded from that. I had made far heavier weather of it than Ayer, but I think I saw that he sensed I had tried.

He showed me consideration on another occasion too, when from our tutorials he must have begun to believe there might be some promise in me. The efficient if tyrannical departmental secretary took care of the seating arrangements for the seminars, placing the few comfortable armchairs facing Ayer at a convenient and respectful distance. They were reserved for the likes of Richard Wollheim, Johnnie Watling, Peter Downing and later Bernard Williams, all members of the teaching staff. There being a chair to spare on this occasion Ayer said 'Let Hannay sit there'. Appalled at this breach of protocol, Lyndsay Darling looked at Ayer and, in something close to disbelief, said 'Hannay?' For myself, I was overwhelmed but also disembowelled by the thought of what was expected of me; it was like Sandy Brown allowing me to play clarinet along with him only much worse. I never presumed to sit there again.

In spite of having become Oxford's Wykeham Professor of Logic, Ayer continued his UCL seminar in the autumn. Now that his future lay elsewhere, the proceedings began to lose their lustre and Ayer perhaps his dedication. When Stuart Hampshire, lately of All Souls, once hired by Ayer as Lecturer at UCL, succeeded him as Grote Professor of Mind and Logic, it was then he who presided. Having earlier deprived Ayer of his wife Renée, people now spoke of him now as taking over chair as well as bed. Assuming he would also be taking over Ayer's supervising, Hampshire invited me to the Grote salon to ask about my topic. I told him but said I'd already asked to be supervised by Bernard Williams, about whose up-coming appointment as Lecturer we had been informed before Ayer's departure. Inspection of the records proved this to be in order and Hampshire left it at that.

Supervision by Bernard Williams proved to be worlds apart from my times of trial with Ayer. Only three years my senior, Bernard was then by some default a mere assistant lecturer. Instead of the spacious setting of the Grote Chair's see-through salon with its larger windows overlooking Gordon Square, we sat high up at the back of the building with a view of the college rooftops. It was said that Bernard had taken this modest position to be on hand for his wife Shirley, already a very active Member of Parliament. Once or twice Bernard came quite exhausted to our meetings after waiting up to provide Shirley with refreshment and perhaps breakfast too after all-night sittings. On those occasions we went to a nearby café and talked there as always over and through matters of common interest, none of which had any obvious connection with the subject of my thesis. The nearest we came to that was discussing J. L. Austin's subtle paper on 'Pretending'. I didn't object. I was in the presence of a mental capacity vastly superior to my own but one that seemed to think in the same direction even if his seemed occupied more with familiar philosophical puzzles mostly known from the time of the Greeks. In fact, when I asked Bernard why he took to philosophy, he said that while reading for Greats at Balliol, it was the famous paradoxes from antiquity that took hold of his mind, the rest of philosophy including its history slipped by unseen. Once, on arriving for my weekly meeting, I found Bernard's board covered in the detailed architectonic of Kant's first two Critiques. He may have been catching up on parts of the history of philosophy that he had to teach, but it is just as likely that he was getting to grips with the Kantian notion of morality of which he later let it be known that he was deeply suspicious. Ironically, I remember him regretting that he saw no work of his own in sight and but that perhaps like Kant he would produce something weighty late in life. Kantian ethics, and the notion of morality that it spawned, were later to become the target of Bernard's ever more Nietzschean attitude and publications.

At that time, the criticism focused on his former teacher Richard Hare, Oxford's White's Professor of Moral Philosophy. Following the then current fashion for reformulating traditional philosophical topics in terms of modes of language and the uses of speech to perform certain functions as in baptism, Hare had developed a 'prescriptive' account of the nature of moral judgments, one that was explicitly opposed to the emotivism of Ayer and others. Prescriptivism retained the emotivist's refusal to accept that there are ethical *facts* about which ethical sentences can be true or false, but instead of construing them as expressions of approval or disapproval (the so-called boo-hooray theory), it sees them as a form of commendation with a commitment attached, saying that what you decide for yourself must be something you would commend to anyone else in similar circumstances. To me that sounded good enough, but Bernard kept insisting that Hare's proposal begged the question of what made sentences ethical in the first place. My analytical powers at the time were too under-developed for me to see this. The same was true of other logical difficulties Bernard saw in philosophers whose views I tended to grasp uncritically simply because I liked them. He conjured up some puzzle about

Bishop Berkeley that had me walking for hours round Kensington Gardens trying to see what the logical point was. I think it was something to do with images implying perspective and the possibility of visualizing something not being seen by someone. Once the point struck home I thought it rather trite and not worth wasting much mental effort on. I have changed my mind about that, while for Bernard it was the nucleus of a central argument in his future collection of essays, *Problems of the Self*.

It took time for me to realize that being adept at philosophy is not always a matter of arguing about something consequential. On the other hand, the hint I received from Bernard at that quite early time was very consequential. His criticism of Hare wasn't simply that he had begged a question, something philosophers do quite often and probably wouldn't get very far if they didn't; it was the idea that immorality is due to lack of reasoning and that the way to improve things is to provide arguments for general conclusions. I felt I shared this scepticism about philosophy as a source of truth even within the purely formal terms to which both Hare and Kant before him confined themselves. It goes with a sense that the grasp we really need of the values that count for human well-being are to be found in actual experience and of literary descriptions of these *in situ*. To some, Bernard Williams' vituperative scorn for Hare's views on ethics must have seemed out of place. Hare was a respected philosopher whose experience as a prisoner of war motivated him to bring ethics onto centre stage in post-war analytic philosophy. To Bernard's own analytically acute mind, Hare's ethical theory begged the question of where to begin, and he came to voice his disdain of academic philosophy in general and scorn for what he referred to later as the 'professional exercises' that abound in the journals. I once heard him on radio advocating good literature as a richer source of moral insight than the thought processes of 'some late nineteenth-century genius' or any latter-day successor.

One result of my tutelage under Bernard Williams was to lose sight of any general conclusion I could arrive at regarding my topic. This was still mental imaging. Everything we touched on tended to fragment into subsidiary topics and finer points, making the idea of a 'thesis', that is to say some point of view to be defended by argument, ever more elusive but also un-worthwhile. A clearer way forward would have been found with Hampshire, who was not afraid to advance general theses, such as those promoted in *Thought and Action*, about which Bernard Williams however remarked that 'Stuart leaves all the spade-work to others'. In the end, and several years later, in order to get the 'thesis' out of the way, I contented myself with criticizing various philosophers' claims, leaving what should be said positively about imaging to a common sense from which the philosophers I took up for discussion seemed to me to provide no good reason to depart. That too struck me as being in the spirit of Bernard Williams.

During this time, I had my first and only face-to-face meeting with John Macmurray. I heard that he had retired to Jordans, a Buckinghamshire village not far from London and with Quaker traditions, although later he moved back to Edinburgh to care for his aged mother. I wrote to Macmurray saying I had been studying under Ayer and asked if I could pay a visit to ask some questions. At the time I had no idea of Macmurray's antipathy to Ayer and he said nothing that hinted at it as we spoke. I detected some wariness however, but that could be due to my request sounding like a snooper's. On my arrival he did begin treating me as if I were a journalist. He ushered me into the living room and placed me on a chair while his wife, Betty, who I was not to meet, stayed invisibly in the kitchen preparing tea and biscuits. On returning with these Macmurray said he gathered that we were related. This was news to me and I suppose something Betty had just told him. After the initial wariness wore off, he spoke openly and interestingly, particularly on my asking how, subsequent to his recently published Gifford Lectures, he now understood the category of religion. I was struck too by his positive attitude to recent developments in analytical philosophy of language. Two recently published books, he thought, indicated that philosophy was beginning to come on the right tracks. They happened to be Hampshire's *Thought and Action* and Strawson's *Individuals* especially in view of the latter's chapter entitled 'Persons'. Macmurray was well versed in Kant and would appreciate the way in which Strawson had adapted his reasoning. When I asked him if he was writing something, he said no, it cost him too much; the recently published Gifford lectures had been particularly arduous.

It was an odd meeting between a rather shy elderly man, conscious of his isolation in the present mood of Anglo-American philosophy, and a rather nervous younger one trying to find a foothold for what it left out.

I was grateful to Stuart Hampshire for recommending my attendance at Ernst (later 'Sir Ernest') Gombrich's seminar at the Warburg Institute. Born into high cultural and social circles in Vienna, Gombrich had come to Britain before the *Anschluss* and spent the larger part of his working life there. At the Warburg he had been in turn Senior Research Fellow, Lecturer and Reader and was now the recently appointed Professor of the History of the Classical Tradition and also Director. I was delighted.

Like so many Viennese, Gombrich was a dominating figure and directed his seminar as though it were a masterclass and he the only true virtuoso. I forget what the general theme was, but it covered the world of artistic creation. When, again all too early, my turn came to introduce the discussion, the subject assigned to me was Ernst Cassirer's *Philosophy of Symbolic Forms*. Maybe it was because I was Hampshire had been asked to send one of his postgraduates to take care of just that angle.

Luckily for me, another postgraduate with a far more appropriate background for this subject, and studying under both Gombrich and Wollheim, attended the seminar. Michael Podro, someone I already knew as a highly cultivated participant at Ayer's seminar, had studied drawing at the Slade. After attending lectures given there by Gombrich he had given up plans to become a professional painter. Later, first as founder of the Camberwell School of Art and then Professor of Art History and Theory at Essex, Podro would be hailed for lifting art history and art theory out of the hands of connoisseurs and dilettantes and establishing it as a serious academic discipline. In our time he was in the group a few of us formed for fortnightly discussions held in various pubs around Soho. Although at first a little scared of his cultured tones and seemingly effortless powers of articulation, I found in Podro friendly and congenial company. Working away at Cassirer's symbolic forms taught me a lot, the neo-Kantianism allowing me, for once, to call on resources I had acquired in Edinburgh. Aware of my nervousness the evening before I was to deliver my introductory paper, Podro invited me to dinner with his girl friend Charlotte, who provided a pork steak with endives, the latter a first for me and a favourite ever since. We discussed Cassirer and how to put across in twenty minutes, to a multidisciplinary audience and without mystification, his notion of symbolic forms and its application. It seemed hardly possible, but just being able to talk about it with Podro was enormously helpful. When the moment came, I went ahead without too many nerves. I even raised a laugh when on Gombrich asking me whether Cassirer had anything to say on Eastern Art, I said I imagined so since his focal idea like Hegel's seemed to be one that covered everything. I sensed his annoyance at the flippancy. As Podro explained afterwards, Gombrich's expectation was that we were the stooges and he the entertainer. I should have delivered a deadpan resumé and left the jokes to him.

Meanwhile with Hampshire continuing the tradition of Monday seminars at UCL, even with the ultra-astute Bernard Williams now present, the atmosphere was less charged than under Ayer. Bernard usually sat silently for long periods head in hands, and when he did speak it was to summarize neatly what had been more wordily said and to offer objections to which he had already thought of possible answers. This had the effect of hurrying things along but also left others wondering what could possibly be added. The atmosphere was, however, less formal and more often than not Bernard's input gave the proceedings the benefit of an agenda. We probed several chapters of William James's *Psychology*, one of them on imagery. But when next we took on Quine's newly published *Word and Object* I was totally at sea. Quine's deliberately circumscribed vantage-point was the polar opposite of Cassirer's wide-angle vision on life as seen through the eyes of culture. His thinking was derived from the positivism that directly opposed the German Idealist tradition in which Cassirer's thought moved. For Quine the world is a world of things simply there for science to tell us all that can be said about them. The institution of language is a mess and too volatile to fit into a properly ordered scientific account of life. It comes, as it were, after the event. What you have to do is get down to where it begins 'in the middle of things' when, with sanitized basic linguistic equipment, you face what the world throws at you, including rabbits, people and their utterances. To acquire some of the vocabulary required for discussing Quine I wrote copious notes.

We also visited Norman Malcolm's *Dreaming* (1959), where the words were clear enough but the arguments so skewed by Wittgensteinian considerations as to appear whimsical in the extreme unless interpreted to the point of absurdity. To me, like most people, the idea that dreams are private experiences and knowable first-hand only to the dreamer posed no special difficulty. However, to twentieth-century philosophers bent on escaping the professional embarrassment of scepticism and the closed circle of introspective psychology it was crucial to relieve any allegedly private experience of their seeming inaccessibility to the world we share. Malcolm did it by insisting that dreams like any other topic of discourse have their 'language', which as such belongs essentially to our shared world. Dreams, then, are not just experiences but also, and essentially, topics of discourse. Those unsympathetic to this way of arguing could agree with Ayer's jibe that on Malcolm's view dreaming is basically 'telling lies at breakfast'. As for me, my Scottish piety led me in vain to catch some deeper point. The effort led me to an experiment in interior architecture. The basement bedroom looked out (if that is the right word) on a darkened and dank back alley. To lighten things up I painted the walls white and bought lime-coloured curtains from the family firm's showroom in Upper Regent Street. This with some effort of imagination could give the effect of perpetual sunshine about to pierce the gloom. Instead of hanging pictures on the walls, I wrote out obscure passages of Norman Malcolm's book in black with a marker pen in the hope that by gazing at them from my bed, I might eventually see that other light.

I left the words there even when they still failed to illuminate, adding others and also several three-dimensional items, including my shoes, preferring to hang them up as provisional art-works rather than lose sight of them in the subterranean darkness. I also hung up a photo of Gustav Mahler from a concert programme together with several small trinkets from Greece as reminders of sunnier climes. A persistent reminder of the actual conditions was provided by an overflow pipe that periodically splashed water onto the paving outside the window from the neighbours immediately above. Contact with these disclosed a bowler-hatted major recently retired from India, his family living on a paltry army pension, the wife a spiritualist who could solve current crises by placing them in a wider perspective — not just centuries but aeons — and two daughters, one about twelve, whose talent for the piano meant she had done some of this 'before', and the other eight years old and whose later habit of dropping down to see me they discouraged.

I have often puzzled over the frequency and apparently accidental nature of my meeting with spiritualists. Either dealers in the supernatural must be thicker on the ground than one imagines or else I have been more often than naturally brought into their proximity. I am attracted to it but just for that reason refuse to believe in it. They might claim that I am supernaturally appointed to meet them.

London afforded fewer social possibilities than a more compact Edinburgh. Apart from post-seminar dinners on Mondays at an Indian restaurant on or near Hampstead Road, we had few opportunities to gather and talk things over. It was to remedy this that a group of us had begun meetings in a series of Soho pubs able to offer conveniently private upstairs spaces for discussion. For want of a better name or worse, we called ourselves the 'Deicticians'. Participants were for the most part regulars of the Monday seminars. To begin with, besides myself they included Dr John(ny) Watling, the department's Reader, a sharp-minded, totally unpretentious and friendly teacher who had ended up in philosophy after physics and a First in Psychology; Michael Podro, the informed and articulate ex-art student who helped me to deal with the two Ernsts, Cassirer and Gombrich; Timothy Sprigge, a dedicated idealist who was completing his Cambridge dissertation, but under Ayer's aegis also working on the correspondence of Jeremy Bentham, the social and educational reformer and seminal utilitarian whose thinking inspired the UCL founders, and finally, Paul Foulkes, expatriate Australian and translator of several Vienna positivists but currently putting together the text of the illustrated *Wisdom of the West*, a popular coffee-table work only ostensibly authored by Bertrand Russell. Occasionally there was also Glyn Seaborn Jones, a leading figure in humanistic psychotherapy and the first to introduce primal scream therapy to Britain. Some years later he was to become more widely known as a consultant psychotherapist on television with members of the public present as his subjects. My fond personal memory of him is encapsulated in a moment when, on remarking on my untamed hairstyle, he described it as 'leonine'. On my saying 'You mean I need a haircut', he replied that he thought he said it 'more prettily'.

In the autumn of 1959 a tall Canadian of considerable presence, and with a refreshingly direct style, joined the group. Inspired by *Language, Truth and Logic*, Ted Honderich had come to UCL to study under Ayer only to find that he had just left for Oxford. After a briefly wary start, Ted entered our discussions with what seemed a clear message that there was still much nonsense to dispose of in philosophy, not only the metaphysics that the Ayer of 1936 had targeted, but quite a lot of what was still being perpetrated in philosophy's name. This had some effect on our meetings, partly sobering but at times disconcerting. If my memory doesn't deceive me, our last meeting was one where Ted responded to some complex view advanced by another newcomer by pronouncing it 'horseshit'. His deep North American voice gave the word extra emphasis, indeed a kind of finality. If not a stopping point, at least it provided a memorable milestone.

Thomas Kremer, the newcomer, certainly never returned. Our kind of philosophy didn't interest him anyway. A Hungarian survivor of the Bergen-Belsen concentration camp, Kremer had first come within my orbit in Edinburgh where he acquired guru status with some Svengali overtones among a group of younger people. These included Vincent Hope, then unknown to me and and Annette Gomperz, his wife-to-be.

Still a teenager in the concentration camp, on its liberation in 1945, Kremer had moved to Israel. He had been studying philosophy there and, now in London, had been given the professional's accolade of the floor of the Aristotelian Society. It was after his paper there that he briefly joined our group. On my making a smart objection typical of the kind I had been trying to emulate in the company of my hyper-intelligent colleagues, he gave me a beady-eyed and well-deserved rebuke ('Very clever'). I found that by marrying Lady Alison Emily Balfour, Kremer had not only acquired some wealth but been further elevated to the pages of *Burke's Peerage and Baronetage*. Although he was to become an international businessman, making a fortune in toy design and manufacture, his contribution to thought continued, as is evident in the well-received *The Missing Heart of Europe*, a work of more immediate significance than anything we ourselves were on the way to accomplishing at that time.

Ted Honderich and Timothy Sprigge, so different in temperament and background as well as in their philosophical approaches, were to remain lifelong friends. Without the relaxed atmosphere of those exchanges in Soho pubs and subsequent mutual visits, it is hard to imagine them and myself becoming so close. In time, having mastered the ropes he needed to progress in his chosen career, Ted charged ahead under his own steam with a high disregard for what thinkers of the past had said on the topics that interested him, the first of these being freedom of the will. Having demolished that idea, he would examine the principles behind the penal system and then attain notoriety for his claims on behalf of Palestinians to the moral right to perform terror. At that time, Ted was still finding his feet, but aspects of his combative personality were already evident.

Timothy, dedicated and approachable with wide sympathies and interests, was the most professional of our debating group and a true philosopher in every sense. He spoke against but from within a background of traditional philosophical distinctions drawn from pre-Russellian idealism. It was a background against which, as his career developed, he also lived out his thoughts by following what he saw to be their ethical implications. Described in the *Daily Telegraph* obituary as a 'courageous eccentric on the contemporary philosophical scene',[5] much more easily than in our cases he could be identified with his own philosophical project. It was one that ended in a view of things of the kind Ted clearly thought philosophy should do without. It took the world at its manifest level to consist in pieces of consciousness whose separateness is only an illusion. Given certain premises, philosophical reasoning leads us to the conclusion that all consciousness is one and the physical world, which we find it so natural as well as logical to separate in thought from the mental, is linked to the mental in a way that makes it, too, mental. Converting Wittgenstein's thought that a musical score is a projection of the symphony we hear and *vice versa*, Timothy was to present his own mature view of the world on the analogy of the heard symphony with the score as the idea we have of 'just things' or 'matter-in-itself' and the world we know as essentially mind. The obituary also described philosophy for Sprigge as 'a matter of life and death, not least the life and death of non-human beings'. He would later become Chairman of Advocates for Animals.

For myself, 'down from Edinburgh', as Ted remarked in his autobiography, I had 'stepped out of at least the pages of a better women's novel, or one for all of us by Walter Scott'. I seemed 'secure in a dignity acquired from a line of severe Scottish thinkers, and possibly well-heeled'. The 'possibly' suggests that Ted somehow believed my shabby clothes were not owing to my having no other choice. As for the lineage a Scot, even of humblest origins, can easily give an impression of original severity. But whatever severe thinkers there were in my background, and there were several, they had no influence on my own upbringing. Any grimness on my part was likely owed, among other things, to the seriousness with which I had opted later in life than usual for a thinker's role and to my impatience at not finding what I had hoped it could offer. Timothy's views certainly appealed to me, as to my ecumenical mind did Ted's. Lacking the former's erudition and the latter's self-assurance, or due to an inability to disguise any deficiency in that area, these two provided inspiring examples.

The three academic years in London were a trial. Towards the end I sensed that it might not be one with which I should be testing myself. But once on course there was nothing to be gained by turning back. Besides, London had much to offer beyond intellectual gymnastics. Just around the corner from Earls Court Square was the Troubadour, a coffee house founded four years earlier by a Canadian couple. I stumbled on it by accident and quickly became a regular. This was an oasis of calm in the Earls Court bustle with its baggage-trailing Australian tourists and offered respite from my struggles with tortuous abstractions, as well as giving me a chance to escape the gloom of my basement. The Troubadour sported a basement of its own, already a venue for jazz, folk- and other culturally current music. It later became famous for aspiring artists, some to be famous, as well as a place where the already famous would come to play informally after their concerts. Bob Dylan, Paul Simon, Jimi Hendrix and Elton John appeared there. At that time, the late 'fifties, it was a relaxed haven for local misfits and others with time on their hands or at their own disposal and with a taste for omelettes and stuffed peppers. If there was talk of celebrity, the big names then were Richard Harris and Anthony Newley, misfits on a larger scale but now on the way to careers in which this could be used to advantage. The present clientele included some who hoped for the same. Bandana das Gupta, from Calcutta, who served behind the counter, had already played small parts in minor movies and on television. Jim Cormack, a Geordie student of composition at the Royal College and basement-playing saxophonist, was an expert with omelettes. Michael Manton, then with a publisher, was biding his time for something more. Jack Sunters, his elder sister Irene a well-loved Scottish film and television actress, had as his own ambition some form of back-stage activity in the theatre world. Dislocated on first arrival in London, and eager to gear into its life opportunities, Jack also dropped in quite frequently at my basement for some encouragement. I didn't always offer it. One day he arrived while I was absorbed in Mahler's ninth symphony, having decided to listen to it twice, which I did with the concentration of a Buddhist. Jack waited patiently, listening to what must have been entirely new music and not what he had come to the Old Smoke for. Three years later a letter from Mike Manton, himself now an academic, told me that Jack did wonderfully well at a teachers' training college and, while still a student, had developed a talent for producing passion plays and television plays for schools. About Mike Manton himself, my former tutor in Edinburgh Bob McGowan informed me later that they were now colleagues at the University of Kent.

There were others, from Stavanger in Norway the long-limbed, hipster-cool Bjørn Apeland, a glass-painter studying in London. His decorations in the Christmas season covered the Troubadour's large window. He could tell me of the Norwegian philosopher Arne Naess, a 'cat' whose unusual approach I recalled Ayer mentioning in class. Instead of tackling the question of truth in his head, Naess had travelled on trains asking passengers what they meant by 'true', 'truth', etc. The result had been a locally published but widely rumoured monograph from 1938, *Truth as Conceived by Those Who Are Not Professional Philosophers*. It could be called a positivist approach though not at all in the usual office-bound sense. Ayer and Naess, I was to discover, had met briefly in Vienna before the war. Sadly, I heard later that 'cool' Bjørn drowned in Spain, the circumstances being somewhat clouded. There was Collin Bates, an Australian Pianist with Bruce Turner's Jump Band, who instituted the Troubadour's jazz sessions. And there was Shmoo' Bob, likeably unembarrassed by intellect, and a sturdy blonde German *au pair* with considerable savvy, as well as several other young women, some sharp-tongued and attached to the above men. There were few unattached women, but one evening the sister-in-law of a celebrated author said she would like to come home with me. She did but took so long bathing herself that little that I remember came of it.

Another exception was the forthright and good-natured Judith, who towards the end of my London stay became my close friend and consolation. We took to visiting each other and going to the theatre and Mahler concerts. She, too, worked behind the bar at the Troubadour. On late evening shifts she would visit me on the way home with elaborate sandwiches. She came one evening when I felt out of sorts and had already gone to sleep. Coming into the bedroom and not waking me though I was aware of here presence, she left the sandwiches and kissed me like a mother saying good night to her child. It spoke more than any volume.

Although then not so widely celebrated, in current records the Troubadour is described as 'one of the centres of London's intellectual life'. Its later fame was due to association with such iconic items as *Private Eye*, early Ban the Bomb meetings and the Black Panthers. For me it was a kind of home with some *déjà-vu* from early childhood. If we came there too early, Mike our large Canadian host told us to get out and do something useful while he swept the pavement and cleaned the floor. He did that every morning, while in the evenings he was just as likely to turn out customers heard discussing share options: 'We don't have that kind of talk here.' A committed socialist, Mike came from Montreal and had a Dutch father. With his wife Sheila he had turned a grocer's shop into what became one of London best-known venues. I read recently that in

1970 they sold their coffee shop and home above and moved their inspiring operation to Dubrovnik. Michael van Boemen died in 2009 aged 79.

Two events during those three years were to mark my life forever, both beginning with communications from friends in the north.

It was in June 1959, the first summer, that I received an unexpected phone call from Fiona, unexpected because she had never phoned me before. It sounded innocent enough. Our mutual friend Norma was going through a difficult time, could I offer her a roof during a short stay in London? I knew that Norma had married some years previously and had been living in Hong Kong. Now, a few years after giving birth to a daughter, an extra-marital affair had put the marriage on the rocks and the husband was suing for divorce. The proceedings were conducted as required at that time in London's law courts. After the hearings Norma was due to return to Edinburgh. I said she could certainly stay over. Norma, as already mentioned, had been a good, but not more than, friend from my early university days. She had been the support that Fiona brought along to form the foursome required of her outing with the mature architect student. Both of us being honorary members of the Failures, and Norma subsequently becoming part of the sailing community, had forged a friendship but not more. It was Fiona, as Norma told me much later, who thinking it might restore some humanity to my philosophically desiccated soul, had put her in mind of me as a more than just convenient contact. She arrived at the door distraught. The judge having decided that her past as an art student disqualified her from having sole care of the child, her daughter had been made a ward of court. Apparently, the husband's elder unmarried sister was cited as an argument in favour of the husband retaining custody. The husband being already considerably older than Norma, the outlook for the daughter seemed bleak. There were tears and comfort was called for. Fiona wrote to thank me for 'looking after Norma just now — she needs it so badly'. Two months later she phoned to say that Norma was pregnant.

It was my turn to be distraught. Any prospects I had for making a living out of what I was doing were in the far future. For every day that I ploughed deeper into my chosen field, that eventuality seemed more distant. I could drop it all of course, but what was the alternative? Yes, Norma and I had common interests, among other things music, but our alliance had been imprecise and unresolved. With no contact for several years I was now more closely attached to those people 'of both sexes', as my grandmother had remarked, with whom I was sharing the various aspects of my less than integrated life. Rather than adding further to these, this new situation was a blight upon all the others. One thought was 'What can I do about it anyway?', while the other, the thought of Norma, the child and their future, was one that I could not escape. For several years to come the insoluble dilemma placed an inhibition upon every occasion offered for a serious and open relationship. Secrecy didn't help either. The person who should know was my mother, but she was now in thrall once more to her moralistic family in the shape of her younger brother on whom she was dependent economically but also psychologically. It would be as acutely embarrassing for her to confess her son's sins, as it was unnatural for me to bare my soul to her. She herself had been brought up to talk of 'good families' and to be conscious of belonging to that respectable *élite*. Also, our relationship, except perhaps in the first few years had lacked the intimacy that makes sharing such confidences the natural thing to do. Not telling my mother meant not telling anyone else, from loyalty but also because once abroad the news could spread to her too. Norma, too, wanted to keep the identity of the child's father secret. It was not until much later, when both my mother and her brother had died, that I told my family. Then my uncle's widow, a more pragmatic soul, was content with referring to me as a 'dark horse'. We remained on good and, in some ways, even better terms.

That summer, I paid an escapist visit to Paris. A previous visit just before settling down in London had opened a new world. I had joined the family of another Edinburgh friend in Brittany for a fortnight's holiday at the end of August. The holiday over, instead of accompanying them home, I stopped off at St Malo and took a train to Paris. There I had come upon George Whitman's Librairie Mistral, latterly re-named Shakespeare and Company. Placed in the quiet Quartier St. Julien le Pauvre on the Left Bank just opposite Notre Dame, it offered a meeting place and also cramped sleeping quarters to poor writers and visiting students. A young Irish poet, who seemed to have some familiarity with the local *gendarmerie*, was taking advantage of a mattress there while in transit to Italy. He and I slipped off in the late evenings to eat oysters at Les Halles, at that time (and until 1971) the central fresh fruit market. With associated bars and restaurants, it came to life during the night. For a poet, he appeared to have an uncanny ability to open locked doors without a key, as returning one early morning to his lodging. Preferring solitude, I had booked in at the Hotel de Flandres on Rue Cujas, a plain establishment but conveniently located by the Sorbonne. I read in the mornings in the soothing cool of the high-arched Bibliothèque Sainte Geneviève and had lunch at the student cafeteria opposite, and then, after a short rest at the hotel, walked down to George's on the Left Bank to help out if need be, or just sit and read or talk. Once a young uptown lady with several friends arrived in a car outside Mistral as though out to show them a curiosity shop. They were looking in my direction and laughing, I supposed at me. Later she came in and asked if we couldn't go out, suggesting Whisky à Go-Go, a high-class dive for teenagers plus. A nice change from my monastic routine, I thought as I dug out my crumpled light-beige linen suit. She drove me to her home on the fashionable Rue Francois 1-er near L'Étoile. Her elegantly dressed mother, seeing the state of my attire, or perhaps it was me, seemed less than delighted. The conventions of polite French greeting were briefly performed but the nightclub and bar proved a welcome diversion and Michèle seemed to think there might be some future for us. She planned to meet me the next day, but when she arrived I was laid up in the hotel with a bad stomach caused by something I'd taken at lunch. This lasted for several days and the only way I could continue helping at George's was by not eating anything after breakfast. There were some frightening seconds in the hotel, about five I would guess, when I became totally paralysed and unable to breathe. It was as if my body and all its works were held in an iron grip, the only occasion I can recall when I could say that it was as if my mind was something quite apart from, and no longer interactively engaged with, my body. The brain, though, was of course still functioning, but its motor departments were terrifyingly on holiday. I didn't see Michèle again. She turned out to be secretary to an Argentinian concert pianist and was about to go on tour. Later she wrote to me in London to say her pianist boss would be there in case I would like to meet them. I never did. That was in the late summer of 1958.

Now, a year later and in a state of personal disarray, a spell at George's Le Mistral seemed good for peace of mind. It became more than that. July saw the publication by the Olympia Press in Paris of *Naked Lunch* (later wrongly re-titled *The Naked Lunch*) and its author William Burroughs was in town. So were other luminaries of the Beat Generation. One was Harold Norse (his name an anagram of Rosen), a Beat poet who died as recently as 2009 at ninety-two. Described as 'a literary beacon in the gay community' and said to be the mentor of a whole range of twentieth-century American writers, Harold had just arrived from Italy and was staying nearby at the 'Beat Hotel' in Rue Git-le-Coeur to the west of St. Michel. Burroughs was also living there. While Harold and I were playing chess outside the bookstore one afternoon, George came out to say that Burroughs had invited us to tea. Half expecting a marijuana session, I was touched to see ordinary tea being poured from a traditional brown teapot. Burroughs had a battered typewriter which he offered for sale, the one on which he had recently finished *Naked Lunch*. I regretted not bidding for it.

Among others invited was Ian Somerville. He was a computer programmer from Cambridge and had come to Paris ostensibly to improve his French, but George had engineered this visit on his behalf with a view to his collaborating with Burroughs and Harold Norse and also Brion Gysin in technical developments of the 'cut-up' technique used in *Naked Lunch*. Ian and Gysin later produced the Dreamachine, a stroboscope driven by a 78-rpm gramophone player designed as an art object to be seen 'with the eyes closed'. It was thought to affect the alpha-wave activity of the viewer's brain. I learned later that Ian, who helped cure Burroughs's codeine addiction, also became his lover. At the time there was no indication of homosexuality, nor even when Ian later in the autumn came to visit me in Earls Court. He had written to say that on his last night in Paris, he and Denise, another helper had been given by George eight thousand Francs to buy a meal at the neighbouring La Bucherie, a fashionable restaurant where Sartre and De Beauvoir were often seen dining. Its kitchen door also provided George's dog 'Butch' with hunks of meat. That he said he got on quite well with Denise put me off the scent.

As for me, I had got on 'quite well' with another of George's helpers, one that he himself rather fancied and for whose favours we played a little flippantly at competing. Jacqueline, a light-haired, slim and lively young student of quick humour and understanding didn't openly object to her nickname 'La Crevette'. We got along nicely but she wrote to me later saying that she was mystified by my not responding more openly to her own less inhibited expression of our mutual liking. I couldn't get myself to tell her why, while attempts on my part to forget the reason were stymied by letters from Norma confirming what we already knew.

I came across two postscripts to that stay. One was to a work by the creative choreographer Merce Cunningham, saying that 'the most interesting of his publications for a student would probably be *The Dancer and the Dance: Merce Cunningham in Conversation with Jacqueline Lesschaeve*'. This 'congenial' interviewer's questions concerning his early dance experiences, his views on art, nature, and the 'spiritual' had been addressed by Cunningham 'at length'. The other was a reference to Ian Somerville's death in a car accident near Bath in 1976. He had been experimenting with heightened consciousness through reproducing a visionary experience Gysin once had due to flickering sunlight.

Creative dance and the heightening of consciousness represented exciting expansions of the distance between the poles of the body-mind relation that far exceeded my own occupations with it. *Tant pis*.

Chapter Eight: Clearing the decks

Clear the deck: getting ready to start something new by putting everything else out of the way.

To scorn this philosophy before proving enough ability in it to show that I knew what I was scorning would be to open myself to a charge of sour grapes. I said to myself 'Onward!'. In another respect, however, there was no going forward. The background for a visit to pay my respects to Norma and her family was not auspicious. She was living with her mother, for whom things were already bad enough with her husband lying in hospital with complications from which he would soon die. I had met Norma's mother in better circumstances. Now her greeting on opening the door was 'Here's that bad man'. Norma naturally enough wanted to talk and we walked endlessly up and down the garden side of Princes Street, opposite the one on which I had passed her some seven years earlier. There were harsh words and tears. Marriage was out of the question. Here there was no going forward.

Not so with the second life-changing event in London. It was a letter from Peter Frøstrup now in Norway. He and Joan had repaired to Oslo where Peter had secured a job with the fledgling university press and had responsibility for its journals. He would send me 'a small pile of issues of a magazine called "*Inquiry*"', which might interest me, though because it was 'mostly American' he had some doubts. When the pile arrived, it included to my pleasant surprise an issue in which Anfinn Stigen, a Norwegian philosopher then teaching at Aarhus in Denmark, subjected Ayer's *The Problem of Knowledge* to meticulous scrutiny. There was also a detailed reply by Ayer himself. That was interesting enough, but there was also a simple clarity in the thought of both that I had missed in the discussions in our seminars. When my grant ran out the following July, I would have to find a job. Jim Haynes, now well established in Edinburgh, was planning to open a coffee house with books in Paris on the *Paperback* model. He wondered if I might consider being its manager. It was tempting but not a way of bringing to fruition all that I had done or tried to do these last five years. But then Peter wrote again asking if I was interested in a temporary copy-editing and proofreading job at the university press in Oslo. One of their English language consultants was on pregnancy leave. He reverted to this journal *Inquiry*. It had been going for only two years and under the editorship of its founder, Arne Naess. Perhaps when settled in this language-consultancy job, which could become permanent, I would find that editing the journal was something for me too? It seemed a long shot, copy-editing perhaps but editing? However, having assembled a distinguished advisory board and commissioned enough papers from the famous to launch the first two volumes, Naess, according to Peter, was leaving the actual work to an assistant with the title of 'managing editor'. It was not impossible that I might take over that role.

I had always looked south or southeast for a change in circumstances. If philosophy was unable to produce light, why not the sun? Yes, but I had seen Norway and knew the sun shone there too. Yes, again, it was high summer where everything was idyllic. And arriving by sea after a hard voyage adds lustre to any shore. But after five years in basements, the prospect of fresh air, blue skies and (mainly) white-painted wooden houses was hard to resist. A job working on manuscripts, some of them even philosophical, would be an ideal pastime for someone who had so far failed to put one together himself. Also, I was told that the press owned an electric typewriter. I might use it out of office hours to put down some of my own sentences.

In the spring of the final year in London I negotiated through Peter with the press's director. He demanded an interview and I needed to know more about the work and the terms. There was also a chance of contacting Arne Naess. With my sister Jane I flew over and spent some days with Peter and Joan in their modern suburban flat, so unlike anything I'd seen them living in previously, and all four of us took off for a week in a rented cabin. We travelled by train to Åmot in Eggedal, spent days basking in an unbelievably hot sun and read Agatha Christie, then a staple of Norwegian cabin-dwellers. Naess was not available on our return but the interview left us agreed on a start from 1 November. The director said if I didn't show promise by Christmas I'd be shipped back to Newcastle by the first boat, a challenge he was to rue. Meanwhile an entry permit was acquired allowing me to work in Norway as an English-language copy editor.

I spent September in Scotland. Norma with Fiona and her friend Kenneth had rented two cottages near Tongue on the windswept and treeless Scottish north coast. Disappointment and bitterness had filled Norma's letters, but I was invited to join them and took the train to Lairg where Norma picked me up for the forty or so extra miles to 'Beechwood' at Tongue. By then Tim, our son, was eighteen months old and it was what my mother would call a 'bucket-and-spade' holiday. The situation was awkward but not too much so: we knew each other well enough. On departing, it was with the sense of a last meeting for some time to come.

Changing trains on the way south at Inverness, I headed for Kyle of Lochalsh, taking a bus from there to Glenelg, on the mainland opposite the Isle of Skye.

There I spent some days with Vincent and Annette Hope and their children and also Vincent's philosophical father. Vincent and I went out rowing one day on the Sound of Sleat when the wind suddenly blew up carrying us away from the shore and it seemed inexorably towards the strait leading north into Loch Alsh. Significant waves also formed and reduced whatever momentum we could achieve. I was rowing and at first didn't say anything, but when Vincent sensed I was struggling and asked 'Hadn't we better try getting back?', I had to admit 'That's what I'm trying to do!'. Making the most of the lulls in the now near gale-force wind, we managed to edge ever so slowly back to the pier. There, a handful of locals had gathered to savour the drama of a landlubber from the south toiling against the elements. When, after a good half-hour of straining at the oars, we did finally reach the pier, one of them came forward to take the rope and said: 'It's just as well ye can row, laddie.' I took it as tacit praise and a signal of acceptance, in spite of my origins south of Ardnamurchan.

Vincent said I'd saved his life. I thought it a little strange that he didn't mention mine. This and other incidents led me later to reflect on Vincent and on our relationship. When I had moved to Norway he and Peter Frøstrup seemed my nearest friends and Vincent my only lasting collegial contact in Scotland. I later became alienated from both or they from me. The circumstances can wait, but the underlying causes were already there to see in Vincent's case if only I had been able to detect them. As I saw it, we were inverse examples of a syndrome mentioned earlier: a form of social incapacity that for want of non-linguistic approaches uses language as the bridge to reach other people. For me speech is the most natural mode of contact with individuals, but it works *only* with individuals. As a verbal version of table-tennis, it can be sociable but also lead people to suspect I am quarrelsome or just contrary. It also happens to be an ideal medium in the forensic atmosphere of philosophical discussion, where it is professional to pick holes in whatever anyone else has said. To me Vincent is the exact opposite. His natural 'conversational' style is that of the speech-maker. With a repertory of ready-made, well-considered views his mind on most things seemed already made up. Besides an exceptionally good musical ear and performing talent, Vincent's social spontaneity takes the form of playful humour and sometimes clowning. It can be a way of keep the social reins in one's hands. If I am right, we have in common a form of social isolation with language as our contact with the world. I may be wrong.

There is another thing. I knew about boats and while Vincent was in my care I could at least row. He was thankful I did not fail him. I returned to Edinburgh by train in the company of Vincent's father, a man always interesting to talk to. We discussed the implications of the latest news. The United Nations Secretary

General, Dag Hammarskjold, had died in an air-crash in Africa. Parting in Edinburgh, I continued to Melrose for a short spell before leaving for London to close shop. There were last rounds, farewells and settlings, though everything in my case was unsettled. No dissertation, no job that would help to bring three years of assorted notes and half-remembered conversations into some kind of order. The prospects were dim enough for me to think back ruefully on Ryle's advice back in 1956. Had the right course been to 'abandon the whole scheme'? Reward for effort or fulfilment began to be the stuff of imagination. It was given food by a chance meeting on Charing Cross Road with Hamish Henderson, Scotland's formidable folklorist, poet and ex-soldier. I told him what I was up to but with little headway so far. He said, on no evidence apart from our casual encounters in Edinburgh's International House, 'Don't worry, you'll write books'. With superstition not totally eradicated from my mind, I was able to take this brief encouragement from a man of such wide experience as a portent of better things to come.

An unfinished lease on the basement in Earls Court had to be taken care of. That was easily settled. Per Ung, a Norwegian sculptor and his English wife Valerie were to be in London for a year from that autumn while he attended St. Martin's School of Art. After a thorough clean-up undertaken by Valerie, the like of which the flat had never seen on my watch, they moved in. I found a friendly roof with some hospitable relatives in Argyll Road off Kensington High Street. My cousin Jos(lyn), a sculptor who works in ceramics had married Joe Tilson, an artist associated with the British Pop Art movement and teaching at St. Martin's. The centre of their large home, which also provided accommodation for Joslyn's mother and a Norwegian model, as well as an unluckily pregnant American college student, was a large kitchen frequented by their aspiring and, at that time, more or less penniless friends and colleagues. These included the later celebrities Peter Blake and David Hockney. The atmosphere of warmth, good food and talented young artists on the way up was invigorating in spite of standing in sharp contrast to my own situation.

Latterly I had become good but entirely platonic friends with Bandana, the aspiring film and television actress from Calcutta who worked behind the Troubadour's counter, and also with her American divorcee flat-mate Jan Vogt. They were intelligent and it was an amiable and uncomplicated relationship. We invited each other to coffee and even tea. When Bandana was due for some Shakespeare part in the summer I went to hear her lines. But she, too, was unsettled. To my surprise, on learning that I was to leave for Norway she asked me to take her with me. London had done her no good, she was tired of being exploited for her looks and having no place to hide or family to lean on. When

Jan had to be away, Bandana asked me to come to her flat and sleep there to keep her company. Not, it seems, afraid of anyone in particular and needing me to warn off whoever it was, it seemed a less determinate fear. She trusted me, which I appreciated and acted with discretion accordingly. But equally unsettled as I was, I was in no state to bear the responsibility of helping her settle in a land foreign to me and which she knew even less. Maybe she looked at Norway rather as I did, a kind of blank cheque for an unspecified better future. The request was so unexpected that I failed at first to see it was an expression not of hope but of despair. The painful memory is infinitely more so for what followed. When I returned to London on a short visit two years later, I was told that Bandana had recently gassed herself in her Kensington basement kitchen.

I left London for Melrose to prepare for departure not knowing quite what or how much to take with me. I packed the few indispensables that would support what was to be a brief spell abroad for recovery of my wits and, most of all, start on that dissertation, perhaps even get it out of the way. I took clothes, including a suit that I never came to use, some books and gramophone records together with the jazz tapes collected after tutorials with Ayer. Unsure of the weather conditions in store, the question of winter-wear was postponed. Financially, I was at ground zero. The primitive tape-recorder had been sold to pay for the ticket. Still, at twenty-nine I was about to take on my first proper job even if it was only a temporary one.

After lunch on Saturday 28 October 1961 we, my brother Ian, our mother and I, drove to Tynemouth where Fred. Olsen's MS *Braemar* was preparing to depart at the Tyne Commission Quay. I went aboard, found my cabin and climbed to the top deck thinking to wave goodbye, but they had already gone. It was a strange feeling. Leaving, I had also been left. Where else to look now than hopefully ahead?

As the Northumberland coastline disappeared astern, so did civilization as I knew it. The ship's turbulent wake was ploughing under all that had entered my mind in the last three years. In a day or two I would be proofreading other people's works, checking not thoughts but just symbols. What had Peter advised? Sever all connections with the past? He, surrounded by all that he had left behind, had become *my* connection.

Part Two: Surfacing

Surfacing — *'to suddenly appear or become obvious after having been hidden for a while'*

(Oxford Advanced Learners' Dictionary).

Chapter Nine: In commission

Commissioning: *placing a naval vessel or commercial ship into service, after which it is said to be 'in commission'.*

MS *Braemar* docked at Vippetangen on Oslo's East Side early on a clearly etched Monday morning on the 30th of October 1961. Peter Frøstrup and Leif Schanche were there to greet me. Working for an oil company, Leif had a car, exceptional in those days, and we drove to Peter and Joan's flat, an artist's fairly limited living accommodation but with a large studio at the back. It was part of an artists' 'colony' with several rows of studio apartments, properly so called, built by the city on the property called Ekely, once Edvard Munch's and where his studio still stood. With the help of Joan's credentials as a former art student, they had rented one such apartment, moving that autumn from the block on the Northern outskirts where my sister and I had visited them in the summer. Another apartment on the row above belonged to their friends Per and Valerie Ung now occupying the Earls Court basement.

The new apartment was small but with an extra bedroom. It too was confined. Until we all moved the following summer to a more spacious top-floor flat in Majorstuen near the city centre, it was my kennel. There was a ventilator above the bed and I could feel for the first time how, brushing your face on its way, cold air cascades invisibly to the floor. I made the sacrilegious mistake of turning off the bathroom switch on leaving that small area, as we always did at home, only to be sharply admonished by Joan, for whom in the everyday climate of a Norwegian home it was her 'sanctuary'. The floors of their bathrooms are comfortably heated.

Peter was still managing the journals' section at the university press. Although the editors with whom it was his job to be in contact were neither poets nor novelists, this was at least literature of a sort produced by hard-working academics, whose efforts he was just as able to appraise. His and Joan's new neighbourhood provided the ambience they sought, certainly a good deal less diurnally bibulous than the Scottish poets, but boisterous enough on occasion and sufficiently unbuttoned to dissociate Peter at weekends from the nine-to-five office brigade to which he now reluctantly belonged and into which he had brought me. As for Joan, there was a prospect of acceptance in this setting as an artist in her own right. She began as a designer of book-covers for the Press.

I had a day or two to wander about Oslo getting impressions and reflect on the fact that career-wise at twenty-nine I had come nowhere. The novelty of an Oslo unfamiliar in its early winter frost wiped clean my memory of everything I had done and half-learnt during those five years. I had thought to start on my thesis as soon as I was settled in but had no idea where to begin or what to focus on. In London the university had me registered as working towards a dissertation on 'Images and Imagining', but I had no practice in writing in the style of my most recent mentors, the only leading marks in my mind being 'imagination', far too broad a subject, and 'mental images', which in the light of day seemed a trivial topic. The one thing I remembered was Ryle's treatment of it in his annoyingly elusive chapter on imagination. One thing was certain: there was nothing in Ryle's whirl of suggestions and analogies out of which to spin a dissertation. Another deterrent was the thought that having come this far, not least in years, I should deliver something more ambitious.

A chance of escape had been narrowly missed. Before leaving Melrose I had a letter from Peter saying that Jim Haynes had dropped by with a Swedish girlfriend on the way to her home in Stockholm. The question of managing his projected coffee-bookstore in Paris had again been raised. With recent encounters still fresh in mind, I could think of no greater contrast to the threadbare life I now saw before me, correcting the barely serviceable English prose of Norwegian academics in an outpost of European civilization. The prospect of setting up in competition with George Whitman in his Librairie Mistral and perhaps even joining forces with him, as of life in Paris in any imaginable respect, was a temptation I would have been far more open to if less obsessed with that dissertation.

The task of settling in quickly overshadowed the dream of Paris. Had something gone wrong at the start, I might have kept it alive, or had Oslo proved a dreadful place to end up in. But so far nothing had gone wrong and Oslo seemed both manageable and refreshing. The truth is that to ditch everything I had been struggling with over the last five years would mean destroying some part of myself. In retrospect, I doubt that I would have found myself at home in the expansive rhetoric of French philosophy. On the other hand, Norway itself didn't seem to offer much chance either of fulfilling whatever promise lay in what I had done. Having left my exceptionally able colleagues behind, my mind was no longer being honed or tuned in the manner required of discussion at their level. Whatever one may think of the relevance of what they were discussing, the fact that the standard of discussion was so high meant I had even more to lose by staying on in Oslo. I told myself I would hang on there just long enough to get that thesis written, yet not so long as to lose what little philosophical literacy I had acquired.

Early on the Wednesday morning Peter and I walked the ten minutes it took from the bus to a late nineteenth-century neo-renaissance house in Josefinesgate. It had served through the years as a duplex private home, a boys' school, a Rudolf Steiner School and during the war a German School. Just then it was the official address of the Oslo Architects' Society but housed the fledgling university press's editorial department. We went upstairs and through a door on which I saw my name already printed, reinforcing perhaps by design a sense of impending permanency. Another name was printed there too, that of my boss, Trevor Chadwick. I was told he had been a schoolmaster in England but after the war, in which he had a chequered career as a junior officer in the RAF, he had contracted tuberculosis and was given a year to live. Sent to a sanatorium in Lillehammer, he recovered but falling ill again on his return decided to settle in Norway for good. In downtown Oslo he joined a group of ex-law students putting together a publishing operation in the basement of the old university building. It was to become the Oslo University Press. Educated at the Dragon School and an Oxford graduate, Chadwick was by now an experienced copy-editor. In a letter earlier in the summer, telling me that he would not be there when I came over to test the ground, Peter referred to him as 'The Corrector', describing him as 'a nice old fellow, utterly harmless and with not too much authority'. That was something of a relief. I was to be his apprentice and partner. Just now my future colleague and mentor was on a visit to Germany.

The office I was to share with Chadwick had two large desks, each by a large window overlooking the street. Before I had time to look at the papers already on my desk, in walked a sprightly Asiatic girl who, looking first at me and then out of the window, said, 'What a nice view you have'. Joanne was a twenty-three-year-old so-called *Sansei*, or third-generation Japanese American, from California and currently working with the sales department. She was also a friend of the Frøstrups and in the winter months to come we would be better acquainted both in the office and at home. After a week or so Chadwick returned and all but literally welcomed me with open arms, saying he was overburdened and needed an extra hand.

Trevor was an out-going man in his early fifties, exuding warmth but with the humour and attitudes of an over-grown public-school boy. He would ring the Paraguayan Embassy on the other side of the road just to see someone move over to take the phone. On hearing Joanne's voice in the hall outside, he would say, 'Ah, there's a Nip in the air'. She took it in good part and everyone did all they could to accommodate Chadwick. Directed at those Norwegian colleagues who appeared to underestimate the true extent and importance of his work on their behalf, Chadwick's bluff humour could be less than affectionate. He would bait people who interfered with his own schedules and mocked his superiors in their absence, although having considerable respect for the two former law students who had launched the Oslo University Press and given him his job. They owed much to Chadwick, but in the very nature of the case were not in a position fully to appreciate what his work meant to them. Manuscripts in a blunt and very basic English, and disfigured by Norwegian syntax, were transformed by his hand into models of English prose that earned for some of their work the Clarendon Press imprint. His sometimes not un-malicious humour was obviously also in part a way of keeping his own spirits up. There were things we only came to know about Chadwick later.

As for myself, fears of failing philosophical literacy were partly laid to rest by the arrival of Eivind Storheim, the first editor to seek consultation at my desk. He was in fact Managing Editor of the recently founded *Inquiry*, proof-copies of which Peter had sent me in London. It became clear that Storheim was happy to discuss the submissions with me. Also, I would be checking the prose as well as the punctuation and, with the high standards set by my recent years in London still in place, I could keep critical track of on-going discussion. Peter engineered a meeting with the nominal Editor himself, Arne Naess. I knocked on his door at Halling Skole, a former secondary school just around the corner and where pupils had once been prepared for the university, but now a provisional home for several university departments. '*Kom inn*', he said, and I went in, whereupon he asked me if I'd seen the philosophy library. Since I'd just come in and his office was lined with books and I had noticed none outside, I wondered stupidly whether this could be it. 'No, where?', I asked, looking at his own bookshelves. 'Outside', he said. This disconcerting way of saying 'please wait' proved typical of Naess's unconventional style.

Once face-to-face with the famous professor, then forty-nine, alert and with a face that gave no sign of professorial pomposity or things held back, I found him easy to talk to and straight as well as quick and amusing in his replies. Not long after this, a manuscript by Naess himself landed on my desk for copy-editing. I began to follow the argument and found a few oddities and lacunae, which I circled in red and signalled with question marks in the margin. Not knowing quite how he would take this from a stranger, I was nicely surprised when he asked me round to discuss the piece with him. He even raised the possibility of my becoming a part-time assistant. That would take some time to arrange but, not long afterwards, Storheim arrived at the office to announce that he would be spending three years at Harvard on a research grant. Since he and Naess would need someone with a background in philosophy to deal with correspondence in fluent English, they had agreed to ask me to take over the managing editorship 'pro tem'. My bosses at the Press disliked the idea of an employee being at the same time a customer, but Naess's fame carried weight and they waived their scruples. I would take over Storheim's responsibilities in the summer. These I discovered were comprehensive, since as Peter had indicated earlier, although nominally Editor, having got the journal running, Naess devoted his wide-ranging energies to other projects. The initial flow of commissioned articles from the famous having come to a standstill, there were as few as thirty-three submissions that year. With at least twenty of these published there was little room for choice and all the more for improvement.

So began my training in the basic practicalities of philosophical publication. Under Chadwick's tutelage I became reasonably adept at language laundering and, in view of my new editing role, benefited not least from his extensive knowledge of the compositor's rules. I was both editor and copy-editor of this journal, following each article from submission through acceptance to correction, final preparation for the printer and correcting the proofs. So effective did I become in the latter role that the director who in my interview the previous summer had warned me that I would be shipped back to Newcastle if I failed to measure up, began to complain of the large number of printer's mistakes I was finding.

Combining the roles of editor and publisher's reader was of course indefensible. As a customer I could demand changes that as an employee of the Press I was in a position to refuse but was nevertheless inclined to accept on behalf of the product's academic reputation. A streak of perfectionism had entered into work with 'my' journal, and it led to printing costs that would have bankrupted it were it not for a subsidy (from the Research Council for Humanities and Science) calculated on the basis of the previous year's costs. This meant that charges for proofing went largely undetected. The directors of the Press were also sufficiently pleased with the rapid rise in subscriptions in the first year of my editorship to leave matters as they were.

Office life under Chadwick's wing gave my exile a peculiarly paradoxical character. Here I was, geographically and mentally, worlds away from an exacting academic ambience that had been putting pressure on me for five years, but still doing things academic and now more comfortably in the role of advisor. Furthermore, although definitely abroad, I was under the wing of an archetypal Englishman; Chadwick's determination not to go native merely emphasized his origins. Every step he took was a renewed territorial claim. Our shared office was a kind of club into which Norwegian colleagues entered as if by courtesy of Her Majesty. English being the territory's language,

Norwegian colleagues were always at some disadvantage. We gave audience to respected academics, many of whom at that time were taking their life-work doctorates just prior to retirement. Their dissertations, several in fine art and in sociology, were given the finishing touches needed to make them presentable to Anglophone editors and readers. At times it was hard to realize that we were, with the press an offshoot of the university's welfare association, employees of the Norwegian state.

It was only on reading an article in the *Observer* some years after his death in 1979 in England at seventy-two that we learnt about Chadwick's earlier past. I had received some hint previously. One day, in explaining a telephone call I overheard him receiving from abroad, he had hinted at some form of collaboration on a book having to do with the war. He mentioned a plane that he had organized for someone and also a failure of some kind on which he did not elaborate.

What the *Observer* article later revealed was that Trevor Chadwick, then a schoolmaster, had been deeply involved in the Kindertransport operation evacuating Jewish children from Europe just prior to the outbreak of World War II. The British Government had agreed to take in ten thousand mainly Jewish children from occupied territories in Austria, Czechoslovakia, and Poland for subsequent re-emigration when conditions allowed. Initially, Chadwick had been in Prague to take two children back to his school in Dorset. He took three but then returned to help others. A London stockbroker had broken off a skiing holiday in Switzerland to organize the exodus and, on his return to England to raise funds and arrange foster homes partly through newspaper advertising, an office was set up in Prague with Chadwick in charge. There he remained for four months and, together with a colleague working for the Czech secret service, was responsible for persuading anxious parents to part with their children while at the same time negotiating with Gestapo officials for special trains and arranging sea transport. Long queues outside the office caused trouble with the Gestapo, but Chadwick and Bill Barazetti, both described as daring and colourful characters, contrived at great risk to thwart any interference. Except among the children in question, and their parents for as long as they survived, the rescue operation received no public recognition. Nicholas Winton, the young stockbroker who started it and who, at ninety-one and in a wheelchair was recently present at a documentary about these efforts, later explained why he never even told his wife. The biggest transport was to take place on 1 September 1939, but that was the day Hitler invaded Poland and all borders were closed. Two-hundred-and-fifty families stood waiting at Liverpool Street Station in London for a train that never arrived. Not one of the children who had boarded it was ever heard of again.

While the picture of the hundreds of children eagerly waiting to board in Prague haunted Winton, Chadwick, who had been responsible in Prague for organizing that train, would have been haunted by the actual sight of them leaving. According to the recent account by his son in *The Rescue of the Prague Refugees 1938/39* [8] Chadwick's sorrow was that out of the thousands of refugees on his list he managed to save 'only' hundreds. One refugee, Gerda Mayer, the third that he had taken with him on that first flight, and who his mother had promised to support until she was eighteen, became a writer and later dedicated a book to 'the memory of Muriel Chadwick and her son Trevor Chadwick to whom I owe my preservation'. In a letter published on the Internet, clarifying that matter of an aeroplane, Gerda Mayer, under the heading 'The Youngest Kindertransport Refugee?' wrote:

> Sir — The late Trevor Chadwick who, together with Sir Nicholas Winton, rescued the children from Czechoslovakia, describes the first of his transports in Karen Gershon's *We Came As Children*. [9] 'I took my first air transport rather proudly, on a twenty-seater plane. They were all cheerfully sick, enticed by the little paper bags except a baby of one who slept peacefully in my lap the whole time.'
>
> Moreover, Trevor Chadwick's family personally rescued three of us, i.e. they became guarantors. Sadly, he died before the Kindertransports became public knowledge and he received none of the accolade now happily accorded to Sir Nicholas. I myself tried to have him recognised by Yad Vashem as a 'righteous Gentile' — one winces at the oddity of the phrase — but was unsuccessful.
>
> Does it matter? Yes, it does. It matters to his family, who are rightly proud of him. And it matters historically. He should not be overlooked.
>
> Gerda Mayer, London E4

I had no reason, then, to ask Chadwick who it was that had phoned him, but his few words suggest it was Gerda Mayer herself.

The truth of the Kindertransport only became public when (by then Sir) Nicholas Winton's wife discovered photographs and lists in her attic. The refugees themselves now adult, and not least their children, could now collect their stories. Chadwick's own subsequent life seems not to have been untroubled. He mentioned his sons but at the time seemed to have little or no contact with them. Soon after I arrived, he married Sigi, a twenty-seven-year-old German girl who sang with him in the choir of St. Edmund's, Oslo's Anglican Church. He was fifty-one. I visited them, sharing a bottle of Scotch with Trevor. It was the second occasion on which I became quite drunk in Norway, this time in midwinter. The first had been in the middle of the summer of 1957 on arriving at Hankø after that first North Sea crossing.

London, and Scotland too, became increasingly remote. Placed in a small world somehow lacking any clear coordinates with the one I formerly inhabited, it came sometimes as a shock to be reminded of it. While still in London, I had been asked by Bernard Williams if I could help an Indian student, Sunnit Deb with his Master's thesis. From Oslo I had written to Bernard on Storheim's behalf to solicit a review of a book on 'freedom of the will' by the Norwegian philosopher Harald Ofstad, then a professor in Stockholm. Nothing came of it, but in replying Bernard could tell me that Deb had passed 'after a protracted viva'. He said I should have some of the credit 'for having improved both his philosophy and his English'. That the thesis had come out 'in very respectable English indeed' was something Bernard doubted would have been the case without my 'efforts'. Any praise, particularly from Bernard, could make my day, indeed several days. But he also asked about my own thesis, saying he 'hoped to see me before long'. Here I was in no better a situation than the Indian prior to those efforts of mine. I had the hopeless feeling that it would be some time before Bernard saw or even heard from me again.

That first winter there was a more immediate and less wrought link with the London past. A letter postmarked Stockholm from Collin Bates, then pianist in the Bruce Turner Jump Band, announced the band's coming arrival in Oslo. This 'thirties-style small-swing-band from the Troubadour was to play at the Metropol. It was then a venue for many famous jazz musicians, among them the legendary New Orleans clarinettist Albert Nicholas, then resident in Paris. Looking like a successful doctor, he was conservatively suited with a neat instrument case. Nicholas played with a wonderful fluency that led me to pack my own clarinet well out of sight. I had just missed Sandy Brown and Al Fairweather at the same venue, and they had been preceded by Dexter Gordon, Ben Webster, Stan Getz and many another famous American musician, some of them resident at the time in Copenhagen. I had spoken with Collin though I didn't know him all that well but realized, or suspected, that our meeting had an ulterior motive. Before leaving, as if entrusted with the question, he asked me if I would be coming back. He mentioned Judith and I thought she might have asked him to enquire. Perhaps there was a personal interest too. I said I had no plans for a return. If it meant he should feel free to strike up a closer relationship with Judith, to me that seemed a good idea. Just recently I read that Collin died in 1991, a year after returning to his homeland Australia. There was nothing about his private life but he left a legacy in his recorded work with various groups, most of all in the Collin Bates Trio with its cult LP 'Brew' from the Troubadour label. I play it regularly on You-Tube.

The set-up in our shared accommodation at Ekely was cosy but confined. We knew each other's foibles and got along pretty well. Joan kept house on a portion of our pay while Peter and I worked at the press. It was a traditional pre-feminist arrangement, for which neither Peter nor I, nor any Norwegians I met for many years to come, had envisaged any alternative. To break the routine, we took the tram every Thursday evening to Theaterkaféen, then more of a regular brasserie than the over-priced tourist icon it later became. It was a meeting-place for the not-so-well-off who could drop in once in a while for a good meal with reasonably priced wine and mingle with writers, artists and journalists along with their usual hangers-on.

At home hidden tensions nevertheless came to the surface. For Peter, the future and that of any family he hoped to maintain had to be forged in a world not of literature but of budgets and accounts, for which he had no taste. As an academic press, our workplace, if a possible stepping-stone to my own career, offered little to the creative spirit that occupied Peter. For this he had to rely on wide contacts made in his spare time and with Joan as his card of entry to the world of Oslo's artists. But Joan's future in that role depended on recognition by those who were already established. One problem here, as I reflected later, was that her special talents depended on quick observation and a sense for human quirks and pathos, something possible only in her own culture. Removal from that had left her in an artistic void. Besides, among the already established artists were several interesting women more than happy to welcome on his own account a lively, appreciative and provocative observer like Peter Frøstrup. Indeed, in their company Peter was at his most engaging. Knowing their language in both senses, he was the focus of an attention in which Joan was not included.

I have often wondered what led Peter to ask me to join them in Norway. Was it to provide Joan with compatriotic support, or perhaps also himself with a bridge across the North Sea? Or did he have a cultural *ménage à trois* in mind that would give the household greater social clout among the artists and intellectuals? He once suggested — I must admit to by disbelief and near-horror — that I should stay on indefinitely in my proofreading and copy-editing job and devote myself to essay writing in my spare time. Yes, there are many instances of writers, even foreigners, finding fulfilment and even fame while keeping some penny-earning job on the side, T. S. Eliot, for instance. For myself, I could think of nothing more mind destroying than reading academic proofs, a killer of creative inspiration if ever there was one. As for essays, to me these seemed a literary indulgence in which art took precedence over truth. Perhaps in old age I might be able to dispense wisdom from afar if not from on high, but just then I wouldn't have known what to write about. In any case I could hardly compete with Norway's own often excellent and well-established essayists.

Most of all, I still intended to write that dissertation. My identity, or to put a better gloss on it, my personal integrity as I saw it, depended on it. My own reason for coming there at all, apart from a job, had been to settle my own thoughts and try to get them down on paper. During that first winter, every weekday after dining in the nearby 'Krølle Kro', a downmarket restaurant frequented by artists, students, single ladies, and with a reasonably priced menu, I spent the evenings on the editorial department's solitary electric typewriter producing what I hoped would be a Williams-acceptable draft of a thesis. Peter was aware that, on arrival, I hadn't written a word of my dissertation, but no doubt he thought this was a good thing, since I could then get down to doing something un-academic and creative instead. He was probably right, but for me at the time that thought was impossible. I told him I appreciated the point but hadn't really planned to spend the rest of my life in this way. Treasuring my own delusions of grandeur for a while was necessary just to keep me warm. Peter seemed to accept that. After all, his own gleanings from academe must have given him some sympathy for my reluctance to live for a gold watch in the proofreading business.

One day Peter asked me whether I didn't think that, with increasing age, we became more cynical about other people's stupidities, just leaving them to it rather than engaging ourselves in any effort to reform. He thought it was not so much tolerance as indifference. I tended to agree but being of a more conciliatory disposition, I had never been so directly concerned with or dependent on denigrating others, something which in Peter's eyes was merely further evidence of the 'prostitute' he once playfully claimed to find in me for not trying to set things and others to rights. To me this principle suggested something even more sinister: genuine indifference to others in the interests of one's own projects. I sensed that in retreating into his own new-found indifference and looking for my support, Peter was acknowledging that he had been forced by his return to abandon his dream and with it his principles.

Cracks in Peter and Joan's relationship once hidden were now visible parts of it. It occurred to me, as time went on, that the real reason I had been invited over had been to help paper them over. But in my involvement I began to develop some cracks too. In a matter of weeks and months I was invited along to more parties than had been my lot for a decade or more. To Peter and Joan's satisfaction, and with their earnest encouragement, I became attached to Eli Silseth, a talented graphic artist with whom I 'danced all night' at the Young Artists' Association's annual celebrations. The liaison was brief. I was, for my own reasons, in no mood to strike up dissolvable relationships and also unwilling to reveal to Peter and Joan a story that, for reasons of my own, I had kept from my own family. In the end I let the graphic artist down, disappointed my hosts, and incurred the wrath of the graphic artist's closest friend and sculptress colleague.

I further disappointed my hosts by establishing a closer friendship with the aforesaid Japanese American girl who had congratulated me on the view from my desk on that first day at the Press. Having arrived in Norway two years earlier on board the SS *Stavanger* with a degree in business management from Berkeley, she had then worked for a year in Sweden assisting the founder-director of an American telecommunications firm. Back in Oslo, after a brief stint with the Norway America Foundation, she had joined the University Press.

Joanne, too, had been captivated by Peter's engagingly challenging presence and was sufficiently soft on him to assume some mutuality. Unknown to me at the time, before I arrived Joanne had been invited home without Peter informing her that he had a wife. Typically, and perhaps it is something Eastern, she kept her disappointment as well as resentment at Peter's lack of openness to herself, redefining her role as friend. Peter had mentioned her in correspondence and I found she was a constant guest though not a member of the artistic circle. As the others spoke interestingly in the sitting room, Joanne stood silently in the tiny kitchen washing the dishes. If she came alone, it could be with a guitar and the conversation would become normal. That the silent, equable and slightly whimsical guardian of their kitchen should capture the attentions of the living-in philosopher was not what they had planned. Later the rift was to widen enough to cause a break between myself and Peter and Joan.

Fantasies of peaceful refuge sprang up as in the past. A small cabin on a beach with a huge double-glazed window facing the sea, a window like the one in the offices of the new university buildings to which I had now transferred — that was how I now imagined my alternative existence. I even thought of investigating where I could get hold of such windows. But then came the possibility of real escape. A letter from Willie Stewart, my generous teacher in Edinburgh, now Professor at the University of New Brunswick, was in the throes of establishing a philosophy department there. He offered me a lectureship at $4,500 a year and said, as if it were an added attraction, that he had already hired a former student colleague, Neil McGill, as Assistant Professor. Was it because I wasn't offered a similar position that I was disinclined to accept? Or because New Brunswick seemed no place to seek advancement or look for further opportunities? In the worst case it could be a career *cul-de-sac*. In spite of the respect in which I held Willie Stewart and all that I owed him, I felt I should decline. For advice, however, I wrote to Ted Honderich but also to Fiona, telling her of my nocturnal typing activities and hibernal hardships.

Now one of Edinburgh's Telephone Samaritans, she felt qualified to offer some. Her first proposal was tentatively in favour.

> I don't know where New Brunswick is, it sounds like somewhere in the Pied Piper, but if it's lots of lolly *and* being called 'Professor' in New Brunswickian accents the while imposing one's opinion forcibly over the opinions of lots of shuddering students I wouldn't call it depressingsville, not for a bit surely?

Slipping more authoritatively into her new role, Fiona raised a more basic question:

> But seriously what do you have to stay in Norway for, or is it just easier? I mean if you don't love it better than anywhere, couldn't you try India or somewhere where they might want philosophy taught in English and would probably give you an electric typewriter, twelve rupees an hour, *and* a mosquito net into the bargain? I can't help feeling (it's the Samaritan — Telephone version — and the would-be social worker in me breaking out) that psychologically Scandinavia mightn't be as good for you as somewhere else, you lean so strongly towards the little-white-room-with-the-wind-howling-through-it and the smell of snow and introverted, abstracted semi-depressiveness that I think you should move to Italy or somewhere temperamentally different for a year or two. Or you *will* end up as an icicle and not on the way to the bus stop either, but in the head.

She was right, neither philosophy nor the frozen North would do me much good. More convivial surroundings would almost certainly have made for a healthier and less egocentric life. But I was, as before, stuck with what I had done so far and so late. Yet another new beginning would only open the door to terminal despair. So, I said to myself, hang on! Ted Honderich's succinct advice was to the same effect: 'By all means take the job if you want sled dogs to make up the front row.'

Another and more permanent connection with the past helped. My brother, now an experienced airline pilot as well as Olympic sailor, took time off to sail the schooner once more over the North Sea. It was late March, absurdly early in the season for such an exploit and although they were a crew of eight, I was worried stiff not least because my younger sister was also on board, taking a week off from tutoring in London.

We were in the dark about their plans and progress, and it was only after they reached Norway that I received news of this from my equally anxious mother. Things had looked bad at the start; the engine had broken down in the Caledonian Canal and the weather forecasts heralded gales and snow. A fishing boat heading for Inverness towed them through, the canal, although in the interests of their safety and fearing he would be aiding and abetting in this motley crew's shipwreck, the skipper had at first refused. The North Sea was no place for amateurs at any time of year, least of all in March. But they persuaded him and, when on their reaching Inverness the weather seemed to improve, Ian chose to start the crossing from there instead of further south. Calculating their progress with no idea of their sailing plan, I followed the weather reports for Forties, Fisher and Skagerrak. Strong winds were forecast for Fisher, but there were no reports of rescue calls on the radio and eventually — it seemed a long time — they phoned to announce their arrival at Kristiansand. They figured in the local newspaper next day sunning themselves in temperatures that kept seasoned Norwegians well wrapped. I calculated the time needed to reach the Faerder Lighthouse at the foot of Oslo Fjord, fifty miles to our south, and Chadwick, now as anxious as myself, was able to ring the keeper who graciously climbed the many steps to have a look from the top. He could report a green schooner with red sails heading north. They arrived. We celebrated. The crew, tired, elated but pressed for time, after showers and food flew back to their jobs. The two girls told me they had kept below during the whole crossing making food while the others kept watch three at a time.

Stationing the schooner in Oslo was a last gasp attempt to enjoy the amenity of this fine vessel. In the long term it was also in every way a hopeless plan and even irrational in the short term. My father had bought *Charm III* in 1955 for a song thanks to a damaging survey; but upkeep of such a large vessel in need of constant repair was expensive, much more than we could hope to manage over any longer period without morphing overnight into well-paid executives or senior airline pilots. My brother was on the way but also planning to manufacture yachts of his own design, something that would absorb any surplus income from his flying career. There was also a time factor. Maintenance work consumed time off in the early months of the year and shortened the period we had for enjoying its fruits. The expedient of covering expenses with charters would still further diminish the period of enjoyment as well as taking time to arrange and administer. Knowing this in advance, I had hastened that first winter to type a longish draft of what I hoped would become a dissertation. In retrospect it was over-ambitious and very immature.

Meanwhile, the approaching summer forced my attention on things maritime. Having joined the Oslo Sailing Club and with the generous help of a fellow member and some old iron procured by Peter's half-brother Kjell, I had a mooring placed just opposite the Maritime Museum on Bygdøy, a fashionable peninsular housing several tourist attractions including Nansen's *Fram* and Thor Heyerdahl's *Kon Tiki* raft. That summer I lived aboard, enjoying the gentle rocking as ferries passed and taking the ferry to the Town Hall in the morning. During the long Whitsun week-end a crew consisting of the Frøstrups and myself, the let-down graphic artist and also her irate sculptress friend went on a cruise down the fjord. Anchoring in a small coastal town famed for its artists, we received a party of these on board. A man who rowed out to us claimed to be the mayor and the atmosphere became joyous bordering on the Bacchic. The once irate sculptress expressed her own glee by jumping overboard fully clothed. I began to see the underlying volcanic nature of the normally placid, taciturn, self-contained and only outwardly excessively rational Norwegian character.

At work Peter was still in good spirits even if most often in the role of provocateur and Socratic gadfly, teasing opinions from us, getting us to see how things might have been done better, who should be praised, who blamed. His persistent questioning earned him from Chadwick the label 'badger'. To us, Peter's infectious enthusiasm, as long as it lasted, was not typically Norwegian (his origins were in fact Danish), and it was not hard to see why the local artists took to him.

Whether as a relic of his service as a military policeman in *Tysklandsbrigaden*, Norway's contribution to the Allied Occupation after the Second World War or a souvenir from the war, Peter had a Mauser pistol locked away at home. Here things were more subdued but not immune to drama. Parties sometimes left him in a bad mood, for which one can think of several good or bad reasons. Back from one of these, he took out the Mauser and began waving it in front of Joan and me. We had given him no cause for jealousy, but maybe she and I had begun to be paired in his mind as a couple of hobnobbing cultural foreigners.

Peter switched jobs, becoming managing editor of a twice-monthly newspaper (*Frisprog*) originally dedicated to opposing the government's policy of combining the two main Norwegian languages (it eventually succeeded in getting the government to abandon the policy), but in effect an independent forum for the discussion of literary and other art forms. The paper was edited by two well-situated ladies: Margrethe Aamot Øverland, wife of Norway's poet laureate, and Sofie Helene Wigert the sister of shipowner Fred. Olsen, and herself a wealthy shipowner. She quickly became an object of Peter's ire. Not just scorn of the high-placed and wealthy in general, there was also his frustration at having to meet her steely will. Many years later I met Mrs Wigert at a party and asked her if she remembered Peter Frøstrup. Her eyes darkened, 'That man', she snapped, 'he didn't come back in time from his summer vacation, yes, something about sailing.'

It had been our last summer with the boat. The previous summer, due partly to problems with the propeller shaft, we had contented ourselves with a short cruise down the Swedish coast. In August, the problem provisionally solved, a charter crew from England took over intending to sail in the Baltic. For weather reasons and their time running out, they had to leave *Charm III* at Varberg, a small port and resort on the lower Swedish west coast. She lay there for over two weeks before I could reach her by train. Spending some days waiting for fierce winds to subside, I enjoyed the company of three other compatriots similarly weatherbound on their chartered yacht *Sea Falcon*. They were Julian Holmes and Mike Beckingsale, officers from the British occupation forces based in Kiel, and Kathie Hibberd, the latter's girl friend from London. It was refreshing to be in English-speaking company. *Hallands Nyheter*, the local newspaper, carried an illustrated piece on us in its Wednesday 29 August number, saying the weather forecast made it likely we would be there even longer. A jovial evening was spent on board a Danish fishing boat whose welcoming crew were tempering their impatience with freshly boiled shrimps, akvavit, and beer. When, next morning, the weather seemed to be relenting, and running short of time myself, I summoned my crew from Oslo in the shape of Joan, though not Peter who was at work, Per and Valerie Ung, Per's father, a retired building entrepreneur, and Tony and Anne-Lo Richardson, he a veteran of a Pacific crossing and she, besides mother of their two children, a former telegraphist on a Norwegian freighter.

With this not entirely unseasoned crew we set off in the gathering darkness in a headwind that the weather report assured us would lighten during the night, but it didn't. Except for Per and myself he crew were confined to their bunks until late next morning by which time we had tacked in headwinds to within sight of the south end of Oslo Fjord. Per and I kept ourselves going on a pot of pork and beans warmed up by the cooks before they succumbed. I remember going below to see how the others were faring. Joan clung to me for a while and said she needed warmth. On reflection, I wonder if she may have had a larger time scale in mind and a more embracing warmth. I recall how, on first arriving in Oslo, having turned off the bathroom switch, as one did in Scotland when leaving that amenity, Joan had sharply rebuked me. Blessed with a heated floor, in a cold world this particular Norwegian amenity was for Joan a sanctuary.

Sailing in the Kattegat at night is not easy. There is traffic with its exact distance and direction hard to make out in rough conditions. We flashed a torch on our red sails to make our own proximity known. Nor was the compass yet entirely reliable. But after a while we could make out the blinking light of Svenner, outside Larvik. For those on and below deck it was in different ways a memorable night. The fifty miles up the Oslofjord allowed everyone to recover and the voyage became a minor legend among those who took part.

The following years meant further postponement of my personal project. But what kept me busy taught me more about how to go about my topic. Still partially employed by the Press, I had become Arne Naess's part-time assistant. He was a generous boss and in spite of my indifferent Norwegian he let me translate a book he had written on Gandhi and then two textbooks, all of which I did in his time, earning a modest translator's fee on top of the income from my job.

Communication and Argument was my translation of a textbook that all Norwegian students then read in an examination, *Examen Philosophicum*, an inheritance from Copenhagen in the days when Norway was a Danish province. The exam was taken in the first year at university and covered psychology, the history of philosophy, scientific methodology, and argumentation. My translation came out in 1965 and in the 24 November 1966 issue of the *TLS* I was happy to read a notice saying that the work's 'main purpose is well defined: to teach people in a democratic society to think clearly, coherently, and, above all, responsibly', and that '[p]robably no philosopher or sociologist now living could peruse this simple manual without learning something from it'. Already translated into Swedish, I found this to be a tidier version than the Norwegian, which over the years had suffered piecemeal tampering at the hands of Naess's many assistants, and I used it instead as the basis of the translation. What appears in the recently published *Selected Works of Arne Naess* as the 'Authors Foreword to the First Edition' was in fact an added introduction of my own. I also tackled Naess's *Moderne Filosofer*, a supplement to his three-volume *Filosofiens historie*, and which offered detailed introductions to Rudolf Carnap, Ludwig Wittgenstein, Martin Heidegger and Jean-Paul Sartre, four philosophers with widely diverging views. I edited the original, supplementing it in part.

A happy coincidence was the involvement of one of the four Vassar students I had met in Edinburgh in the editing and marketing of this book by Chicago University Press as *Four Modern Philosophers*. In the course of preparing the text with Margot Schutt's help and advice, I had to acquire both Heidegger's and Sartre's permission to quote extensive passages from their works. With a philosophically indefensible piety of which I am not ashamed, I treasure their brief letters of acknowledgement. I helped Naess with several articles and shared some lecturing with him on the Pyrrhonian Sceptics. My first ever lectures, still in English and on epistemology, focused on Ayer's *The Problem of Knowledge*.

In applying myself to the journal's future with zeal, the job became my further education in philosophy. I wrote to Ryle, then Editor of *Mind*, seeking an exchange of advertisements and journals. He agreed, telling me in typically schoolmasterly tones not to bury copies of *Mind* 'in a locker'. I wrote long and detailed letters in response to submitted manuscripts, secure in the knowledge that their authors had no inkling that I had been in their august branch for little more than five years. There were at that time still fewer that fifty or so submissions annually and it would take a year or two before the average rose to well over a hundred. Refusals and acceptances could receive equal treatment. Reading these essays and finding out what might improve them, whether or not sufficiently for acceptance, I learnt a great deal and engaged in several lengthy correspondences, establishing contact with a far wider circle of philosophers than would have been possible had I stayed in the UK. Publishers began sending review copies, far more than we could handle, and a large library of current literature began to accumulate both in my office and at home. The office itself, a tiny affair with a large window covering the wall at one end and with bookshelves on either side, was shared with Hans Skjervheim, an enthusiastic as well as chain-smoking opponent of Naess's 'positivism', which at that time was held to dominate both psychology and social science, particularly the latter as locally conducted in the recently established Institute for Social Science. This institute, heavily influenced by several visiting Americans and the expatriate Norwegian political scientist and sociologist Stein Rokkan, previously he too one of Arne Naess's assistants, was part of a transatlantic network. *Inquiry* (its original subtitle 'An Interdisciplinary Journal of Philosophy and the Social Sciences') had been established with its products in mind. The prestigious advisory board included three expatriate Norwegians and several famous pre- and post-war figures including Carnap and my nemesis Gilbert Ryle. The sociologist Robert K. Merton and Charles W. Morris, a semioticist, had also been co-opted as well as the Swiss developmental psychologist Jean Piaget. There was also Ernest Gellner, once an assistant to John Macmurray in Edinburgh and now a professor of philosophy and scientific method at the London School of Economics but essentially a social anthropologist.

As far as I could tell, their advice had seldom been sought and, except in areas where my ignorance was significant, I chose to be my own referee. Today this would be academically 'incorrect' if not scandalous, but I felt the circumstances justified a central hand and Naess didn't mind. The journal's interdisciplinary and open-ended approach was something to which peer-reviewing, to say nothing of lordly advice from the already established, was in any case antithetic, each in my view contributing to conformity and stifling any renewal. I began what is known as 'active' academic journalism, commissioning special numbers and searching widely for suitable contributors.

An early special number was on 'Marxism and Alienation' and among its contributors was another colleague with whom I was to share that office, Lars

Roar Langslet, then while doing military service learning Russian in the King's Guard. A leading light among the young conservatives, but with wide interests, he was in uniform when I met him in a small café to go over the proofs. Later he would be Minister of Education and Science, but being Catholic and the State Church Lutheran, the cabinet position's responsibilities had to be revised from that of 'Education and Church Affairs'. Where Skjervheim had emphasized his presence by persistent coughing due to chain-smoking, in Langslet's case it was constant telephoning to his political contacts. But I was happy to have their company. Skjervheim, with whom I had many an interesting and spirited exchange, thought I understood the local philosophers better than they understood themselves. For his part, Langslet once fortified my ego by saying I should have been awarded a medal for what I did with *Inquiry*.

Apart from gaining valuable insight into the nuts and bolts of philosophy by editing copy and reading proof before working in the afternoon for Naess, I could use scholarly contacts from abroad. When I felt that a short paper bringing attention to seemingly psychologistic tendencies in Wittgenstein's *Tractatus* called for comment, I drafted a reply suggesting that in a certain sense this should be expected since logic in use is the mind at work. This was one aspect of the 'Logical Idealism' I had sketched in so amateurish a fashion in the abortive draft for Bernard Williams. I sent my reply to David Shwayder in Berkeley, a noted commentator of *Tractatus*'s 'Picture Theory'. His unpublished dissertation on the *Tractatus* had become an object of scholarly pilgrimage to the Bodleian Library. Shwayder wrote appreciatively of my comments, and my first publication, a very slight and disgracefully dense affair, appeared in the 1964 volume of *Inquiry*. Naess was on a climbing expedition in the Himalayas and not consulted. I wonder if any other editor would have accepted it. I may have abused my editorial freedom but consoled myself with the thought that such a brief reply to a small discussion piece was but a minor sin.

The journal's broad approach gave room to topics that had been programmatically dropped in the circles I tried to become part of in London. I came to realize, however, that form and style were paramount considerations and that nothing off the beaten track could be introduced or re-introduced unless it satisfied the standards of clarity brought to its pursuit by the philosophers I had come to know in London. It was their great virtue to introduce such requirements into a profession that so easily provides opportunities for vagueness and obscurity masquerading as depth. Published philosophical thinking, I thought, must be lean, with every vestige of what my colleague Jon Elster has called inner obesity (*indre fedme*) burned off in the process of coming to clarity.

Domestically, as mentioned earlier, the three of us moved into a larger flat, the major part of its redecoration undertaken by Joanne and myself. Joan was at the time having to cope with the coming birth of their first child. Peter was busy in yet another job, this time at the press bureau, selecting news flashes and translating them into Norwegian. Since he found dealing with money tedious, it was Joanne who attended to the financial details of the purchase and redecoration. Peter had other aversions. He was extremely sensitive to smells and could throw up when he had to clean drains and sinks. But I remember helping him lay the linoleum on the floor of the tiny triangular room that was to be the baby's bedroom. 'Here I am', he said with despondent humour, 'laying the floor on which some pimply youth will one day take my daughter's virtue.'

Touching was the way he arranged his desk in a corner of the best room with a view through a gap made by the street and with the famous ski-jump just visible. The floor was painted regulation Frøstrupian green, the desk ready with pens, paper and pad. But work and his demons always got in their way. Another of Peter's aversions was his mother. Although only a short distance away, he never paid her a visit. An American receptionist at the publisher told me of her shock when one day Peter, though possibly just to shock her, said he hated his mother. I, on the other hand, the 'prostitute' that I was, could engage his mother in friendly conversation when once in a while we met at our shared post office. That, like all who knew him before he left for Edinburgh, she referred to him as 'Truls' rather than 'Peter' is a tell-tale fact. Truls had left for Scotland but it was Peter who returned, or so he thought. Even today, if I mention him here in Norway to an ageing school-comrade or a retired journalist, I have to bear in mind which of the two Frøstrups they knew.

With the arrival of their first-born imminent, Peter and Joan needed more room. Joanne, though no longer Peter's colleague, was still mine and had become part of my own fledgling circle. We were both invited by Arne Naess to his mountain cabin for a typically Naessian weekend in the bleak but spectacular heights of Hallingskarvet, mid-way to Bergen. It meant a long climb of several hours from the railway station in the fresh snow guided by Naess, who carried a cast-iron stove on his back to aid our comfort in the chilly heights. Joanne and I spent an hour one morning preparing a slalom course for Arne above the hut. He used it just once. I was forbidden to gather snow for water since melting it would squander calories in the cabin. I had to find my way instead to a brook running under the ice and snow some way off. I found the brook by falling into it, my drying off consuming at least as many calories as were saved. Any food left in the pan from one meal was the basis of the next, usually the same. But we enjoyed this unusual stay and appreciated our participation in its rigorous regime. I noted Naess's large library up there in the mountains. It was here he had written his *Filosofiens historie* and several textbooks known to at least one generation of Norwegian students. Memorable too was the breakneck journey home in Naess's rattling East German Trabant.

That Joanne and I became a pair in the eyes of others strengthened the sense we had of being that ourselves. Both of us felt we had helped the Frøstrups enough by installing them in their new home. Although keeping my room for the time being, I began spending longer periods with Joanne in severely cramped accommodation in her landlady's otherwise capacious ground-floor apartment in an old villa not far from the city centre. She, Fie (Anna-Sofie), was also a proof-reader, working for a weekly magazine that published the Norwegian edition of Donald Duck. Reading these I found was an entertaining way of adding colloquial Norwegian to what up to then had been academic jargon learnt mainly through translating Naess's textbooks.

It was in the city centre one day that I ran into Peter, who could proudly announce the birth of their daughter. They had decided to call her Mariella, though for some time, when very small, she was familiarly referred to as 'Wong'.

As for Scotland, I had kept in desultory touch with Fiona. She in turn kept an eye on her friend Norma on my behalf and reported our son Tim's progress. But Norma had been doing the same. By plying me constantly with photos I assumed she was still envisaging a future together. Living as I was in a limbo of uncertainty about almost everything, I had so far refrained from saying otherwise, letting my departure for Norway speak louder than words. When I told Fiona about my friend Joanne, her response was characteristic. Recalling that in my plunge into the dead world of thought-crunching I had started giving people 'cold, abstract, calculating looks, as through a microscope' as if one was a 'miserable streptococcus, and annihilating any feeble little social-type chat one might make with a bit of crushing Logic & Metaphysics or chilling Moral Philosophy — or something similar', she said it sounded now as if I had 'one foot back in the human race'. 'Welcome back', she wrote, 'long time no see'.

Although I told Fiona that nothing had been said, let alone decided, as to how our relationship should develop or end, she felt that the fact that there was anyone at all in the picture was something she must communicate if only to put an end to Norma's dreams. It seems she also informed her of my mother's impending visit to Oslo. Norma's response was to say she would take the boat to Oslo and bring Tim with her to confront my mother. I told her my mother knew nothing about either of them and that it would be a hardship for her as well as me. She stayed at home.

Why my mother should visit at just this time was at first unclear to me. The house and farm in Melrose had been sold and my elder sister and husband had found a new and economically sounder replacement near Banchory in Aberdeenshire. Maybe my mother's move to London made it easier to visit us? She had bought a house in Pembroke Square, not far from Kensington High Street and previously owned by Arnold Toynbee, and before him by the novelist Neville Shute (whose real surname coincidentally was 'Norway'). Properly established there, she could travel without complication.

But there was something else. On returning from the University one afternoon while still staying part time with Peter and Joan, I found the post still lying on the floor inside the main door. On picking it up, I caught sight of my younger sister's handwriting and opened the envelope assuming it was for me. On reading 'Dear Joan' I was about to replace the letter when Joanne's name caught my eye. Curious as well as taken aback, I let my eye fall on a sentence about my 'poor mother' having to bear the thought of our alliance. I may have missed the context in returning the letter hurriedly to its envelope, but what I'd seen was enough to activate anger as well as sympathy on Joanne's behalf for being considered in any way an unsuitable companion. There was also guilt for not having made things clearer both to Joanne and myself about what our closer companionship meant for the future. I never mentioned the letter to Joanne, nor of course to Joan. But the moment was one in which, from a mixture of motives steered by sympathy and fondness, I suggested to Joanne that we live together with a view to marriage.

My memory is unclear on this point, but I may have suggested to my mother that she pay a visit with the intention of introducing her to that idea when she arrived. My motives were so intertwined that it is hard to say what action subsequent events represent. On hearing that I was unlikely to return and there was another woman 'over there', Norma was, as Fiona told me, constantly in tears. So was it to put Norma out of her misery that I attached myself to Joanne? Or was standing up for Joanne a way of escaping my own misery on Norma's account? I like to think that I stood up for Joanne to vindicate her in the face of accusations of unsuitability. But when it comes down to it, would a life in Norway be best for both of us? More to the point, did she think so? What if it was just the loneliness of two immigrants? In the event, my mother arrived but met Joanne only briefly. After a few days in which I arranged a meeting with the Rudolf Steiner School and she witnessed the National Day celebrations, she succumbed to influenza and was confined to her hotel. On returning to London she wrote me a short letter referring to 'the Joanne situation', something we had not discussed. She said that in the time since she had been with us this would have 'diminished or grown'. I wondered at that, the interval having been quite short.

Something in the letter led me to guess that she had taken counsel for advice on the prospects for a union such as ours with her anthroposophical friend

Evelyn Derry. She knew me fairly well from my first year in London. Did I know enough about the Japanese character? The American part would be due to environment and education. 'Undiluted Japanese is so totally different that contact with it could be stimulating or disastrous.' The remark can seem ironic today as I write, her grandson by her second son having been married with three daughters to a native Japanese for many years. Anthroposophy verges dangerously on the treacherous ground of racial distinction, however, and my mother would be impressed by such fears. She hoped Joanne would for her own sake go home and 'hear other points of view'. Wisely enough, she concluded that Oslo would be 'too small a place for you to escape one another even if you wanted to'. In predicting the dangers of isolation in the case of failure my mother was showing good practical sense. Two misfits from diverse backgrounds in a foreign land could end up doubly out of place if they decided they had to part. She then asked me to look at this situation 'objectively', and then in a phrase that greatly disturbed me, said that she could wish that some of my 'contemporaries showed the least sign of encouragement'.

What could that mean? Was it simply that no one had actually spoken up in Joanne's favour? Or had my contemporaries been speaking discouragingly behind my back? I thought immediately of the letter referring to my 'poor' mother's anxieties. What had they been saying?

I speculated. Both Joan and my sister had spent some days the previous summer together on the schooner. Perhaps, on that occasion, some impressions had been received or views exchanged between the two. Joanne had been on board because, with Peter fully occupied in his new domesticity on top of his job, it was Joanne who in the spring and well into the summer had spent evenings with me scraping, painting and varnishing the hull and deck-work. *Charm III* had been laid up on an island to which we took a ferry every weekday after early dinner. Although Peter occasionally helped and in early June my brother Ian flew over with parts for the drive shaft, it was Joanne who provided most support. Another time, one early afternoon in the autumn of our first sailing season, a fierce southerly gale caused *Charm III* to drag her moorings. A telephone call said she was only a few yards from the steep shore outside the Maritime Museum. Joanne and I hurried there in a taxi and found the stern so close to the bank that we were able to jump on board. The police patrol boat had been alerted and arrived, but to attach a towline we needed the help of two young men in a nearby dinghy with its outboard. Eventually we were towed to a safe berth in the lee of a small island. That evening Joanne and I went and visited the young men to thank them with some bottles of wine.

It was natural, given Joanne's close association with the boat, that the following summer when we set sail for the Swedish coast that she be invited along. Peter and I had to leave *Charm III* at Marstrand, he returning to his desk at *Frisprog* and I repairing to London to search for my dissertation. Joanne and Joan were left together on board with the small 'Wong'. To join them Jane flew in from London together with her friend Margaret, so that it was these four ladies who kept harbour-watch for perhaps a week before Peter could join them. Joanne would be exceptionally reserved under such circumstances, thinking Joan hostile to any closer association between her and Jane's brother. She would in any case be careful in Jane's company not to seem to presume any such thing. I have a photograph of Joanne sitting with her legs over the side of the boat reading. Her silence would be natural, isolation the wrong interpretation.

It also occurred to me later that Joan was more alone in Norway than Joanne, who made friends easily and was already socializing with three adventurous SAS 'air hostesses' outside our circle. There were also close contacts through working for the Norway-America Foundation and older connections, one of them a concerned common colleague, Mrs Evensen, not in her circle, but who came up to me at a party and murmured in my ear that I should look after Joanne. Besides, both she and her other friends would have felt out of place in the company of Peter and Joan's artistic and semi-intellectual circle. Of Joanne's own circle, Peter and Joan knew nothing.

Whether or not the undiluted Japanese character differed critically from the European, and to whatever extent we were *bona fide* representatives of our separate cultures, Joanne and I got along nicely outside the special constraints of marriage. These, after all, can be too much for anyone whatever their ethnic origin. Joanne was my one local confidant regarding Norma and Tim, though I refrained from telling her that Norma was plying me with letters and photographs. Nor when that time came did I mention her threat to confront my mother.

Later, when we were married, Joanne related that Joan had said to her — though in what spirit I have no way of telling — that any marriage she contemplated with me would last no more than six years — or was it months? It could have been a bit of friendly advice drawn from her own experience; as Peter's friend I might even be tarred with whatever brush had made Peter a difficult partner. She also knew something of my chequered past. But saying this to Joanne was disastrous on all counts, By putting her constantly in mind of its possible truth it became a self-fulfilling prophecy. Worst of all was the possibly shaming interpretation that I was too good for her — not what they had had in mind.

Although Joanne never lost her liking for Peter, her respect for him dwindled as long as he did nothing to repair the breach. Of Joan she would seldom speak.

Our marriage would be spiked and, should it fail, Joan would be partly to blame. I blame myself for not trying to convince Joanne that Joan's interference might just possibly have been a piece of friendly if clumsy advice.

I flew to London. I had sent a draft of the dissertation to Bernard Williams, but as the months passed with no reply began to wonder what had happened to it. I wrote to Katherine Backhouse, the new department secretary, who reassured me that my thesis was not at the bottom of the North Sea but in the hands of Mr Williams: 'He thought you were in no hurry to get it back: he understood that you would discuss it "when you came to England". She asked if I would be returning and what I wanted Bernard to do with it.

I was rather hoping he hadn't bothered when I visited him this late summer of 1963 to discuss it with him. Bernard and Shirley Williams were then living in a large house in Essex Place near Kensington High Street, or perhaps it was Phillimore Place. When I got there Shirley was nursing their daughter Rebecca. Bernard fished the bundle out of a drawer in his desk and we took it with us to a small café in Phillimore Gardens. I recall no comments that might have indicated what he thought of it, so the discussion must have been very general. Twenty years later in California, talking about the time when he had been my official supervisor, Bernard remarked that I seemed to have difficulty finding a way to do philosophy, a 'methodology' as he put it. It was quite true. Maybe the crash course I had taken in Edinburgh had shown me too many different ways, while in London I lacked the practice and experience needed to tackle philosophical questions in a new and quite different way.

Bernard himself was not exactly a model to follow in this respect. There was something casuistic and piece-meal in his needle-sharp but omnivorous mind, with puzzle (and fault-) finding its central drift. Since I had been unable under his tutelage to acquire any clear notion of how to handle the topic of imagination philosophically, I now decided to shelve that draft and postpone the project until I became clearer about how to proceed. The considerable piles of notes I had accumulated on the subject had begun to gather dust and were to stay there as a perpetual reminder of a task to be undertaken some day in vindication of my existence. My very presence in Norway, my whole life, indeed who and what I was, had all been defined by the goal of fulfilling this project, as also, further back, by that fateful decision six year earlier to return to academe.

Things went quickly after my mother's visit in May that following year. *Charm III*, now a financial burden we could no longer bear, was put up for sale. After failing to interest a Greek ship-owner, she was sold to an Englishman who came over in June with his crew to sail her to Plymouth, his home and my birthplace. Noting some trepidation on their part, I persuaded them to take on Gunnar, a seasoned sailor we'd met at the Theaterkaffé and who knew the ropes. I joined them down the Norwegian coast, and at Arendal waved farewell to a seagoing transport that for nine years had played a large part in our lives, bringing and keeping many people together.

Her last trick had been to bring my sister Jane into contact with her future husband. On the Swedish coast that previous summer, a yacht crewed by several German medical students returning to Kiel from Iceland happened to moor alongside *Charm III* at Marstrand. Intrigued by a crew of four young women, one with a guitar and another with a baby whose diapers flapped where usually one saw flags, they made their introductions. One was Jens Wiebel. Two years later he and Jane ran into each other at London's Aldwych Theatre at a performance of 'Six Characters in Search of an Author'. They were married in London in April 1966 and Jane moved to Hamburg.

Seeing *Charm III* head out of the Skagerrak into the North Sea brought no sorrow. Indeed, the sense of freedom at being spared a burden of responsibility that hung over all else, and not least my personal mission, was euphoric. So elated was I that in my euphoria I engaged two elderly ladies in a feverish conversation on the train all the way to Oslo. As for *Charm III*, although I guessed that this was my own last glimpse of her, more than half a century later my brother Ian, when cruising the Caribbean in his own schooner, moored next to a gleaming white apparently new vessel whose owner invited him onboard. An immediate sense of *déjà vu* was confirmed on hearing that this was *Charm III* then virtually rebuilt and to this day a regular winner of the Classic Regatta at Antigua.

Among things waiting for us in Oslo was a job not unlike that of restoring a wooden boat for the sea. We had bought a run-down house in a small village halfway down the Oslo fjord, in those days a good hour's drive from the city. It was a distance in which awkward questions could wait and into which the Frøstrups could meanwhile effortlessly de-materialize. But although our circles were no longer concentric, since nothing had been said there was still a sense of being within orbital hailing distance. How Peter and Joan were reading the situation we had no idea. When my mother heard of the house we had bought and our plans to marry later that year, she gave Joanne her full support and had her own engagement ring adapted to suit her future daughter-in-law's hand.

Chapter Ten: Ghosting

Ghosting: making headway when there is no apparent wind; also a form of identity theft.

One weekend on the local train back from Asker, a growing satellite town to the West of Oslo where the prices proved too high, we saw a newspaper advertisement for the sale of a house in a small village half-way down the East side of Oslo Fjord. It was within our price range. The following Sunday the lawyer who was the seller's property agent drove us there. The house was up a narrow lane, red-painted and two-storeyed with an outside stair to the upper level. It nestled on a slope between two other houses, a large ugly yellow one on the right with a garden, and the other smaller and white-painted immediately to the left. The month was July and the small property was surrounded invitingly, though in the long term deceptively, by seasonally protective greenery.

From inside, over a neighbour's low roof, the upper floor offered a panoramic view of the fjord. At that point it was only two kilometres across, with the heights of Hurumlandet rising opposite to the west. We decided there and then to buy it, in our impatience all too readily accepting the seller's price, excessive according to our new neighbours, who comfortably took our side. There was neither water nor electricity, nor any connection to a sewer; the kitchen arrangements were modest and antiquated, the windows far from winter-proof. Estate agents in Norway describe such places as 'idyllic', which may often mean close to the sea and habitable for the month of July and the first half of August. But the house had something of that quality and looked as though it might be restored to full-year habitability. Once a religious meeting-house, and on its upper floor a morgue, from its outside staircase to that upper floor it was known locally as 'Trappehus' (Stair House). For many years it had been rented to an Oslo family as their summer dwelling. Meeting them on that occasion, it seemed a binding condition of sale that the family be re-accommodated in a room at the far end of a large shed on the other side of the path and whose near end housed the delicately named 'outhouse'.

In the summer immediately after signing the contract, and until late the next summer, we commuted by bus from Oslo at weekends to work on the house. It was the first hint since both of our arrivals that roots might be set in this foreign land. But it meant more than just digging a hole; there were neighbours and bureaucracy. Applications had to be made for connection to the public water supply and for electricity to be brought in. Negotiations with the neighbour in the big yellow house had to be conducted to dig a pipe through her garden to reach the road from a septic tank. An unaccommodating lady who was to cause more trouble, she agreed on condition that she have free access to the new system. That was not all; Norwegian bedrock had to be dynamited on both properties as well as on the road to make way for it, not something to delight those prone to be suspicious of interference by foreigners.

To be able to set things in motion, Joanne resigned her job at the publisher. With the municipality engineer's go-ahead, she set off from Oslo one rainy day in the early autumn in gumboots and sou'wester to find a man reputed to have an excavator and access to a dynamiting expert. She was told he was excavating somewhere in the woodlands owned by Fred. Olsen, the shipowner whose vessel had carried me to Norway. Hvitsten's 'big house' as his family home, and his shipping empire had begun here with the exporting of ice and wood to Scotland. Joanne tracked the man down in the woods and secured his future services.

We started meanwhile on the house itself. On Thursday evenings we boarded a small bus in Oslo's East Side taking us and other weekenders directly to Hvitsten. We had two large cans, one of paint and the other of soup. Starting with one room, where we could sleep and plan further operations, we gradually tore out old linoleum, removed tired wallpaper, scraped window frames, and began rebuilding the interior. An inner staircase was put up, floor coverings laid, and paint applied to ceilings and walls. Our willing neighbour on the other side lent his house-building skills, something nearly all Norwegians have. He fitted cupboards and installed a large double window I bought in Oslo, which vastly improved the view of the fjord. By then we had a second-hand Volkswagen and could fetch and carry. Arne Solberg, the kindly neighbour, also laid the concrete floors for two WC and shower rooms that had been storage spaces. Water and electricity came fairly soon. The septic tank and its drainage at a considerable regulation length out into the sea took longer.

It was a way of becoming acquainted with the locals. They might easily have viewed with hostility the invasion of their settled life by two obvious foreigners. They were a small population with under eighty permanent residents. Until recently the smallest town ever in Norway, physically it occupied little more than a tenth of a square mile. It was due to this that town status had been withdrawn and, as recently as January 1964, brought under the rural municipality of Vestby, itself a larger town on the main Oslo-Gothenburg rail route about ten kilometres inland.

Though small, the population was cosmopolitan. Like many other locals, the plumber had learned his trade at sea. Betraying their knowledge of far-off places, he and his colleagues referred to Hvitsten (White Stone) as 'White Rock City'. Further down our lane was an English widow from Liverpool, her late husband a Norwegian sea captain. Nearby, in the other direction, lived an elderly spinster who had spent most of her life in New York with the Salvation Army. She still played guitar and sang. Further up the hill, a ship's purser from a well-known freight line came home with a Brazilian wife. Quite soon we could identify ourselves as members of the local community as distinct from the 'city people', who came on holidays and behaved as if White Rock City was theirs, the locals a skeleton crew that kept the place going for them and could be paid, or underpaid, to paint their houses.

Joanne and I were married on 25 November 1964 in Oslo's grandiose Town Hall with only Joanne's landlady and my brother in attendance. That evening, since they too, naturally enough, had to be informed, the Frøstrups arranged a small party. When it had already begun I made so bold as to suggest that we invite Arne Naess, who to our surprise though, knowing his unusual party manners, also alarm, accepted. True to form, the famous professor arrived quite quickly in pyjamas and climbing boots, explaining or accusing us for the fact that it was rather late. In the brief period that he devoted to the proceedings he dominated them completely, adopting his Mephistophelean mode to such effect that after he had left, Joan, who had not met him before, remarked 'That man's the de'il himself!'. While present, however, the same devil invited home the next day to look for a present in his cellar. There we rummaged around with Arne's sister in a sea of old furniture and picked out a wicker chair.

The wedding was a mere incident in the larger 'event' of putting the house in order. We moved in during the summer of 1965. There were setbacks. The 'city people' who occupied the house immediately below suspected that dynamiting the bedrock had led to leakages into their garden from the new drainage system. They sent samples to the medical faculty in Oslo for testing. It proved to be subsoil water that had found new ways of reaching the sea, bad enough that original Norwegian bedrock should be disturbed by foreigners. The neighbour who had got her sewage system at our expense complained that a bush had not been re-planted properly. When, after a further attempt on my own, she complained again, having come on speaking terms with Fred. Olsen's Danish head gardener, I asked this professional, also called Olsen, to settle the matter once and for all. He did. Later the same neighbour asked Joanne if we needed money to buy curtains, since as yet we had not put up any on the side facing her house. It was said maliciously and with sarcasm. It helped that she had a bad reputation among our other neighbours; we began to feel we could rise above these signs of petty pique on the part of itinerant 'city people' who behaved like visiting landlords.

A visit to Joanne's family in California had been on the cards for some time. We decided to fly there that summer. To be presentable, I took out and dusted a suit I had brought with me to Norway but so far had little opportunity to use. I looked forward to my first visit to the United States and California in particular. Since Joanne's time was her own, she would fly over first with me following a week or so later. There was another thought behind the timing. That Joanne had left home at all had something to do with her relations with her mother, probably a stubborn unwillingness to follow in her mother's footpath.

Following Pearl Harbour, like 120,000 other Japanese Americans, the majority of them United States citizens, the family had been wrenched from their home and livelihood and sent to a 'War Relocation Camp' at Topaz in Utah. California was declared an 'exclusion zone' so that internment elsewhere was the only way in which residents with Japanese ancestry could remain in the United States. For a generation born in the United States, already conscious of their American identities, this was a blow to which only two responses seemed possible once the crisis was over. One was to bend over backwards in becoming ultra-American and secure unquestioned affiliation with the new homeland. The other was to see the misery of an America that could allow things so un-American to happen. So successful was Joanne's mother in pursuing the former alternative that she now had a position in the military establishment at Fort Mason in San Francisco. There she decided the fates of high-ranking military personnel on the basis of their efficiency or were really needed. Her husband took it differently. Before the war he had run an insurance agency with his father. The agency naturally vanished. Having been forced to spend the time of internment away from his family labouring on a dam-construction project in Idaho, his re-action was to merge unobtrusively into on-going life by way of Berkeley's municipal park authority. He devoted much of his spare time to reading in the Richmond public library. Joanne, herself part of a new multicultural generation looking optimistically into the future, had no thought of conforming to her mother's conservative life-style. Inspired by a teacher in Berkeley's Department of Scandinavian Studies, she had set off with her guitar for freedom. The question now was how would the reunion go?

Joanne duly left and I cleaned up the house and started packing. She phoned after a week to say I must not come over. Alone in Hvitsten and with clear images of San Francisco and Californian skies already firmly in mind, I was disappointed and asked why. Was it a recurrence of whatever drove Joanne from her home in the first place? Was it her parents' concern that she was to marry outside the Japanese American circle? Although Anne Ichiyasu (born Akimoto) was now well integrated into the American system at a level where ethnicity was not a factor, Japanese Americans in their home-circles were acutely conscious of their ethnic identity. You would think this was normal in the United States, where identities have too little history to be able to take care of themselves; but here, in view of what had happened to them in the war, there was an additional need to preserve in the wider American mind a sense of the major injustice perpetrated on a particular section of the community. In practical terms, it also meant membership of a group contesting the legality of the internment. It wasn't until Ronald Reagan's presidency, in 1988, that Congress signed legislation apologizing on behalf of the United States government for an action based on 'race prejudice, war hysteria, and a failure of political leadership'. It was agreed that all surviving internees receive reparation.

In the summer of 1965 my only thoughts were of having to meet my new parents-in-law, that it would be nice if Joanne and I could both get on good terms with them and, not least, that California would be a wonderful escape from the drudgery of house-restoration and speaking Norwegian. I told Joanne I was coming anyway. She said we shouldn't live with her parents. I asked her to think it over and call me again. Perhaps we could stay with them for a while but spend time in Los Angeles with her uncle's family, known for being more relaxed in these matters. Uncle Min had escaped internment by being seconded to General Douglas MacArthur's staff as a mediator with Japanese business in the process of rebuilding the Japanese economy. Reaping the rewards of his contacts, he now presided over a firm selling fishing gear from San Diego to the whole South American coast.

And so it was. Joanne met me in a fog-hidden San Francisco with a large Dodge Pontara. Perhaps delaying the critical crunch as long as possible, she seemed reluctant to take me straight home. We looked at those parts of San Francisco still visible below the fog before crossing the long Bay Bridge to Oakland and heading north along the freeway to El Cerrito.

On being introduced, I immediately got on good terms with Joanne's sharp-as-a-diamond mother. Her father, very different in temperament but with a solid portion of humour, was warm in his welcome. In almost painful contrast to our own home, theirs was in impeccable condition. We had a spotless air-conditioned bedroom facing the road. Through the closed windows in the morning one heard the sound of gas-guzzling automobiles whishing past and the distant bray of the Santa Fe Railroad, recognizable from a thousand westerns. It was atmospheric.

I took a bus to the Berkeley campus and introduced myself to two members of *Inquiry*'s Advisory Board, Benson Mates and David Rynin. I had already corresponded with them. At that time the university had summer vacations and they found me an unused office in Dwinelle Hall. Facing an atrium where no people came and with some tropical plants as props, it was cool and I had a sense of being a withered growth transplanted from the back of beyond to a peaceful refuge in the centre of learning. I read and wrote and soon discovered near neighbours in Bill Craig, a well-known logician, and Paul Feyerabend, an iconoclastic philosopher of science, both of whom had time to talk and share lunch. It was while talking to Feyerabend one morning on the steps of Dwinelle that I first met Avrum Stroll, a Berkeley graduate then teaching at Simon Fraser University in British Columbia. Two years earlier, with some changes at my suggestion, he had published a piece in *Inquiry*. To my surprise, he recalled the correspondence and thanked me for my comments. I was to keep contact with all three.

Such prestigious connections at the famed campus may even have helped my credentials as a son-in-law. A friendly reception at the famous campus did no harm. After some local tourism into Marin County and San Francisco itself, Joanne and I flew down to Los Angeles on a brief visit to her uncle Min, his wife Dorothy and cousin Clifford. They lived in Gardenia, a suburb identifiable in the vast sprawl of LA only by its name on the map, their home the typical one-storey construction of pasteboard on a wooden frame with a small lawn, but well-appointed and with for its time an enormous television set. They were pleasant hosts and rather more relaxed than their relatives in El Cerrito.

We returned to Norway via Boston for a reunion in my case with Lee Proctor and her family. Lee, then Wakefield, had been one of those four Vassar girls studying in Edinburgh in the early 'fifties. Now, more than ten years on, a mother and the wife of physician Monroe, she lived in a quiet rural setting near Concord in New Hampshire. In Boston we reunited with Gene Sharp, the non-violent activist, just lately deceased, an expert on strategies for dealing with authoritarian regimes. Before moving to Hvitsten we had met in Oslo, where Gene at Naess's invitation had been charting the resistance of teachers to the Nazi occupation in World War II. While forced to ransack Gandhi's writings to unearth unreferenced quotations in translating Naess's small book on Gandhi, I had grasped enough to make talking with Gene rewarding as well as congenial. We had also been treated to his excellent cooking. If my memory serves me, he published an article in a special issue of *Inquiry* put together in the light of this interest. In Boston, Gene was establishing himself in a rehabilitated apartment not far from the Boston waterfront.

There was a sense of creases from the distant and near past being ironed out. Some remained, our Hvitsten home was a refuge in a time of need but if the idea of permanency underlies any house-building project engaged in personally, establishing ourselves there had no place in a realistic future. Only in the light of a dream of the kind that used to support my depression could it be permanent. But California, too, was a dream if less unrealistic in terms of the future. As it was, we returned to our reconstruction work and prepared amenities appropriate for the arrival of a third member of the family.

Our son, Jo Erskine, was born on 18 February 1966 after a heavy snowfall and it was approaching midnight when signs of his imminent arrival became unmistakable. The Volkswagen's wheels wouldn't grip even on the flat level of the path outside, so we knocked on the neighbours' door and the family of five came out to put their shoulders to our four wheels. The appointed place of birth was twelve kilometres along a country road that luckily had recently been ploughed. We got there just in time. Jo was born shortly before 2:00 a.m. After persuading the midwife that I was unlikely to faint and being told to keep well out of the way, I was allowed to attend. In my anxiety and the general excitement it didn't occur to me to wonder whether we had got a boy or a girl, the truth came simply as an added detail. Everything had gone, and continued to go, well. When, after two or three days, I drove mother and infant home, we stopped off at Hvitsten's general store to show our product off. The proprietor, Fagerli, insisted we put the infant on the scale to check his weight, thereby, I thought conferring on this new resident full White Rock City citizenship.

As an environment for the early years of a child of a mixed-race marriage between foreigners, Hvitsten at that time could hardly be bettered. We were made to feel part of the community; the neighbour children took to Jo and, although older, treated him as one of them. Through restoring the house with their father's help and that of his contacts, and with Joanne's close contact with his wife, we were on greeting terms with a wide selection of neighbours as well as others in the wider municipality, including the municipal engineer and the sheriff. Being little more than a hamlet, Hvitsten lacked certain amenities. There was no kindergarten the nearest school in Vestby. Within three years Joanne had provided both. Gathering the support of some other young families with children around Jo's age, she established a kindergarten in our own garden, albeit just below my working space and, when the time became opportune, she arranged a first-year class in a disused school building donated to the community by the wife of an earlier Olsen generation. Somehow, she secured a shipment of small wooden chairs made in Hungary. Her polite and quietly insistent nature worked wonders. For a hippie carrying a guitar who began by attending to flowers in her window box, she was proving to be an indomitable and creative social genius.

How much this was a matter of basic character or education and environment I don't know, but Joanne's sense for the communal must have found its roots in the way her family coped during World War II. Born in 1938, she spent her own formative years in surroundings where communal activity was perforce a way of life. Mothers, their husbands removed to work on public projects elsewhere, had to run the family collectives on their own and for children, though perhaps for many of the mothers too, the result may well have been a socially and even personally more fulfilling way of life than that of a nuclear family in those typical self-contained homes behind whose lawns Americans play out their ideologized individuality. Whatever part it played in making Hvitsten a fine setting for the formative years of her son, Joanne's acquired community sense and distaste for garden hedges and isolated homes had found its proper setting.

Where I belonged in this setting was less clear. During terms I drove to Oslo once a week to give a lecture, for which I received some extra income. My half-time assistantship was confirmed until the end of 1968. At home I was occupied mainly with editing *Inquiry* as well as performing, for a while, the duties of editorial secretary for the *Journal of Peace Research*. The distance between me and the editor in Oslo proved in the end too inconvenient. We had occasional visitors. I invited Erik Stenius, a visiting Finnish scholar well known for his views on Wittgenstein's *Tractatus*, to come down on Sunday. Troubled by the absence of hospitality shown by my colleagues to visiting academics, I thought it would save their faces, as well as Stenius himself from the tedium of a day in which nothing much happened in Oslo. To reach us he had to take a hydrofoil to Drøbak, where I would pick him up. He seemed awestruck by this new-fangled means of progress down the fjord, and I realized the fare must have cost most of the modest fee he received for his lecture. A very reserved man, he was not easy to engage in conversation and I wonder what he thought of this Sunday in our small home with a child calling on our attention and little scope for intelligent conversation.

A regular visitor was Tommy Gavigan, an adventurer from my home country's West Coast. One of a large family, a trumpeter, and a seeker, we met him in Oslo at some friends of Joanne. Then driving for a stationery firm, Tommy dropped in on us occasionally leaving packages of foolscap. These proved very convenient for plotting chapters or courses of argument. Tommy was also a budding sailor. He bought an old Colin Archer, a solid sailing vessel designed as a life-saving boat by the son of another immigrant from Scotland. With a newly acquired wife but little experience, he sailed it from Nordfjord north of Bergen to Kristiansand in the south. At one point he had left his even less experienced wife adrift while rowing ashore to get help for the motor. Tommy later worked as an assistant to the brain researcher Per Andersen, assuring me that the latter would one day receive a Nobel Prize, which was not so unlikely. Tommy alas would be unable to see his prophecy confirmed. I read some years later that he had drowned in a diving accident in southern Norway. A man of active fantasy, he talked of building a raft on which he could sit and listen to Wagner in the middle of the inner Oslo fjord. Compared with his, my own life was almost a caricature of the dourness proverbially ascribed to the Scot.

My 'old' sailing friend and fellow musician Mike Pollett visited with his wife Dorothy, and some relatives also came by. In the summer following Jo's birth we had a visit from my mother and from Hamburg my sister Jane and Jens, recently married in London. Two years later we would entertain my cousin Beatrice and her husband Brian Tinsley. Beatrice was the second of my mother's older sister Jean's three daughters. They were all brought up in New Zealand but, by now, Beatrice was a member of the astronomy department at the University of Texas at Austin. She would later move to Yale, but in the very year of her promotion to full professor she was diagnosed with malignant melanoma. The exceedingly bright and cheerfully optimistic Beatrice died at the tragically early age of forty but not before having left her mark on cosmology. In 1984 the American Astronomical Society established the Beatrice M. Tinsley Prize for outstanding creative contributions to astronomy or astrophysics. We hadn't met since she was a mere child, her family having left for New Zealand in 1946. That we should do so in out-of-the-way Hvitsten was due to Norwegian astrophysicists having chosen a nearby agricultural college for their turn to host an international conference.

The distance to Oslo was no real obstacle. Naess was seldom to be found and the work he gave me was more than enough to keep me busy at home. When, on one rare occasion, I found him in his office, he handed me a pile of four lectures that he had been touring with on Pyrrhonian scepticism. We had shared a seminar on the topic and he asked me to look through them with a view to re-casting them as chapters in a book. Along with other chores, including a search in Sweden for an agent to sell my brother's yachts, this one would take some time, but I managed to persuade a sceptical Ted Honderich to agree, on the advice of Bernard Williams, to publish the result as *Scepticism* in the Routledge Philosophy and Scientific Method series. It came out to Arne's considerable joy in 1968. Although first reviews were generally hostile, an English philosopher, asked by Ryle to contribute one in *Mind*, wrote saying two reviews that had already appeared made him ashamed. Their authors had made no attempt to grasp the book's unusual approach and had failed entirely to see its point. He added that had Naess been his fellow-countryman, he would not have written this letter since it 'would savour too much of flattery'.

I had by then received a three-year research grant allowing me to pick up my own threads again. It was through yet another lucky chance. After the not unexpected refusal of an application in 1965 with the hopelessly vague wording 'Philosophical and Psychological Consideration in the Approach to Mental Activity', on my second attempt a telephone call from a member of the grants committee set things rolling. It was Knut Erik Tranøy, professor in Bergen, he said my project sounded interesting enough but I would need to elaborate on my plans before he could advise his committee-members on its merits. I jumped into my car, raced to Oslo to meet Tranøy during his sandwich break.

But for two things he might well have passed over the application. First, Naess had written a very positive letter of recommendation to the committee, saying I knew more about Anglo-American philosophy than anyone there. Secondly, that spring I had been invited to join an examination committee responsible for adjudicating a candidate for the Master's degree in Bergen. The evening's entertainment following the candidate's successful defence of his dissertation took place amid considerable conviviality in Tranøy's home. We got to know each other and, as I later found out, had rather similar backgrounds.

Born and bred in Oslo, Tranøy had studied abroad and like me had found his way to philosophy later than most. But his story was a lot harsher than mine. Together with up to seven hundred other students he had been arrested in 1943 and sent to Buchenwald. After his release and return, he spent a year as an attaché at the Norwegian Embassy in Washington. It was there that he became interested in philosophy. He took a Master's degree at the University of North Carolina and after a year in Paris went to Cambridge, where in 1953 he received his doctorate. At Cambridge he had been greatly influenced by Georg von Wright and became friendly with Ludwig Wittgenstein. It was a background that invited scepticism about the state of philosophy in Norway. In September he wrote to say he was 'of the opinion bordering on conviction' that I would receive the grant, adding that the information I'd given him was 'most important'.

In December I received a letter from the Research Council awarding me a one-year grant for 1968 but renewable for two more years depending on funds and progress. The grant carried with it an obligation to give a two-hour lecture every week, but with our home budget shaky after a period with only a half-time job supplemented by a weekly lecture, I asked if I could give an extra lecture to supplement it. This was granted and in a mixture of relief and hope but not undue optimism, I dusted off the intimidating pile of papers that had accumulated during my first attempt at a dissertation and began looking for some easier way into the 'images and imagining' area that would justify the letter of my application.

That was not easy; I needed a style and since the dissertation was for London it had to be analytic. I had little practice in the analytic style and there were more than one model to choose from. Ayer's classically clean and John L. Austin's fresh and occasionally impudent style both appealed to me. The latter was a classy thinker far above my level, so I decided I would try some middle path between deadpan analysis and something livelier if only to sustain a head of steam. After looking wearily at the old papers for somewhere to start I came quite by accident on a discussion piece by Alan R. White. Its unspoken but fashionable assumptions so antagonized me that I immediately set to work in an attempt to undermine them. This took me back to Ryle and what I found so elusive in his treatment of imagination in *The Concept of Mind*. So the grand project was shelved for the time being and mental images became the focus. It was the topic I had been registered under at the University of London. I decided to use the grant to get the dissertation quickly out of the way before taking on the grander theme that the Research Council was paying me for. Retrieving the handwritten note Willie Stewart had given me at a party in Edinburgh, written on ordinary stationery, I rehearsed his argument there against Ryle, and then fished out my old notes on Sartre and read some recent articles by philosophers whose own arguments about mental imagery owed much to the later Wittgenstein. They were all campaigning against what they claimed were conceptual illusions about 'inner objects' due either to Descartes or to misleading analogies inherent in our undisciplined speaking habits. I thought their 'methodologies' concealed unquestioned metaphysical assumptions.

Within two months of intense scribbling I had a draft.

During that time tensions already inherent in our home-life had come to the surface. They grew into an undercurrent of irritation as well as open conflict. Working at home is inimical to family life at the best of times, but the pressure I had to maintain to stay in focus and write with the mental energy needed to keep track of arguments placed me outside the home while still in its environs. These included, under the window of my study, a kindergarten that in pursuit of her excellent communal aims Joanne had arranged for local children. As spring approached there were attacks of asthma, mainly in the early morning, which meant I woke before six. I would go downstairs and read. I particularly remember reading slowly through Tolstoy's *Kreutzer Sonata*, another book from my grandmother's library.

By late June the attacks came at any time and the inhaler I had been given seemed only to make matters worse. One day in mid-July, Joanne had to call the taxi in Vestby. The taxi driver's wife was a trained nurse, and Vestby's only taxi served as the local ambulance. Before the oxygen equipment could be used, however, a doctor had to sign some document. In Norway's mid-summer a majority of general practitioners are on vacation along with everyone else. As we searched the district for one still on call, I lay on a stretcher with my face very near the roof of the taxi unable to see anything. Finally, a doctor in nearby Drøbak gave the nurse his blessing and with the oxygen helping slightly we drove interminably the fifty or so kilometres to the district hospital. There I was quickly taken care of and kept for two weeks while allergy and other tests were taken.

I could now take an outsider's look at our situation. Joanne arrived with my manuscript on request and I was able to correct some of the draft. I was struck by how well some of it sounded but how unlike me. I remember saying to myself, My God, this is like some of that stuff in *Mind*! If I hadn't found my own method it seemed I could at least put on the style.

Noting the pages strewn over my bed, the doctor remarked that here was part of the diagnosis. From this distance Hvitsten began to look like a sideshow and it became clear that the fact that Joanne and I were not combining well would have to be faced. The stay at the hospital also put me in a wider context of normal people, the most intellectual being elderly teachers. We discussed the weather, for me a welcome climate change in itself. I became acquainted with the kindly ladies of the Norwegian Women's Public Health Association. They did rehabilitation work and provided recovering patients with coffee and biscuits, but also strawberries and cultured milk, the latter having an unexpectedly relaxing effect on my windpipe. In general, I bathed in an atmosphere of un-committing care and kindliness.

Diagnosed as allergic to 'Danish house dust', and given assurances that my heart had not suffered under the strain, I returned to Hvitsten to complete the dissertation and make plans for our near future. These included shaking the Danish house dust from our heels in exchange for the on-shore breezes and blue skies of California.

I wrote up a fairly decent draft; or rather, the arguments being more or less clear in my head, it wrote itself although in a style that echoed voices I had heard in seminars and debates in London. None of these could be my own since a voice was something I still lacked. Some practice at this academic form of ventriloquism had been procured in putting together Naess's book on scepticism. Here the arguments were at least my own, or perhaps I should say extensions of one particular argument that, more than a decade earlier, Willie Stewart had given me in his handwritten comment on Ryle.

Happily unaware that Ryle would be one of my examiners, I waded into him with relish. In March I had sent an entry form to the Senate House for the Ph.D. examination and in April wrote to Richard Wollheim, then Grote Professor at University College, to ask after all this time with no supervision if he would glance at the dissertation and comment on its general approach. He delayed answering until May, saying that he might be called in as local examiner, but in July wrote that he had managed to make some 'scanty remarks' in the margins, adding that I might revise the introduction. A remark that 'at many points the argument is of great interest', this being a standard palliative in the hands of an editor refusing a submission, was not encouraging, but I wrote to thank Wollheim, dealt with his comments and accepted his advice on further literature as well as on points of structure. I submitted the thesis in the required three bound copies on 10 September and on 30 September received a letter requiring me to attend an oral examination at Brian O'Shaughnessy's room at Bedford College in Regents Park, at 11.15 a.m. on Tuesday the 8th of October.

Arriving there in a state of understandable anxiety I had no indication of how things might go. In spite of the corrections made on Wollheim's advice, the dissertation had been spun out of my own head with no collegial feed-back and only my editorial experience to guide me in the way of effective presentation. There was also an element of cheek, or if you like unprovoked irony, in the un-revised introduction, including a remark about a series of blind alleys the first of which was Ryle's way with imaging.

It was with some consternation therefore that when O'Shaughnessy opened the door I found Ryle standing there ready to greet me. After the usual polite preliminaries they got down to business and I answered as best I could, nor too badly I thought. But when, in conclusion, Ryle looked at me with folded hands and said, 'I don't want to sound huffy, Hannay, but perhaps you can tell me where in *The Concept of Mind* I talk about psychology?', the unexpected question left me fumbling. It occurred to me that the only reason for asking it was that he thought I had read only the one chapter, on imagination. Or was it that I had missed some qualification to his dismissive conclusions about mental images or their wider background? With some foreboding I went out into the corridor and stood waiting the best part of half an hour. When I was eventually invited in, Ryle took over and said that the dissertation focused too one-sidedly on criticism of others' positions and lacked arguments for my own view or on views these positions opposed. However, he said, they both thought the dissertation could be salvaged if I could re-submit it in a significantly revised form.

It was a blow. Later that day, in an attempt to allay my despondency, I phoned O'Shaughnessy to gain some clearer idea of what went wrong. He said they had discussed my case at length but that Ryle thought the dissertation suffered from my not having received any decent supervision 'over there in Norway'.

I knew he was right. There was too much self-indulgence and uncalled-for smartness. Tough arguments were still to be found. I tried consoling myself with the thought that the disappointing séance had at least given the thesis a touch of the supervisory assistance it lacked. Not long after, I wrote to Ryle saying I didn't want to sound huffy either, but his last question had seemed to insinuate that I had not read *The Concept of Mind* in its entirety. All he said in reply was that I had been 'a bit too impressionistic' in my 'exegesis' of the 'all in strategy or background metaphysical assumptions of, e.g., Sartre and myself'. Somewhat puzzlingly, he also said this didn't really matter. I was left wondering what did. Many years later, in correspondence with Brian O'Shaughnessy, I asked him if he remembered me and the occasion. He replied:

> Of course, I remember you, and very well too. You were the first Ph.D. I ever examined — I only examined four in all — and always regretted that I did not stand up a bit better to Ryle, whose insistence on re-writing seems in retrospect quite absurd. But he was a headstrong old boy, and very pernickety about things like presentation.

After this debacle, I returned to Oslo and prepared for a grant-supported year at Berkeley. Before that failed oral but not long before we left for California, Peter and Joan moved to Ireland with their now three children, Mariella, Danielle and Aksel. We had a farewell lunch at a workaday brasserie frequented by employees of the Norwegian Broadcasting Company, appropriately in view of Peter's proletarian self-image. It was a summer day and we sat outside in the sun in a district where we had once lived together. The previous four years we had met only intermittently and awkwardly, although one Sunday, Peter, by then press attaché for SAS, had arrived in Hvitsten armed with a camera. We chatted amiably as if nothing was wrong. A few years ago Joan told that she never saw the photos and knew nothing of the visit.

Unresolved tensions remained. In the summer following Jo's birth on my mother's second visit, and in an attempt at renewed contact, the Frøstrup family had dropped in with their hired motorboat. Having some inkling of the breach, for my mother the happy relationship she had enjoyed with Joan during the two years she and Peter had lived on the farm, seemed now ended. In a last-ditch attempt to keep their cultural and artistic ambitions alive, Peter and Joan befriended a theatre group from England. This sociable set of gay young thespians, living in a large house on an island in the fjord, staged classy but, I thought, narcissistic plays at the Maritime Museum attended mainly by tourists. Their sales manager assured me it was an artistic success.

As for my own performance, the Frøstrups' departure would mean leaving their once supporting actor alone on stage. But my one-man act was coming along and, having provided the lines, the journal Peter placed in my hands had now opened the door onto a wider stage.

Chapter Eleven: A good deal

Good deal: in the timber trade a cut wooden plank was once called a 'deal'. Someone lucky enough to have one of usable quality had a 'good deal'.

The tension and excitement in the air were there from the start. Berkeley's Free Speech Movement had ended three years earlier but the student protest had made it impossible for the university administration to exercise a ban on political activity on campus. The counter-culture was in full swing and noisily there every lunch-time on Sproul Plaza. There was strong local support through the currently influential *Berkeley Barb*, a weekly newspaper with its anti-war and civil rights messages, and advocacy of radical social changes demanded by the youth culture. The Black Panthers from neighbouring Oakland made their presence menacingly felt on Telegraph Avenue, and the university faculty composed largely of academics who had sought a fruitful career in the safety of their departments, could hardly escape being caught up in it. On my first day in the department's library, the building housing the philosophy department was 'liberated'. Fire-hoses were used to drench the corridors and the contents of offices that had been carelessly left unlocked.

Other adjustments were called for; for instance, clothes. At my first meeting with Wallace Matson, the chairman, I arrived in a fairly new suit, which I caught him eyeing in a way that I took to indicate that it was conspicuously out of place. I quickly reverted to T-shirts and jeans. We stayed some weeks with Joanne's parents at El Cerrito, a fair bus ride from Berkeley, long enough to become friends with a young Hungarian family opposite and an equally young Norwegian mathematician along the road, an assistant professor at the university.

Established on Milvia, two blocks north of University Avenue and a short walk from the campus, we arranged for Jo to attend a school while Joanne began evening classes in Oakland. For her this was a new California, politically alive with old barriers swept aside. She made friends, among them a Black fellow student, someone her family would have advised against in her previous California existence and might still. I had a permanent place, a carrel, in the Bancroft Library, where I worked in the morning and afternoon. My hope, originally, had been to continue my exchange with David Shwayder, chairman when arrangements for my visit were first made, but due to some disagreement over promotion he had recently moved to Illinois. I was in fact lucky to be admitted to exchange visitor status at all, since it was reserved for scholars with their doctorates behind them. I hadn't told the Norwegian Research Council that I had been refused at my first attempt, only that I had submitted my thesis. Matson said they would waive the restriction in my case.

Rather than revising the dissertation straight away, I looked around to see what the faculty were doing that might help me in the longer term. Stephen Schiffer was working on his Oxford D.Phil. thesis under the recently appointed Oxford philosopher Paul Grice whose work focused on 'speaker's meaning'. At the opposite end of the philosophy market, with some help from David Rynin, I delved into the Absolute Idealism of the late nineteenth-century Californian Josiah Royce. I browsed randomly in the bookshelves, to which there was unlimited access, and there was a general sense of finding bearings in ways impossible in Norway and not least at Hvitsten. I met faculty members, the old guard and the young Turks: Thompson Clark, Barry Stroud, and John Searle. We attended a solo concert given by the legendary Earl Hines playing with still magnetic power on a white concert grand in the Berkeley Community Theatre. I also hit it off with Ruth Anderson, head of the departmental office, who seemed to welcome the chance to talk to someone to whom she was not responsible and with no part in whatever local factions she had to deal with. To me, she could also vent her feelings about the behaviour of those students who had 'liberated' Moses Hall the very day I set foot in it. 'Savages', she said. We continued a correspondence after my stay in which she described her travels, until in September 1972 Ruth wrote to say she had finally quit her job.

I usually returned to our apartment for lunch but sometimes joined members of the faculty. Paul Feyerabend brought his caustic humour to our lunchtime conversations. He also employed it in connection with a graduate student who had interpreted my friendliness as an opportunity for something more. She told me later that Paul had advised her not to be misled by my friendly demeanour since among other misdemeanours I had murdered my aunt. Back in Hvitsten, I did once enter our bad neighbour's house with an axe in hand after she had set her dog on Joanne and Jo, but luckily I didn't find her, and of this Feyerabend knew nothing.

One person whose company I particularly appreciated was Stanley Moore on sabbatical from San Diego and living nearby. In 1954, Stanley's interest in Marx and former membership of the Communist Party had attracted the attention of the House Un-American Activities Committee. As a result of a hearing in Portland, where Stanley took the Fifth Amendment and refused to answer the charges, he was dismissed from his teaching post at the prestigious Reed College by its trustees. After some ten years picking up part-time work he received an appointment at UCSD, arriving there at the beginning of Herbert Marcuse's years at that campus — not quite un-coincidentally since Marcuse's previous appointment at Brandeis had been terminated for similar reasons. Now on leave, Stanley was in Oakland with his wife and adopted child, and he took part in seminars, which is where I first met him. His life-experience and the preoccupations that led to it made him a warm and interesting conversational companion. I read recently that it was as late as 1981 that Reed College issued an apology, and it was not until 1997, just four years before he died, that they invited Stanley to lecture there.

It was from Frank Xavier Barron at the Institute of Personality Assessment and Research that I felt I had most to learn. Barron was a pioneer in the study of creative thinkers and artists. With a background in philosophy, the chance experience of a summer job as an attendant in a hospital for the mentally ill turned him to psychology where, instead of exchanging the one discipline for the other, he found an area in which the basic questions of philosophy came alive and were, as he later put it, 'embodied in human suffering'. Barron was intrigued by my interest in imagination and came to the point of suggesting I might try for a job at the new Santa Cruz campus to which he had recently been appointed. Joanne and I even went to the extent of driving there so that I could talk to the Principal of the open-ended college to which Barron was to be attached. It turned out to be more in the way of an informal interview. We had a pleasant but, on his side guarded, and on my side (by American standards) over-modest chat that left things so open as to be virtually closed. I still had no doctorate and only a meagre list of publications, all of them in an area that Barron himself would regard as abstract talk. However, I was able from our conversations to see this kind of talk, and my own participation in it, in a clearer perspective. On creativity, Barron spoke of the role played by facing the unknown and taking risks combined with a strong urge to find order in chaos. That sounded closer to my own original thoughts in sharp contrast to the style and mind-sets of the philosophers I knew. Hitting upon order in chaos was also a fair description of my own disorganized *modus cogitandi* if not life itself. Talking to Frank Barron not only gave me some encouraging insight into my own way of getting along, it also put me in mind of where I had once thought of going.

Following Barron to the new and innovative campus at Santa Cruz might also have helped to resolve our home situation. Our various occupations, their contacts, and the warm welcome we received from Joanne's wider family in the Bay Area and Los Angeles made our situation easier. Joanne was taking courses in Oakland and Jo enjoyed lively and friendly company at a local school.

Arthur Cody, somewhat of a renegade in philosophy, with a doctorate from Berkeley and who I knew through a contribution to *Inquiry*, came and took us to visit friends in San Francisco. We, too, were mobile having arranged with my sister in Hamburg to import a Volkswagen 'bubble'. With its one-and-a-half litre engine it coped excellently with the California traffic. We visited Yosemite, meeting a bear that seemed to arrive on cue. Joanne, her father and I drove to Reno, winning enough at a casino to pay for dinner and the petrol. I arranged for Timothy Sprigge, my postgraduate colleague in London, and now visiting at Cincinnati, to give a talk to the weekly student seminar, after which we all drove down to the Monterey peninsula. In February, before the People's Park confusions, the three of us together with one of Joanne's aunts drove to Los Angeles, where I looked after a stand at the Los Angeles Boat Show displaying my brother's new 22-foot 'Galion' sailing boat. There we were accommodated once again by Joanne's welcoming Uncle Min and his wife and son. This, and finding agents for the boat, brought me into contact with people with quite other mind-sets than those of my academic colleagues.

Not that the colleagues presented a uniform front. On the way south at UC Santa Barbara and at UCLA I talked with two philosophers who could not have differed more. I had arranged to meet both in connection with the journal. Paul Wienpahl combined his interest in Zen with Spinoza, whose collected works he had translated. He spoke for a radical empiricism that merged with mysticism, and his manner of speaking was that of a military commander. He looked in fact a bit like a grizzled veteran and was a no-nonsense man totally clear in his utterance and easy to talk to. With Harold Garfinkel at UCLA conversation was less than straightforward. A professor of sociology, he had invented 'ethnomethodology' as a way of addressing social phenomena shorn of the theoretical constructions and interpretations that sociologists are wont to give them. He too spoke for a kind of radical empiricism, but since it meant eye-balling the phenomena in such detail that their contextuality was all that came into focus, even ordinary situations became radically peculiar. To illustrate his approach Garfinkel tried describing his first visit to Italy, or rather his arrival at da Vinci-Fiumicino airport. Its complexity was such that I wondered how he ever made it through immigration. I left UCLA with a strong sense of the contrasting small-town simplicity and seeming transparency of life back home in Hvitsten and how easy it had been to adjust there.

Back in Berkeley we went through the usual cycle of colds, influenza, rain and fog, all of which once it was over made us feel that we somehow belonged. I even had a sailing boat stationed at Sausalito, one of my brother's for which I was to find a Bay Area agent. Thompson Clark, a philosopher famed for his examination of the conceptual intricacies involved in grasping how we see a tomato was also a sailor and we enjoyed a spell in the bay. As time to leave approached I had to return to my dissertation. But then events of a more eruptive nature prevented any concentration on these.

Our apartment was located directly between 'People's Park' and its later 'Annex'. The former was a less than three-acre plot of cleared university land that owing to delayed implementation of development plans, students with the support of local people and politicians proposed should be a public area. The students were particularly interested in establishing a space for free speech that was not subject to surveillance, impossible on the campus itself. Locals as well as students began planting flowers there and to transform it into a public park.

However, ever since the 'sixties Free Speech Movement the Berkeley campus had acquired among the republican brass in Sacramento a reputation for unpatriotic dissidence. For Robert Reagan, the state governor, it had become a 'haven of communist sympathizers, protesters and sex deviants'. So when, in the light of local interests and to allow for negotiation, the campus leadership itself decided to hold back for a short period on its revised plans to turn the area into a sports field instead of student quarters, offices and parking, which would be a compromise, Reagan intervened by having two-hundred and fifty Highway Patrol officers sent in to fence off the area and guard it against intrusion. In the eyes of Reagan and his political supporters it was a symbolic matter of upholding the property rights of the university against a pernicious leftist challenge. The face-off deepened through people climbing the fence at night to plant flowers to be removed by guardsmen during the day.

The demonstrations grew in numbers. A state of emergency was declared and, against the City Council's vote, two thousand seven hundred National Guardsmen were sent in to occupy Berkeley. The streets were fenced off with rolls of barbed wire and tear gas was directed at any groups of more than two people. A curfew was imposed, hundreds of arrests made and serious injuries caused by over-zealous police officers. A student died from shotgun wounds and when several thousand people gathered on 19 May at a memorial meeting on campus, National Guard troops armed with bayonets and wearing gas masks surrounded a crowd that included elderly people and children with a helicopter dropping tear gas on them. To the injuries suffered, there were added those to people working in the university hospital and their patients as the gas drifted in its direction. Less critically but tellingly, the gas penetrated to the small corner of the Bancroft Library where I was attending to my dissertation. Many in the crowd outside suffered from the gas as well as in the panic that ensued.

The hard line was extended when the National Guard, some of them students at the campus, began to show sympathy with the locals. Guardsmen from a more conservative area in southern California, who would be better able to withstand the force of 'Flower Power', were sent in as replacements. Undeveloped land about a mile from the now fenced off park was appropriated by students and others as a 'People's Park Annex'. Here, their faces grotesquely masked and without their badges, Berkeley police were known to beat up anyone who dared venture there by night. The Annex was just down the road from our apartment so that processions of demonstrators frequently passed by during the day. On 30 May we joined a march sanctioned by the city in protest at the occupation and passed rows of National Guard troops, down the muzzles of whose bayoneted rifles girls placed flowers while a small plane flew overhead with a banner, 'Let a Thousand Parks Bloom'.

Around that time we had a visit from Arne Naess. He had dropped in at Berkeley on his way back from a periodic peace-seeking sojourn in the Nevada desert. It didn't seem to have quietened his restive soul, for when he met up with Paul Feyerabend, who was also not one to take life as over-seriously as they imagined others took it, the pair tried to out-compete each other on Telegraph Avenue. Just when everyone's nerves were on edge, and not least those of the police, Arne chose to grab a cash register in a bookstore and make as if to dash for the door. He was quickly dissuaded. Feyerabend, on this occasion, didn't try to outdo him. Another side of Arne was revealed when we took him to see *Guns of the Magnificent Seven*, a poor sequel to the classic itself. A gratuitously graphic scene of brutality where horses trample on the heads of captives buried up to their necks in sand brought forth a sigh of horror and disgust.

When things had sufficiently calmed down, we played out our time in Berkeley. I put my revision in order, had it bound in three copies as before and sent them off to London. All I did in essence was to write an extra chapter providing the arguments Ryle found lacking and make some minor revisions. I re-entered for the exam. A date for the oral examination on our return was fixed. When the time came, due to an eye injury Ryle was unavailable on the appointed day. The external examiner this time was R. F. Holland, editor of a series in philosophical psychology. With the earlier session in mind, this one proved an anti-climax and can be well described as bathetic. Holland dozed off while O'Shaughnessy plied me with some desultory questions. Both gave the impression that it was a formality. Many years later, meeting O'Shaughnessy's two charming daughters at a party in San Diego and jokingly remarking that their father had flunked me, they looked slightly shocked. It was after this that I wrote to O'Shaughnessy asking if he remembered the occasion. He had ended his letter by saying: 'I was very pleased your thesis sailed through on re-submission, and remember your rather splendid elation on receiving the (very well-deserved result), which you expressed by offering me a cigar.'

Corrections made according to the examiners' advice, and the oral a matter of going through the motions, such was the contrast when I left the dreaded room this time that for the first time in my life I didn't know whether to laugh or cry but ended up doing both in the Leicester Square cinema, but not after buying myself an orange-coloured shirt with tie to match at Simpsons on Piccadilly. The film was *The Battle of Britain*. Its packaged pathos combining tragedy, heroics and victory was more than enough to induce tears. The shirt and tie were never worn, though for several years I kept them as symbols; celebration itself never seemed in order. Those who have struggled with doctoral degrees know about this special version of post-partum depression. It is a complex state of mind in which triumph is overshadowed by the realization that much valuable time has been wasted and unnecessary damage incurred for something that may be of benefit only to oneself, and whose main impact is on those near who have suffered in the time it took.

Chapter Twelve: On the beach

On the beach: usually said of a temporarily unemployed seaman awaiting another job at sea.

Returning to Hvitsten was less re-starting the camera than reeling the film back to its beginning. This fjord-side village's role as a hide-away in which to limber up before facing my equals was over, Joanne's California relationship had been recovered, and except for Jo, for whom the fjord-side village held his earliest memories, the place no longer had the acquired familiarity that makes almost anywhere a home. We would need an alternative in any case; at the end of the following year the research grant would run out.

Santa Cruz might still be a solution. Nothing had come of my meeting with James B. Hall, Provost of the about-to-be opened College V. However, Barron wrote to me in November 1970 saying I could apply for a visiting fellowship to the History of Consciousness programme at $1,250 per month. Just up my street, but it struck me as too much of a makeshift and I didn't apply. A year later I tried to elbow my way into a more permanent niche in Santa Cruz through Maurice Natanson, phenomenologist and now chair of the philosophy department. I had reviewed a book on psychiatry and philosophy that he and two other similarly oriented writers, Erwin W. Straus and Henri Ey, respectively psychologist and psychiatrist, had edited. I wondered if he could put in a good word for me. I don't believe the reason he declined was that I had described the book as 'richly illuminating but on many points philosophically unsatisfactory'. By then they had doubtless established the faculty they wanted. Later, by way of farewell to this sunny option, and after writing a long and appreciative though again also critical review of Natanson's *Journeying Self: A Study in Philosophy and Social Role*, for *Inquiry*, I had a letter thanking me for a 'fair as well as perceptive account'. There followed a copy of a poem he had written, 'Crossing the Manhattan Bridge':

> Near the Yiddish Forard Sign
> A billboard testament
> Says in black and white:
> The Wages of Sin is Death.
> Occasionally, the Sea Beach Express stalls there,
> Waiting for a grunt of current.

> To signal it on to Canal Street,
> The tenements, blackened loaves,
> Are deserted, the pigeon-coops flown.
> Beneath their roofs, an apostate
> Announces a red-letter edition for Jews — gratis.
> And between the boroughs
> The rails tremble and the cars grate.
> Below, the river fish circumnavigate.

Natanson kindly wrote on the cover: 'For Alastair Hannay, an excellent critic of my work.' A footnote revealed that the poem was written in mind of his father Charles Nathanson, an actor in the Yiddish theatre on Second Avenue 'during its golden age'. Independently of my personal ambitions I regret never meeting this articulate exponent of phenomenological and existential thinking whose temporary office in Berkeley I had occupied some summers earlier. Natanson, who later left Santa Cruz for Yale but returned in retirement, died there in 1996.

One outcome of the Californian visit was an issue of *Inquiry* on mental health, with contributions from Frank Barron, Paul Wienpahl, Herbert Fingarette also at UC Santa Barbara, Gerald Mendelsohn in the psychology department at Berkeley and Brian O'Shaughnessy, all with broad and in a proper sense 'spiritual' interests. Also included was my piece on the book Natanson had edited on psychiatry. In general, academic editors should not publish their own work, but in the case of a book addressed to a wider than normal audience, and for which any competent reviewer would be hard to find, on topics I was interested in myself I felt justified in making the occasional exception.

Back in Hvitsten with the doctorate secured but somehow unimportant, and certainly no solution to our lives, we could only bide our time. The autumn of 1969 and next spring and summer were spent there. Having sold the Volkswagen, to Feyerabend's disgust at a slight profit to a student in Berkeley, with some money over from the liberal travel grant together with exemption from income tax, and under the pretext of being a visitor to Europe, I had bought a Volvo from a dealer on Berkeley's Shattuck Avenue. It was a deep yellow, unusually exotic for Volvos. On seeing one parked at Los Angeles airport, it gripped me, no doubt like that model tyre ashtray I whipped from by headmaster-to-be's drawing room in Carlisle as my parents were trying to impress on him my suitability as a pupil. To pick up the car we returned to Hvitsten via Gothenburg. Having no permanent job in Norway, and able in principle to leave again for the States at any time, I could at least in practice if not entirely legally import the car free of duty, keeping it untaxed in Norway for two years. Due to another trip abroad, this time to London, it would be four years before I had to pay up. By then I had a tenured job and although still a Brit had, according to the law at that time, become a Norwegian state functionary.

Around this time there were some refreshing sea interludes. Tony Richardson, an unemployed millionaire who in his out-board-motored dinghy had chanced on our schooner one day, had become a good friend. A periodic enthusiast with maritime experience both in the war and from crossing the Pacific in a sailing boat, now having lately dropped in turn first Buddhism and then photography, he was ready for a return to the sea. I went with him to Jutland in search of a boat. When he had decided on one, we later sailed it back to Oslo. I also crewed for him when, having found the single-handed voyage down the Swedish coast to Lysekil in Sweden hard-going, he asked me to come along on the return voyage. I sensed that, to keep this hobby going, Tony was counting on my being similarly enthusiastic. The pain of letting my academic obsessions come in the way is one I still feel.

Biding time was also interrupted by a welcome visit from Arthur Cody and his friend Wendy on a European tour. There were other bright moments. On receiving notice that the degree of Doctor of Philosophy had been conferred on me (as an 'internal' student even after all those years), I was astounded to read that the examiners judged the thesis 'suitable for publication'. They had added the words 'in a modified form,' but that was in lighter print. A modified version was eventually published in 1971 in the Muirhead Library of Philosophy as *Mental Images — A Defence*. It is some consolation for the trouble entailed in producing it that it survives to this day as one of seventeen volumes reprinted in 2002 under 'Philosophy of Mind and Psychology'. Forty-seven years on I was even able to buy it in a paperback version from 2013. To me, reading it now, the style is so alien that the author's name strikes me as a pseudonym. Later, when taking part in a *viva* at Cambridge, my co-examiner said he thought it the best book he'd read on imagination, so maybe that alter ego had managed to embrace the grander topic after all.

Another bright moment just as Ryle's long editorship was about to end was his acceptance of a version of the additional chapter ('To Be a Mental Image') as an article in *Mind*. Gilbert Ryle has a special place in my affections and disaffections. The first chapter in the personal saga of my dealings with him had been with his well-intentioned advice back in 1956 to 'give up the whole idea'. The last chapter came nigh on twenty years later in the autumn of 1975 at a week-long international conference chaired by Ryle at Christ Church. The two invitees from Norway, Knut-Erik Tranøy and myself, found ourselves in a group of thirty-seven colleagues including nearly all the great names in the fashionable and predominantly analytic strain in philosophy. Seated next to a mellow Ryle at the celebratory dinner, I engaged him and him me on several topics. These included Dan Dennett, who along with Ryle had been the target of some snide remarks in my dissertation. Dennett famously carried to its 'natural' if not logical conclusion the letter of Ryle's campaign against, in his own famous words, the 'ghost in the machine'. He let the machine stay but refurbished it with its own ancillary 'semantic engine'. Of Dennett, who came to Oxford from Harvard to take his DPhil. with his ideas already firmly in place, Ryle said he'd never had a more effective student. On the subject of editing, in which I too had gathered some experience, Ryle confided that he looked sceptically on papers submitted with covering letters in green ink. I saw the point: why should anyone spend time looking for green ink when blue or black were there for the taking? I was reminded of several such covering letters I had received and now wondered whether their authors had tried Ryle first. He also asked about Jakob Meløe, a Norwegian and maverick philosopher whose single-minded and round-the-clock Wittgensteinian approach to life had made him something of a celebrity in Oxford in the late 'sixties. I could tell Ryle that, formerly at Bergen and Aarhus, Meløe was now professor in far north Tromsø and applying his language-game analyses to local conditions there under the title of 'praxeology'. Recalling our exchange at the oral examination, I bravely asked him if there were 'mental images?' 'Of course', he replied but without expanding. I was emboldened to mention that earlier negative advice about a career in philosophy. He had of course no recollection of that correspondence. The only answer I received was a typically gruff, 'probably the wrong advice'.

Looking back I can see it may well have been the right advice. And in any case, I didn't decide on a career in philosophy; it had seemed out of the question. I simply slid into it, the career attaching itself to me in a loose kind of fashion. Generally, I would say that I have managed to weave my own way through it and that it is to Ryle that I owe the manner best suited to me, inviting incredulity at what such a notable thinker would have us believe. Ryle was also a better stylist and more broad-minded in his approach to philosophy than many of his famous English colleagues. Few of these would be able to see in that famous book *The Concept of Mind*, what in Dennett's language might be called a hetero-phenomenological appendix to Heidegger's *Being and Time*. Ryle knew his Heidegger. He was exceptional. Born the same year as my father (1900), he died the year after this last meeting.

A glimmer of light in this time of limbo came from another direction. The colleague to whom I owe most for an opportunity to find what, for me, was a more constructive approach was Ted Honderich, my almost exact coeval and post-graduate colleague at University College. As an influential editor, Ted's commissioning was now ranging widely. Even before that year in Berkeley he had written to ask if I knew anyone who, for the princely sum of two hundred and fifty pounds, might translate 'well' and 'extensively introduce' Kierkegaard's *Concluding Unscientific Postscript* for Pelican. Possibly at a party, I must have mentioned my interest in Kierkegaard to Ted in passing. I had scarcely looked into that book at the time and my Danish was certainly not up to it. So I discounted myself from the start though able to offer some suggestions gathered from my own recent editing. Not finding any there to his satisfaction, Ted then asked if I'd consider doing it myself. Though prone to setting myself impossible tasks, there was enough to do already. Editing *Inquiry* unassisted was a half-time job in itself and for the next three years I was committed to my research project. After that I would need to look for a reliable source of income.

Two years later, after a spell in London, Ted asked me if I knew anyone who could write a book on Kierkegaard himself. Probably several could have done it, but at that time I was too out of touch to be able to suggest any names. Then, in October 1971, he wrote again asking if I wanted to write 'the Kierkegaard book' for his Arguments of the Philosophers series. My first reaction was to say no, but having thought it over the task struck me as not entirely impossible. By then I knew enough to get started and could read Kierkegaard in Danish. I said yes, subject to knowing how long I could take and more about the intentions of the Arguments series. Ted informed me that the 'official' delivery time would be two years from signing. After reading the general intentions, though not knowing quite how Kierkegaard would fit them or vice versa, and certainly far from qualified at the time to write such a book, I said yes and signed a contract with Routledge and Kegan Paul on 6 March 1972.

Contact with Oslo was confined to lecturing once a week as Naess's deputy. In the summer after our return there was a three-day seminar where Imre Lakatos and Paul Feyerabend were planned to lock horns on scientific method with Richard Popkin in attendance. True to form, Feyerabend failed to appear but there were lively exchanges between Lakatos and Naess. After the sessions Lakatos suggested I visit them at the London School of Economics. Eager not to miss this chance of temporary escape from Norway, Joanne and I decided to spend the remaining period of my research grant and a little besides in London. Arrangements were made through Lakatos to be given academic visitor status from September to January. It gave access to the Senior Common Room and the part of the library reserved for academic staff. No office, but since I was mainly interested in meeting people this seemed more than good enough. There was a weekly seminar and ample opportunity to talk to colleagues. My mother agreed that we could stay with her. It was something like a parallel to

Joanne's Californian 'home coming'. Like that one it was to prove not entirely successful. Used to living alone with her thoughts and a few family contacts of her own generation, it proved too much for my mother. Just before we left for Norway she had a breakdown.

The inner strains I can only guess at, but sharing her temperament in some ways I felt I understood. She was something of an involuntary loner, forced into solitude by thoughts of a world better than the everyday, one that she tended to face in a generally defensive way. Being a firm believer in homeopathy, she accepted her doctor's diagnosis that her breakdown had a physical cause related to some aspect of here tripartite nature. I am fairly certain the main reasons were situational and had to do with her relations to us and in particular me.

As for Joanne and myself, the stay was a case of life goes on. She was occupied with Jo and his nursery school. I was in daily contact with new colleagues. Asked to provide a paper for discussion at the weekly seminar I went into panic mode: it wasn't to be until just before we left in March and it hung over me obsessively during the whole stay, during which I formed a brief and cordial but only partly collegial attachment to an American Ph.D. student. The complications and attendant pressures plagued me during the latter part of the stay.

Joanne and I did some social visiting. We called on Timothy and Giglia Sprigge in Lewes, and on Ernest Gellner in Petersfield. I went sailing with Gellner at Hayling Island. Our own daily lives became disconnected and life together non-committal. Perhaps some awareness of this contributed to my mother's breaking out at last in tears, but the emotional strain of re-relating to a long-absent and outwardly much-changed son cannot have helped.

The weekly seminar initiated by the now retired Karl Popper was still named after this illustrious initiator of Critical Rationalism. It also retained notorious features due to his manner of conducting it, most of all the habit of interrupting speakers so insistently that they scarcely began their papers let alone finished them. The current protectors of his image and myth religiously upheld this unpleasant custom. For Popper, it was his insistence on terms being used in the way he used them, together with the assumption that his own works provided the terms of reference for anything worth discussing. I had seen this technique enacted by both Imre Lakatos and John Watkins. The seminar itself focused on scientific methodology, a topic Popper had famously contributed to in his *Logic of Discovery* with its thesis that it is a scientific claim's ability in principle to be falsified that makes it meaningful, not the ability of more evidence to support it 'inductively'. Besides being followers of the Popperian tradition in scientific methodology, and developing it in various intriguing ways, Imre Lakatos and John Watkins also owed allegiance to Popper's other main contribution, namely political philosophy.

Karl Raimund Popper was a Viennese, born in 1902 into a family of Jewish origins but with both parents Christianized. He left Austria before the *Anschluss* and, while a lecturer in New Zealand, wrote the influential *Open Society and Its Enemies*. As Professor of Philosophy and Scientific Method at LSE he became widely known as a vigorous defender of liberal democracy. The philosophical direction known as Critical Rationalism grew from an amalgamation of principles underlying these two main preoccupations. LSE being the erstwhile base of Friedrich August von Hayek, the Austrian-born economist and defender of free-market capitalism, had traditions to which Popper's political leanings were well adapted. Under his growing influence its philosophy department became something like an anti-collectivist counterpart to New York's New School of Social Research, where European émigrés in the Marxist Frankfurt School tradition had established themselves.

Imre Lakatos, originally Avrum Lipsitz, was twenty years younger than Popper. His mother and grandmother had perished in Auschwitz. A mathematician, he became a senior communist official in the Hungarian ministry of education but after a period of study in Moscow was imprisoned for three years on charges of revisionism. On release, he continued to be active in dissident circles and after the 1956 Hungarian Revolution fled to Vienna and then England. At Cambridge he wrote a dissertation demonstrating how mathematics conformed to Popper's falsifiability criterion. From there it was but a short step to the LSE.

As a failed conservative politician, John Watkins' route was less direct, but not before having completed a career as a naval officer with a DSC for successfully engaging German E-boats prior to the Normandy invasions. It was von Hayek's *Road to Serfdom* that convinced Watkins of the dangers of socialism. He began studying at the LSE while von Hayek was still lecturing there, then turned from Government to Philosophy, and later became President of the British Society for the Philosophy of Science.

My journal *Inquiry* had just published a long and polemical review of *Criticism and the Growth of Knowledge*, a collection edited by Lakatos and Watkins. Consistently an expression of Popperian correctness, the book was savagely seized upon by Joseph Agassi, himself by upbringing a Popperian, former lecturer at LSE, prolific author, and at that time a professor of philosophy commuting between Tel-Aviv and York University in Canada. Now a renegade, he had entitled his review 'Tristram Shandy, Pierre Menard, and All That'. Agassi's style in print and as teacher — it could be called Socratic

— was severely contextual, taking up issues as they came and looking at them provocatively and not according to the programme of any 'school', not even the one in which he had been schooled himself. That *Inquiry* had published this review seemed to amuse Lakatos, who treated me in a very friendly way, but it clearly rankled with Watkins, who I overheard referring to me as 'that stinker' while we were standing in the queue for lunch in the senior common room. On his companion pointing out that I was standing close behind, Watkins remarked less than convincingly that he'd never say such a thing in the person's absence. I have heard many academics saying nasty things of their colleagues. Indeed one of them called Arne Naess a 'loathsome creep' to his face. That was unusual and with no academic basis. As for absent fellows, I once heard Hugh Mellor refer to Feyerabend as a 'wanker' and Judith Jarvis Thomson to Bert Dreyfus as a 'twerp', both of them colleagues that I confess I owed more to than to their denigrators.

Administrative obligations kept Lakatos away when it came to my turn at the seminar. The topic was a concept devised by Popper himself in a memorial lecture included in a collection, published a few years earlier: *Of Clouds and Clocks: An Approach to the Problem of Rationality and the Freedom of Man*. It was designed to justify our ordinary belief that someone's present location can be explained by their purpose, by their intention to be there. The scientist himself, the American physicist Arthur Holly Compton whom Popper's lecture had been commemorating, nicely used himself as illustration. In giving his own lecture at Yale, Compton had asked his audience what right they had, considering the extreme improbability of this event seen in purely physical terms, to expect a phototropic, or heat-seeking, organism like himself to leave 'sunny' Italy to come to 'chilly' New Haven to give a lecture.

Quite rightly, Popper had already rejected the Heisenberg uncertainty principle as a way of introducing the required freedom into a physical system; it was not the kind that action guided by reason should exemplify. But he thought he had a viable alternative and called it 'plastic' control. In effect, however, or so I argued after much cogitation, all the models of this kind of control that his paper offered could show was how certain outcomes remain indeterminate while under the influence of a given control, and that the activity specified by that control, for instance keeping a promise or not disappointing expectations, can become unspecified by being brought under another and higher control, for instance avoiding pneumonia. Neither possibility allowed room for what Popper required, namely volition. It would require that subjection to a particular control was itself something over which one had control.

I still don't know whether my arguments actually destroyed Popper's notion. But the talk went down well enough and Lakatos told me that Watkins had said it was a success. I had the feeling that, so long as they themselves had some non-plastic control over the critic, they didn't really mind having Popper made a target of criticism. They may even have relished it. But for me the main achievement was to complete the talk at all, something that would most certainly have been impossible if Popper himself had been present. The trick was to tell Watkins at the start that I had a criticism of his own interpretation of Popper's concept of 'plastic control' at the very end of the paper. Whenever someone in the customary manner interrupted, Watkins would break in and say, 'No, let Hannay get on with the paper'.

An expanded version appeared in the *Canadian Journal of Philosophy* in December 1972 as 'Freedom and Plastic Control'. I sent it there because the editors were seeking papers to get their journal started. Stuart Hampshire, to whom I sent an offprint, said nice things about it, but I have never seen a single reference. If 'Popper' had been included in the title there might have been a response; as it stands it sounds rather like an advertisement for preventatives.

The talk provided my only real opportunity to return to Britain as an accredited academic. Sitting in front of me as I gave my talk, and to my alarm with his eyes mostly shut, was Stanislav Andreski (or Stanislaw Leonard Andrzejewski), the Polish-born head of the sociology department at Reading, one that he had recently founded. Still on the lookout for likely colleagues, and with a long-standing relationship to LSE, he may have plied Lakatos for suggestions. Or maybe he was just visiting. Although to all appearances sleeping off a good lunch, Andreski, in his relaxed style and attire slightly hippie, found nothing to object to in my talk. If actually asleep, he may have made up his mind already. He asked me if I was interested in a job at Reading and invited me to come there and look around. I went. The sequence of events is lost to my memory, but one experience still stands out. Lining up for lunch in the Reading University senior common room cafeteria, I thought, no, I quite definitely don't want to be here, these are not my people, it's like being back at school.

Was it cowardice? While working on my paper I had turned down an invitation to talk to the philosophers' senior seminar at Warwick. That was stupid, since I could have given my thoughts a trial run there. But I felt untried in the procedures, and to tell the truth, with my efforts over the years to speak Norwegian, English was no longer at the tip of my tongue. A sense of insecurity in academic circles in general was something that never left me and now it took over. The reason I gave myself for not pursuing this unique opportunity was that my engagement with problems of the mind and consciousness was vocational. It was the only reason I had for persevering with philosophy. The prospect of having to bone up on sociology, a subject known to me largely through the colossal amount of routine research produced by Norwegian sociologists, would mean more delay or even indefinite postponement. Back in Norway a letter from Ernest Gellner said 'the people at Reading were very sorry when you decided to withdraw and had been looking forward to having you with them'. It seems I lost an excellent chance to pursue a more widely focused career. Only recently I remembered how a review article by Gellner in an issue of *Inquiry* that Peter Frøstrup had sent to me in London had opened the door for me to the problems and procedures of sociology and social anthropology. Had I known more about 'Stan', who died in 2007 at eighty-eight, he could have been an inspiring mentor. Described in the *Guardian*'s obituary as an outstanding scholar, 'politically astute' as well as a 'polyglot' and 'internationalist', a 'British scholar with eastern roots and a word-wide perspective', Andreski wrote on contemporary issues and developed a critical theory of capitalism and its roots. Owing nothing to fashions or trends, his career was of his own making. The books in which he first read Max Weber were paid for by food and cigarettes as a member of the British occupation forces in Germany.

That was the outcome of a story on its own. A student in economics at Poznan, on the outbreak of war Andreski had been mobilized as an officer cadet and sent to the eastern front. He was captured by the Soviets but escaped before the Katyn atrocity, in which at Stalin's command practically all of his comrades were murdered. Dressed as a tramp, he managed to return through the Soviet and German occupation zones to Poznan, and together with a school friend crossed into the less strictly controlled Slovakia. Travelling now by train to Hungary without documents, he eluded suspicion by reading German newspapers. On reaching Britain he joined the Polish forces and after the war became an extra-mural student at LSE, taking his Ph.D. in 1953.

In Reading I might have overcome paranoid fears about British university life. It would also have provided a convenient escape from the abstract niceties of analytic philosophy in its already increasingly scholastic vein. Still, as Timothy Sprigge in sympathizing with my decision pointed out, it would require a change of course. Again, I felt it was too late for that. In any case the die was cast. My exile in northern latitudes looked like becoming permanent.

Chapter Thirteen: Long shots

Long shots: in old warships the muzzle-loading cannon were charged with black powder of uncertain potency and the odds were therefore against a hit when firing a 'long shot'.

A long-term alternative to Norway was not to be abandoned without a struggle. In late July 1970 one more cast was made at sunnier horizons. While Joanne and Jo were crossing the United States by Greyhound to visit her parents, I flew to Athens. There had been difficult times at home. Conversation tended to end in recrimination. In deciding to sell the house, the reasons were largely negative. I know my own part in this, the provocation in my own reticence and edginess not to mention obsession with my work. All of it was upsetting for Jo.

I had written to Maria earlier saying I was thinking of a job at the British Council in Athens, teaching English and writing on the side. Visions of a small house on an island with best sellers flowing from my pen was just another of those desperate dreams that crop up in critical times. I arranged to visit Athens for a week from the end of July. It was in the Junta time and I stayed with Maria and her two children.

Now divorced and not yet remarried, Maria had a married friend in the offing and we agreed there was no future for us together. As for the British Council, their representative was surprised that anyone with a London Ph.D. should want to teach forty hours a week. He looked at me with suspicion, as if perhaps I had some connection with MI5. The teaching load closed that option and with all ideas of a future with Maria scuppered I headed home with a melancholy tear. As a buffer before reaching home, I stopped off at Rome. With a hire car, and armed with detailed instructions that I had been given beforehand, I visited my cousin Joslyn and her husband Joe Tilson holidaying on their Tuscany farm, not far from Cortona. I hadn't seen them since we were lodging in their house in London prior to departing for Norway more than ten years earlier. There was comfort in their company and we all visited another cousin there from New Zealand. Rowena Hill, now resident in a disintegrating Venezuela, was living in a historic house on the hills outside Firenze. It was a strangely disturbing step back into my own past and left a sense of regret at losing touch with so much of it in my pursuit of whatever it was I was pursuing.

With the choice of channels now clear I returned to Oslo. While Joanne and Jo were away I lived in the luxury of a new house in Oslo overlooking

Bunnefjord and owned by our friends Tony and Anne-Lo Richardson. Tony had left for the States and another woman and Anne-Lo asked me to look after the house while she too was away. Rather than experience the loneliness of living in a house up for sale, I accepted her invitation to stay until Joanne and Jo returned. The sense of independence was euphoric and insinuated into my mind the thought of finding a place to live by myself. I worked enthusiastically on a paper for a conference to be given in Oxford in the not far-off future. When Ann-Lo returned, I vaguely recall and hesitate to attempt to describe an agreeably unbuttoned evening in the company of Thor Heyerdahl's son, also Thor, and his girlfriend.

It was early autumn when we moved to the new apartment in Oslo. It meant driving a large rental van twice in one day, with Jo as passenger, transporting all or most of our belongings. Once there, the novelty and convenience of living in a city with all its amenities was refreshing. There was the liberating fact that it took only twenty minutes to walk to the campus or, indeed, almost anywhere. The flat was small with only one bedroom, which was given to Jo and his electric train. Joanne and I slept in the living room on a convertible sofa. It was absolutely necessary to find rented space nearby where I could work uninterrupted. At the university I was still sharing an office.

That autumn it was John Searle who used the other desk. Dagfinn Føllesdal, my usual office companion, was fulfilling his permanent part-time commitments at Stanford. Searle had come from Berkeley to teach action-theory and the visit was a major event in many respects, not least in so far as John was the only colleague in my experience to arrive on campus in the morning on skis. Hoping to live in an airy modern concrete and glass Scandinavian-style building, it was a disappointment to be assigned an ethnically correct small-windowed timbered house as dark inside as out. Almost on arrival, John had to be taken to the emergency hospital to treat an eye after crashing into a half-open door.

Nor was the campus in 1971 all that it might have been. In the grip of a sorry rehearsal of the student unrest that had originated in Berkeley and taken a more seriously disruptive turn in Paris, forces not to be outshone were at work that led two years later to the establishment of a Norwegian Maoist party with 'armed revolution' as its slogan. Halfway through Searle's course there was a student strike. Faculty were urged to join, but few did. The immediate grievance was the state budget's poor provisions for the university, something at which all academic parties were aggrieved. Mostly, it was a political stunt to widen support for the overthrow of the corrupt Norwegian way of life.

Searle, by an unlucky chance or naïve mismanagement, had been invited on a NATO scholarship. Once this became known, there was a move to boycott his lectures. The leader of the boycott was none other than Naess's son Ragnar. Since the visit had been at his father's suggestion while in Berkeley, this unfortunate turn of events was one that Searle could understandably sense as discordant. When, in a Socratic spirit, he invited a delegation to his seminar to discuss their reasoning, their performance proved no match for his, and all they could do was resort to mind-numbing slogans. Although the boycott was partially successful, colleagues, myself included, rallied in support of the seminar, with the result that not only was attendance satisfactory but the level of discussion higher than if Searle's audience had been confined to students with only a mediocre command of English. Due to his famously punchy style, the lectures were invigorating in themselves, not least because this was clearly a trial run on a topic that had newly interested Searle himself. It meant that he welcomed participation.

There would be more discord. Naess while in Berkeley had mentioned his mountain cabin and led Searle to assume that he could have the run of it. But now the cabin was equipped for expeditions and not 'family weekends'. Other things reinforced Searle's antipathy. Sharing our office, he gained some idea of my own activities and discovered that I was doing all the work for a journal the editorship of which, Naess not yet the guru of deep ecology, was his main claim to international fame. I also let slip un-diplomatically that Naess once remarked to me that it was just as well I was not ambitious. Ambition being the very bread of American academic survival, Searle was deeply indignant on my behalf and his eye falling on the manuscript of my forthcoming *Mental Images* he began to take an interest in my future. I said I had made some overtures to Sussex, and he told me to jump at the chance. The following year, this and all other attempts on my part at escape having failed, after speaking with a Norwegian colleague who had passed through Berkeley, John wrote saying he 'figured' I was still getting a 'raw deal'. Although it was, as he said, none of his business, he thought they should 'stop exploiting' me, adding it was still a 'project' of his to get me to California.

Another visitor from the USA at that time was Karel Lambert, known as 'Joe' to distinguish him phonetically from his wife Carol. Joe was professor of logic at the Irvine campus of the University of California. Since his once-a-week lectures were devoted to the esoteric topic of free logics, he escaped the scrutiny of the campus revolutionaries. He also kept a lower profile than Searle, for whom that would be uncharacteristic. Joe wrote to Maurice Natanson suggesting I might be suitable for Santa Cruz. By this time, however, Natanson had colleagues he would have to convince, and for whom Norway would be close to Greenland. After some tentative efforts on my own for positions nearer home, again lacking both reputation and supporters, I was no part of any candidate 'pool'. I naturally fell by the wayside as one of sixty applicants for a job at the Open University. In my naïveté, on seeing an advertisement for a lectureship at LSE I had written to Lakatos. As a man of wide political experience, he would think I was crazy to suppose they hadn't already earmarked the position for one of their own.

In Norway now it seemed for keeps, the future had to be adjusted accordingly. There was much to attend to. At his first kindergarten Jo suffered for not being sufficiently Norwegian, a situation he had never encountered in a fjord-side village among only friendly children. Oslo was and is not the cosmopolitan city it likes to believe it has become. When Joanne accompanied me to see Jo off on the local train to a replacement kindergarten on the hill behind Oslo, he seemed clearly embarrassed by what his playmates would say. But then many children in the company of their coevals find their parents embarrassing. He told me later that he was unprepared for the tough exteriors put on by Oslo's well-off youngsters. Things went better when he began school near home, not least thanks to Joanne's efforts in activating the school orchestra. He played his violin in concerts given in Oslo's new concert hall by the city's combined school orchestra and was admitted some years later to the Norwegian Academy of Music.

Worse was the failure of his parents to produce harmony at home. Some harmonious streak in his own being must be why he didn't suffer more than he appeared to. As it was, Jo showed a kind of sad understanding that put us both to shame. We had bought a television set and watched the several BBC and Granada series shown on Norwegian television, including memorably *A Family at War*. Watching a scene in which after some set-piece acrimony the mother and father sat beside each other on a sofa holding hands, six-year-old Jo came up behind us, grasped our heads and pressed them together. Words could not have said more.

Back in 1964, correspondence with the mother of my first son on my informing her of Joanne and our engagement had come to an untidy halt. Norma had even planned to settle in Oslo to be near me, writing at one point to say that she and Tim were taking next Tuesday's boat from Newcastle. I dissuaded her, although I imagine that our mutual friend Fiona had a hand in that too. The exchange had ended on a high-pitched note, anguish on her part followed by well-directed comments on my immaturity seasoned by some admission of her thoughtlessness. I was told not to send her more money. Now, however, seven years had passed and Tim wanted to make contact. He was twelve years old. A visit was arranged and he was to arrive by Pan Am in Bergen. I drove over and picked him up. We spent a couple of days driving through scenic mid-Norway, rowed on Vangsvatnet, the lake on which the tourist town Voss stands, passed through the Dovrefjell mountain range, and threw stones into the Glomma River at Otta. In Oslo, in spite of a five-year difference in age, Tim and Jo got along together. For us both, and not least for Tim, the situation was strained and the tension could be felt on our drive to Oslo. I noted traits I recognize in myself: a tight-lipped manner of expression and a short fuse under stress. They were features I also recognized in his mother: all three of us were much alike. However, the exercise was generally successful and a basis established for future contact. On a visit to Edinburgh the following summer I stayed over with Tim and his mother.

Having signed the contract with Routledge in March, I began reading Kierkegaard in earnest. Once started, I found in him an odd mixture of radical and conservative, making him difficult to pin down, though to the author himself this seemed to be something to relish. The more I read, the more impossible seemed the task of collecting his thought into a volume on a series devoted to recognized philosophers and their arguments. Challenged, I felt the only course would be to focus on this task exclusively, apart that is from editorial duties, until it was completed.

For that I needed a job. A readership in political and social philosophy became available at Oslo. I applied in spite of these not being my topics and Kierkegaard obviously having no well-defined place in them. In the event I came second in the 'competition', as is the nature of appointments in Scandinavia, with reasons given by a committee for the order in which qualified candidates pass the line. I had to look further. With a week in Paris on my own to reflect on the situation, I entertained airy thoughts of finding some way of eking out a living there even, in the hope of finding cheap accommodation, re-visiting the street where the old hotel had been where Leif and I put up far back in the 'fifties. Both the place and the hotel had been rehabilitated into up-market apartments, the more fashionable for being fronted by their old *façades*. I asked an estate agent how much they cost. It was not out of the world. I would take these thoughts back with me.

While dining there one evening in a Japanese restaurant just off rue St. Jacques, not far from George Whitman's (now) Shakespeare and Company, I overheard two Americans, evidently mother and daughter, energetically discussing the latter's plans to study philosophy in Paris. We got into a conversation that ended with the daughter taking my address before rushing off to some other appointment while her elegant silver-haired mother asked if I would like join her at an organ recital at the nearby Église Saint-Severin. I would and did. When we parted I told her I would, if needed, help with whatever plans her daughter Jeanne came up with.

Back in Oslo that autumn, a chance meeting with Ingemund Gullvåg, former student of Arne Naess and a philosopher well versed in the locally unpopular analytic tradition, led to the next step in my career. Gullvåg had recently set up a new philosophy department in Trondheim, a former Teacher Training College being upgraded to a College of Arts and Sciences (later fused with the prestigious Norwegian Institute of Technology to form the present Norwegian University of Science and Technology). With experience of the higher professional standards of philosophy abroad, both in Sweden and the UK, he was on the lookout for non-native talent. There would be two new positions in Trondheim, a readership and a professorship and he said he had thought of me in connection with the first. Not asking why I shouldn't try for the second or who he had in mind for that, I decided there and then to apply for both. They would be advertised successively and the process of appointing would take at least a year. Meanwhile I was still deputizing for Arne Naess. Joanne, together with her friend Anne-Lo, signed up at a school for social workers.

In October a letter came from Paris. Jeanne Brody reminded me of our brief meeting in Paris that summer and concluded with the hope that the letter didn't 'seem like incoherent babbling from a stranger'. She regretted not having had a chance to talk but had been encouraged by my telling them I had left university for two years before returning again to study philosophy full-time. She, too, was taking a break although, to enjoy the benefits of a student card had signed up at Nanterre. In New York her courses had been haphazard — she mentioned Heidegger, Wittgenstein, Austin, Searle, Lévi-Strauss — there had been 'no firm foundation in Descartes, Kant, just to mention a few'. This to me was a typical result of the way philosophy is too often presented to university students. To be 'in' philosophy they are made to skim a wide selection of currently visible thinkers whose real claim to fame is that they devoted their own lives wholly to working out ways of seeing things according to their individual lights. No better method could be devised for actively preventing students from finding their own way, or from seeing the deeper point of pursuing the quite distinctive paths these famous figures followed or themselves forged. I had been fortunate in this way. Edinburgh gave us a solid background in the traditions from antiquity to Descartes, Spinoza, Kant and not a few others, while in London I had been confronted with the locally accepted rules of the game. In France, Jeanne was lucky to be there at a time when Marx was still an influential background thinker. She said she had been trying to fill the political holes in her education and was reading Fanon, Han Suyin, Mao, and Jan Myrdal, and was about to embark on a study of economics. She said she thought the benefit of her university education in the USA had been to put pressure on her to read things that she would have not found the motivation to go through on her own, while now she was quite prepared to go it alone. I had told her mother that I edited a philosophy journal and Jeanne would like to see it. She suggested we keep up a pen-pal relationship and I sent her some copies of *Inquiry*.

In her next letter Jeanne thanked me for these but said she found them hard to tackle. I had told her my own story and mentioned my reservations about academic philosophy. She agreed but said the American system was tolerant compared with what she had seen of the European; the former did not discourage spontaneity and creativity in the way the French system clearly did. In two minds about pursuing her 'maitrise', which would require a dissertation, she felt she might learn more and teach others more effectively on 'the streets'. She was focusing on Marx and thought of writing her dissertation on the Marxist notion of alienation. It wasn't easy to study on one's own without the pressure exerted by a university course and I felt life was going to be hard for her. I had said I might be returning to Paris some time and she had told me to say when. She would arrange something for me.

The more the Trondheim committee took its time, the less my thoughts dwelt on the north. To balance what looked increasingly like an inescapable move to even more northern climes, I had arranged with Maria to look for some property in Greece. It should be by the sea or in Athens itself. After some discussion we decided on Athens and I opened a common account there, transferring the amount of money I could spare for the project and which Maria would pay in instalments as building progressed. She informed me not long afterwards that an architect and engineer friend was building a new block of flats in a quiet area near the north end of Patision, a short tram-ride north of the city centre. A down payment for a flat of fifty-four square metres at 1-3 Salteli on the first floor up and with a back balcony was made in early February. Later in the month I visited Maria and her family in Athens. In a shared taxi I also met Takis, her 'professor', a surgeon who she later told me was jealous of our easy relationship. I can understand that.

In April a letter arrived from Jeanne Brody in Paris expressing dislike of an article in *Inquiry* by Jason Xenakis. I disliked it too and don't recall why we published it except that, as still nominal editor, Naess had met Xenakis at a conference in the USA. Jeanne said she hoped to see me soon in Paris. She told me that in these two years since we briefly met she had become part of a 'politically oriented collective'. Her plan was to exploit the connection academically by making it the theme of her *maitrise*. What interested her was the relation of the collective to the individuals who formed it and their relation as individuals to it. On arriving in Paris I was to meet her at the collective's 'librairie', where she worked in between giving English lessons. I was told about the collective and its plan to go on a collective walk the following Sunday. This would be a good opportunity to talk. I said I'd like to join them little realizing that this was a stage on a progression already begun on the way to even greater hikes. More modest distances had preceded it to enhance endurance, thus allowing the collective gradually to work its way up to the big one from Paris to Orleans. Luckily my visit came before that.

This Sunday's hike was from Ile de la Chaussée on the Seine to Versailles and back. It took a 'green' route which meant trudging a distance of some twenty-five kilometres. After meeting near their collectively run restaurant, La Gavroche, we were crammed into two closed vans and driven to the starting-point. It was in late spring and we went in groups. I spoke with a lady, I think a teacher, about philosophy. There was no point saying 'French' philosophy since philosophy was whatever French philosophers of the day were known to proclaim. For her it was Foucault, for me then only a name. But it was a friendly occasion. As to the purely athletic aspects of the walk, I hung on as best I could. Driven back to the restaurant, I hobbled along to my hotel to rest having planned to go to a concert that evening. But on waking I was unable to get up from the bed. There was nothing of its political aspect to note in this outing, yet it was well organized and there was some sense of the group forming a core of co-operative activity, rather like that on a ship though here with the city the element to contend with. In non-political terms it was easy to see that whatever political notions were shared with the organizers, the collective was a constructive resort for the otherwise isolated and lonely. For me the exercise did wonders for the circulation in my legs, and for some time after, quite unusually, I had no problems with long periods of standing still.

In our further correspondence on my Kierkegaard project Ted Honderich could tell me of a job in moral philosophy at Glasgow. He gave me names to contact, but I made no move. It seemed like going backwards or sideways. To end up in Glasgow would be like a rocket landing too near its launching pad. Worse, it called for the mental re-tooling that Timothy Sprigge had agreed was a good reason for withdrawing from Reading. My target area was bounded by Trondheim and Athens with Paris as a transit station.

A holiday in Britain was no infringement. My cousin Joslyn and her husband Joe asked if we could take care of their large Wiltshire home, The Old Rectory, at Christian Malford near Chippenham while they spent their usual summer in Tuscany. That seemed an opportunity to revisit the old country, but we chose to make a decent journey of it and drove to Bergen through hitherto unvisited parts of Norway, including Lærdal where we camped and Joanne got badly stung by a horsefly (known as a cleg or *klegg* both in Scotland and Norway). The car ferry from Bergen took us to Newcastle and the journey, so far as I recall, went via Carlisle my old home and Birmingham to Wiltshire. Once settled we bought a bicycle for Jo who enjoyed the company of a young minimalist poet and his wife living in a cottage on the property. It was a quiet time, the only hitch being Joanne's discovery of fleas in the large and comfortable bedroom. I don't believe I ever saw one, but we ended up sleeping on the large kitchen table. I found in their library the Hong translation of *Either/Or* and began to think about Kierkegaard again. There was a quick visit to my mother in Kensington before we returned to Oslo by way of Harwich and Esbjerg on the South Jutland coast, and then from North Jutland to Larvik in Southern Norway. Joanne and Jo then left once more for two weeks in San Francisco while I again stood guard over the home of our friend Anne-Lo.

I had hoped to spend those two weeks in Athens seeing to plans for the new apartment. But Maria said she would be away at that time. I flew there at the end of November instead when teaching was finished and stopped off in Paris on the way to find Jeanne immersed in the activities of the collective at the bookstore and the restaurant's kitchen where I spent an evening peeling potatoes. For her it was a deliberate 'plunge head first', as she called it, to test her limits. She had also helped to establish a new collectivité in Grenoble. Her full engagement meant she could no longer take the dispassionate attitude required of a dissertation on the collective's meaning for its co-members. She was having instead to take a dispassionate look at herself. Seeing a 'shrink' twice a week she had decided to write on alienation in connection with the artist in modern society. Even here it was hard to escape a personal element, or perhaps it was what she needed. Her father had died early as a struggling artist in New York. I asked her to send a copy of the dissertation if she thought I could help when it reached a stage where comment might be useful. She said she would. I felt on leaving that I should not have visited her just then and later she said as much: the visit had 'thrown' her. With no clear self-image, I can be blind to the effect I have on others and, as a consequence, insensitive to timings of meetings and their expected nature.

Equally unfortunate was the timing of my arrival in Greece. Two days after arrival there was a counter-coup within the Junta ranks. It followed the Athens Polytechnic uprising in early November and was organized by Dimitrios Ioannidis, head of the military police. After overthrowing Papadopoulos, he put the presidency in the hands of one of his friends, Phaedon Gizikis. Martial rule was installed and for several days I was unable to leave the hotel. When at last I could talk to Maria other than on the phone, she said that her lover Takis had invited her to Vienna. Having battled with him constantly to take her rather than his 'other half' on his travels, as she put it, this was more than she could resist or refuse. On later apologizing for her absence, she said Takis had treated her 'very well'. I said that in return for her indispensable help with the new flat she could treat it as hers.

I don't wink or give women the eye or in other ways try to draw their attention. But, in general and certainly over the long term I find women more rewarding as conversation partners and friends than men. Between collective locker-room talk that skims over individual hopes, fears and woes and the self-important chat with which they tell you what *they* think or have done, men with the exception of good neighbours and school friends are less good at mutual exchange. Whether by nature or situation, women at least in my experience seem better at it. The result may be more than conversational and not to everyone's benefit. My temptation is to say, 'So be it'.

As we flew north towards the lengthening day my Greece exploit seemed to assume the quality of yet another dream. Within a few years and due to another combination of coincidences, it was to seize me by the scruff of the neck and plunge two people into the rude awakenings of a twenty-three-year relationship that included a second marriage that lasted seventeen years.

Part Three: By and large

'If the wind was blowing from any point in the half-circle eastward of the line from north to south, from nearer the stern, the ship was said to be sailing large. *... To some extent sailing ships were able to make progress into the wind, that is, with it blowing from forward of the beam. In such cases, the ship was said to be sailing* by the wind, by *here having the sense of "towards".'*

Dave McClathchley

So as you see,' continued Harris, 'it is quite impossible to sail both by and large at the same time. It is a contradiction in terms...'
' "We do say by and large," said Jack. "We say a ship sails well by and large when she will both lie close when the wind is scant and run fast when it is free." '

Patrick O'Brian, The Truelove, or, Clarissa Oakes.

Chapter Fourteen: Higher latitudes

High latitudes: *latitudes around or above 600 N magnetic latitude. E.g.: Oslo: 59".53' 01.00" N.*

In December 1973 word came that I had been placed first for the readership in Trondheim. The remaining procedures were purely formal and arrangements were made for me to begin teaching in February as a visitor. Once appointed, I would be there for periods of ten days returning to Oslo for a long weekend every fortnight. This would reduce the pressure at home and I could focus on teaching and research as well as the editorial work that now took up a large part of the week. The philosophy department in Oslo agreed to reserve my desk in the office shared with Føllesdal. Retaining the journal's official editorial address was no drawback for the department and in picking up the mail every second Friday I would keep in touch with Oslo colleagues.

Soon after returning from Athens that spring I learned that Ben Lassers, the Californian medical student and now physician who had shared the apartment in Edinburgh, had died accidentally through carbon monoxide poisoning. The cause was a faulty Ascot water heater and lack of air. I could recall how careful Ben had been to insulate the windows and doors against the cold, and imagined how this may have contributed. It was a sad fate for a sun-loving Californian who only partly to escape enlistment had come there to study philosophy and became a respected cardiologist. Was there another parable here for those who look for new places to start over?

First impressions on a visit to Trondheim in late January were ominous. With its impressive cathedral and frontage on an expansive fjord to the north and east, and a horizon of distant hills, it was an attractive enough city. However, the department was situated (along with others) in a building that looked as if it could be converted overnight, or maybe re-converted, into a factory. It lay in the shadow of an iron foundry from whose four smoke stacks there belched billowing grey clouds. I had seen these before in a photograph. It showed my father and some fellow officers reclining on a hill above Trondheim while on an autumn cruise in 1930. Somehow that helped to make both the transition and the poor amenities more acceptable. But there had been another omen. Although on that first trip I had been told that I would be giving a lecture, on arrival I found that no one had told the students. What kind of operation was Gullvåg running up here, and how could they afford to fly me there just for a chat? However, some words with a colleague had the happy outcome that I would rent one of his rooms, not a place to sit and be at ease, but my quite large and airy office was nearby. The smoke stacks in full view would help to keep my thoughts down to earth.

In February 1974 with office gear, relevant books, clothing, radio and tape deck packed into the car, I headed north. It was like aiming at an arctic oasis in the wilderness on the way to the North Pole. Trondheim is only five hundred kilometres from Oslo, but to a non-Norwegian who has been no further north every mile can seem an adventure. In driving there that first time, it was with the expectation that this was an expedition from which I would return in about two years, not more, just long enough to get that book written.

Recalling similar hopes regarding the dissertation, ten years later I was still travelling that distance. Not however by car, since by then it had been wrecked one autumn evening on an over-hasty journey to the academic year's first departmental meeting. I was by then chairman or 'chair' as one is urged to say. It was a job I held for five years and which, together with increasing editorial labours, pushed the completion of the Kierkegaard manuscript into an ever-extending future. Another time-consuming novelty was teaching in Norwegian, in some cases to two hundred students at a time. That meant spending many hours carefully preparing my lectures and simultaneously improving my colloquial Norwegian.

But no intimation of these hazards disturbed my thoughts as I traversed a landscape that, aside from variations in altitude, was now made uniform by the white blanket of winter. Foremost in my mind was my Kierkegaard project. It had been pushed there more forcibly the last few weeks by the fact that I had been sharing that same office now with Barry Stroud, another Berkeley philosopher. Barry had a contract for a book in the same series, his on David Hume. Lecturing in Oslo on Hume, he would be using the occasion to polish up his manuscript chapters of which were splayed triumphantly like a fan across Føllesdal's desk. The sight of them concentrated my mind, and it was in a state of combined panic and determination that I drove northward trying to imagine a fan of my own. I had indeed started, beginning, however, at the end. I had written a chapter on the 'abstract' individual, thinking to protect Kierkegaard from Marx-inspired criticisms, but also using the comprehensive nature of Marxist thinking as a way of keeping in mind what I now guessed might be the equally wide embrace of Kierkegaard's own very differently angled thoughts.

Arriving in Trondheim tired and hungry in the late afternoon, I found a fried-chicken parlour in the town centre and then drove to the philosophy department to unload my books and make myself known. It was late and the only car still parked there was the personnel manager's. He was just getting into it. Seeing my own car loaded with luggage, and perhaps reflecting that had I been moving house it would have come as part of a larger load in a mover's van, he said he hoped I would be coming up there permanently. Words of a more welcoming kind would have been in place — if nothing personal at least some routine sentiments on behalf of the institution, a little comment off the bureaucratic cuff just to mark the moment. But Norwegians are better at set-piece celebration than casual settings calling for a sense of occasion. They are not social improvisers, nor is there a repertoire of habitual friendly phrases like 'Good to see you, come away in'; they seem to regard such forms of social lubrication as both redundant and false. Where, for instance, in France it is natural to acknowledge sharing a space however briefly by saying 'bonjour', Norwegians will steadfastly avert their eyes from fellow-shoppers or passers-by to avoid infringements of private space. There is a rule that for eyes to meet or tongues to wag you must first have greeted the other and shaken hands. It may, after that, become an insult not to say hello. I recall the horror expressed by a visiting Norwegian-American couple in an Oslo supermarket at the way in which the natives, aiming for whatever was next on their list, headed straight for it and if they dodged each other it was by virtue of some built-in reaction device more suited to an indoor sport. If static, as when meeting someone they know, they will stand there quite impervious to the possibility that they are in someone's way. But yes, once you are on hello terms, there is no end to Norwegian friendliness. What others find missing is a habit of courtesy. Barry Stroud commented to me that Norwegians seemed to move around in telephone kiosks. At least in my experience, Americans count on courtesy, while Norwegians are over-suspicious of social artifice. I used to put it down to a long history of sparsely inhabited valleys, but I remember a similar situation in New York. I was sitting alone at a café close to a bar beside group of Italian-Americans quite oblivious of my presence. Surrounding my table, they shouted at each other over my head. It has to be said for the less vociferous Norwegians that, to behave like that, they would have to be drunk.

The cool welcome reinforced my determination to shorten my stay as much as possible. Several things were to frustrate that intention, and it would take a ten-year conflict ending with my resignation to bring it to an end.

For eight of those years, home was a small room with an adjoining kitchen with one burner and no refrigerator. There was a small bathroom adjoining. My host, a taciturn but kindly colleague and at that time single, slept in the neighbouring room. We could hear each other's snores. The outside walls were badly insulated and in winter the chill could be felt if I rolled over in bed. Prices in Trondheim being much lower than in Oslo, I did think briefly of buying my own flat or even a small house, but a brake on that thought was the intention to stay no longer than necessary.

If that was one reason for scorning comfort, when necessity extended the stay I was led by a change in circumstances in Oslo to another thought, that of penance. In fact, with the Kierkegaard project at the back of my mind, I began to conceive of my northern exile as an experiment in existential independence and even self-chastisement, at any rate a means for investigating the rigours of existence itself, a time of fruitful suffering that might initiate me into the relevant psychology that could justify my rash acceptance of Ted Honderich's rash invitation.

Apart from the Spartan accommodation, a constant factor until near the close of that decade in Trondheim was on returning there from Oslo in the winters late on Sunday nights. Stepping off the airport bus to brave the icy winds sweeping through the dark and deserted streets, dragging my luggage the kilometre to my chilly room, was an experience designed to make the most sanguine person disconsolate and to provoke in any foreigner thoughts of 'why on earth here'? But luckily the workaday week with good colleagues was too full to allow such brooding and there was more than enough in life's detail to keep me occupied also at weekends. The short spells to Oslo, where the situation there was not that of a marriage, meant that 'home' had to become a variable that travelled with me.

For a while it took root in Trondheim. I became friendly with an about-to-be-divorced student, married and with a child. She had returned to the university to begin a career in teaching. But, for reasons that will appear, another attachment quite soon replaced that one. It, and several other factors, made my stay longer than anticipated, but shorter than it seemed at first destined to be. Looking back, other things been equal I might have found it in me to settle in this historic university town with its sense of independence and a lively population given to succinct humour. It also had a tradition in philosophy well ahead of Oslo's. I have before me an 1872 offprint of an article by the orthodox Hegelian professor in Oslo (then Christiania) M. J. Monrad taking to task an 1839 essay by Schopenhauer 'On Freedom of the Human Will'. It had been awarded first prize in a competition sponsored by the Royal Norwegian Society of Sciences and Letters with its seat in Trondheim and founded almost a hundred years before Oslo's Norwegian Academy of Science and Letters.

The official appointment to the readership came through in March 1974 in the form (as was then the custom) of a scroll signed by the king. Thus, at last, at the age of forty-two, I had a permanent job in a profession irresponsibly entered upon as a direct consequence of some wretched weekends and some chanced-on books in Bradford some eighteen years earlier. I celebrated with a lonely dinner ruminating on the turns of fate and directions of tidal drift that had landed me in this town in what was, for me at that time, furthest north.

In the Easter break Joanne and Jo joined me to go even further north. We embarked on a round sea-trip on the Express Coastal Route to Kirkenes at the Russian border and back. I began to realize, as the days and nights onboard ship went by, just how much more of Norway there was. Apart from being a fine way to spend the traditionally long Norwegian Easter break, it gave all three of us a vivid sense of the greater and more magical part of that country. Tensions were for the most part subdued and we revelled in the novelty.

Shortly before that Easter break Maria wrote to say that her husband Nasos had died of a heart attack while mowing the lawn at his new house. Although they had been separated for thirteen years, Nasos was still only in his early fifties. She expressed sorrow and was worried about the effect it would have on her two children. My flat would be ready at the end of June, so I suggested I visit them in the summer. Maria asked if Joanne might like to come along too, but the Easter exploration of the North Norwegian coast had been only a brief reprieve. The ripples on the smooth domestic surface had been duly noted by the ever-observant and sensitive seven-year-old Jo. He rightly called me 'umulig' (impossible). Recalling the word is almost worse than hearing it at the time. To add to the deficit, my obligatory medical check on becoming a member of the Trondheim faculty revealed serious hypertension. A friend in Oslo recommended a specialist and I began treatment. The medication sapped my energy further but when, after a summer catching up with editorial work and making some progress with Kierkegaard, I was asked by a colleague in Oslo to launder the language of his doctoral dissertation on David Hume, I could hardly refuse. On top of this I had begun to be targeted in connection with promotions and appointments abroad. Flattering but time-consuming.

Good news came from Paris, where Jeanne Brody had completed her maitrise, now more in the nature of 'prolegomena' to the study of alienation than a direct treatment of the topic. She had lots of 'ideas and plans' and thoughts of travelling, but spoke of a black cloud hanging over her head and wanting to shake it off. Her hands and feet are up, she wrote but her head is down. 'Nu?', she exclaimed, explaining that this is a Yiddish expression for 'What's new?' The books I'd sent her by Bertell Ollman and Richard Bernstein had been useful. I don't recall what I wrote in return. My mind was focused on Greece.

I flew alone to Athens for three weeks in August, finding furniture and kitchen equipment for the flat and indispensably helped by Maria's son Pericles, or Peri, still lamenting the death of his father. We bought an antique bench in Plaka and, there being much less traffic in Athens at the time, it was delivered on a cart. I stayed for a few days with Maria before moving in, days in which Peri gave full vent to his 'agony' and general discontent with life, while his sister Elektra remained dangerously silent. Then sixteen, she became an accomplished artist but also schizophrenic. Her life would end seventeen years later with an overdose. Three years after that her mother organized an exhibition of Elektra's poems, paintings and porcelain decoration. In 1994 she sent us an illustrated book about her daughter, published with Peri's financial support. North and South, it made no difference. There was misery everywhere.

In October the professorship was confirmed, but then hotly contested by a group of politically active philosophy students on the grounds that I lacked qualifications in practical philosophy, this being the area in which the position had been advertised. Behind the action were some of my own students. They assured me there was nothing personal in it; after all I already had a tenured job there. When it was pointed out to them that the main external member of the appointments committee was the Finnish philosopher Georg von Wright, the most prominent 'practical' philosopher of the time, they were forced to relent. That he was not a Marxist but an 'analytical' philosopher was not to the point, either, for von Wright was also a philosopher in the wider humanist tradition, writing for a general public on social and moral problems that affect everyone. Once this was made clear, peace was restored and a threatened boycott of my lectures cancelled. As a gesture to their genuine if less well-informed interests, I agreed to give a course on Neo-Marxism and the recent work of Jürgen Habermas.

In February 1975 a letter from Jeanne Brody in Paris told of some progress and plans to publish part of her thesis as an article, though with doubts because it criticized the 'super intellectual' magazine in which she had in mind to publish it. She said it would be nice to talk again. The long Easter break was in mid-March, which I spent in Athens, the only time I can recall making proper use of the apartment. On returning to Oslo via London I flew first to Paris for two days and, although my memory of the visit is vague, Jeanne wrote to say she'd enjoyed our evening together. I noted she was not in the best of spirits, and she said that she noted that I noted it. She spoke in her letter of life's rocky road but said I'd been a help.

In retrospect, I see the relationship as one that worked well enough because we were both struggling with our own quite specific problems even if in quite different situations and at a distance. She was going through what I might have undergone had I chosen to start off in Paris instead of Oslo. The same difficulties of loneliness, and yes, alienation also from oneself —

Jeanne talked of disliking herself. I was open with her and I doubt if either of us would have been so forthcoming in the complex switch-board of daily contact. Perhaps, not so strange to say, it was because our contact was mainly through correspondence that we came in a manner so near. Like me, she said, she was making her way as best she could. Her December letter had sounded miserable, but work at the bookstore ahead of Christmas and preparations in the self-help restaurant for a New Year dance had kept her going. Now twenty-eight, she would 'hang in there' for another nine months until her work card was renewed. There was one bright spot: she enclosed a copy of a letter that appeared in the *International Herald Tribune* on Martin Luther King. For some years we kept up a correspondence. In 1976 she sent me a copy of an article she had written for the political and cultural weekly *The Nation*. She asked if my Athens flat was available in September. It would take a tremendous effort to get out of Paris and face the world, but if she managed to pry herself out of her depression, she would try.

Jeanne reached Athens. She had said that she never felt lonely travelling. I feel much the same, sometimes lost perhaps but not lonely. In Athens she met Maria who, with typical Greek forthrightness, admonished her for staying in the apartment instead of exploring the sights. Writing afterwards Maria asked me please not to send her any more people like this 'sweet, lost and somewhat psychologically not quite right friend of yours'. Jeanne for her part spoke of the 'shy sweet Electra', someone with whom she must have had more in common. Jeanne also dined with my lawyer Haris Calpouzos, though what impression she made on him, or vice versa, I never discovered, but at least both were fluent in French. At Maria's she met Ian, my brother, then flying for British Air-Tours and a frequent visitor. She flew back on his flight to London. She thanked me for the flat saying I was a 'sweetheart'.

The Nation described Jeanne as now a journalist and novelist living in Paris. Subsequent letters came in envelopes stamped with the names of firms for which she worked: Merrill Lynch, Pierce, Fenner & Smith, dealing in 'wealth management', and which she described as 'pretty god awful'. There was also Publications Filipacchi, a multimedia firm feeding 'consumers' passions and lifestyles'. She worked for UNESCO in its world heritage branch and wrote asking about Bergen's famous quayside, Bryggen, though I couldn't help her there. In the late 'nineties I had a card from Toulouse, wondering if we might meet, since I was holidaying in Collioure. Nothing came of it. I suspect that was as well. A meeting in our later versions might spoil the memory of a mutually constructive past. The Internet recently told me she is now professor of anthropology at the University of Toulouse-Le Marail and specializes in the Diaspora.

It was in Oxford late in the summer of 1975 that, together with Knut-Erik Tranøy, I attended the symposium that proved to be my last meeting with Gilbert Ryle. Eager to put on a reasonable show on this all-or-nothing we call the 'mind' I returned to this, my first topic. The talk was supposed to take twenty minutes to half an hour with discussion to follow, but to clarify what I had in my own confused mind to say on this theme I needed to write a longer piece. Ted Honderich had been working in the same area and since it included a comment on his views, I sent him a draft. Ted wrote back with some quick but apposite comments, to which he added I need pay no attention. He told me to be less 'self-critical' and 'have confidence in the paper'. He found my style less forthright than his own.

The Oxford International Symposium took place at Christ Church from 29 September to 4 August 1975 under the auspices of the University itself and the German Academic Exchange Service. The number of participants had been kept low to give the debates the feel of a seminar. They came from Finland, the UK, France, Germany, Norway, Canada, Sweden, Yugoslavia and the USA. In being picked out as one of the two participants from Norway, with Tranøy and I both having connections with UK philosophy, he with Cambridge and Wittgenstein, I detected the hand of Gilbert Ryle. He was the chairman and it was in the Dining Hall at Christ Church on the occasion of the Symposium Banquet on 2 October that I found myself sitting, as recorded earlier, beside a friendly and convivial 'Uncle Gilbert' as he was known to visiting students who were grateful for his help and hospitality.

For me the whole symposium was a mixture of stress and wonder at being thrown into the company of some famous members of my ill-chosen profession. I enjoyed a comfortable room in Christ Church and was woken every day with early morning tea. The surroundings were idyllic, a world away from the smoke belching iron foundry under which my own 'campus' sheltered. To find calm and some mental repose I decided to attend evensong at the cathedral. On the way I found myself in the company of three others doing the same. One was a practising Catholic, Wittgenstein's most famous student and literary executor Elizabeth Anscombe, another Hilary Putnam, a former radical interested now in Judaism and widely respected logician, from Harvard. The third was Zeno Vendler, former Jesuit priest, a Hungarian philosopher of language and then professor at the University of Calgary in Canada. Their treating me as one of them mitigated my innate but carefully concealed sense of inferiority, even if the thought of having to speak in front of these celebrities sent quivers down my spine. There was reason. Miss Anscombe was noted for her merciless treatment of those whose views she found wanting. I had just seen her reduce a mild-mannered Canadian philosopher to red-faced confusion for daring to say something about which she believed she knew better. Worst of all, my talk was to be the last of the whole symposium. It meant that while listening to others' I was half-thinking of my own. But it went off better than I feared as later related to Ted Honderich:

> Well, it wasn't so bad. Neither the 'symposium' itself nor my modest contribution to same. You were right about the general discussion after my paper becoming a discussion of the paper — which in the circumstances I would rather have avoided. The circumstances included lousy acoustics —the final day's papers were held in something resembling an Indian Imperial railway station (called Examination Halls I believe), and extreme tiredness, and also something to which I myself am exceptionally prone: de-programming of the mind by over-exposure to other minds (my version of the 'other minds' problem). There was something a little surrealistic about it. Elizabeth Anscombe asked some slightly puzzled, probing questions, and a German told me I would have to accept the transcendental ego. Oh, yes, perhaps the most challenging remark was by Putnam who said it looked as if I'd have to accept subjective idealism too if I didn't distinguish my conscious arm-raising from my consciousness of arm-raising. We have four weeks to revise our papers, so I'll try to make it all clearer. Your notes were invaluable. I realise how much I miss and need that kind of first response.

The most satisfying outcome of my talk was being invited home to a reception given by Peter Strawson, the central Oxford philosopher at the time. He was intrigued at hearing such 'good English' emanating from someone from Norway and had asked John Searle, also in the audience, to invite me along. I scarcely recall the reception or my return to Oslo, but more vividly a chance meeting on the street with Hywel Lewis, the Welsh philosopher and theologian who was also editor of the Muirhead Library of Philosophy in which my revised dissertation had been included. My talk had given him the impression that I was an unforgiving materialist. Lewis, whose works then included, in order of publication, *The Elusive Mind*, *The Self and Immortality*, *Persons and Life after Death*, to which was later added *The Elusive Self*, must have understood the dissertation's 'defence' of mental imagery as a definitive siding with a Cartesian version of dualism of the kind that these titles suggest. Focusing on the first-person point of view, I'd argued its inseparability from whatever physical events come within the orbit of active intelligence. Its target had been the physicalist scenario that sees no need to make room for that point of view. So I wasn't as bad as Lewis suspected, it was at least a beginning on the way back to the soul. Just before leaving, I ran into him outside Christ Church.

He looked concerned and said he gathered that I didn't share his belief in the separability of souls. I hadn't actually said so and considered the matter still open, if not quite in his terms. There was some correspondence in which I tried to clarify our differences in a way that brought my view closer to his, but it was frustrating not to have time and opportunity to deal with this issue more personally.

Ever to be regretted, in my state of decompression I dropped plans to stop off in London to visit Ted Honderich and also Johnny Watling, the latter also a friend from my UCL days. Instead, I recuperated at my mother's new home at Ham Common near Richmond.

Soon after this, the autumn of 1975, I was amazed to receive an invitation from an organization calling itself the International Cultural Foundation. It was to a conference in Washington. Never having heard of them, I wondered, why me? As many others know, it was founded by Sun Myung Moon, the 'spiritual' leader of the Unification Church. I assumed it was because I was an editor that I came into their picture. This was confirmed when Arne Naess told me that he too had been invited, both of us associated with *Inquiry*. It felt like being part of a religiously inspired globalizing conspiracy. The world, according to the Church, required a renewal not only in religion but also in science and culture in the light of absolute values. Whatever scruples may have briefly caused hesitation, and in my joy at this prospect of a brief escape, the chance to attend all expenses paid proved irresistible. When Arne asked me to travel with him, since at that time the famous mountaineer had qualms about travelling alone, my conscience was satisfied and the matter decided. Greeted at Washington's airport by smartly suited young men who might have come from wealth management, as indeed they did, I became uneasy. They were as immaculate as Seventh Day Adventists but with an impersonal efficiency that gave them a sleek corporate feel. There was something reminiscent of Moral Rearmament only worse, much more professional, sinister, less good-hearted.

The conference was officially dedicated to finding absolute values through a 'dialogue' between the sciences and the humanities. The several hundred participants included Nobel Prize winners and many philosophers I knew by name. Agassi was there and also, whether by default or design, Kai Nielsen, a militant atheist perhaps invited to show an open-minded spirit. I don't recall contributing anything, the most vivid memory being a sightseeing taxi ride round Washington before the sessions began. There was little dialogue of the kind advertised. Scientists and philosophers were as usual exploiting the occasion to do their own things in their own languages. There was, however, some common focus on values. At the time, and in the light of the publications that ensued, I did feel that there was a good deal of openness in the attitude of the organizers. There was no censorship. The fact of the matter was that the Church, with its colossal funds at the time, provided a unique forum for top scientists and some philosophers to talk about values. It was only later, on a similar occasion, that I felt we were really in the grip of an attempted global take-over. That was at a Moon conference in San Francisco in 1987, where it became more evident that they were after our journal. A sociology professor, Irving Horowitz, remarked that these conferences were 'one of the great brilliant marketing strategies in the history of religion'. For me, just a small fish in the strategists' huge net, it was a useful experience with no ill consequences.

The contrast between the grass-roots collectivist movement that Jeanne Brody had found in Paris and this top-heavy meeting of intellectual celebrities was something to reflect on. The former struck me as a kind of anticipation of how a good society based on identity-building co-operation and respect should look. But it had no way of extending its influence except by a proliferation of the same, something that would eventually come up against the barrier of individual greed that propels the shared economy on which even collectivists depend. Of course, no such collective intention is embedded in the ideal of unified sciences, and organizers of academic conferences don't usually expect it either, except in the sense of herding diverse personages into a single space. If the idea of a global society did find its place on this occasion, it did so somewhat grotesquely in the shape of the Reverend Moon himself, who appeared to us at the appointed happy hour. Not only was he the founder of the Unification Church; rather like Napoleon on a horse, he was the symbol of an ideal global collective. At the time this might be said to have existed as a kind of anticipation of the real thing with its stage-managed mass marriages and what were virtually claims to exclusive rights to the choice of what we can properly call love.

Back in reality, after consultation with Maria I decided sadly to sell the flat in Athens. Originally, I had planned to convert its capital value into something even more idealistic and unreal, a house on a Greek island. But it had a prudential as well as a provisional aspect as a fixed point on the map marking a spot where I might, if need be, start over again within reach of a long-standing friend. However, now that I had a permanent job it was unlikely that Greece would be my next stepping-stone, should there ever be one. Its sunshine would still always be in demand and a modest home by the sea might be a permanent asset. I wrote to Maria along these lines. She said her affair with the surgeon had unravelled the previous autumn and ended in acrimony, his assurances in the face of Maria's increasing insistence that he divorce his wife proving empty.

Like many, or most, men in that situation he tired of the pressure and found that protecting his reputation was the prudent course. The worst altercation had occurred in the flat itself and the memory of it had left her disinclined to set foot in it again. Since I had little use for it myself, we agreed that it be put up for sale. Maria would scour the papers for a place by the sea. She subsequently found one. But before I had time to go and see it for myself, I had hit upon a more complex alternative not wholly to Maria's liking.

It was in the year following the Oxford symposium that I took over the chairmanship of the Trondheim department. This meant learning the ropes of university bureaucracy and as far as possible perfecting my Norwegian. Norway is a land of decision-making routines, a tradition going back to the annual parliaments on Iceland in Saga-times. It is their way of keeping on track and, one has to say, avoiding personal responsibilities. The routines and the way they are arrived at are effective, but make for discussions of a kind to which the academics involved, their minds on other things, tend to lend only half an ear. Since the momentum tends to lie with the administration, it takes time and energy to support the cause of one's department. My predecessor Gullvåg had built up a department from scratch and had been especially effective in this respect, relying largely on the responsibility laid on the department to teach the propaedeutic course taken by all humanities students. I found, on taking over, that my chairs from other departments thought Gullvåg had outwitted them for too long. Now, with a half-articulate immigrant as his successor, it would be their turn. Several, especially the historians, had little respect for philosophy in any case and were unable to apprehend that it had become an extremely wide discipline touching also their own fields — or unwilling to let the university spend its precious resources on philosophy at the expense of their own well-established areas of study, history and language being strong contenders in a land still conscious of having only recently established its nationhood. I looked like easy meat and it would be an uphill task to secure further positions, or even keep the ones we had when they became free. In the event I was to retain the chairmanship for five years and in that time managed to keep the department heading, at variable speed, on the course Gullvåg had set. During that time we hired Audun Øfsti, himself from Trondheim but then teaching in the world's northernmost university in Tromsø. From Oslo we hired Helge Høibraaten, an inspiring lecturer able to think as he spoke, but too wound up in his thoughts to sit down and commit them to paper afterwards, or even before, thus until then due to the regulations disqualifying himself from a permanent teaching position. By virtue of a new rule that temporary personnel could not be fired once they had held a position over a certain period, I got him a tenured job none the less. Helge was to become Humboldt Professor in the Free University in Berlin, a visiting position of some prestige. The atmosphere in the department itself in my time was cordial, both among the few faculty members themselves and also between these and the more advanced students. Some of the latter were adults returning to the university as a break in a career or having brought up their children to school age. I settled into that routine, commuting back to Oslo every ten days for a long weekend with Joanne and Jo in the rather confined quarters that space-wise suited them better when I was absent.

Chapter Fifteen: Top of the tide

Top of the tide: a time of slack water when the tide at its highest is about to turn and fall again.

In Oslo, early in the New Year, I mentioned my Grecian plans in passing to a fellow émigré from Scotland who I had known slightly in Edinburgh. Maureen was a distant relative and a school friend of my elder sister. A prize-winning art student in Edinburgh, she had married an architect student there, a Norwegian from whom she was now recently but amicably divorced. She said Erik had spent that summer on a Greek island with a new friend, an actress with a house on Skyros. Perhaps I should speak to him. I visited Erik in his office and he seemed pleased at the opportunity to ring his new friend, which led me to sense that perhaps the summer relationship had not extended into the winter. This would be no surprise in a land where the short and often intense summer has an unreal quality that Norwegians actually exploit, its events often being acceptably extra-curricular. The lady in question invited Erik and myself to dinner in her West End flat. She was tall and striking with lively brown eyes, by no means the Scandinavian prototype, and quite lacking in the affectations people often associate with celebrity and particularly with acting. During a dinner of *pinnekjøtt*, a Norwegian speciality (rather than delicacy) of steamed salted lamb, the conversation turned from Greek islands to her own immediate plans. As one of a group of in-the-news Oslo actors she was to bring new life to the Rogaland Theatre in Stavanger under the artistic direction of an up-and-coming theatre director. When I asked what she intended to do with her nicely appointed flat, she said she'd thought of renting it but wasn't sure how long she'd be staying in Stavanger. In any case she would still want to visit Oslo when free to do so.

After dinner, Erik and I drove to his home. Finding I had left my knitted snow cap behind, not by design but because I was still unused to such headgear, I drove back to collect it. We used the occasion to talk a little more. I told her I was looking for a workplace and she said I looked honest. Since sixteen-year-old Tori would be going with her to Stavanger, she appeared happy to accept an arrangement in which I could use her daughter's bedroom as an office. I would pay her rent and keep the place spick and span. She sounded strict but was friendly and forthright.

It would be, and soon became, an excellent solution. I worked there when in Oslo while for 'baby-sitting' purposes I was within easy distance of Joanne and

Jo. Finally moving my belongings there and settling in gave a sense of freedom more intense than I had ever imagined possible. I celebrated by going out on the town. I saw Ken Russell's 1974 poetic film on Gustav Mahler and felt the glow of freedom in doing something on my own. The intensity was short-lived but the freedom something I cherished and was determined as far and long as possible to preserve.

The ensuing summer proved bizarre. The proprietor of my weekend flat and I had now become more than friends and this time it was I who would accompany her to Skyros. The previous summer she and Erik had come to an agreement whereby he would lend his professional assistance to the repairs of the crumbling roof of the old house high on the Skyros acropolis. Perhaps it was a way of keeping open an option on another 'summer flirt', as the Norwegian saying has it, or even something more enduring. I had some work to complete and would join them a week later. On their way, Bente and Erik spent the night in my Athens apartment. One may easily imagine it was there that Bente first faced Erik with the facts. There was a curious symmetry in this. Prior to their departure, his former wife Maureen had an appointment in Trondheim and asked if she could stay over with me, which she did. To avoid misunderstanding I thought it best to declare my interest in Bente. When told of our new relationship and plans for the summer, Maureen expressed anxiety on Erik's behalf. It had been too late for her to speak with him and when Erik mailed me a list of materials I should buy in Athens for the roof repair, and added that this kind of job was now mine, I detected in this 'official' transfer of responsibility a tone of both soreness and resignation. I was unsure how the holiday would go.

Arriving in Athens in sweltering heat, to secure the materials I engaged the help of Tasos Pikionis, the architect who had been responsible for my apartment. He told me where to buy the necessary articles. I collected them, took them by taxi to the bus station, this being the only public means of transport to the port of Kimi on the East side of Evvia (Euboia), from where the ferry to Skyros departed. The driver stacked them on the roof along with luggage and other packages. After a longish journey, first on the highway to Chalcis and then through Evvia's mountainous terrain, I lugged everything onto the ferry. As we headed for the empty horizon I could finally relax in the comparatively cool sea air. Eventually, through the summer haze, the hills of southern Skyros appeared and we berthed at the west-coast harbour of Linaria. Bente was waiting there with friends. A very old bus took us up to the town. With a splitting headache I spent the whole of the next day lying on the earthen floor in the comparative cool of Bente's very traditional house.

There were several others. Besides Erik, there was Martine, a French student who had been there the year before and was welcomed this time with her cousin, along with the latter's red-headed French boyfriend. They were a lively group. Bente's daughter Tori had struck up a friendly relationship with the local bus driver, who also had a motorcycle on which he took her on tours. The house was one that Bente and her husband had bought several years earlier. On their divorcing, to put things behind her she had spent some spring months there with Tori. More than mere tourists, they were now in some sense part of the local scene and Bente was the object of more than one Skyrian's amorous phantasies. In our presence this may of course have led to some untold jealousies. As it was, in our numbers we were something of a collective, so that any inner jealousies were underplayed in general holiday activities which included, besides swimming and relaxing evenings in the tavernas, some serious roof-repairs. Erik seemed happy to engage the attentions of Martine. My own most lasting memory is of the slight breeze that filtered providentially through the open window in the night.

It would be two years before I revisited Skyros. The following summer I decided to get to serious grips with the Kierkegaard manuscript. The saga of delays and missed deadlines makes depressing reading, only partly offset by the publisher's and series editor's severely tested good will. I had said as early as October 1973, four years previously, that I hoped to finish it within a year. When that proved impossible, I thanked Routledge for their continued optimism and asked for an extension of 'six months or so'. When all of twelve months proved again too little, they asked me to stop playing the 'this year, next year, some time, never' game and to refrain from giving a definite date until I could ensure them that I could devote one more long vacation to the work. I said that under that condition December 1976 looked 'not impossible'. The new friendship and Greece had unexpectedly intervened, but this next summer, after four to five weeks closeted in the Oslo flat, I felt I had coped with some of the most difficult aspects of Kierkegaard's writings and could send three chapters to my then editor, David Godwin. I even thought I might have broken the back of this intractable project, so there was no need to read resignation in his typical editor's 'looking forward to seeing the completed manuscript'. Luckily at the time I had no idea it would be not until August 1981 that the long-suffering publisher (in reality a succession of shorter-term-suffering editors) would receive the completed typescript.

Joanne and I officially separated in the spring of 1977 after enduring the obligatory counselling meeting, intended as a last-ditch attempt to prevent such breaches. It was more like a farce framed in tragedy, or vice versa. Usually matters are by then already settled and, if not, the setting is hardly suited to repairing what has so far proved irreparable. However, official policy and official morality require this final shot at reconciliation in the presence of someone not at all qualified to succeed where others have failed. For us it was a harrowing experience, not so much for what was said and the foregone conclusion, as for the fact that the very exercise emphasized the implied failure on one or both parts. When the session was over and we had returned to the car, Joanne wept and I felt no better. Joan Frøstrup's prophecy twelve years earlier stirred in our memories. There was also the plain fact that we had a son and that his home would lack the comfort and support of two mutually adjusted adults. For Jo there was to be even less sense of a home when, that summer, Joanne completed her social studies and began working in a nearby school taking care of variously disabled children.

In October 1977 an opportunity arose for Jo and myself to travel together to San Francisco, where we and especially he could once again meet his grandparents. The occasion was that second invitation, all expenses paid, to attend a conference sponsored by the Unification Church. This time to my eternal shame, knowing that a switch to Moonian theocracy would never influence my editing, I had no illusions about the motive behind the invitation. It was an opportunity — perhaps heaven-sent nevertheless — to make temporary repairs to our disjointed family life. We flew via Seattle to Los Angeles and stayed overnight with Joanne's Aunt Dorothy before taking the one-hour flight next day to San Francisco. Jo was picked up by Joanne's parents, while I made for the Fairmont Hotel on Nob Hill.

Except for some additional participants, the story there was much as before. In the hotel bar I ran into Howard Hong, who with his wife Edna was already well known for the on-going translation of Kierkegaard's collected works. In a white suit and smoking a cigar, he called to mind a familiar photograph of Mark Twain. On hearing that I hailed from Norway, he seemed to recall a railway station with his name somewhere in that land, so perhaps that was where he came from too. Aside from a well-known Danish cheese brand, Høng is a railway station in a small town on the west coast of Zealand, the island on which Copenhagen stands. But there is no Hong in Norway. Niels Thulstrup, another dedicated Kierkegaard expert was also attending the conference. There, too, was Eileen Barker, the sociologist of religion I'd met at the London School of Economics. A local newspaper had published criticism of the conference and the Church. Journalists in the hotel lobby tried to elicit provocative comment. I let slip that I did not hold with the principles or motivation behind the conference and should of course have been ready to explain why I was there at all. But they didn't pose that tricky question.

Eileen was non-committal with a purpose since she was there for professional reasons. She planned to infiltrate the Unification Church itself to test claims made against it that members had been brainwashed. She was later criticized for being too soft on the Church, leading some critics of her 1984 *Making of a Moonie: Brainwashing or Conversion?* to claim that she herself had been brainwashed. Others blamed her for helping herself lavishly to Moonie conference money with the intention of taking the lid off the movement that provided it. Those most offended by Eileen's well-documented conclusions proved later to be the Church's opponents. She pointed to the huge financial rewards 'de-programmers' and 'exit counsellors' enjoyed by exploiting the simplistic notion of 'cult' spread by anti-cultists. I read later a piece in *The Guardian* by the now retired and respected Eileen Barker in which she said 'cult' means 'a religion I don't like'. She founded the Information Network Focus on Religious Movements, which was controversial because government supported. In this article she admitted that some religions identified as cults were known to have engaged in 'heinous criminal activities' but the 'vast majority' did not. Due to media bias we are more likely to read that a cult member has committed suicide than that an Anglican has done so. One of the few lasting memories I have of the conference is wandering round San Francisco's 'tenderloin' district and disputing with Eileen whether we should watch a 'live show'. For some reason, embarrassment or lacking the sociologist's cultivation of distance, I backed off and we didn't.

It had been a long time since we had heard anything of Peter Frøstrup. Word filtered through of his success as foreign editor of the Irish Times, and Joan had sent cards from their new home at The Stables, Kilmacanogue near Dublin, an address that seemed to fit their lifestyle. In the autumn of 1972 Peter had been in Oslo in connection with a referendum on whether Norway should join the Common Market. Friends said they had seen him on television but no contact was made. Some years later, after Joanne and I had divorced and Peter was no longer with Joan, he came over from Ireland for a second time and included Joanne on a round of visits to his old friends. I was in my freedom apartment and Joanne called to say Peter was with her and would I join them. It was like going back ten or twenty years. When I asked what his plans were, he said he wouldn't mind a job with a Norwegian newspaper and mentioned *Nordlys*, the Tromsø paper. Back again to basics? Dreams? I told him I still edited that damned journal he had lumbered me with but refrained from accusing him of having left me in the lurch. He had no regrets about lumbering me with the damned journal.

Joanne phoned soon after to tell me that Peter had died without warning in Dublin after a heart attack. It was on the 29th of April 1978 and Peter was forty-six. It was a terrible shock, exceedingly more so for his sixteen-year-old daughter Mariella, then staying with him. With his persistent search for something better for himself and to have others along, Peter was more than anything else alive. His demons led him to drink and smoke too much and, with a thorn in his own flesh, he had a beguiling way of converting it into a concern for those around him. Behind his friendly provocations, and in my case, constant teasing, there was an innate kindliness.

I had by then settled into a three-cornered commute. It required flying rather than driving. I had for two years driven the distance to Trondheim and back every ten days, always something of an adventure. The changing seasons added to the variations in landscape, and the drive was never dull. I played music, especially Bruckner since the journey took over six hours. I could prepare my next-day lecture in my head as I drove. I would pause at Alvdal, about three quarters of the way, for a meal prior to the last climb and long descent into Trondheim. Usually the winter was the testing time for driving, not just the snow but also the extreme cold for which even a Volvo's heater sometimes proved inadequate. Once, after the Alvdal meal, I found a pair of recently laundered trousers in the back frozen stiff. Another time I foolishly left the car to visit the cafeteria without putting on my coat. When I came out again the lock had frozen and I had to fight my way in a minus twenty degrees centigrade northerly wind to the nearest petrol station to buy some lock-releasing fluid.

But it was summer rather than the hard winter that put an end to driving, at least for a long time. I had returned in mid-August to Oslo from Skyros the day before chairing our autumn term's briefing session. Our terms start that early — and I left Oslo at five-thirty in the evening, which was late, but hoping to arrive at my digs by midnight. Keeping up a good pace I stopped as usual for a break at Alvdal and speeding happily thereafter on my way I was soon passing three large lorries, anxious in my hurry to put them behind me. With the extra acceleration required to overtake the last of these, and with no time to decelerate, I came upon an unexpected hairpin bend. With no warning signs, it connected the familiar road to a stretch of straight new highway that had been constructed during my absence, the temporary surface covered in gravel. I took the first bend without trouble, but the tyres would not respond to the second and we slid off the road at some pace and down a slope, luckily treeless, rolling over but landing upright again. My seat belt was in place. I tried to restart the engine but the radiator had collapsed into the engine and nothing turned. The large intercontinental lorry I had just passed stopped and its driver came to assist. Seeing the sorry state of the car, and on hearing that I was on the way to Trondheim, he offered me a lift and advised me to remove everything from the car, since otherwise others would do the same in the night. He phoned the local sheriff to say he had seen the accident and I was not drunk and that he would take me on to Trondheim. He expected me to experience delayed shock but I didn't and haven't so far. What I felt was annoyance.

There was a taxi waiting for me when we reached the outskirts of Trondheim. My saviour had ordered it on his phone, calculating the timing exactly with the result that I arrived at my door only half an hour later than planned. I rang Bente to tell her the car was gone and she mistook my matter-of-fact tone to imply that perhaps it had been stolen or taken from me by the authorities. Whether a lack or simply a trait, I may have inherited it from my mother in whom I detected an acceptance born of an undercurrent of resignation. The insurance company decided it would cost more to repair the car than to compensate me at its current value. I had visions of my mustard yellow Volvo in the crusher. Not very long after I saw it cruising around Trondheim as good as new with fancy attachments. I learned that two brothers who restored cars had bought it from the insurance company.

After this commuting was by train or, more frequently, air, six hours in the one case and one in the other with a bus-ride added. Teaching and administration kept me in Trondheim from Tuesday to Friday, and after my propaedeutic course on Friday afternoons I flew to Oslo, the airport at that time only twenty minutes from the city centre, the bus depositing me just outside my door. On Saturday I picked up the journal mail at the University and kept contact with Jo and Joanne. Late on Sunday I flew to Stavanger to visit Bente and on Tuesday mornings took the 'milk route' to Trondheim, so called because the plane stopped at several west-coast destinations on the way. It was time-consuming, but the travelling was on the whole relaxing and helped to keep my various occupations apart, an advantage when dealing with their variety.

To catch up with research I applied for and received several periods of leave without pay with my colleague and host Sverre Sløgedal kindly deputizing as chairman. The best memories are from such periods when in Bente's rented apartment in Stavanger I would write all day and look forward to her return from rehearsal in the early afternoon. I also enjoyed meeting her colleagues, who were quite unlike mine and on the whole offered more volatile company. Under its new director the theatre in Stavanger was enjoying a renaissance and attracted several visiting directors from the continent. Bente was their star actress and played a wide range of parts from Ibsen (*The Lady from the Sea*) to Dario Fo (*Accidental Death of an Anarchist*). I learned a lot about the theatre and saw the hard process of gestation that ends where, for the public, it begins. They are tough people too. Just before the Dario Fo piece was to be brought to an audience on a nearby island, Bente fell ill with influenza. There was no talk of cancellation. Normal people would have taken days off work, but acting commands loyalty and these people, often with rather slippery private lives, manage the impossible. Once again this was a many-sided and creative world that if only I had met it earlier, I could wish I'd tried to become part of.

In some ways the theatre's rehearsal period resembled my own project of trying to put a publicly acceptable typescript in order. My performance took ten years, theirs six weeks. Many things got in the way. Editing *Inquiry* without secretarial, or any other, assistance took up much of my time. During the term I had to confine journal work to the weekend, whether in Oslo or Trondheim where, there being little else to do, it helped to fill the time. Most of the work on Kierkegaard was done in my head while travelling, or in restaurants where I scribbled thoughts on the backs of restaurant bills, menus and sometimes on paper napkins. While still driving, Alvdal's excellent cafeteria was a place where I could sit for some time writing and I stopped there often. On making my first trip after a summer vacation the proprietor would greet me with 'Ah, the migrating bird'. In Trondheim, with minimal kitchen equipment in my quarters, I was a frequent customer of the city's excellent cafeterias and restaurants. On Sundays I might find Gullvåg writing there too before taking his family to the cinema. On Saturdays we could sit together in the nearby supermarket cafeteria scribbling philosophy amid big-buying natives from the surrounding districts with families in tow. Creating a typescript out of scribbled notes was a laborious process involving many drafts and much re-typing.

Desperate to speed things up, I applied for four-months of unpaid leave in 1979 from January. When it was granted I set to work with greater concentration in the Oslo apartment with weekend visits to Stavanger. As the deadline approached and pressure mounted there were symptoms of exhaustion. In April, deciding not to accompany Bente and her daughter on the conventionally long Norwegian Easter break, I remained in Oslo struggling with the finer points of Kierkegaard's notions of faith and knowledge. The strain began to tell. There was a recurrence of those feelings of incipient heart failure that had begun as far back in 1954 when I began studying philosophy. I described it some days later in my notebook.

> Saturday between Good Friday and Easter Sunday. A quarter past two, afternoon. While typing the latest sentences on Kd., sudden dizziness, feeling of a physical hiatus, the works stopping, breathing requires effort, impulse to move in order to get things going gain—rapid pulse. Psychologically, panic. The date doesn't help. I'm to make dinner for Jo. What if I collapse *this* side of the door? Better to go out and get a doctor. Begin to ring the first aid station—but then put the receiver down. Rest a few minutes — it seems to have gone over. But no, again

— two or three times again. Think of ringing Joanne (at Anne-Lo's). But then, due to need of fresh air, decide to go out. Head towards the emergency station at the Red Cross Hospital — don't feel I'll make it. Write note 'Ring Jo Hannay, tel. 46 23 34' — and put it in pocket in case I don't. Shaky, become dizzy two or three times (especially when I *think*!), but come to emergency station (only 10 to 15 minutes away). Place crammed full of old ladies and young children. I tell the receptionist and get instant attention — am told to lie on a stretcher, am wheeled into a room and wait. Peace! No more dizziness. Eventually doctor — hears symptoms, checks, suspects hyperventilation over-breathing, breathe out too much carbon dioxide (immediate cure is to put a sack over one's head and breathe it in again, he says). ECG test — OK. Friendly nurses, staff, get prescription—Take bus to Majorstuen to get pills. Upgrade narco there trying to persuade the lady behind the counter to give him some prescription cough-mixture without a prescription — his doctor is on Easter holiday. She is firm. He gets a non-prescription bottle at 25 or 23 kroner. He stumbles out with a 'Continued Happy Easter'. I take the bus back. Jo comes, we eat. No problems. Next day begins the same around midday. I take the pills, wonder whether the brain needs extra fuel and eat honey. Helps. Stop work on Kd. (which brings the spells—*Angst*?!) and read proofs. No problems. Weak. Relaxed. Maybe the pills.

At that time hyperventilation was, if you will forgive me, much in the air, young doctors being especially on the lookout for its symptoms. I am fairly sure the diagnosis was wrong; air was above all what I needed. Whatever the physical circumstances, it must surely have been a matter of stress related to intellectual activity engaged in by those not necessarily best suited to its demands. It was to happen again, on one occasion in connection with another book, though at other times it may have been caused partly by the medication I was taking for hypertension. Whatever the causes, there was something cathartic about the occurrence itself. I wrote two 'afterthoughts':

> There's no doubt that like the thought of tomorrow's rendezvous with the hangman, this experience wonderfully concentrates the mind. We evade the truth of our existence as much as we can, but a properly human existence is one that has been 'concentrated' by the thought and experience of nothing and found a security in itself afterwards on that basis. A confusion ends without a solution being given.

Needless to say, the manuscript was not delivered by May the 1st and not even by the beginning of the following year, as Carol Stevens noted in the spring of the year after, reminding me that the book was originally due for delivery in October 1973 and 'several extensions' had been granted the last date given being 31 January 1980.

When, at long last, on 20 May 1981, I could promise in good faith that Carol would have the typescript by the end of August the house on Skyros had been sold and we were spending the summer on Mykonos with a colleague of Bente and his wife. It was at their beachside house at Agios Sostis, at the north of Mykonos, that I wrote the preface. The saga of a seemingly never-ending project came to its belated close on 25 October the following year. On that day a copy of a letter to the bank arrived informing me that one hundred pounds 'advance' had been credited to my account and I could read that the book would be published 'on Thursday of this week'. In context the word 'advance' seemed out of place.

The book had a mixed reception. Mary Warnock gave it a thorough going over in the *Times Literary Supplement*, finding the discussion interesting but the 'arguments' I looked for in Kierkegaard insufficiently rigorous to count as such. They are certainly not up to then current Oxford standards. Later surveys of Kierkegaard's reception placed those 'arguments' in their proper continental context. One described my account as 'debatable in detail' but so 'sympathetic, painstaking and essentially philosophical' as to be a 'milestone in British Kierkegaard studies'. [10] Another said that in 'placing Kierkegaard philosophically' it was a 'turning point', having a 'breadth unequalled in any previous contribution'. [11] Later, in the USA, when I was regarded as a possible colleague at a university, a member of the department told the chairman, as he revealed to me later, that the book was 'practically worthless'. I recently saw it displayed as a text for a quickly expanding interest in Kierkegaard in Slovenia.

Ending my five-year stint as 'chair' at Trondheim coincided with Bente's return to Oslo. Having made his mark in Stavanger, the theatre director went on to grander things in Bergen while Bente joined Oslo New Theatre's permanent ensemble and, except for three years as director of the National Academy of Dramatic Art, would remain there until retirement in 2004. Tori, her daughter, came back to Oslo so I had to find alternative accommodation. I was due a sabbatical and I needed a place to concentrate in any case, so in the early spring of 1980 I bought a 'loft' apartment of the kind becoming fashionable among the young middle-class generation soon to be labelled 'yuppies', or 'young upwardly mobile professionals'. Old attics originally designed for drying clothes and storing heirlooms were turned by pop-up building firms into 'penthouses' with sloping roofs and sturdy but architecturally interesting beams. The new owners were typically in their 'twenties and early 'thirties. Approaching fifty I was by their standards already well over the hill.

My own 'pent-house', appropriately plain, was peaceful and within walking distance of the Oslo campus. It was also not far from Jo and Joanne who were still occupying the flat we had bought on moving from Hvitsten. It was in the summer of this sabbatical that Joanne and I were officially divorced. By now Jo was fourteen and, under both Joanne's guiding hand and that of a dedicated teacher, was already a more than competent violinist able to play in the city's youth orchestra. We entered into a stable pattern: I drove Jo to his teacher and when the time came taught him driving. At Joanne's request I also practised kicking a football with him on the university grass, this competency being something she was afraid he might be ridiculed at school for lacking. For me, it was a relief not having to travel and the commuting pattern would be simpler when the sabbatical was over.

The shorter distance between Bente's home and mine meant that questions kept on hold now became topical. Until now I could have been a husband forced to work away from home, but living separately in the same city brought the question of a more lasting bond into focus. The natural solution would be to live together, but since I was now well integrated with Bente's family, all of whom lived in the area, the next step from their point of view would be to formalize the relationship.

We did both. The sabbatical over, Tori moved out to find her own independence and I moved back in. We were now sharing on what looked like a permanent basis an apartment that must have reminded Bente vividly of her divorced husband. A gifted architect, he was responsible for its excellent interior architecture. Bente had been adventurous enough in marrying this exceptional character, but she must have thought the apartment might now serve its marital function more dependably. Returning to the apartment had for me quite other associations. It was here that five years earlier I had that inspiring sense of my life being once more in my own hands.

As it turned out, we were together for twenty-two years and officially wed for nineteen. Before marrying, having quite a lot in common, we were living in harmony and both getting on with our jobs. We travelled to Morocco and also Tenerife, where I too hastily put down some money on an apartment in an as yet unfinished building project that went bankrupt. Apart from that foolishness on my part, it seemed a good start. There was no thought of further children and unlike Bente I was under no pressure from a conservative family. I should have been reflecting on my ability to remain in such a relationship. My father had remarked that married life calls for a change in attitude, something he must have known all too well. For some, that might be fairly straightforward, and even convenient in terms of life's stages. But in others some alteration more than just the way of looking at one's own life is needed. It may have been a sign of weakness to say to ourselves, as we both did, that things will turn out well if we just keep going. The sheer momentum of the *status quo*, an insidiously comforting default factor that says the course is straight ahead, can in favourable circumstances keep a relationship going. Yet it is exposed to the temptation of making light of the formality when expedience upstages traditional ideas of the sanctity of marriage.

One such occasion arose in the autumn of 1981. Bente's stepmother's death meant that Greek holidays were a thing of the past. Now responsible for her father's summer vacation at the family cabin on the south Norwegian coast, she had to sell the house on Skyros. But just a glimpse of alternative sunshine suddenly appeared in the West. John Searle had spoken of 'getting me to California'. I was invited to Berkeley as a visiting professor, the height of my career, as I saw it and still do. It was also a time for which fate and the furies had been waiting. California and our marriage in December 1981 became fatally linked. The preamble is briefly told. Rather than waste time while I coped with a kind and level of teaching to which I was quite unaccustomed, for Bente to have any benefit from our stay, she could attend the very active theatre department there. Not doing so would be to lose a great opportunity. We learned that as my 'spouse' she could 'audit' the department free of charge. A banal pecuniary trifle based on a merely bureaucratic rule became the excuse for the pretence that a decision to marry was the right one, something we both now recognize to have been a mistake.

The simple wedding ceremony took place in the Oslo City Chambers in the presence of the best man Arild Brinchman, Director of the National Theatre with his actress wife Monna Tandberg as maid of honour. They treated us to a sumptuous lunch in their home. When Joanne and I had been married in Oslo's Town Hall eighteen years earlier, the celebratory meal had been a late breakfast for two in a tiny café bar named 'Ritz'.

The bareness of the formalities this time suggested an underlying reluctance to submit to the potential disaster of married life. For some a wedding ring, however discreetly decorative on the finger, can become a millstone around one or the other neck. Norwegians dispense with wedding rings and make do with an exchange of engagement rings. We dispensed also with these. I admit the thought of a ring never occurred to me; after five years together, there would seem little point in telling the world we were to be married. Some people may have thought we already were. A sense of the indecency as well as unreality of the occasion lingers regarding both what I owed to Bente and appreciated in her and a deeper sense of my own inability to live up to what was promised. Marriage according to some is a way of harnessing the sexual drive within socially advantagious limits independently of the nurturing of children. Others see the latter as its only real function. In a world where securing a social identity has become a more complex matter, that function may be a form of self-effacement that can masquerade as self-sacrifice in the interests of the next generation. In optimal conditions, a married couple may be in a situation of mutual help in overcoming native inhibitions against their own personal development; they may even arrive at a greater understanding of themselves in a way that finds expression in their separate activities and by doing so may help offspring on the way to doing the same. Either way, some such shared central project must surely help. Providing a helpful environment for the bringing up of children is the traditional example, and personally I see no real reason for marriage outside that aim. Gay marriage is a sentimental farce that misuses a tradition in need of self-scrutiny and made no better by the egotistical and face-saving adoption of children. The first thing to think of when contemplating having a child is how the child will benefit from having just these parents whatever their sex. To talk of a woman's 'right to have a child', and the plea that a woman is unfulfilled unless she has one, is to place the burden of personal fulfilment forcibly on an as yet non-existing human being with no say in the matter.

We were married on 17 December 1982. I left for San Francisco on 5 January leaving Bente occupied at the theatre until she could join me in March. At Berkeley my academic expectations or hopes, if not dreams, were met to the full and more. Friendly colleagues, equally amiable, enthusiastic and hard-working students for once with a welcome respect for their teacher, and not least the wholly liberating experience of thinking aloud in my own language, all this was for me euphoric. I taught for two quarters and was asked if I might stay for a third, but for domestic reasons had to decline. Behind the faculty's invitation was the need to fill a social and political philosophy requirement. Due to the political ructions that had made Berkeley a hotbed of student unrest, they were wary of having a permanent political philosopher in their midst. The one man who had seemed destined for that role was refused tenure, this causing another demonstration. He was now teaching off-campus. The policy was therefore to hire visitors to do the job. I was one such. By no means an expert in this field, I had to prepare myself for the role. Knowing by now where to look, I was able to assemble enough discussion in my mind for the period in which it was to be put to this use, rather as an actor learns a role. Once performed it can be picked up again later, even if other parts have had to be learned and stored in the meantime.

The first Berkeley lecture was to a class called 'Philosophy and the Social Sciences'. I was to give a partly historical and partly systematic introduction to the special nature of social sciences. At the time, John and Dagmar Searle were kindly lodging me while I looked for accommodation. Arriving only a few days before teaching began, and with the combination of initial disorientation, jet lag, searching for an apartment and trying to organize the lectures in my head, all of this made for a tense start. With no exact idea where Tolman Hall was, I scrambled in a state of high anxiety along paths, through trees and around bushes and arrived breathless, and in some confusion, some minutes late to find a large number of students waiting. To excuse my sorry state, I gave a halting speech pleading jet lag and then explained more or less what they were to expect if they chose to show up again. A 'student' sitting on the front bench proved to be an already well-known philosopher who, I suppose, was hoping to pick up some pearls of wisdom from a hardened expert. This I was not. Yet by the end of the quarter I had almost become one and the verdict on my course was generally positive. In preparation I had made careful notes for the students and for myself, and it was a treat some time later to be told by Donald Davidson, who was called upon to give that same class the following year and knew even less about the topic, that he had got hold of a copy of my notes and found them useful.

Panic before lecturing has never left me. But I realized from the odour filling the men's lavatory in the minutes before lectures that I was not the only nervous teacher in town. A mind detector would sense everywhere a hurried atmosphere of concealed anxiety. On another stay I was given an office near enough the gents to hear the unzipping of flies as tenure-tracking teachers sped to clear themselves of bodily constraints before devoting an hour or two to dis-burdening themselves of lately rehearsed wisdom. But then many seasoned stage actors experience the same every time they face their audience.

My other course that winter quarter was the first I ever gave on Kierkegaard. For several years Bert Dreyfus had been giving a basic Kierkegaard course. I was now entrusted with those students of his who wanted to hear more. It soon became clear that based on a small selection of texts, Dreyfus had been giving them a very special version of Kierkegaard. By relating the works to contemporary life, and in particular that of students in the Bay Area, Dreyfus presented a systematic Kierkegaardian background against which students could grasp the dynamics of addiction and commitment. The latter was treated as the kind of decisive step needed to get oneself out of addiction in the familiar 'detoxing' programmes, but also as the sort of self-chosen dedication to some goal or model that gives the chooser an identity in an otherwise nihilistically conceived world. As noted earlier, I had come across something of the same in Moral Rearmament circles. Since what Dreyfus gave them had obviously made an impact, the students were rattled at my suggestion that he had got Kierkegaard wrong on several crucial points; I began to wonder whether the more text-true account would hold any interest for them. Bert had a knack of making hard-to-get-at philosophers excitingly topical. As it was, we worked away at Kierkegaard with a wider exposure to his texts than they were used to, and I left them at least a little more open-minded as to what Kierkegaard's contribution to contemporary life might be.

There was also an invited talk on Kierkegaard to the Pacific Division of the American Philosophical Association meeting at Sacramento. My paper collided with another that Bert wanted to hear. Choosing the latter, he diplomatically left a recorder at mine under a wide-brimmed hat on a front row seat. At the back row sat a tall man, thickly dark-haired, taking notes. He approached me at the end and introduced himself as Ed Mooney. Ed, one of my still lingering friends in academia, was then chair of the philosophy department at the State University campus at Rohnert Park in Sonoma County, north of San Francisco. We became frequent correspondents and were to meet on several occasions, the last a decade ago in Copenhagen at a conference belatedly celebrating my seventieth birthday. Ed was to edit the papers given there in what was a Festschrift except in name and published in 2008 by Indiana University Press. The commentator on this earlier occasion at Sacramento was Paul Dietrichson, from Washington University in Seattle, a Norwegian by birth he had been visiting at Oslo when I first arrived there in 1961. Now, twenty-one years on, after airing our differences in the discussion, we retired to his motel room and, with increasing amicability, consumed a large quantity of whisky.

Much of the inner tension that dogged my earlier weeks in Northern California is filtered out in the telling though also in memory. Sensing I was overstaying the Searles' welcome, I moved to the Faculty Club, a timber construction of some beauty with creaking floors and thin walls. I liked it a lot and stayed there on several later occasions. In preparation for Bente's arrival, I found an apartment on Haste Street close to Shattuck Avenue, not a very long walk from the campus where I enjoyed the spacious office left for me by Barry Stroud, the very man whose chapters on Hume lay accusingly on Føllesdal's desk when I moved to Trondheim. Now, eight years on, my own book at last published, Barry was on sabbatical leave. With the well-stocked Howison Library upstairs, I worked well and in peace. As usual when alone, I adjusted fairly naturally to the new circumstances. Bente's arrival was something I was looking forward to because she was Bente.

On her arrival we began by being happily occupied in our separate departments. Bente's contact with the theatre faculty also offered me wider contact with the university. There was a moment of sadness. Shortly after her arrival Bente received word that her former husband had died. Only fifty-one years old, he had been a man of much enterprise and talent but, part genius and part romantic, had placed a heavy burden on Bente. His death naturally brought back positive memories. Our apartment was opposite a veterinary complex where every week a garbage truck without a canopy took on a load of carcasses of euthanized pets. I turned Bente carefully away to avoid seeing this visual analogy.

She soon adapted to Berkeley's strange blend of international academic workshop in what is otherwise a thoroughly parochial setting. We were invited home to colleagues, attended experimental productions in San Francisco and Berkeley, met innovative theatre people both local and visiting, and in the short Easter break managed a week of humid Hawaiian luxury on Maui. In mid-April, thanks to Dagfinn Føllesdal, who loaned us his vintage gas-guzzling car, we drove down Central Valley and through Los Angeles to San Diego, stopping frequently to replenish the engine oil, which seemed to evaporate rapidly in the heat. Through Avrum Stroll's good offices I was invited to give a talk to the UCSD philosophy department's Friday seminar. The talk is something I hardly remember, and no doubt left little impact. Inevitably it was on Kierkegaard, not a topic to arouse interest there at any time. Only one of the faculty, a former student of the Kierkegaard scholar Louis Mackey, was versed enough in the Danish thinker to be curious. Having to deal with family matters that afternoon, he could only meet me at the pre-seminar lunch, where he gave me a copy of a classic article that I only got down to reading several years later. By then I felt moderately confident that I had a grasp of Kierkegaard's goals and method in *Concluding Unscientific Postscript*, the work that article draws on and which it reads as a seven-hundred-page how-not-to-do-it joke at the expense of Hegelians.

Two balmy nights at La Jolla's old-style Colonial Inn (as it was then called) and a welcoming party in the evening given by Jerry Doppelt and Sharon Weremiuk, where besides Avrum and Mary Stroll we met among others George Anagnostopoulos, Fred Olafson, and Nick Jolley, made for a memorable break in our Berkeley stay. They would all be close colleagues and friends when, in years to come, La Jolla became a regular destination.

Back in Berkeley there was drama in a visit by Arne Naess and Kit Fai, Arne's third wife, whom he had met while teaching in Hong Kong. While we were sitting drinking coffee in the popular Pavilion on Bancroft Way I caught sight of John Searle and remarked this to Arne, who said he must introduce himself. Having failed to do so on Searle's visit to Oslo he may have wanted to repair this discourtesy. Searle's deep-rooted response was far from courteous. As Arne told it on returning to our table, he was stunned. On asking what wrong he had done, Searle asked him to come to his office at four. We waited on the lawn outside to hear what Arne could report after this meeting. He said little but was clearly upset. My guess is that Searle named the grievances listed earlier from the time we shared an office in Oslo. There was the refusal to allow him use of the mountain cabin. He may have mentioned what he considered to be Arne's indefensible exploitation of me in connection with *Inquiry*, though less likely that he should refer to Arne's son's contribution on behalf of the radicals who had arranged the student boycott of his lectures. Searle himself, who Feyerabend assured me was a 'softy' at heart, and more sensitive than the tough exterior he presents, would have been hurt by the plain discourtesy of not being welcomed by his official host. His ebullient, even Napoleonic self-image would have been dented even more by being told that the expedition cabin he had envisaged occupying was not for 'family weekends'. On reflection, I wondered whether more than ten years of indignation on Searle's part was a main reason why Arne, whose connection with Berkeley went back to pre-World War II days, had not been re-invited there.

There was some tragedy in that, fastened in my memory later when on a later brief visit on my own I was sitting on the same lawn and caught sight of Arne standing just above Wheeler Hall gazing up at the Campanile and then at nearby Moses Hall, where the philosophy department was located. He didn't approach it and after some minutes turned and went away. Sensing a private moment, I refrained from calling out to him. He was returning from one of his regular mind-restoring visits to the Nevada desert.

In rather different circumstances, it would soon be my turn. Classes and examinations kept me there until 20 June, but in May Bente had to return to Oslo for rehearsals. Cocooned once more in my own world, I faced two quite demanding classes, one of them in social philosophy again. For some reason I chose a text beyond the limits of my grasp of its nevertheless absorbing topic, namely functional explanation, the difficult idea that what causes apparently rational or purpose-driven arrangements in natural evolution or in society is the fact that it turns out that they work, not that they are in some mysterious or predetermined way planned. The other course was a seminar for postgraduate students on the 'mind-body' problem, a topic for which I was better prepared, my only disappointment being that when we came to a critique of the views of Donald Davidson the latter declined to take part. There was some consistency in this. Davidson disliked having to reply to criticism, even in print, on the grounds that his critics tended to misunderstand his real aims. It could be that he failed to make these altogether clear.

Due partly to my teaching assistant Lynne English, the course on social philosophy went better than expected. But here too there was some sense of failure: being so much drained after each hard session that I only wanted to retire to my office and keep everything else out, I felt I failed her. She even wrote me a note asking if anything was wrong. I had of course to say no, nothing, it was just me. We ended on a friendly note and later exchanged cards. At the close of the course she and a student drafted a two-page letter to the chairman asking that I be re-invited. I detected in it a continued attempt by the students to have a politically wary faculty hire a permanent member of staff to teach the history, methods and ambitions of social science.

Dear Dr. Sluga,
The purpose of this letter is to express our appreciation to the philosophy department for offering courses which examine the philosophical foundations of the social sciences and to encourage the department to continue this practice. In particular we were both helped a great deal during this past year by two of Alastair Hannay's courses: Philosophy of the Social Sciences and the course on functionalism.

As graduate students in the philosophy of education, we have found little interest among human science faculty members here at Berkeley in sustained discussion of the serious difficulties facing the social sciences. There have been important exceptions to this. Tony Stigliano, a lecturer in the education school, has offered a number of good courses in this area, but he will be leaving next June. Dr. Feyerabend's philosophy of science course, while not dealing directly with the social sciences, has nevertheless been valuable to a number of students we know in the education school. The 290 seminar given last winter by Hubert Dreyfus and John Searle aided many of us who are interested in the question of whether or not an objective social science is possible. Finally, Dr. Hannay's 138 and 141 courses, as mentioned above, were the most thorough we have taken in this area.

The philosophy department has taken the lead in offering such courses, a practice we strongly urge you to continue. Many practicing social scientists apparently see it as a weakness to admit their enterprise in general suffers from its inability to answer a number of theoretical and methodological questions. We believe these questions are best considered through slow, deliberate study and open discussion. Because the philosophy department has no vested interest in defending or attacking the work done by social scientists, it may offer the most objective forum for the consideration of these issues.

In closing, we would also urge you to invite Dr. Hannay back to teach. Besides his patient and thorough teaching style, we were impressed by his ability to help us talk through and understand one or two important books each quarter, an approach which taught us and, we believe, many others in the classes, much more than if we had raced through four or five works in ten weeks. Finally, Dr. Hannay's willingness to entertain basic questions over and over again, both in class and during his office hours, until the questioner understood the matter at hand convinced us of his genuine interest in helping us grasp some rather complex theories.

It may take some time for the philosophy department to attract large numbers of students to courses dealing with the philosophy of the social sciences, but we firmly believe the interest among students is there.

Please feel free to contact us if there is any work we could do to make such courses come about and/or bring Dr. Hannay back to teach at Berkeley.

Sincerely,
Lynne D. English
Leo vanMunching III

The letter, quoted here in full because I am rather proud of it, was dated 16 July, by which time I was back in Norway. Not unexpectedly the department continued its policy of caution, using visitors, or one of their number, in general philosophers hired for expertise in quite other areas. That I was not re-invited is natural enough since such invitations are prized opportunities that occur seldom in a lifetime.

Something else also altered my fortunes. Bente's earlier departure from Berkeley eased several pressures, one of these my reluctance to visit Joanne's parents either with or without Bente. My relationship to them was awkward enough, but to visit them alone would have offended Bente's strong sense of what is owing to her. What stuck most clearly in my memory when I visited them was Joanne's mother saying she was worried about who would now look after her daughter. If only I could have told her that Joanne is still a very active 'head' of the family.

Another release was having time to engage with colleagues as well as students. It was refreshing to be able to talk 'shop' and become better acquainted with them personally. Among those I spoke to and befriended was a colleague's research assistant, frequently to be seen walking at his side on campus. As many had guessed, and I later discovered, the relationship was close enough for steps to be taken not to have it made public. At conferences they took different planes. Perhaps for the same reason she was never invited to this colleague's home, misguidedly I imagine, since his wife certainly knew that the tall young woman was her husband's assistant and must have wondered why he didn't ask her along, unless of course she knew and told him not to.

She also did research work with a psychologist on consciousness, which was my topic. We had some lunches together and I quickly became her confidant. She could tell me of her boss's annoyance rather than pleasure at Bente and

I inviting him and his family out to dinner at the famous Spenger's Fresh Fish Grotto. He hadn't time for that, and the restaurant was one where you usually had to wait for a table when you were only four. Bearing this in mind, I had booked a table for six and told the waiter at the last minute that two had unfortunately been forced to cancel. In the event we were able to sit down to eat straightaway and it all passed off amicably. The assistant and I took a Sunday walk in the woods above Berkeley, and since she was the only person I could think of inviting out to celebrate my fiftieth birthday, we did so at a Chinese restaurant on Shattuck Avenue. The colleague and his wife had by then left to visit another university and would be away until after my departure. Hearing that I was on the lookout for lodging during these last weeks, they asked if I could take care of their home, water and mow the lawn and feed the dog. Out of curiosity or revenge my new friend was eager to see their home and I could hardly refuse even if I had wanted. We made dinner and she stayed the night. There were several nights, not many but enough for serious warmth to enter our relationship. Since, as she also knew, these were the last few days of my stay, the whole thing affair had a tragically episodic aspect. She drove me to the airport in the car also kindly put into my care. Stopping on the way at Harry's Bar on Fillmore, both of us well dressed, the barman said we made a good couple and asked if we were on a honeymoon. The mixture of exaltation and near ending was too much for my new friend. On our parting she wept. My feelings more confused, I said I would write.

I did and she replied. Knowing there was no future in the relationship, for both this exchange was a fairly friendly winding down. Not deliberately asking for trouble but disliking concealment, I left some of her letters on my desk in their envelopes. Bente, her suspicions easily aroused, opened one or more and said I must stop.

It was a defining moment. Bente, without warning or asking, wrote to my correspondent in terms the latter found 'hurtful'. When I wrote asking who knew of the relationship besides ourselves, to my alarm she said the colleague himself. For want of a better address, Bente had sent her letter to the philosophy department at Berkeley. On noting the Norwegian stamp, the colleague had 'got into' it. Although he himself never came to mention this, I feel sure that either later or at the time others too knew. My new friend was on good terms with another colleague, and in a department office it takes little for such things to become common knowledge. From there it can spread to the department as a whole and further. Being in the open, it must have had domestic repercussions.

The story acquired mythical proportions. Some ten years later in San Diego, on telling Paul Churchland I was about to visit Berkeley in connection with an

APA meeting, he intimated with a slight wink that there had been some scandal up there. Surprised, I chose bewilderment, something I also felt, and began to wonder what effect this brief encounter had on my chances to build on my good experiences at Berkeley. Was this why, for example, I failed consistently to have quite well-supported applications accepted by the Centre for Advanced Study in the Behavioral Sciences at Stanford? Warmly encouraged by San Diego colleagues to apply, I had relied heavily on the support of others from Berkeley whose work was nearer mine. For me the 'scandal' was finally dissolved when, on seeing me at an APA meeting, the colleague and his wife came over to me and gave me a diplomatic greeting.

Norway after this unwanted excitement proved more stifling than ever. One welcome whiff of fresh air came with a visit by my sister and her husband and another in the form of a request from Penguin Books to translate Kierkegaard's *Fear and Trembling*. This proved fortuitous in the best possible sense; it opened the way to an occupation in which I could put my abilities such as they were to better use and with less strain. I completed the translation in six weeks while holidaying on the coast. This was before word-processing technology came my way and I translated by hand before typing. Starting before breakfast, from the window I would watch the rope we had strung up as a handrail for Bente's father to climb up from his separate cabin below. When it began to quiver I knew the time had come to shut down. Bente's solo kayaking also gave me time to write. I enjoyed the peace that rowing by oneself provides. There were glorious surf-rides in the small fibreglass dinghy. Attaching an extension to its outboard handgrip I could sit in the bow and keep the boat surging along on a wave and found myself singing 'A life on the ocean wave, a home on the rolling deep, let the scattered waters rage and the winds their quarters keep'.

Chapter Sixteen: Off and on

Off and on: when daylight fails a careful master would sail back and forth, toward and away from the landfall, roughly maintaining his position until daylight would again permit him to see where he was going as he sailed into ever-shallower waters.

Shortly after that shadow over my visit to Berkeley, there were complications in Trondheim. A graduate student had asked if I could help with her dissertation. She arrived at my office with a half-empty bottle of red wine and in a state suggesting her immediate need was counselling rather than tuition. An art student, she was taking a Masters in philosophy in order to grasp her own activity in the wider context of aesthetics. She also had a child and the father worked in the free theatre world in Oslo, so that she too was away from home — or was it he? Although her life seemed difficult and even tortured, when putting its current state into words, she proved to be exceptionally fluent. It introduced a ding-dong mutuality into our relationship.

There was also a vicious streak directed on life itself but also on those responsible for hers. I became included in the mix but with a role having little to do with who I was. She said she would like to meet my mother at my funeral. Torn between attraction and a sense of responsibility for her welfare that went beyond the quality of her dissertation, but also inhibited in both directions by the fact that I was married and allergic to a double life, the relationship stumbled between several stools without our getting to know each other. We corresponded in our absences, she in Italy, I in Montreal. The exchanges came to an end with a missive—'not a letter', as she wrote, but a poem honouring us both for escaping thirty years of 'devilry' in 'an un-friendship'. Its first line went 'There are many ways to checkmate ...' and the 'letter' was signed caustically 'Baby Doll', a name she knew my colleagues had given her. Some weeks later while I was in Oslo the phone rang. Bente took the call and received details of all our more than academic encounters.

I have wondered since whether free of the reins that keep husbands and wives mutually in each other's hands, but which they can also use as excuses for not prolonging adulterous asides, it would have been better to risk the devilry and live out the problems and dreams. Or did inhibition halt the development of some longer-term misery? The affair came to a dismal though mutually agreed end. Chancing to meet some time later, we agreed it was good to meet again. It was as though a deep trough in separate wave systems had met at one point, but the surge had eased and we were now buoyant again on our own crests. The once baby doll is now a successful graphic artist.

With neither of my marriages could I say that I had reflected on these matters. With the first, we were both newcomers to a foreign country, each there to make a fresh start but with no clear idea of the future. That the way forward should be shared was a gamble we hardly considered. With the second, both parties were looking for what their previous marriages lacked. This time it was a matter of each taking little or no account of the active lives in which the other was already separately engaged. The pressure of combining both under one roof proved at length to be a strain. Explanations here can sound like excuses, but it would be strange if they could not also to some extent serve that end.

In quite different contexts, neither of us had nine-to-five occupations. The theatre, when you have work, is totally absorbing. Bente, as a leading member of the permanent ensemble, was constantly employed. There were other engagements. After a late night at the theatre she could begin the next day early rehearsing for radio or television and then later make her way to the theatre, either at noon for rehearsal or in the late afternoon in time to go on stage. In many periods she was rehearsing and on stage on the same day. Seldom was she free in the evenings, and Sunday from just recently was the actors' only guaranteed day off. What kept us together was the time we devoted to projects outside working life. In the 'eighties this included six-week holidays on the Norwegian south coast and in Oslo rehabilitating a large apartment in a building that had seen no renewal since it was built a century earlier. Shortly after that work was completed we were constructing a 'loft' apartment from scratch in the same building. Later there would be months and several visits planning a new house in the south of France. This was extra-curricular work at which Bente excelled and for which she had unlimited energy. Nest building, she called it. She described my daily occupation, indeed my life-style, as that of a 'recluse'. Because my hermetic activity consumed as much of my free time as I could afford, there was less sharing in the nests once the cooperative work of building them was done.

Although Bente showed more respect for my work than I felt it deserved, I found it hard to explain what it was and what it meant to me. And why should that be so hard if it was supposed to matter so much? As for what mattered, on becoming more familiar with the theatre and its ambience I often found it more congenial to the interests that first drove me to philosophy than anything I ever came across once in the cave or endless tunnel in which scholars of the subject proceed, some in the delusion that they are seeking light. In fact, I doubted whether my abilities lay in that direction at all. Perhaps no amount of effort could outweigh the frustration caused by my overload of tunnelling.

Yet, to repeat the old refrain, at this late stage I could hardly abandon my chosen vocation. I was receiving commissions to write and translate, even opportunities to submit proposals for books on subjects of my own choosing. This on top of normal academic duties and the eternal editing, made me a sorry cohabitant. It had also a disruptive and even seditious side. Or rather two such sides: one of these was that even inhabitants of philosophy's catacombs need someone to talk shop with now and then. Bente's own keen mind grew from experience and dwelt on situations grasped intuitively with what she called her 'antenna'. She was driven by feelings, not thoughts. But if she couldn't tell Socrates from Sophocles, her replies to interviewers were articulated with a precision that would be the envy of any good philosopher. For the latter, however, such directness or visible self-assurance are not typically a panoply protecting an inner fragility.

Like so many of those I have met in adult life, Bente's too was marked by the war. She was just under nine when the Nazis arrested her mother for helping Jewish families to escape to Sweden. Tortured and imprisoned in a concentration camp near Oslo, Lise Børsum was transferred to Hamburg and then to Ravensbrück concentration camp. Surviving hardships that she described in *Fange i Ravensbrück*, she was among the surviving Scandinavian prisoners repatriated on buses organized by the Swedish Red Cross. Finding on her homecoming that the experience had disabled her for family life, she was welcomed into the company of psychologists and wrote of her experiences, leaving her two children in the care of their good-natured father.

The young daughter's longing during those two years of her mother's absence was accentuated by having to spend them with another family out in the country. After that, she was sent to a boarding school. The impact of this experience came to artistic light in her overpowering autobiographical 'one-man' show *Min Forestilling om Mor*, literally 'My Show About Mother' — in its English version simply 'Mother'. Apart from captivating its audiences in a quite agonizing way, its belated cathartic effect on the narrator herself would be hard to dismiss. Bente was recently taking part in Italy in a meeting of those whose mothers were interned in Ravensbrück.

Lise (Milly Elise) Børsum died in 1985 at the comparatively early age of seventy-seven, her death accelerated by her experiences but also some needless surgery. Beginning her adult life as a well-off middle-class housewife, and married self-effacingly to a physician thirteen years her senior, her almost casual plunge into resistance work had overturned her life completely. Afterwards she turned to journalism and authorship and toured the country with her message, working later as administrator of an organization concerned with rehabilitating war victims. We sat, on one remembered occasion, round Lise's dinner table together with Joseph Agassi and his wife Judith Buber, granddaughter of the Jewish philosopher Martin Buber. Her mother, too, had been sent Ravensbrück. Leo Eitinger, a Holocaust survivor born in Czechoslovakia, was also there. Now a Norwegian psychiatrist, he was dealing with the delayed traumas of concentration camp survivors. Lise also had musical gifts inherited from her father Eyvind Alnæs, a noted composer. Less poignant gatherings included summer days on the converted Normandy landing barge on which, in a sheltered bay at the southern end of Oslo Fjord, Lise and her journalist friend Harald Øye spent their summers with good food and not a little gin and tonic.

It is an irony that concentration camps have affected both my marriages. With Joanne, it was the experience of a makeshift un-American communal way of life wholly for women and their children. For Bente as a child it meant separation from her family. Was it a dread of being abandoned that made her appear so obsessively protective? In the war she had no family, while Joanne's camp life was exceptionally familial. Her rules of domestic conduct had to do with the way I behaved at home; alliances or friendships outside the home were matters left to me so long as the family and its home were preserved. Less than a matter of keeping up appearances, it was a matter of keeping the home intact. When I told Joanne of my intention to marry Bente, she asked, 'Why on earth do you have to do that?'. When I did, she left a bottle of wine on our doorstep.

Fortune was later to spare her some momentary panic. One day, or evening if I remember correctly, a man with a Bergen accent rang me at my office. Was my name Hannay? 'Yes, Alastair Hannay.' Jo's father? My heart missing a beat, I said. 'Yes.' Jo hadn't been in that day. Finding the Music Academy too stressful, Jo had taken a degree in information theory at Oslo University. Now with a temporary job at an insurance firm in Bergen, it was his boss calling. They had waited until after lunch on Monday, but when he still hadn't shown up they tried calling his mother. Unable to find her, they were trying me, to hear whether Jo had been in Oslo. He hadn't and I had heard nothing from him. Jo had told them he planned to go on a mountain hike that weekend. They had spoken to the tourist office, and yes, sure enough, Jo had been in there on Friday and they had recommended a route — two hours' bus, a good climb and overnighting in a cabin and then a long walk on Sunday and finally down to the railway. It was vital to find out if he'd gone with anyone. Was his girlfriend in Oslo?

Not knowing her family name, I couldn't check, but Joanne would know. I drove to where her office should have been, but they had moved. After a long walk I found the new place, but she wasn't there either. They phoned other places where she might be but wasn't and I drove to those other places — no sign of her red car, so I went home to call Jo's boss. The local sheriff had been alerted and they had spoken to the bus driver, but without a sure description the sheriff wouldn't start a search — what if he was not there? It's getting dark soon, they said, we need to know if there were any others. I rang various friends of Jo who weren't in. I looked up trains, thinking helplessly that if the police wouldn't look, I would do so myself. We were to go to the theatre after Bente returned from rehearsal but I cancelled it.

At about 7:00 p.m. the phone rang. It was Jo from Bergen. He'd been ill but, without a phone, had assumed the office would guess he was in Oslo. This was before mobiles. Fortunately, I had not been able to contact anyone, not even Joanne. Jo gave me her beeper number and she called back. She had been spared those six hours. As far as omens go, an optimist might sense that however bad things may be, they will turn out well in the end. An Athenian coffee-ground-reading lady at Plaka seeing agonies in store had once predicted as much.

There was now some cause for personal optimism. Due another sabbatical, I had been invited to teach a quarter at San Diego. In March came a letter from David Daiches, the Director of the Institute for Advanced Studies in the Humanities at Edinburgh University, saying I had been awarded a Visiting Research Fellowship there. It would be for two months in the spring of 1985. I arranged to spend these months in Edinburgh immediately preceding the three in California. Spring in Auld Reekie turned out to be bitterly cold in a stone-built house where the generous coal fires once warming the large rooms in Buccleuch Place were replaced by small gas-fires endlessly greedy for small coins. But of warmth there was plenty among fellows drawn from Denmark, Germany, Poland, New Zealand and the USA as well as Edinburgh itself.

It was strange to be listed as a scholar from Norway in my own hometown. Vincent and Annette Hope kindly offered me a bed, and along with Timothy Sprigge, my ex-colleague from London and now Edinburgh's Professor of Logic and Metaphysics, they came to listen to my paper on Kierkegaard at the weekly 'work-in-progress seminar'. Peter Jones, the director, said it was just the kind of paper they needed, by which I think he meant it was in generally intelligible English.

As in Edinburgh, I began alone in San Diego, or rather La Jolla, where the UCSD campus overlooks the Pacific Ocean. Compared with the nostalgic, low-key return to grey and familiar Edinburgh, arrival there was like crashing into a bright new world. The stay itself proved to be an exciting chapter in an unfinished book.

There was as usual no time for acclimatizing. After a short week in Oslo to arrange my visa, I had arrived in San Diego on a Friday, the day after term officially began and there was much to do before my teaching began. Even if accommodation has been arranged, it is typically unfurnished. To deal with that requires a visit to a rental firm, for which in turn you need a car and some knowledge of local geography, and that a visit to a car insurance firm, which then requires someone else's car and a good map. If you are lucky, the dealer will give you temporary coverage. A telephone account has to be opened, the furniture has to arrive, and you have to learn the way not just to the campus but to those remote parts of its vast area where your teaching is to take place.

Avrum Stroll met me at the airport and, after a short visit to his home discussing plans, took me to the La Jolla Village Inn where the department had booked me in until Monday. On Saturday I had lunch with Bob Pippin, who had volunteered to show me La Jolla. At the Chart House overlooking the Pacific we drank cool wine. These people knew how to make one feel at home, as did the Faculty Wives with whom for a token fee I arranged on Sunday to rent the kitchen equipment, dishes and cutlery I would need in the apartment waiting for me and the furniture on Monday. On that day, I made my way on foot from the Village Inn to the campus, its vast space hidden behind a ridge of woodland. I was shown my office, to my pride once Herbert Marcuse's and now Zeno Vendler's, one of the three 'big shots' I had attended Evensong with at Christ Church ten years earlier. Avrum drove me to a car dealer who had been helped out by his son on a summer vacation, and I ended the day at the cost of four hundred dollars in a vast green Impala, with amazing directional stability and you could steer with one finger. Insurance was arranged on the spot, a telephone account opened with Pacific Bell. On Tuesday I was ready to prepare for my class beginning the next day.

Given the luxury of teaching only one class, for me a unique situation so far, I could focus on it fully. Billed as 'Phenomenology and Existentialism: Sartre and his Critics', it had to be trimmed if fitted into two lectures a week for ten weeks. We focused on Sartre's *Being and Nothingness* and followed with a discussion of Foucault, whose post-structuralist anthropology pointed a dagger at the heart of Sartrean freedom. With little time to prepare this course before arrival, I bought two beach chairs, one of them for Bente when she arrived, and drove to Del Mar beach where I scribbled lecture notes in the afternoon sun. I continued to do this during the full ten weeks on the three days I didn't lecture and at weekends as long as my hospitable hosts allowed.

The students were full of questioning and suggestions, especially when it came to identifying cases of *mauvaise foi*. They put newspaper cuttings in my mail shelf with humorous suggestions as to what could count. It came to them questioning their own 'roles' as students, seeing in this too an instance of the adoption of a part that relieves them of the embarrassment of their freedom. Perhaps they were too polite to ask whether my job was also a case in point. As for theatrical roles, we had the assistance of the theatre department, some of whose students were willing to devote half of one lecture hour to a performance of the latter part of *Huis Clos*, or 'No Exit' with its sting line 'Hell is other people'. It was also part of the drama students' training in learning parts at short notice and a good example of a cross-fertilization that, in my experience, is all too rare in the academic world.

As usual when the word 'existentialism' appears in the list of course offerings, they were a mixed lot. One, as I discovered later when meeting him in his new role, co-founded the local Sledgehammer Theatre, a group dedicated to modern theatre. Another became a senior researcher at the Søren Kierkegaard Research Centre in Copenhagen with untold publications to his name and, at the time of writing, is a senior researcher at the Slovak Academy in Bratislava. A third is a poet who later became a painter. He sent me a collection of his latest poems. Others continued in academic positions, though none in philosophy but some, as is normal today, ended up in the software industry.

As in Berkeley I had become so used to arranging my own life that Bente's presence felt more like a visit than a re-creation of home. But there was plenty to keep her occupied too. The theatre department had agreed to her taking part in its activities. As a result, we both attended student performances and the more professional stagings at the on-campus La Jolla Playhouse, an important part of the Californian theatre 'scene' founded by Hollywood and used in the past to try out a large number of successful plays and shows. Contact with the theatre department's chairman and his wife led to their visiting Norway. There were explorations in the Impala to the nearby Anza Borrego desert. Some of Bente's colleagues, together with Charles Marowitz, a stage director and playwright who had worked in Oslo, were staging an experimental play in an offbeat district of Los Angeles, so we visited them. Bente's daughter Tori came in June, having flown to Miami and crossing the continent by Greyhound. There were visits to San Diego's Sea World and the Wild Animal Park, and after a few days she boarded the Greyhound again and returned to Oslo by the same route.

Life offers its share of lucky coincidences. Wild Animal Park provided a stellar example. On returning to the car park I found I'd lost the car keys. With no idea of where in that vast and much trampled area I might have dropped them, and already late for a visit to some friends, thinking an enquiry at the lost-property desk would be a shot so long as to be absurd, I went there as a matter of form at the very moment a couple were handing them in.

Maybe coincidence plays a larger part in life than we care to think. Like the latter, some have only anecdotal interest, but others can tap forgotten history. My grandfather's next eldest brother Peter McDowell Hannay had left Scotland to find his feet in a shipping office in New York, but soon decided to move to Riverside, a city lying southeast of Los Angeles, to try his hand at cultivating oranges. Unsuccessful in this, he moved to La Jolla. With only the Pacific Ocean before him, and accepting that this was where he would pitch camp, he wrote to his fiancée in Scotland to say she could now follow him. Apparently, by the time she had made the long train journey from the East Coast, Margaret Witherspoon Reed had got on such good terms with the train's conductor that there had been some hesitation about disembarking. We know that she did. The couple started a farm located where the Birch Aquarium lies just outside the university campus. It supplied the nearby Scripps Institution of Oceanography with farm produce. Photographs from that time show a small village round La Jolla Cove with empty land north to the Institution and a small path leading to it. The area is now filled with luxury homes and summerhouses, many for inhabitants of Arizona who find their summer too stifling. Peter and Margaret later built a tavern on the shore called Spindrift. I read somewhere that Hollywood actors and directors in the early days of the cinema would visit La Jolla at weekends and savoured Margaret's famous pancakes. Close to the high-tide mark, the tavern suffered from winter storms and its windows were regularly replaced. Nowadays a restaurant bears its name in a more solid construction with 'Beach and Tennis Club' as its label together and with a nine-hole par 3 golf course attached. The Spindrift room offers a 'tradition of sophisticated dining on the sands of La Jolla Shores'.

Using the phone book I contacted their granddaughter. Her parents had moved to nearby Ramona, a reputedly redneck area, while Mariel, whose fiancée had been killed in Viet Nam, bred horses in nearby Del Mar. After initial suspicion on their side, having been approached by other more distant root-seekers with the same name, on consulting her parents and seemingly delighted she said I must be Erskine's son. We met several times and talked of their past. Patrick, then still an aircraft designer and working on matters of stealth, had lived in La Jolla all his life. They moved some years later to Texas. Patrick died at ninety-three. Marie who died in 2012, reached a hundred. Mariel still keeps horses.

This invigorating and educational stay ended with a two-day drive up the coastal highway to San Francisco and Berkeley. We spent a night at Ragged Point Inn north of the Hearst Castle, followed by a lunch stop at Fisherman's wharf in Monterey. At Stanford we were guests of Dagfinn and Vera Føllesdal. In Oakland, after a night at the Berkeley Faculty Club, we managed to sell the Impala in time for the flight home from San Francisco.

Already before this Californian visit we had moved into our comprehensively redecorated fourth-floor apartment in the fine 1870's building adjoining Oslo's then University Library. Bente did much of the restyling, while I had done what I could between commutes to Trondheim. Height consigned me mainly to the job of painting the high stucco ceilings. With the California experience fresh in mind, the prospect of continued commuting was to say the least uninviting, and after a summer on the south coast with Bente and her father I would have to resume the constant to-and-fro. The administration was also opposed: two years earlier a circular informed 'all employees' that the university's council had agreed to establish rules concerning 'special arrangements', the norm being that one live within 'daily commuting distance of the university'. Those affected were told to make such arrangements by 1 March 1983. I pointed out that the council's ruling was not mentioned in the conditions of my appointment. Would this mean my dismissal? Risking the administration's discontent, perhaps even provoking it, I asked my colleagues to let me lecture every second week, doubling up the hours each time. They agreed.

I was now sharing my Spartan accommodation in alternate weeks with another travelling colleague, his travel regime having so far escaped the administration's eye. When our visits began to coincide, I rented a larger room in the spacious home of Bob Esdaile, a Canadian professor of architecture and his wife Elin, both Marxists and fans of Fidel Castro. I joined them with the professor's students in their cellar for evenings devoted to free fantasizing with various materials but was less than impressed by a biography of Brezhnev that Elin placed hopefully on my bedside table. I moved soon to a suburb and lodged with a lady colleague with whom some years earlier I had been 'together' but now had another friend. It seemed quite natural. Later still, I took a room for four days every fortnight in the town centre in a temperance hotel, once the district's notorious Gestapo headquarters.

There was a growing sense of the sheer meaninglessness of my work in Trondheim. The propaedeutic course could be done better by any of my colleagues. Resuming a topic I had discussed with imaginative and intelligent post-graduate students at Berkeley three years earlier, there was a seminar that autumn on mind-body problems attended by only three or four students. Either they lacked the background, imagination or intelligent curiosity that the topic requires, or I was too dejected to inspire them. In sharp contrast there had been the interest aroused by an off-the-cuff talk I gave to my then architect host's students at the Technical University, under the title 'Method or Madness in Creation?'

To postpone what looked like being a showdown, I had applied for leave without pay for the 1984-85 academic year. The outcome had been that revelatory Californian experience. With no motivation to stay on in Trondheim, when asked to deputize for Føllesdal in Oslo in the spring of 1985 I jumped at the chance. The leave granted, I sent in my resignation and received an 'honourable discharge', the diploma so inscribed by my early office colleague in Oslo, Lars Roar Langslet. With an article on the 'young Marx', he had also been one of the first contributors to *Inquiry* under my editorship. A right-winger, he was now Minister of Culture and Science in the Conservative government.

Without a job after the spring term in Oslo, I applied for a six-month research grant for the first half of the following year and wrote to the Penguin Classics editor asking if there was any interest in further Kierkegaard translation. The grant was approved and in April the following year Penguin agreed to a translation of *Sygdommen til Døden* (The Sickness unto Death). I was by then also in the happy position of fulfilling an invitation to teach for a month in Stockholm, while the following spring, thanks to the influence of friends there, I would be once again in San Diego. In the two years following my departure from Trondheim, not only had I plenty to do but could make ends meet.

If a jagged note was heard from time to time, our separate involvements kept dissonance at bay. Feeling I must make up for lost time, I was taking on ever more assignments while Bente, besides classics by Oscar Wilde, Bernard Shaw, Edward Albee, Anouilh at Oslo New Theatre and plays by modern Norwegian and continental playwrights and reviews, collaborated with Juni Dahr, a freelance colleague, in the Finnish author Maria Jotuni's 'Det kalles kjærlighet' (They Call it Love) on unwanted children left to die in care by 'angel makers'. In 1988 this series of wry cameos was 'staged' in a restored East End apartment where, in lieu of scene shifts, a small audience moved from room to room. This select show was later held in a historical building in Oslo's National Museum on Bygdøy. Later, at the Winter Olympics at Lillehammer in 1994, Bente joined forces with several colleagues in a staging of Sigrid Undset's historical drama *Kristin Lavransdatter*. For myself, in the time to come I would be spending weeks and months 'in the line of duty' in California and elsewhere. On vacations there were activities we could share: lying in the sun, net-fishing, rowing, and generally keeping house in her father's cabin by the sea. Back in our apartment we were more like two people meeting in coffee breaks while working in different departments of a firm.

Whenever Bente had a new part another team of colleagues would be invited to celebrate the opening night or final rehearsal. Without similar access to my own colleagues, she may easily had felt excluded when I took part in social extensions of my own working life. To her, in professional terms I was a closed book, just as my father had been to my mother, though they at least had a family in common.

According to Bente the only time I tried to explain what philosophy was about, as if that were at all possible, was with pencil sketches on a paper tablecloth in Montmartre. I should have tried harder, but to tell the truth my heart was no longer in my job.

That was on a Christmas and New Year break, where we went in order to escape conflicting family commitments. On another occasion we fled to Rome. There, during the first of three intervals in Verdi's *Don Carlos*, we came upon Paul Feyerabend with his new friend Grazia Borrini. On our admitting to not knowing the plot, they insisted on meeting at the further two intervals for briefing. Sharing a taxi with us afterwards, Paul confessed he couldn't remember my name. Having known him for twenty years, I didn't like to look too closely for the reason. It happens. But Paul's death not long after from a brain tumour suggested, I rather hoped, that this might be part of the reason. His company over the years, his provocative friendliness, mordent optimism, humour and not least sympathy for Kierkegaard, all of this gave me much needed moral support. Of his own family name, he told me that it was originally Fabian. No one who met Paul Feyerabend could forget *his* name, which he liked to translate as 'knocking off time'. One exchange of views in Berkeley proved so engaging that Paul found on glancing at his watch that he was fifteen minutes late for his lecture. A poignant memory is of Paul falling into a shallow ditch outside his house on stepping out of my car on a dark evening when I had driven him home. He lay there, this person of immense presence and energy, just a crumpled heap. Before I could help he had pulled himself up with his walking stick and with a smile wished me good night.

Happy now to follow the Kierkegaard thread, I kept my discontent with philosophy secret. In my new freelance situation two invitations were particularly welcome. In July 1986 there was a three-day conference in Sunderland on 'The Ethics of Kierkegaard in Relation to Contemporary Thought'. Kierkegaard scholars from the UK, the USA, Canada, Denmark and Germany met there, among them George Pattison, alumnus of Edinburgh as well as Durham, at that time a vicar in Suffolk but at the time of writing at Glasgow after a period in Cambridge as Dean of Chapel at King's College and Professor of Religion at Christ Church, Oxford. There was Daphne Hampson from St Andrews, a strong-minded woman with it appeared an abiding interest in Schubert's Lieder. Sitting ahead of me on the small train that took us from Newcastle to Sunderland, his back turned, was Ed Mooney, who I had first met in 1982 far away in Sacramento. I talked to a German student, Georg Rädes, then studying at St Andrews, and we later kept up a correspondence that continued after he announced he had contracted Hodgkins Disease. We wrote until he died not long after. His letters from hospital were poignant. In one of the last, he wrote that Kierkegaard had been of no help at all. And it is true: Kierkegaard is less about comfort than about misery.

There was nevertheless something comforting in this northern assembly so close to my origins in the presence of so many like-minded from areas I had visited in wanderings abroad.

The second invitation took me eastward. I gave lectures in Stockholm in March and April 1987. The warm hospitality shown there by the teaching staff and students was welcome balm. I left for Stockholm alone. Mobility reduces with age. It took time to get used to a strange apartment in an unfamiliar city. I had been asked to provide the students with 'new perspectives'. Ignorant of their present perspectives, I began without an idea of how to proceed. When I said I'd like to deal with consciousness, Hegel and Kierkegaard, they said this was 'all news to them'. Naturally they knew more than they let on and we got along well.

Bente arrived for a long cultural weekend. We saw Ingmar Bergman's production of *Hamlet* with Peter Stormare as the troubled Dane and in a disused welding works complete with cobblestones and London drizzle, a *Pygmalion* in which Eliza took a bath which emptied onto the feet of those enjoying the view from the front row. An indignant Doolittle smashed at least ten wine bottles against the wall — empty ones happily. There was an experimental theatre performance of a play based on *Either/Or* set in a Parisian bistro with Sartre and de Beauvoir among the dramatis personae, along with Merleau-Ponty and Camus. This was an experience I could recommend to the students.

The lectures were for three hours on two days in the week, with another two-hour seminar on a third day. This gave me two weekdays and the weekend to prime myself and relax in spite of screams and cursing from a lady in the flat from below. She had been spared institutionalization because she did no harm. For Bente these days offered a rare opportunity to meet her cousin, a sculptor who lived at Gripsholm not far from Stockholm. An artist, he too was used to a life where focus and relaxation easily alternated. He and his wife took us to visit the nearby Gripsholm Castle. The first warm day of spring brought a slipped disc in helping to bring out the garden furniture. It withstood the visit to the castle but not the train back to Stockholm. I stood all the way and back in the apartment had to lie all day on the sofa. On the days I lectured a taxi took me to and from the university. Strangely, when lecturing the pain eased and I had no difficulty in walking back and forth. It occurred to me at this time that in two months I would be fifty-five, the age at which my father had died almost exactly thirty-one years earlier. With relevantly morbid associations but no thoughts of comparison otherwise, I realized that well over three hundred years earlier René Descartes had died in that same city at about the same age.

Oslo now seemed unpromising. In a year or so I might begin looking for part-time employment in the USA. Still unwilling to abandon philosophy altogether, I thought I might try braving the 'prevailing winds of doctrine'. This was an expression used by Dan Dennett to describe the current of anti-Cartesian air sweeping over discussion of the mind. By treating the conscious mind as fundamentally unphysical and even non-spatial, but also as our direct access to things mental, Descartes had everyone for centuries pointing inwards and blinding us to what psychology and neurobiology can tell us about what we assume to know about what we do and why. The wind prevailing today blows full blast in the opposite direction, as though in antithesis to a Cartesian thesis, as in a Hegelian dialectic. Just as in Hegel, however, both may be equally wrong with the new jet stream blowing away everything that we think we know directly, and even the 'I' that thinks it does the knowing. Since machines or biological creatures with other kinds of brains might cope just as well or better, for scientific purposes the subjective side can simply be shelved and left to poets and in daily discourse to the simple-minded metaphors of 'folk psychology'. Under contract to submit a manuscript for a Routledge series, 'The Problems of Philosophy: Their Past and Present', I wrote a brief article surveying some contemporary approaches to consciousness and took the liberty again of publishing something of my own in *Inquiry*, though not before seeking approval from colleagues including Dreyfus, now on the editorial board. Like the earlier book projects, due to other commitments this one too was to lie too long on the in-tray.

The Sickness unto Death translation was due by the end of 1987. But there was also a contribution to be made to a volume on John Searle. Rashly bent even more so than Searle on spiting the prevailing currents, with what I took to be encouraging words on my article from both Searle and Dreyfus, I looked forward to puffing in the opposite direction on a visit to San Diego scheduled for the spring of 1988. There Paul Churchland was now chair, and with Stephen Stich and Paul Kitcher on the faculty the focus was very far from traditional philosophy analytic or continental. Paul's programme was, along with his wife Pat, to convince us that we should bury any concept with no place in a 'mature' neuroscience. Far from merely spreading their sails to catch the prevailing winds of doctrine, they were injecting a lethal puff of their own.

Completing the *Sickness unto Death* translation in seven short weeks to keep its December 1987 deadline, I was now ready for this second visit to San Diego. The consciousness book was now first priority and I hoped to get a better grip on the subject in the presence of a philosopher with a developed project diametrically opposed to my own thoughts. But instead of being asked what I would like to teach, the courses offered were ones that others preferred not to. The Churchlands being now the focus and Paul the chair, I suspect the invitation was due mainly to lobbying by friends and to lighten the load on other colleagues.

Generous and approachable, Churchland exuded a serene superiority filtered through a clearly well-intended show of modesty. Seemingly deaf to the questions that have perpetually perplexed philosophers of the mind and essentially a physicist, Paul approached the mind-body problem from the toes upward with the brain the highest one need go, or from top to toe. Of course, it makes much sense and is a refreshing corrective to a discussion of the mind-body that had for centuries found itself stuck in a quagmire and was now reaching just about the limits of epicyclical nicety. 'Reductive Materialism' was a slogan that promised to let some fresh air into a thoroughly scholastic debate. The problem, in an alternative metaphorical element, was that here the Herculean torrent cleansing the Augean stables flushed out all the questions and possible insights that a top-down perspective might still provide if properly examined. Ted Honderich, citing his own remarks on introducing a Jacobsen Lecture at UCL, described Paul as (like himself) 'an escaped Canadian, escaped so far to La Jolla, California', and as 'that satisfactory kind of philosopher, a proselytizer for a young and promising cause … very roughly … the proposition that the philosophy of mind has its future in a kind of association, or more than that, with neuroscience'. Tactfully put by one who recognized the missing dimension, Ted wrote that although liking Churchland, he found 'close to universal agreement that the lecture' had 'next to zero philosophical content'. Only Ted himself and Oxford's Christopher Peacocke had found it expedient to ask questions, perhaps out of perplexity in the one case and courtesy in the other.

The San Diego visit took off to a bad start. Since Bente would be occupied at home during the term, we agreed that she come with me and stay for the ten days before my teaching began. Arriving at Los Angeles on 24 March, we continued to San Diego on a commuter plane. Either the aircraft was too small to take our baggage or it left too early to have it loaded. That was a minor setback. Obviously used to this, the airline's routines for delivering delayed baggage were impeccable. The problem for me was that our social obligations during Bente's brief stay excluded the period of adjustment and preparation vital in such sudden changes of context. Sharon and Jerry Doppelt housed us the first night, since the apartment reserved by the university was not yet available. They took us to C & M Chevrolet, where Avrum Stroll, participating at an APA meeting somewhere else at the time, had prepared the ground for our rental car, this time a nondescript Chevrolet Cavalier 'compact'. With that we could look for rental furniture and by the evening of our first full day we found ourselves established in Lebon Drive at the opposite gate of the same university property on which I had rented an apartment earlier. We spent these few days doing things we could do together. As the day of reckoning approached, I became increasingly worried about the teaching. I had already been thrown into confusion over one of the courses. Hoping to use the occasion to rehearse some thoughts on consciousness, I deduced from a textbook sent by the ever-helpful Avrum that I was expected to teach the regular introduction to theory of knowledge. A problem with textbooks in such courses is that they are the product of someone else's experience of giving them. The level in this case seemed also to imply that the thoughts the students would be capable of grasping were complex enough for them to be able to see the point of the author's examples without much help. Not having given a course like this for many years, I should have been devoting these few days to planning with my teaching assistants. On one of those days, while we were driving to the La Jolla Shores for a sandwich, I had to stop the car due to a repeat of the sense of heart failure that had dogged me in the past.

For me Bente's departure was traumatic. Watching her walk from the departure lounge at Lindbergh Field and board the flight to Los Angeles left me feeling on the edge of nowhere. Looking through the shaded glass until she had gone and the plane had rolled away, the mood was something more complex than loneliness. For her to stay would only make things worse. Later Bente told me that she realized it had been a bad moment when she saw me standing there behind the glass. My only thought on leaving the airport was to find some means of distraction. Searching among the books on display in the shopping area, I chose the fattest paperback I could find, an English translation of *Das Boot*, the harrowing account of a U-Boat crew on patrol in World War II. With it I returned to the apartment and began reading with children noisily kicking a football in the garage below while their parents tended a grill on the balcony opposite.

There were sixty fifty-minute lectures to be given in the course of the ten-week term. It meant two lectures three times a week on Mondays, Wednesdays and Fridays. The morning lectures were Philosophy 1, 'The Nature of Philosophy', a topic that could be impossibly broad and complex but was intended here to introduce students to 'the major questions with which philosophers deal, through the reading and analysis of classical and contemporary works'. It all went off well enough, thanks largely to the support of Jon Stewart, my teaching assistant, who had followed my class on Sartre three years previously. Fortunately, I had prepared the agenda and made copious notes. But Philosophy 15, the afternoon lecture, was something else. It came after a one-hour and ten-minute lunch break, and unlike the first lecture was actually billed as an introduction. It was a course designed, as I discovered too late, for students taking only a certain number of points in philosophy and so far lacking any background at all in the subject. The notes and thoughts I had prepared proved entirely useless. Finding myself in a large auditorium confronting well over two hundred students expecting me to start them off from scratch, I began by sketching two opposite approaches to the question of what knowledge is, the traditional approach stemming from Plato and Descartes, with its emphasis on avoiding scepticism, and the newly fashionable Wittgensteinian approach that sees it as a matter of how we actually use words like 'know' and 'believe'. My two teaching assistants, Neelam and Bill, burst into my office immediately afterwards and said I couldn't go on like that, it was far above them. We sat down and re-tooled the course on the spot. The students had already bought the introductory book, so we kept the first few chapters. For the rest, we would begin with something easier to grasp and more relevant to their other studies. Since for many these included science, we put Popper's *Conjectures and Refutations* on the list together with some critics and rebuttals of Popper and some text from David Hume on induction, a topic that Popper himself addresses. Popper's idea that scientific theories are conjectures and inherently fallible, and that fallibility is what marks off science from pseudo-science and metaphysics, went down well, at least with those students who came to discuss the lectures in my consultation hours after the Monday afternoon lecture. We turned the series into a kind of narrative, where Popper, as one mature and engaging student, a Vietnam veteran, put it, seems to have got it all 'in one bag', but where the difficulties of Popper's proposal and its limitations are then brought to light. That seemed to set them thinking.

Making up new lectures every second day for nine further weeks was strenuous. I woke early, walked the half hour from Lebon Drive to the campus and worked there until 10:45 at which time I would walk the considerable distance to Peterson Hall and talk briefly to Jon Stewart before getting down to the rewarding enough business of explaining the nature of philosophy to students already geared to find out. The time between that and the next lecture was devoted to a sandwich and V8 juice in my office while I tried to ignore the loud music that broke out regularly in lunch hour on the Revelle Plaza just outside. I would then penetrate to the inner depths of Galbraith Hall, the same building in which the philosophy department was housed, and find my way to the large auditorium. The vast blackboard, though as usual green, was always covered in text left by the previous lecturer. I spent at least a minute, sometimes wishing it were longer, with my back to the audience scrubbing away and trying to think of a good line to start with. I gradually overcame the dread and in defence put on a suitably authoritative demeanour. I told those who insisted on asking question from the back of the auditorium to come to the front if they were that interested.

When the afternoon lecture was over, or after consultation hours, it was with a huge sense of relief that I walked back to the apartment via Ralph's supermarket. There I shuffled endlessly up and down the well-stocked shelves leaning on a trolley. Choosing my dinner from Ralph's shelves took time even though it nearly always ended up with the same, some fish (usually orange roughie), spinach and potatoes and white wine. It was a diet that suited me, and if I lived alone I could live on it forever with a little cheese added. I continued to read *Das Boot* and listened to the BBC World Service with the aid of a long wire stretched over the room as an aerial. In the days between lectures, after some editorial work I would spend time on Del Mar Beach, walking up and down its several kilometres and reflecting on the next day's lectures. Sometimes I had a sandwich and beer at the Poseidon Restaurant at the north end of the beach. On cloudy days I would be in the office and buy sandwiches on campus, or occasionally on the Shores where they were especially good. I enjoyed the system of calling your name when the sandwich was ready and experimented with a variety of names. 'Alastair' seemed out place there, so I tried to get the feel of having alternative names like 'Joe', 'Jake', 'Nate', and 'Hank'. In spite of eating all I needed, when the term's teaching was over I had lost eighteen pounds. It came home to me how much I owed to my two teaching assistants. Already well on their way, they later got jobs at Notre Dame and Cornell. A third had been conscripted to help out. As a recent Oxford graduate and knowing I had come from Norway, he generously congratulated me on my command of English. Not averse to praise even just for its sound, I thanked him and left it at that.

Of the students I remember only those few who came for discussion. The morning course left its more personal imprint. After the last lecture, a delegation asked me out to an afternoon dinner at the La Jolla Inn. It was a friendly and relaxed gathering, leaving an impression of combined respect and openness, something I never found in Norway where first names were normal and everyone at roughly the same level. Here, however friendly our interchanges, I was always 'Dr Hannay'.

There was a darker side. During the term one of the students had died. A quick-witted young man, who once assured me that he had crossed Trondheim

Fjord with his parents, while waving a knife on the street outside his home was shot dead by the police. It was reported that he had rushed out following an argument in the kitchen with his parents, one of them a professor at another San Diego university. There was talk of drugs. Perhaps. But we read every day of the USA's ill-prepared trigger-happy police.

A brief visit to a sunny Montreal in August was a welcome change. There Alastair McKinnon demonstrated his programme for charting word clusters in Kierkegaard's collected works as a way of illustrating Kierkegaard's authorial mind digitally. As I saw it and tried to point out, it left no toom for all-important subtexts. As part of a group invited to test its skills with his computer game I ventured to say so but an unstoppably enthusiastic McKinnon seemed unfazed.

In New York, on the way back, we focused on food and exploring the depths of Manhattan's vertical sided valleys. A warmer side of American life revealed itself on the way to the airport. We had badly miscalculated the time needed for the bus-ride and when Bente inquired of the bus driver how long it would take, that large and equable black man said 'Don't worry darling, we're all going to get there together'. We did and due to airport delays on time.

Chapter Seventeen: With the flow

Going with the flow: sailing in the direction of the current.

Odd how a memoir can drag its feet over the past but go into fast camera when closing in on the present. With fresh memories replacing old ones, you would think it went the other way. However, when the past is being recalled to explain the present, or excuse it, the imbalance makes some sense. Consider, too, how the structure imposed by a relatively single-minded purpose can fall apart when unanticipated consequences of its achievement take over. Not only is focus blurred, there is a loosening of the several threads that held the fabric of a single-minded purpose together. Losing that integrity, they are exposed more openly to life's vagaries and the blindness of habit. Latent collisions surface.

One of these concerned the journal. Later that autumn complications arose with *Inquiry* when a commissioning editor from Blackwell asked if I might 'explore' a link with that publisher. Given the limitations of the local university press in matters of advertising and distribution, I was more than tempted. There were obstacles. The university publishers were eager to regard the journal as their own. Helen Pilgrim's letter set in motion a protracted and legally complex process: if there was no immediate possibility, in 'possible circumstances' there might be one in the course of the next two years. A meeting was arranged with Helen Pilgrim in London in early December to coincide with a visit to Ted Honderich, editor of the series for which the book on consciousness was intended and which I would like to discuss with him. The journal having been the personal initiative of Arne Naess, *Inquiry*'s copyright status was a tricky matter, but the journal was dependent economically on support from the main Norwegian research council. The council's annual contribution supplemented *in toto* the deficit left by what at first had been a meagre income from subscriptions. By now the journal's publisher was an independent business concern and had little interest in looking into questions of ownership and rights. When questioned, they claimed total ownership. Since for a quite modest fee I spent a third of my working year, including holidays, editing 'their' journal, and had managed to provide it with an international status that brought in a considerable subscription, I disputed that claim. Having rather better relations with the research council's representative responsible for underwriting its continued but now smaller contribution to publication,

I asked him whether the council itself might be interested in this matter of rights. An international expert in matters of copyright was hired and a complex verdict assigning certain rights to the editors was delivered. I checked the agreement between the council and the publisher for some indication of the conditions under which it might be possible to sever our ties with the latter. There was a possible loophole concerning matters of efficiency in production and effectiveness in distribution.

I met Helen Pilgrim for coffee on Tottenham Court Road and we agreed to pursue the matter. Upset having just visited Verso Press in Soho to complain that Feyerabend's recent book included at least one chapter straight from the copyrighted pages of our journal without acknowledgement or request, and already somewhat stressed when I met Helen, on walking back to the hotel on Gower Street I had another, and this time alarming, attack of apparent heart stoppage. I sat for a while on a conveniently placed bollard in a side street and after some minutes' concentration made my way to the hotel, where I lay watching a snooker championship on television. The short step to University College and Ted was beyond me. I spoke to him, but he said he couldn't get away. Staying in my room until checking out time I then walked gingerly to Leicester Square, taking the underground to South Kensington, changed to the Richmond line, and on arriving at Richmond Station found a seat on one of the round benches just inside the draughty entrance. Commuters pushed past. My brother had agreed to meet me there, so that we could visit our mother together, but he was delayed and I hung on for dear life in what seemed an eternity before he finally arrived. After we joined our mother the attacks miraculously stopped. No longer missing a beat I flew back to Norway the next day exhausted.

Attempts at that time to re-locate the journal were complicated by the fact that complaints made about the production of the journal tended to be pinned on the publisher's editor responsible for its production. This was George Drennan, a Glaswegian and a good friend with whom I had worked amicably for many years. The editor in charge of the journals was an ambitious and wily man who finally contrived to have all the English-language journals and himself bought up by the present British publisher. George was already under some stress and, in his wiliness but also concern, the editor suggested that this might be the last straw.

The long-awaited crisis over ownership would climax some time later with the takeover of the university press's entire English-language journal production by the London based Taylor & Francis. By then I had good offers from Blackwell, Sage and Cambridge. In an attempt to wrest ownership from the sellers, I engaged a law firm upon which the sellers engaged theirs. Before long mine advised surrender. There was a case to make, but apart from the expense of going to court, the journal would in the meantime lose subscribers. I agreed, not least because I would have to cover the galloping legal expenses personally. Playing the few cards I still held, I threatened to hold articles back unless the new publisher paid my lawyer's bill and insisted that the journal appear under the respected Routledge imprint. In London I met Stephen Neal, the journals director. He agreed to my terms and to the further condition that the editorship be in the hands of a governing board nominated by myself.

This led to a prolonged struggle with Norway's bureaucracy. Earlier, to secure rights of ownership and copyright for the editors, I had established a foundation that could stand as legal owner in possible disputes with the publisher. It later appeared that to be registered the foundation had to own capital. In the register I identified this as a large number of unsold issues now stored in our cellar. To wind up the foundation and replace it with a governing board I was required to send in accounts, which I was told we should have kept all along, having them certified annually by an authorized accountant. After considerable correspondence with the registry situated somewhere near the Arctic Circle, they agreed that the only expense would be the accountant's own expenses certifying that they had been met out of our own pockets. In the end, they decided un-bureaucratically and with excellent pragmatism that we should forget there had ever been a foundation. Its non-existence gave immaculate birth to the new governing board, from which I later resigned after the remaining members, rather than pursuing the open-minded approach instituted by Arne Naess, chose to bring *Inquiry* into line with other academically correct and correspondingly uninspiring 'trade' journals. Having tried previously to avoid this fate by finding an editor who could keep it in its tradition after my more than forty years, I had to accept that after his noble ten years he, Wayne Martin, would be replaced by a dyed-in-the wool 'analytical' apparatchik of Norwegian birth who was willing to take on the job. Clearly it was more important that the journal contribute to Norway's endemic need to be recognized 'internationally' than that it perpetuate Arne Naess's universal ideals.

There was the matter of a job. Of two openings in Oslo, one presented a paradox in so far as a candidate was the department chair largely responsible for the job descriptions. A specialist in ethics, he had, as he admitted, thought that particular position suited to his own qualifications, but was kind enough to mention me as a candidate for the other. This was in 'theoretical' philosophy. In the actual 'competition' for the ethics chair he came second. Consisting of Jon Elster then at Chicago, my old office companion Hans Skjervheim and Lars Bergström in Stockholm, the committee placed me first on the basis of the last four chapters of my long-in-gestation Kierkegaard book. They thought my work, though neither specializing in ethics nor giving evidence of any 'strong' competency in 'practical philosophy' or moral philosophy, had the 'greater depth' if 'less breadth'. When, at a conference in the mountains at Ustaoset early the following year, Hans Skjervheim approached me at the bar and expressed enthusiasm for my book, I felt I'd somehow made it at last. Never confident that something I have written is up to standard, I respected his word. It was sad in the extreme that it was the last I should hear from this engaged and engaging thinker always good for a discussion. Shortly afterwards he suffered a severe stroke that left him speechless, a state in which he lingered too long for one whose vigorous Socratic style was his infectious manner of being.

The appointment was to begin in March 1990. It was a relief to be earning pension points again. At fifty-eight, I had nine years to go before reaching the lowest official retirement age. As it turned out I was to hold the position for only six years, the remaining three supported by a research fellowship. These six years included a sabbatical, so the final count was five. They were years in which thinly concealed tensions surfaced in ways that led to a final unravelling of much of both Bente's and my own life.

Three of these were spent chairing the research council's 'philosophy and history of ideas' group reviewing applications for research grants. Work on the journal continued, although now with an assistant. There was committee work dealing with proposed changes in the department dictated by politicians anxious to assure voters that academics were visibly contributing to the taxpayers' welfare, and there were lectures to be given though now on topics of my own choosing.

Human Consciousness was published in 1990 just after the appointment. It received mixed reviews: at one extreme it would become a 'classic', which it never did, while at the other it was a reason for sacking the series editor. More sober judges pointed to defects I could also see. Clearly more time should have been spent on this attempt to face the winds of doctrine, and more sympathy shown to the mind-sets that set the winds in motion. In October, immediately after its publication, I gave a paper entitled 'Why Not Control at the Top?' at a mini-conference on artificial intelligence in Bergen where the main speaker was Douglas Hofstadter, who together with Dan Dennett had edited and contributed to a widely known coffee-table anthology entitled *The Mind's 'I'*. The following April there was a paper at the Dubrovnik Inter-University Centre's seminar on Psychology, brought to a rude end by the impending disruption of Yugoslavia. Among the last to manage a flight home, soon afterwards I read a newspaper report with a picture of the now roofless hotel in which several of us had stayed.

The seminar overlapped the start of a UCSD term in which I was at last to give a course on consciousness. Avrum Stroll and Paul Churchland had kindly agreed to take care of the first three lectures, the latter's introductory *Matter and*

Consciousness being a useful opener, mainly because it dealt only briefly with questions that needed resurrecting. The course, vaguely labelled 'Knowledge and the External World', was devoted more specifically on this occasion to the challenge of Churchland's eliminative materialism and Dennett's less rigorous but more insidiously attractive 'hetero-phenomenology'. The lectures lasted just one hour in the late afternoon on Mondays and Wednesdays. The students were first-rate and came up with many original suggestions. Dennett himself spoke to the weekly departmental seminar. In the course of a short exchange outside the locale he observed that I was 'living on the edge'. Why not? Where else can you see both ways?

There were three other visits. One was from Bente, now principal at the Norwegian Drama College. She could spare only a few weeks but had an independent invitation to follow teaching in the drama department. Bernard Williams, now installed at Berkeley, came to give a talk at the Friday seminar. For me, it was a first meeting in a very long time and for Bente a first ever. From appearances she remarked that Bernard should have been a French actor. Several less enlightened philosophers might agree though on other grounds. A third visitor was Arthur Cody, who flew down from Santa Cruz to San Diego's Montgomery Field in his small private plane. We spent a peripatetic afternoon on Del Mar beach discussing my views on consciousness. Arthur had many critical comments to make on my work. Outraged by a summary of them that appeared later in a review in *Inquiry*, a Kierkegaard colleague was prompted to write to me in my defence.

With exams in progress, I flew to Berkeley to join a mini-colloquium on consciousness arranged for my benefit by John Searle and Bert Dreyfus. I assumed it was a diplomatic gesture signalling that past embarrassments were over at least as far as they were concerned. At a department party in honour of a departing secretary, I nevertheless had a sense of being cold-shouldered, but staying at the Faculty Club I was happily joined at breakfast by the logician Bill Craig, one of those I had met on that first visit over twenty years earlier. Now alone, a kindly and welcoming man with vestiges of his German origin still to be heard, he lived nearby and breakfasted there. I read only the other day that he died in 2016 aged ninety-six.

To complete the academic circle I called on Bernard in Berkeley with his new wife and two children in the hills behind the campus. My transport in the Bay Area was a monster Chrysler 'Fifth Avenue' with velvet interior, a luxury vehicle hired at the price of a compact by courtesy of a UCSD special arrangement for faculty visiting other UC campuses. Much admired by Bernard, it gave me a rare opportunity to feel superior when I followed him driving Searle's aged

Volvo to Searle's house to deliver a mattress, the ex-fighter pilot struggling valiantly and at first vainly to have it climb the steep hill behind Berkeley.

This period brought me in touch with similarly interested colleagues with diverging approaches and views on consciousness. While in Dubrovnik I had shared the now roofless hotel with Alex Oliver and David Owens, both studying at Cambridge. Alex was secretary of the University Moral Sciences Club and home from San Diego I found a letter from him asking me to consider giving a paper during their coming season. He offered me dates in the Lent term of 1992, early spring, and in spite of the normal qualms I could hardly refuse. Hesitating to put on show my relative backwardness, not to say waywardness, in the now much-contested matter of consciousness, I asked Alex whether anything on Kierkegaard might go down well with the members. He didn't think so and I had to sit down and prepare a thirty-minute talk on why I thought experience could tell us something about the mind even in activities that to all appearances required nothing but open eyes, trained routines and physical agility. I called it 'How Much of My Mind Do I Have to Know to Cross the Street?'. Horribly worried about what the big guns would say to it or think of me, I was even more worried when, in the event, they said nothing.

Prior to the meeting, a hospitable Hugh Mellor hosted a get together where we sampled single malt from his excellent collection. He said, in chatting, that he supposed my answer to my own question would be 'nothing'. That, according to the prevailing doctrinal weather, would mean going downwind, but I was trying to battle the breeze. Never have I felt more nervous before giving a paper. Before the single malt I had spent the morning enjoyably with Alex, but as the time approached I became increasingly uneasy. In the actual session, though, my nerves became settled through sheer resignation and the need to get on with it. I was a little disturbed by the sight of an elderly lady asleep in a comfortable armchair in front of the fireplace. During the discussion she occasionally opened her eyes but said nothing. I learned later that Dorothy Emmett was a permanent fixture at the meetings and went there mainly for the company. A noted philosopher with practical concerns, she had been influenced by among others John Macmurray. For many years she headed the philosophy department at Manchester and had once taught Plato to unemployed miners in the Rhondda Valley. I hesitate to think what she might have made of my talk had she actually listened. Had I known at the time of her likely presence and her interest in Kierkegaard, I might have angled the talk in a more existentialist direction. As it was, when Alex later wrote to thank me for 'entertaining' the Moral Science Club, he kindly added that he thought the discussion 'very productive'. Several people did in fact contribute, including one who said he suffered from *petit mal* epilepsy, a condition I used as an example to distinguish conscious from unconscious management of the surroundings. But the big guns, as I said, remained silent. Timothy Smiley, my kind host whose home offered me a warming bed and breakfast, said I'd dealt well with the questions. I left with the sad feeling that here was a street that at least I could not cross.

There was to be more traffic dodging on the topic of consciousness. A symposium was held in Oslo in June 1992 for Dagfinn Føllesdal and myself in celebration of our almost simultaneous sixtieth birthdays. Each asked to invite four speakers, Dagfinn chose his old teacher at Harvard, Willard van Orman Quine, probably the most prominent exponent of analytic philosophy of the day, and three other experts in his area: the logicians Dag Prawitz from Stockholm, Jaakko Hintikka, then at Boston, and David Woodruff Smith, now from U. C. Irvine. From my UCL days I invited Ted Honderich and Timothy Sprigge, the former now Grote Professor of Mind and Logic there and Timothy Edinburgh's Professor of Logic and Metaphysics. I also invited Bert Dreyfus from Berkeley and Jon Elster, then at Chicago. They spoke on our respective topics and we were both called on to reply.

Olav Gjelsvik on the left; W.V.O. Quine, Ted Honderich and myself centre; Jane O' Grady on the right. Knut Erik Tranøy and Ingemund Gullvåg in the background, Norwegian Maritime Museum, June 1992.

In my after-dinner speech I noted that these former fellow-postgraduates at UCL were my continuing link with British philosophy, the fact that both spoke on consciousness and one now held the Grote chair at UCL, once Ayer's and the other the Logic and Metaphysics chair at Edinburgh, must mean things weren't going so badly back in Britain. I thanked Ted for urging me to write things that but for his encouragement I would never have ventured on. When it came to Bert and Jon, I recalled the reply given by that earlier Grote Professor, John Macmurray when asked why he hadn't mentioned Wittgenstein's famous *Tractatus* to his students. On noting the first sentence, 'Die Welt ist alles was der Fall ist', he immediately closed the book, since 'manifestly the world is everything that is not the case'. That was to take the practising agent and street-crosser's vantage point very seriously.

What Macmurray meant by this had become clearer when he lectured on existentialism. The focus here on the acting individual gives the notion of a 'world' a special sense, one in which choices are continually to be made and whose significance will never be exhausted. This tied in with Bert Dreyfus's distinction between a 'universe of interrelated facts', which it is the aim of science to uncover, and 'worlds' in which we respond in our different ways (instinctively, expertly or calculatingly) to those aspects of 'what is the case' that come relevantly our way. This again tied in neatly with Jon Elster's focus on rational and irrational choice. I remarked also how, as a way of escaping philosophy, the present company proved beyond doubt that my flight to Norway had been in vain.

There was some irony that my final disenchantment with philosophy in London had been due to a seminar on Quine's then newly published *Word and Object*. My comment on Wittgenstein had some relevance for Quine who was now sitting there listening to our speeches. His book was directed precisely at grasping, in exact or 'canonical' terms, our ordinary talk of physical things, in other words how to put what 'is the case' into words. An added irony was that thirty years earlier, and a hundred yards from where we were sitting, I had been living aboard the schooner that first brought me to Norway. Even now I recall the sense of freedom every time I climbed out of the hatch into the fresh morning air. Odd, too, that the colleague whose office I was to share for very many years in Oslo was known as Quine's favourite pupil. When, after the dinner, I managed to speak to the ageing Quine, he was all kindness and we could even agree that Dagfinn's career-long efforts to join Husserlian insights to Quine's beginnings were doomed. I refrained from saying: 'So much the better for Edmund Husserl.'

The meetings went down well. For David Woodruff Smith it had been 'terrific': 'Good vibes, good fun, good philosophy.' Ted apologized for the length of his paper but said it was 'really lovely' seeing Bente and myself, and an added pleasure to see me in my 'natural habitat'. Timothy called it a 'wonderful occasion', describing our private dinner afterwards as pleasurable to the extent even of being able to put up with Ted's 'banter' when Ted's then wife Jane could no longer 'control him'. Ted's mockery of Timothy's pan-psychism was a constant feature of their relationship, perhaps a sub-intellectual reaction to the old-fashioned intellectual expertise and energy that Sprigge brought to his advocacy of a quite unfashionable view. I too envied Timothy's professionalism.

There had been Kierkegaard sessions on either side of the celebratory symposium: in March an 'author-meets-critics' session at an APA Pacific Division meeting in Portland, Oregon, and in the autumn a conference in Denmark in Aalborg by the International Society for the Study of European Ideas. In Portland the author was Ed Mooney and the book his *Knights of Faith and Resignation*. With his literary skills Ed is able more than anyone to exploit Kierkegaard's thoughts beyond their explicit range, and in directions with clear echoes in our present selves. My talk was called 'Into and Out of *Fear and Trembling*'. In Denmark Bente and I met my future colleague and fellow translator Bruce Kirmmse, a historian devoted to Denmark's early-to-mid nineteenth-century 'Golden Age'. On this occasion, having borrowed a biography of Georg Lukács from Jon Elster while we were holidaying in southern France that summer, I could speak on 'Two Ways of Coming Back to Reality: Kierkegaard and Lukács'.

Later that autumn I was to comment on a paper by Michael Theunissen from Berlin at the Norwegian Academy of Science and Letters. It dealt with the actual drift of Kierkegaard's thought in *The Sickness unto Death*, something that Theunissen claimed the text did not properly represent. A reference to the meeting in a note to the preface of his *Kierkegaard's Concept of Despair* admits that he had not properly distinguished what Kierkegaard wrote from what he really meant. What Theunissen himself really meant was that there was an inconsistency between what Kierkegaard had in mind and the way *The Sickness unto Death* put it, hence the need for some corrective text-editing. With this straightened out I could argue, I thought quite convincingly, that Kierkegaard meant what he wrote. Another German Kierkegaard scholar present, Herman Deuser, supported my reading as did two commentators recently when advising publication of my final statement on this question published in 2018 in de Gruyter's on-line *Open Philosophy*.

The lone consciousness trail would continue with two talks late in 1992, one at my old department at University College London and the other in Lund, Sweden. But from the spring of 1993 I gave up on the topic until, just before early retirement at the philosophy department, I gave a ten-lecture series to the

Nordic Inter-University in Oslo. Now, thirty years on, there have been some sporadic articles, two on consciousness commissioned to honour my friends and former fellow graduate students, Timothy Sprigge and Ted Honderich, and a long review of Ted's *Actual Consciousness*. Timothy died in 2007. Their quite opposite views, Timothy's idealism and what has now become Ted's 'actualism', have always formed two ranks on either side of a valley down which I try to forge a middle way. But until a decent calm falls on the prevailing winds there is little point in shouting at a wall of prejudice in the hope of loosening the hold of a current paradigm so uncritically impressed by so-called scientific journalism upon the minds of unreflecting people.

Apart from alerting me to Lukács, that briefly mentioned summer vacation in 1991 in southern France put in motion developments whose outcomes even those who read cards and coffee grounds would find hard to predict. After Bente's ninety-six-year-old father had been moved to a home for the elderly we could again go south for vacations. We decided to look for a house in which to spend some summers to come and possibly even retirement. This was to be yet another combined operation that kept us together: we both enjoyed homemaking. For me there was an element of escapism; there would be a place in the sun where fresh thoughts would stream into my head and poems gush from it like water turned to wine.

I almost bought such a place. Our first stop that summer had been at Saint-Cézaire-sur-Siagne in the Alpes-Maritimes. We were visiting Bente's colleague Minken Fosheim who, with her French husband and their son, had a summerhouse there. A property agent showed us a well-appointed two-storey building near the historic village's centre from which it was sealed off by a high wall. On the inside, with a swimming pool and platform, the house was perched above a deep gorge over which the once fortified village hovered. The price was well beyond my means but the prospect was in every sense tempting. Later in Oslo I offered the asking price, but the owner phoned soon after to say the sale was off. A lawyer, a friend of Bente from her Paris *au-pair* days and recent visitor to Skyros would help to assert buyer's rights. The costs of going to court quenched my enthusiasm, and by then we had hit upon a more realistic alternative.

Chapter Eighteen: Coming adrift

Coming adrift: Breaking loose from a mooring, anchor or docking, or losing motive power

Continuing our journey west we stopped off for two days at Martine's, another Skyros friend now married, it seemed somewhat shakily, to an easy-going Hawaiian with whom she had run a pancake joint at Papeete in French Polynesia. Living now near the coast not far from Marseilles, Martine expressed the frustration of an itinerant by nature when stuck, it seems all too finally, in one place. We enjoyed their lively hospitality and moved on to a built-up area of neat villas beside a nearby oil refinery. It was here that Bente had spent unhappy months in her first *au pair* days. In her 'upstairs' role she was not supposed to go out in the evenings with the maid as she dearly wished, while the daughter for whose welfare she was responsible received the strap from her father when the mother deemed she had misbehaved. We travelled on from these memory-tinged destinations to Perpignan and the small coastal town of Collioure, once the haunt of the Fauvistes. An attractive town with more amenities than Saint-Cézaire, not least its location on the then main Madrid-Barcelona-Paris railway, this was a tempting rival to the former. Jon Elster had an apartment there, rehabilitated and re-decorated by his wife Elisabeth. We had warned them we might drop in and, after some days luxuriating in a well-appointed hotel, the Elster family agreed that we would be acceptable neighbours. We left with plans to buy a half-built house, the details of whose completion we could decide for ourselves.

Bente's father, a man of charm, humour and fondness for life, had died in November, just two years short of the hundred he had planned. It meant some inheritance and we decided that Bente should own the house in the south. Further details were drawn up to be implemented in the winter. They included a swimming pool with adjoining pavilion. It was going to be perfect. Some inkling of an underlying conflict of motives nevertheless left a feeling that it would not work. But just now more immediate tasks put such doubts far back in my mind and by the end of 1992 I had already made three preparatory trips to Collioure.

A traditional week's pause in the spring term provided an opportunity for the first of these. I flew to Barcelona with a computer and printer as well as other necessities needed in the summer to get on with a translation nearing its deadline. Arriving in the so-called off-season was a revelation. The train from Barcelona didn't stop at Collioure and I had to disembark several kilometres to the south at Port Vendres. It was late evening and dark. Half expecting a line of taxis, naturally I found none. With no change to call for one, I began trudging through Port Vendre itself. In the summer and autumn its streets a flood of blazing lights, full restaurants and ambulating visitors, now only a few isolated lights shone and with no one in sight. Under my load of equipment in addition to normal baggage, I tramped on to Collioure. The house stood high up on the far side of the town. After climbing the concrete steps leading directly to the street on which the house lies, I sank down exhausted but elated at seeing how far the swimming pool had come. On neighbouring fruit trees blossom was already glowing in the dark. It felt good. I stayed long enough to check progress and report back that everything seemed to be coming together.

The next trip was arduous in another way. We boarded the Oslo-Kiel ferry on 1 July and, after briefly visiting my sister and her husband in Hamburg, set off south with warnings about the main highways in France being blocked by striking lorry drivers. Keeping inside Germany and Switzerland as long as possible, on reaching the French border we found lorries in endless rows blocking off the main and also some minor roads. Even on some still accessible minor roads farmers had painted out the signposts. Diversions were signposted that sent us up into the mountains in a direction opposite to that of our destination, and to places no tanking vehicle ever visited. It was alarming but I found it quite stimulating and an unwillingness and lethargy that had overtaken me at the start gave way to a mix of panic and excitement. Helped by an uncommitted native taking his dogs for a walk at a roundabout around midnight and other French drivers with local knowledge or better maps, we found our way back to the main road near Orange. On reaching the main highway again after midnight, however, we found the blockade had begun there too. However, tourists, or certain tourists who the strikers thought had nothing to do with their grievances, were being allowed to enter the main highway through a few guarded gaps. Among the favoured, we were ushered onto the main highway to Perpignan and able to refuel just in time. Arriving at Collioure at five in the morning just before sunrise, to catch some sleep we parked on a hill overlooking the house before looking for the key the architect had promised to leave under a stone. The key was there but the electricity had not been connected. Realizing this, a kind neighbour had stretched a cable from his own garage into our garden so that we could get started.

It was an auspicious start. Monsieur Liébart was a retired producer of champagne from the Marne Valley, the friendliest of men and touchingly devoted to his dementia-afflicted wife. He was just one of several generous people living nearby. During the six following weeks we scoured the region to find fixtures and furniture and also two bicycles. We quarrelled occasionally and my shameful impatience with detail surfaced not least in our interminable visits to Perpignan's largest superstore: I had so much undone still to do. A *croque monsieur* and beer before returning to the house with our gains generally lowered the temperature.

At the beginning of August Bente had to return to Oslo. I stayed on for a week, leaving the car to be picked up later. In September she came back alone and I flew down to join her so that we could drive back together in time for an already noted Kierkegaard meeting in Denmark. By then she was on good terms with our builder, a French divorcee but of Italian origin and a bit of a recluse, his easy style and low-key manner suggesting melancholy and depth. His effect on Bente was not unlike that of the strange mariner on Ellida in Ibsen's *The Lady from the Sea*, a part I had seen her play convincingly in Stavanger. Perhaps, like my dream of a place alone in the sun, this man would be Bente's fanciful projection of what she missed in her life with an in-house recluse. If that is how it was, it took four years to materialize as such. The beginning was a bill that came in the post for work completed to date on the swimming pool. The house being hers, Bente thought it fitting that she pay in person and drove to Perpignan to do so at his office, the response to which was an invitation to lunch. They lunched together on a number of occasions, sometimes over the border into Spain. I had no idea what their relationship amounted to and my imagination was not idle, particularly when Bente said that our master builder expressed surprise that I didn't object. She, too, must have wondered. Had I played the traditional part, I should have been humming the words of a Bill Broonzy song (originally from Huddie Ledbetter but also in Eric Clapton's repertoire): 'Keep your hands off her, keep your big mitts down, do you hear what I say, she don't belong to you.' The lyrics exude possession but I felt none. Was it a matter of too faint a heart or, worse still, detached realism? Neither, it was a sense my own inadequacy, a resignation that my preoccupations and shortcomings should lead Bente, as I myself had so often done before, to project satisfaction on an elsewhere.

The preoccupations were self-imposed but inescapable. A contract for a translation of a selection from the Dane's journals and notebooks had been signed three years earlier with delivery specified at 'not later than 30 September 1993'. The plan was to prepare the way for a biography through selecting journal entries with clear reference to Kierkegaard's life, but by the time it was completed the selection had acquired far wider scope. I was also co-editing a

'Companion to Kierkegaard' for Cambridge University Press. In February 1994 I had a letter from Gordon Marino, then teacher of psychology as well as football and boxing at a military college. We had met in 1984 during the time Gordon spent with his wife and young family in Copenhagen completing his doctorate for the Committee on Social Thought at the University of Chicago. Asked to edit such a volume, he felt the project might go more smoothly if I joined him. I agreed to do so and after the necessary soliciting and reviewing a contract was signed in July 1994 with delivery due in the summer of 1995. With a background in the Bronx and a career in boxing that included a bout with Joe Frazier, like me Gordon was a permanent visitor in the world of philosophy. He is now a long-standing but due to retire professor of philosophy at St. Olaf College in Northfield, Minnesota and Curator there of the Hong Kierkegaard Library.

In mid-1994 the humanities editor at the Cambridge Press, Terry Moore asked if I might consider submitting a book on Kierkegaard to a series of 'new philosophical biographies'. The thought of a biography had been the motive for translating selections of Kierkegaard's journals but now, with so much to do, I hedged. I'd be happy to have a go so long as the deadline was 'reasonably relaxed'. Terry said he would work to my schedule and asked me to send in a prospectus later that year to submit to the all-powerful Syndicate. But then I heard from my colleague Bruce Kirmmse, a true connoisseur of Kierkegaard's life, that he too had thought of writing a biography, so I hedged again. But, Bruce being a historian rather than a philosopher, Terry urged me nevertheless to proceed. I agreed and after dealing with some questions and comments from reviewers, a contract was signed in May 1995. With some prospects of a three-year senior research fellowship beginning the following July there was a practical motive. The three years would see me through to early retirement and a biography of Kierkegaard would be a strong argument for being given the fellowship.

So much for the French paradise planned from 1991. Apart from welcome interruptions, including spectacular fireworks and aerobatics on the fourteenth of July, the focus had been on completing the house and not least the swimming pool. Once that was done we could welcome visitors, among them my son Jo, and return the hospitality shown to us by the Elsters. We could also explore a region full of history from the medieval Cathars to modern art with Salvador Dali at Figueres, just over the border, and others including Picasso memorized at Céret on the French side. We visited Vincent and Annette Hope at Vernet, but for me it all ended one day in Paris.

In the autumn of 1996, both of us spending some weeks in Collioure, Bente stayed on after I returned to Oslo to resume teaching. We were to meet in

Paris on her returning. We did. I arrived at her hotel on a day in pouring rain as I recall. There she told me that lunches with our builder had led to more, more than I could cope with just then. For other couples such revelations can bring them together, but for me it was the denouement of a plot that had been hatching for years. The man had been phoning Bente but I happened to be out whenever he rang, though I learned later that he had planned to visit. I don't blame anyone, least of all Bente. To blame myself I would have to go a long way back, perhaps far enough to find excuses.

There was another side to it. During that first teaching spell at San Diego in 1985, we had been invited after a concert to join a professor of classics and theatre with her friends at a Japanese restaurant. On two subsequent visits, in 1988 and 1991, we joined guests at dinner in her spacious hacienda-style house in Rancho Santa Fe. There, besides colleagues, we met members of her family and a several distinguished guests, but also made friends with her new consort Adrian, a physician 'in waiting' when we had met him at that restaurant. With her now divorced Japanese husband, Marianne McDonald had a son Hiroshi, and there were several other now adult children but also a teenage daughter who died in a drug-related shooting accident, an added tragedy to a life already acquainted with grief. In the 'sixties Marianne's brother, closely linked to freewheeling Hollywood circles through close friendship with Peter Fonda, had also died in a drug-induced state, slashing his wrists before shooting himself.

Marianne challenged the fickle gods with what seemed ferocious optimism and seemingly unlimited energy channelled in directions not unduly constrained by conventional codes. She had a reputation for capturing men but also keeping them as friends. Bob Pippin had asked me on one occasion if she had seduced me yet. She hadn't. A rumour, designed among students, it seems to present her in a less glamorous light, was that her wealth came from a well-known international restaurant chain. She was in fact the sole heir of a more impressive concern. Her father, Eugene McDonald, of Irish descent, had been a World War I naval officer specializing in intelligence. In World War II he was able to provide the war effort with sophisticated technology to which, like other similarly patriotic businessmen, he added important industrial patents. Shortly after the war he had founded the Zenith Corporation and, based in Chicago, it became a leading manufacturer of radio, television and consumer electronics. On his death in 1958 the company was one of the largest in the business. Marianne, her early school days spent in a convent, had continued her education in classic studies at Bryn Mawr. With a doctorate from the University of California's Irvine campus she became a respected classical scholar with a special interest in ancient Greek drama.

Apart from academic responsibilities as professor in the drama department at UCSD, Professor McDonald spent considerable time and money in local ventures, generously supporting both opera and orchestra in San Diego, as well as repertory and amateur theatre. She had also founded the Scripps McDonald Center to help combat the effects of drug and alcohol abuse that were all too familiar to her. On top of that, she financed the digitalizing of the entire corpus of Greek classical literature, setting up a base in a house just below the Acropolis in Athens, and then did the same for the Irish literature that she associated with her origins. There were other origins too. Her mother Elba Inez Riddle, a concert pianist and composer, twenty-three years younger than her father and living at this time in Bel Air, had a partly Amerindian background. Marianne was a karate black belt and also a harpist. As a translator of classical Greek drama, she shared with Bente an interest in the theatre and they got along well together – to begin with.

With a sabbatical from June 1993 I decided to spend the last three months of that year in San Diego and was admitted as a Visiting Scholar. Planning to round off my largely ineffectual work on consciousness, I wanted to leave the future open for two further Kierkegaard projects. The university apartment I rented was in the same La Jolla del Sol complex as twice before, still within walking distance of the campus but just a little further away and close to a still undeveloped area where I could exercise. I arrived there late at night from Oslo on American Airlines with 'flu symptoms and seated beside a large and voluble lady. During the New York stopover, feverish, I found people celebrating Octoberfest with quantities of sausage and beer. After good helpings of both the 'flu symptoms magically disappeared. On arrival at San Diego's Lindbergh Field, I was welcomed by Avrum Stroll, but the key that I was supposed to retrieve by means of a code was not to be found. It was now dark and we had to call the campus police to open the door to the apartment. In a period of typical Southern California heat it had not been aired for some time and several days passed before it became even moderately habitable. In time everything went well. A car was hired through Avrum's contact, this time a Mustang.

One day, driving back to the parking lot, I saw what I took to be a newspaper deliverer leaving something at my ground-floor doorstep. She didn't see me but when I got there I realized it had been Marianne. She left an invitation to a lecture on the planets she would be giving in some weeks at Balboa Park. When we later met on the campus, I didn't tell her I'd seen her there but was heartened by this apparent concern for my welfare. Soon after, she invited me to lunch but I was unable to accept at the time. Later, however, remarking that I needed rest from my tireless research, she offered to take me on a picnic. Half envisaging a trip to the shore with her son, I was a little surprised when she arrived at the doorstep alone with a small hamper of food and drink. We drove up to her 'cabin', a palatial wooden villa with a Samurai-inspired interior on the heights of Mount Palomar. The food was exquisite and the drink included an unspeakably good Irish whisky. Some recreation and a pleasant walk in the woodlands followed the refreshments.

Bente would arrive in a few weeks and I began to entertain the faint-hearted hope that this escapade had been a passing whim not to be repeated. It was not so, and the more we became in a generous sense friends, the less faint became my heart. Bente arrived the day before a talk I was to give. There was a revision to normal friendship and we attended Marianne's sparkling lecture in Balboa Park: 'A Cosmic Soap Opera: Mythology in the Sky'. To get there we borrowed her vintage Rolls and were later invited regularly to dinner at her home. When my sister Jane and her son Markus visited from Hamburg, I shanghaied them into attending a concert straight from the airport before jet lag overwhelmed them – an overzealous attempt on my part to show appreciation of Marianne's generosity, the seats being hers. They, too, were invited to Rancho Santa Fe. After a day or two they drove the coast route to San Francisco for their return flight, the ever-adventurous Bente wanting to accompany them. On Jane's request I dissuaded her. For her, the whole trip was a chance to enjoy something new with her son.

There was more entertainment both before and after Bente's departure. After a Thanksgiving party a group of us went to see *The Remains of the Day* and at the boisterous gathering on our return Marianne too was inspired, indeed 'smashed' as she said. There was a fund-raising Moonlight Ball at the downtown Hyatt in support of Scripps Hospital. My table partner was a German physician who specialized in hypertension. He told me of the good effects of ACE-inhibitors, which information I took back to my physician in Oslo. It later led to difficulties. On my own way home I flew first to Oakland, stayed over with Bert and Geneviève Dreyfus and the following day flew with Bert to Atlanta for an APA meeting. I was to return via New York and Marianne and I met once more there.

If considered under her favourite rubric of friendship, or 'philia', which according to her was the core of anything to do with love, Marianne remained friends in a generous sense for four years and in her core sense remains so. We met later periodically in Europe, but just now she was on her way back from visiting her eldest son in Philadelphia. In New York we stayed at the Hotel Plaza Athenée and attended *Salome* at the Met. Later, when the time came to deliver my translation of Kierkegaard's papers and journals to Penguin in London, Marianne arranged a scheduled visit to coincide with mine. She accompanied me to the Penguin offices, both of us registering Paul Keegan's surprise verging on horror at the unexpected size of the typescript. Whatever his misgivings at the time, I hope he listened into Radio 3's 'Speaking Volumes' in November 1996 when Bernard Williams and Jonathan Rée named the work one of two 'philosophy books of the year'. That same visit included a theatre binge in which we attended five plays in three days and dined in exclusive Mayfair restaurants. In these it became clear that Marianne was a well-known guest. We stayed as always in separate rooms at the comfortable Berkeley Hotel in Knightsbridge.

Scotland also provided an opportunity. I had told Marianne I planned a trip to Dumfries to inspect my grandparents' gravestone at nearby Sweetheart Abbey. My mother, then in a retirement home-cum-hospital at Hildenborough, near Tonsbridge, had wondered if she might join them there. Marianne suggested we meet in Edinburgh for a few days.

She hired a car and driver and at New Abbey took photos there and of my old home in Melrose on the return journey. The new owner, James V. Paterson, a Borders Sheriff, was out. His wife, couched by Alzheimer's, was there in what was once my father's study. We spoke to a lady looking after her who remembered my family well and my farming sister Mariot in particular. On the road back to Edinburgh, Marianne, an expert on opera, took pictures of the Lammermuir hills from a vantage point populated with wind turbines, a sight denied to Lucia, née Lucy Ashton. She seemed to enjoy the trip. We joked with Fred the driver, remarking on reaching the shores of the Solway that on a bad day one could see England. Marianne is the only person I know who would dare to drive up to a large mansion and, not knowing who owned it, ask if she could use their bathroom facilities.

In August that same year there was some discussion as to whether she should accompany me to Vienna and Graz. Due to a misunderstanding I went alone, which was just as well: I was to give a paper in Graz on Nietzsche and, not because of Nietzsche but due to the normal stress that precedes any public performance I would have been bad company. When Marianne had some academic business in Rouen and I was in Paris on a self-appointed mission to secure French interest in a new Kierkegaard Research Centre in Copenhagen, I stayed at the Ritz for two days before she arrived there herself. We dined at René Lasserre's more than splendid restaurant. There were to be two more rendezvous in London the following year, the second a mixture of farce, disgrace and disaster.

For me these were breathing spaces when fresh air seemed in short supply – a kind of 'time out' but at the same time excursions from reality, wonderful but fantastical. It was like living out one of those unrealistic daydreams I had when everything seemed to split asunder under the pressure of other people's demands. Now it was real and the demands included what was owed to other people in a shared reality. Possibility at a certain mental rather than biological age, instead of being a promise of better times and places, becomes a kind of overdrive that brings the illusion of their being already there. It was parenthetical and had to end. But not altogether: whatever her own feelings, there has been a consoling sense of Marianne's presence even in absence.

Fate took its revenge. In Oslo I had visited both the dentist and my ear doctor with ear-buzz an increasing problem. Instead of streets cleared of newly fallen snow, I walked back through the snow-covered palace park. On a slope descending again to street level, the snow concealing ice, I slipped and fell on my side. The key clip in my right pocket struck the ground first, causing a crack through the hipbone. I could pull myself up but not move to a nearby lamppost for support. There were few passers-by on the park side of Drammensveien. To those that came by I must have appeared intact. Efforts to explain my plight were ignored as if the mumblings of a disturbed person. When a frightened looking man agreed to cross the street to call a taxi from a tobacconist on the other side, no taxi came and the timid individual never returned. I must have been standing on one foot for over twenty minutes before a more imaginative pedestrian came by and helped me to the lamppost. He waited until we could hail a passing taxi and helped to squeeze me in. I was driven in some pain to the downtown Emergency Station where there was a large attendance. The city council must have economized on clearing snow by letting the state health authority carry the burden of repairing broken bones. There was a long queue. I joined but, beginning to grow faint, I lurched to the reception and informed them I was about to collapse. I was immediately wheeled into a bay for inspection and transported soon after by ambulance to the main hospital.

About to perform in a play to coincide with the winter Olympics, Bente was packing for rehearsals. She hurried down to join me on the ambulance but had to leave immediately on arriving at the hospital. At two-o'clock the next morning, under the influence of an anaesthetic that left me half awake but exceedingly cheerful, the cracked end of the femur was put together with long titanium screws by two seemingly equally cheerful night-shift surgeons. I came to in a euphoric daze while they were still finishing the job, one of them holding a screwdriver. When I asked them to do the same on the other leg, they said they'd consider it if I sang them a Scottish song. I thought of 'Westering Home':

> And it's westering home, and a song in the air,
> Light in the eye, and it's goodbye to care.
> Laughter o' love, and a welcoming there,
> Isle of my heart, my own one,

but was too hazy to be able to mobilize my vocal organs. Eager to get out of hospital as quickly as possible, I exercised my leg that same morning tottering about on a support frame and two days later was sent home to look after myself. Bente would be away for two months. House-bound for about four weeks but visited by a helpful nurse, who checked the stitches and eventually removed them and also bought provisions to restock the refrigerator, I fell into the role of patient with what might seem suspicious ease.

It was a reminder of that time getting on for thirty years earlier when a prolonged stay in hospital brought me into a world where I felt better on my own although surrounded by human life-support. Now at home and literally alone, I had to arrange to have my university mail delivered. A student who had studied with me as an undergraduate did so. Just now she happened to be working on her doctoral thesis in the United States. I could still have visitors and during my convalescence I also invited a visiting lady colleague from California home to dinner. There was a welcome freedom in this captivity and, as usual once I have become accommodated to single life, brief visits at weekends by Bente again felt like intrusions on my privacy – an illusion of course, since the home I was alone in was Bente's. There was nevertheless an increasing sense of being superfluous there. At first, allergic to exaggerated expressions of sympathy from any quarter, I refrained from contacting friends in California. But after some weeks, perhaps simply demonstrating the privation of privacy but now mobile enough to take a taxi to my office, I called Marianne. She received the news with what sounded like sobs, though maybe it was the connection. Still, it was heartening. The news must have spread. Only a day later I received an email from the UCSD philosophy department's administrative staff:

> Dear Alastair, we just heard about your accident and we all send you good wishes and well soon greeting. Now's the time to read all those trashy novels you've been saving! If you run out, let us know — we'll send you ours. Please take care of yourself and know that your friends in sunny California are thinking about you,
>
> June, Gale, Jean and Catherine

With such warmth radiating from the West I was put in mind of where home might be – whether this side of dreaming or beyond. Within the loosely knit associations of Marianne's dependents, close colleagues, friends from diverse walks of life, she herself with her wide-ranging involvement and unending generosity was 'at home' to all of them. No need, or even time or place, to feel too much alone there. Anyone living even at the periphery of Marianne's world would be sucked into the centrifuge of her ferocious engagement. There was something else. Energetically optimistic and open-minded herself, and impressed by Bente and her career, though perhaps also with thoughts of preparing a local welcome should she choose to change continents, Marianne nominated Bente for a Living Legacy Award from the Women's International Center, a local non-profit organization 'dedicated to women and their great contributions to humanity'. Marianne had a hand in the organization as well as the nomination. Her award was duly made. Along with several others, Bente received hers in March 1995 at a gala held at San Diego's Coronado Hotel.

We had made a video in preparation showing a selection of Bente's film and television appearances with my commentary. The trip was by British Airways first class to Los Angeles at Marianne's expense and we were limousined to San Diego and back. At the gala Bente made her prepared speech and we mingled with other awardees. These included Ginger Rogers and Peggy Lee, both in wheelchairs, the latter from some permanent disability and Miss Rogers having recently fallen down a stair on Ronald Reagan's yacht. There was also an Irish Salvation Army general and Aldous Huxley's widow, who from her appearance must have been a child bride and was now being celebrated for something to do with dancing. I was guiltily pleased when, on being introduced to a friendly Ginger Rogers, she remarked to Bente 'What a nice husband you have'. It was after the speeches and she told Bente that she had been the only recipient to say anything sensible.

The generous Marianne had rashly invited several of my philosophy friends with their wives. I abstain from mentioning their names since, sharing a table and evidently scornful of the congratulatory style on show, they provided ungratefully, I thought, and certainly impolitely if not childishly, an increasingly noisy and irreverent accompaniment to the proceedings. For them it was evidently social kitsch of a kind with which, as *bona fide* intellectuals, they should be seen neither to others nor among themselves to engage. It was indeed hard for a non-American to stomach the effusion of superlatives showered in turn on each celebrity. In my case incipient nausea was kept at bay by looking down at my feet and trying to see the cake beneath the sugar candy. Bente, too, apart from carrying off the required show with aplomb, took it all with a healthy pinch of salt, as no doubt did the long-feted and down-to-earth Ginger. Her secretary gave us a card but, sadly, Ginger Rogers was to die soon after in her ranch of congestive heart failure at the age of eighty-three.

My mother had died in January aged eighty-seven. The news was not unexpected. I visited her a few weeks earlier along with other members of the family. The occasion was one that she clearly gave us to believe was a farewell. Much of the sadness here was the loneliness that my mother had faced following the death of our father nearly forty years earlier and her own family's subsequent diaspora. Not long before she died she had written that she had 'lost' me. I worry still over in what sense or why.

The news of her death came an hour or two before I was to give a paper at a conference in the snow-covered hills behind Oslo. The old heart problems had recently recurred, doubtless due to anxieties but also the ill effects of too quick a change of medication for hypertension. I tried to relax by walking in the fresh winter air. Before the talk, the Danish priest Johannes Møllehave, author and lecturer and Denmark's Shakespeare expert, lent me his room to recover. He said he had once suffered the same. I nerved myself to give the talk, which went without drama. It targeted a recent Danish author's attempt to rephrase Kierkegaard's thought in ways that would allow a modern audience to grasp it. An Oslo newspaper's review of the book was headed 'Kierkegaard for Everyone'. To me, the difficulty of Kierkegaard's texts lies not in deciphering them, but in our unwillingness to break with habits of thought our weak-willed attachment to which Kierkegaard was so good at diagnosing. I remarked afterwards to Joakim Garff, already engaged on a debunking biography that would domesticate the man – a constant aim of Danes in the face of their still unburied nineteenth-century irritant – that maybe Kierkegaard was for 'the very few', to which the quick rejoinder was 'or none'. On recently reminding Garff of this, now head of the Kierkegaard Research Centre he was smilingly ashamed. For me, Kierkegaard's texts open doors we still try to keep closed. Jerry Cohen, from Oxford, called me a 'Kierkegaardian Fundamentalist'. So be it.

California still beckoned. There would be more visits. I was to spend two weeks or so looking after a Californian colleague's house. After mastering the alarm system under its owner's meticulous supervision, but before I could settle in, Marianne came to inspect the accommodation and found the bedroom I had been offered wanting and the mattress too soft. She decided I should have a guest room at her place. I rather hoped the colleague and his wife would not mind this discourtesy, but even more that they wouldn't find out. The student who brought me my mail when I was recuperating, and whose dissertation the colleague was supervising, did find out. She was supposed to ring me occasionally to tell me what mail had arrived. On most days I managed to reach the house early enough to catch her before she left her office. Later, when our relationship had taken a more familiar turn, she said she had tried calling me at other times too and knew straightaway I wasn't spending nights there.

The sadness of this visit was in the departure. Both Marianne and her protective Mexican factotum Ignacio had met me on arrival at Los Angeles. On my leaving she insisted on driving me back alone. She told me later she had driven out of the airport blinded by tears and managed to miss the freeway. There was a much longer history to her sadness than this parting. My own was in losing close contact with an exceptional lady whose generous welcome had given me a home in a sense that I realized had for too long escaped me. But it was not a last farewell.

Chapter Nineteen: Taken aback

Taken aback: *when the wind shifts suddenly, causing the sails to fill from the other side, stopping the ship, and endangering the masts and rigging.*

Left alone in Collioure that summer, liberated rather than marooned, I kept up a correspondence with Marianne. The overnight delivery brought me material she thought might be useful for my work, mainly Aristotle as I recall. Looking out for the vehicle that periodically brought these packages added spice to a plain breakfast. Rehearsals had called Bente home in August and a weekend meeting was arranged with Marianne in London on her way to visit her son in Ireland. She picked me up at Heathrow, as usual with a driver, and we checked in at the Berkeley Hotel. We were just starting dinner when Bente called on my mobile to say she was free that weekend and could she join me in London? Was she making soundings? We made a quick decision, or rather Marianne did. She would fly to Ireland in the morning and Bente could take over the theatre reservations made for the weekend.

With or without suspicions, Bente arrived and we set out on the heavy theatre programme with a matinée. In the evening show, which was the musical *Five Guys Called Moe*, the guys eyed Bente out for audience participation and, to the evident admiration of the players, she engaged in some professional repartee on stage. But by then the strain on my nerves was telling. Leaving Bente to take in yet another show that evening, I started home for the hotel on foot. Familiar heart problems and dizziness soon forced me to take a taxi. Cardiac tests in Oslo showed no physical defects and the specialist said that had the symptoms been physically caused I'd have died several times. The strong medication for hypertension advised by that physician in San Diego may have had something to do with it. There was also the strain of duplicity.

Yet it was with recuperation in mind that early I embarked on yet another Californian visit early in 1997, this time to prepare for a talk at a late-March Pacific APA meeting in Los Angeles. It became, instead, a time of hurt feelings, recrimination and bad conscience. For several reasons of the kind already touched on, I wanted to be alone. The ever-generous Marianne, when she heard of my plans, booked me into a condo at Solana Beach directly overlooking the Pacific. There I found a fully stocked wine cooler and, soon after, Marianne having returned from Europe, I was told I could use her old Rolls Royce. On top of that, she would send her Mexican housecleaner with daughter once a week to clean up. What a start!

Under these ideal conditions I settled into a solitary routine, working in the mornings, walking in the afternoon and occasionally even running, then relaxing in the evening. There was journal work as usual. An extra task I took on in view of Marianne's attentiveness was to edit a manuscript she had prepared on operas based on classical themes, the least I could do in return. For this I was provided with a Dupont fountain pen and a bottle of red ink. There were some visits from colleagues. No shadows were cast by impending academic duties of my own.

In her e-mails Marianne had revealed how little she liked the liaison with my former student, her dislike provoking some splendid sarcasm couched in luridly adapted Catholic symbolism not to be repeated here. Rather than jealousy playing any part, she was simply disappointed at my stupidity. During a dinner at the end of January, in honour of a wealthy investment manager with books on pre-Aegean history to his credit and presidency of the American Academy in Rome, Marianne opened a discussion on passivism, which she opposes and I defend. She quickly came around to attacking Hannah Arendt as a case of a bad thinker who was also a passivist. Arendt, as Marianne knew, was the subject of an essay the said young lady was writing. After some minutes she turned to me and said 'Maybe I'm saying this because of ————!' I told her that ———— was also critical of Arendt and that the paper had nothing to do with passivism.

The same day she had sent me some extracts from oriental astrology which showed the young lady in a bad light and how we two, on the contrary, could even under quite different signs get along amusingly. It can sound like a mixture of resignation and perhaps even despair, but the fuel of Marianne's life force is always in the end hope. She said, more or less, that when I 'got tired' of this liaison I should come back to her. 'Go for your new love,' she said, 'and drink the wine until the cup is empty, and then find another, perhaps an old one, it improves with age'. Of course, she was right.

Two interruptions disrupted the prospective idyll of a three-month stay, the one catastrophically amplifying the other. I had suggested to the young lady a weekend in New York as a way of consolidating our so far only epistolary commitment. A short escape from each of our locations was accordingly planned for the end of February. At first doubtful about coming at all, Bente was nevertheless due to visit but before that planned escapade. She may have thought that, insulated from this new threat back home, my presence in California offered an opportunity to repair our relationship. It could also have been a welcome break from the Norwegian winter with a chance to keep up with our friends.

She arrived towards the end of January when the run of Albee's *Three Tall Women* had ended. An email print-out verifying the secret assignation had fallen from a pile of paper that the Mexican ladies had placed too near the edge of a coffee table. When Bente picked it up and read it, all hell broke loose. Although minimally mollified on hearing that there were no plans for New York to be followed by California, the fact that the threat now came from where she thought it had been left behind must have come as a blow. She said that she should never have come. For her sake and mine I agreed. The four weeks we were together were tense and relieved only by a weekend trip that she shared with a colleague's wife to the southern tip of Mexico's Baja California Sur.

It was a time for weeping. On leaving Oslo, I had wept thinking of Bente sitting alone at the kitchen bar where we had our meals – the price of a vivid visual imagination. At the departure lounge at Lindbergh Field, San Diego's airport, she wept realizing that the years of reliance were over. That was bad enough but at our hotel in New York my friend also wept, though I still don't quite know why. The few days we spent there were enjoyable enough if, in their artificiality, predictably unsatisfying. There was *La Traviata* at the Met and lunch with Jon Elster, who although a good friend of Bente seemed intrigued at this new acquaintance. But there were bad signs. In the taxi to Kennedy for the return flight she became nauseated and at the airport was plagued by a cigar-smoker. I first took her to her check-in and she then followed me to my earlier departure to San Diego. Her own diagnosis was that her body was resisting departure. I said it might be reminders of things past and present still un-faced. We went our different ways with more in our minds about each other than before.

When I told Marianne that I wouldn't be back by the following Saturday from a brief sortie to Berkeley for the APA meeting, by which time she would be leaving for Europe, she too broke down and cried in her living room. She would be occupied the coming week with Alexander Cockburn, a well-known journalist and long-standing contact. This would have been our last chance to be alone. We managed nevertheless to be together at a dinner she gave for Alexander, who she described to me as her 'guarantee against loneliness', and the Strolls. I noticed how he seemed to assume the reins, so much so that on the pair emerging from her private quarters, the new chef announced them as 'the McDonalds'. But she too cherished independence. She asked me: 'Why declare freedom and give the key to another jailer?'

Most evenings both before and after Bente's visit I dined with Marianne alone. Partly, it was to keep the soon-to-leave chef busy until his notice ran out, but I could see that Marianne in all her activity was lonely. We regularly took evening walks down the tree-lined road to Whispering Palms and back. It took about an hour and she talked of the day's problems, life's problems, mine and of Bente. At dinner, with wonderful food served, she sat dressed in jogging clothes in preparation for the walk. One evening a car stopped and the days being quite short, its driver said he had seen us 'guys' on several evenings and thought us foolish not to be more visible. He proved to be a physician at the hospital where Adrian worked. Ignacio was instructed to buy road-worker reflector-jackets. With bands round our feet and staves shining brightly, we became a more visible curiosity. Drivers would scarcely have recognized the usually impeccably dressed public benefactor.

Marianne's quality can be captured in a cameo drawn from a reception at the Hyatt in San Diego a week before I left. The State Governor Pete Wilson and his wife were also in attendance. Present, too, was a state official concerned with overseas affairs, obviously an old beau and still a friend who occasionally helped Marianne to cut corners for visitors in matters of immigration. Since it was clear I was there as her escort, he would draw the obvious inference. Having done herself up in glittering attire reminiscent of a flapper, Marianne radiated presence. Introducing an Irish nun with her usual partisan panache for the Republicans, Marianne was totally convincing and looked amazing. The former beau stood with me watching her admiringly and remarked, 'she's priceless!' I said 'Yes.'

The APA meeting was held at the Easter weekend in late March 1997 at Berkeley's Claremont Hotel. I gave the talk but firmer in memory are a colleague's diplomatic handshake and it being an occasion to introduce a colleague and former student of Henry Allison to Arthur Cody. He had driven up from Santa Cruz in his old brown Cadillac. 'Cool Arthur' was to be good friends with Michelle. I flew back to San Diego and the following day, just before boarding her London flight, Marianne rang from Los Angeles Airport offering some kind words on the paper I had given on Kierkegaard and Nietzsche. She told me I should lead my own life and not think of or live for others' as she thought I always did. Bente was being childish but would get over it. As for the current attachment, I sensed she knew it would not last.

And what about Alexander? They had left for Los Angeles together, so I read her calling from the first-class lounge as an opportunity contrived by losing her boarding card. Alexander was already boarding and she knew that with her baggage on board they wouldn't leave without her. I looked at my watch when she rang off, 1800: departure time, closed doors, fairly typical. No fluster either. Priceless indeed.

This roller-coaster ride in reality was to continue. In the following spring, 1998, yet another APA Pacific Division meeting called. It was in Los Angeles's Westin Bonaventure Hotel, for many a familiar film location with Clint Eastwood and John Malkovich tussling decisively in one of the cylindrical glass elevators in *In the Line of Service*. For me the tussle was with a colleague who sixteen years earlier had given me an offprint of his essay 'Christianity and Nonsense'. Since then I had seen that its once fashionable claim that Kierkegaard's *Concluding Unscientific Postscript* is an elaborate this-is-how-not-to-do-it joke has no basis. He and his wife sat in the front row, he with his usual beaming smile, she concentrated. Afterwards he allowed that he hadn't meant to imply that the work had no serious intention, a near platitude on which we could both agree.

On this occasion, too, Marianne played vicarious hostess. She put me up in a Del Mar hotel for the two weeks but insisted I spend the last evening at her home. It was Easter and in the absence of her chef she made breakfast for us both – bacon and eggs, surplus bacon fat carefully removed. As if sending me off on a long and unending journey, she sketched out my future. I would write the Kierkegaard biography I told her I was planning, then an autobiographical novel I had mentioned half (but only half) jokingly, and there would be a new book on consciousness. With support from Avrum Stroll, Zeno Vendler and Fred Olafson, she had used the old one to try to get me a job at the university even donating money to the philosophy department for a position in so-called continental philosophy. Wishing, not unnaturally, to avoid suspicions of giving in to money-backed pressure from outside, the department decided otherwise and appointed someone else.

It was basically farewell not to *philia* as such but to anything more. The leaving involved a large afternoon whisky that propelled me at good speed in my rental towards the airport in Los Angeles. In the freeway tangle north of San Juan Capistrano I lost my way but unaccountably arrived at the airport in time for an earlier flight than the one I'd booked.

It later occurred to me, during their regime, that the Churchlands could also have had a hand in my not landing a job in San Diego. On top of its several defects, my book had no appeal for them. If they had bothered to read it they would even have found some snide remarks aimed in their direction. There was also an unresolved personal relationship. Whenever I happened to run into Paul on later visits, he would talk of inviting me home but never with a follow-up. I wondered at first whether Bente had been the attraction and our separation now the obstacle. But Pat may have seen me as an undesirable; the only occasion Paul subsequently invited me over was when she was away. We then had a good heart to heart chat in his jacuzzi. It set me wondering. I had earlier, and in a show of friendliness, approached Pat with that half cheek-to-cheek embrace now all too common in Europe and not least Norway, as a form of greeting. She was clearly surprised. Paul was there too but it was none the less as though I had wantonly invaded Pat's private or even intimate space. Those rumours from Berkeley must have by now reached them and, if not a serial seducer of Don Giovanni's format, I might be something of a habitual lady's man.

Paul too had his sensitive spot and I foolishly touched it. I was allocated to his office while he was on leave. A student knocking on the door took me to be the man himself. Later I told Paul this and added jokingly but untruthfully that I'd told the student that my views about the mind had changed. I had of course done no such thing, but the joke was quite misplaced and Paul's immediate reaction was to believe that it was true. Pat and Paul formed a sectarian mini-cult dedicated to a belief in the theoretical power of neuroscience to explain all that should ever need explaining. Of the two, Paul struck me as the more open minded and as, in a wide sense, a man of this world. By no means paradoxically, he proved also to be a keen stargazer. This being an interest I shared I once asked him how to begin some astronomy of my own. He advised me to buy a decent though not too ambitious telescope, say a 60 mm refractor. On a visit to Oslo I also warmed to his appreciation when I played him some Bunk Johnson, a New Orleans trumpeter who most jazz connoisseurs consider too primitive. Although admitting that his own favourite was the sophisticated Bill Butterfield, Paul could sense the elegant subtlety of the more primitive performance. Pat seemed more the teacher-preacher and I heard her refer to her students as the 'kids'. Someone told me she used her classes to disabuse them of their inherited religious inclinations. The 'kids' in my own class included some Vietnam veterans. To them the valley of death probably revealed more about the origins of religion than any neural excavation. Paul seemed less than enthusiastic about his name translating into Danish as 'Kirkegaard'. But that word also means 'graveyard', and in view of what this dedicated couple hoped to bury for all time, it is not entirely inappropriate.

There were other motives for not wanting to settle in California, not all of them positive. I see my own history as a constant attempt to get out of situations that prevent me from fulfilling a vague goal definable only by what it seemed to me evidently not to involve, as if the time has not yet come. Also, teaching large classes is not my metier, though I have sometimes reached the point of realizing why entertainers are so tongue-tied in cooler company: panic opens the way to a hidden talent that taps into parts of the brain one hadn't realized were there. On the other hand, I found it much easier and more rewarding to 'talk shop' with my collegial friends in California than back in Norway. In that respect I would have warmed to a place in the sun. The warmth of Marianne's own welcome and the opportunities for reflection as one walks the lengths of those wonderful beaches, here too there were motives for wanting to stay. But there was the danger of being swept up into her tornado and ending at its edge. Perhaps my present escapade was an excuse to avoid that prospect. As it happened, with her own imagination riveted to reality, Marianne found a real musician to join her circle, one who could help in the creative development of her violin-playing son, and a dramatist who could join her in her own engagement in the theatre. She remains a warming memory and friendly contact.

Otherwise my life seemed to follow its own schedule. The application for an early retirement fellowship was accepted. Other things changed. It was now late spring 1997 and that Easter Bente visited Collioure alone. She had gone to meet my friends Vincent and Annette Hope in Cadaquez, a small Spanish coastal town associated with Salvador Dali where the two were taking a spell away from their nearby holiday house. Bente's tale of infidelity so affected them that Vincent wrote to say he was withdrawing his friendship. Bente's return from France almost coinciding with mine from California, back in our apartment she insisted that I leave without trace within three weeks. Meanwhile she would borrow the apartment of a vacationing colleague. This move, she later disclosed, was intended give me time to reconsider. I had known all along that this must happen and, having left mentally, I was in no mood to backtrack.

Knowing Jon Elster kept an apartment nearby, I asked him if I could rent it. Even though it meant turning out a colleague, he agreed. I moved my things and injured my back carrying sacks full of books down the five storeys to the car. They more than filled the modest space available in Jon's already crammed bookshelves, so the remainder had to be stored in the car's capacious boot, which would function for some time as a mobile library.

As I wheeled my office-chair to the car, I looked up to see Bente looking down from the balcony, her head and shoulders silhouetted against the sky from the top-floor terrace. The image is stuck indelibly in my memory. I drove not to the apartment but to the farm belonging to the mother of my new friend, about an hour's drive north of Oslo. I went there alone and began working on the Kierkegaard biography. The house itself was large and attached to the farm though not part of it. I worked hard for a week compiling a detailed chronology of events in Kierkegaard's student years.

Having promised to bring back certain belongings that included Bente's bicycle, I took the ferry to Kiel and drove south towards Collioure. Never before or since have I motored for such long stretches at a time at such breakneck speed. Not so much ecstasy as urgency to get things done. The roads were not yet full, and with a motel night-stop at Beaune, the wine capital of Burgundy, I arrived in Collioure twenty-six hours after leaving Kiel. That included a short stop on the way in a spasm of masochistic conscience at a Rhone-side village. It was another place where Bente had spent time as an *au pair*. I stood for a while agonizing over the fate of a hopeful teenager looking forward to a better life and happy future.

After a week or so, my friend flew down to Barcelona. I met her there and we drove back to Oslo via Kolmar and Kiel. The bicycle and several others items that I had crammed into the car had to be delivered and for that to happen Bente said we could meet at her apartment. Still with a key, I arrived there before her. A note on the kitchen table informed me in direct terms of what kind of person I was. No mention was made of the fact that I had travelled several thousand kilometres to fetch her belongings, nor, and doubtless there was more than a touch of self-pity here, that the next day would be my birthday. When I was about to drive off Bente arrived and stopped me, saying she had meant to speak to me. Having just read the note, I was not in a mood for that. It might have occurred to me in a better moment that it was written earlier and that she still hoped I might reconsider.

The official separation came a year later. We had been together for over twenty years. Bente says even today they were more than just meaningful. We both agree that we should never have married. For the next three years, except for an unhappy and inconclusive attempt at reconciliation with a psychologist, there was no contact. That last attempt had been at the instigation of my sister Jane after Bente had visited her in Hamburg. She said later it was to find out more about what kind of person I was. Jane had told me she had been accompanied then by another man. Later still, Bente said a much younger one.

There are several indelible memories of Bente, but one stands out in particular. After our summer visit to Mykonos, where the last touch had been given to my first Kierkegaard book, we had visited Naxos, a large island nearby and famous not only for Ariadne and Dionysus but also for its huge potato harvests. Bente was determined to make a bicycle tour of the island. We chose our bikes, mine rather small for my size and with a chain that slipped with every turn of the pedal. We rode off into the hills with Bente leading. A significant breeze helped us on our way even uphill, which thinking of the return I found a little alarming. Being her intrepid self, Bente would no doubt have thought little of it any way. We ended up after an hour or so at a beach with a taverna inviting us from its distant end. Reaching it meant passing an outcrop of rocks and we decided to wade the last stretch in the sea. As we emerged just below the taverna, its customers burst out laughing. One of them said we looked like emissaries of Poseidon emerging from the deep. On the return trip Bente, in better form than myself but also with an undeniably better bike, forged ahead. Trying to narrow the distance, I thought of heart attacks. None came and I merely collapsed with exhaustion on arrival. This too ended in laughter, ours. Yet there was something symbolic in this exposure of the disparity between the cave-dwelling wimp and a true warrior of the north.

The ensuing years kept me busy. The bulk of the first draft of the biography was written in two concentrated spurts, the first from October to December 1997 in Jon Elster's apartment, and the second from January to April 1999 in a newly acquired apartment of my own. Besides editing the journal I had several other things to write, papers for conferences and a hundred-page translation of Kierkegaard's *A Literary Review*, something some friends attending a conference in July 1999 near Monterey had suggested I do, and which without a contract I hoped Penguin would agree to publish. To their later regret they did, as of now it has sold only in the hundreds. Unusually, unlike my previous books, all of which landed me in hospital or casualty wards, the biography went surprisingly smoothly. I had to thank my friend's presence for this – a supportive figure in the background and companion on days off. From November 1999 to January 2000, assisted by reviewers' comments, most of them from George Pattison, I made extensive revisions to the typescript and mailed the final draft to Terry Moore in New York on January the 26th.

By then the unreal and inherently precarious infrastructure of my life had begun to fall apart. I had planned to celebrate the book's completion by inviting my friend with me to New York. We could combine celebration with handing over the typescript in person. For reasons I failed fully to grasp at the time she was reluctant and succumbed to a nicely timed bout of influenza.

It had seemed to start well enough: knocks on the door, small wolf-whistles, smiles, eulogies to the grey-head, many teasing and promising coffees. In this there was a refreshing simplicity. She had the idea that we were born to meet: on my guardian angel reading news of her birth I had been shipped to Norway by hers. The initial feedback from friends, doubtless diplomatic, was not discouraging. 'No, not old-man's disease, it seems wonderful,' was Jon Elster's answer when I asked him if it looked like that on the three of us meeting in New York. 'Intelligent and beautiful', said Arthur Cody after we had visited him in California. 'Worth staying in Norway for', was Jerry Cohen's comment when she had slipped off to the rest room while we were dining in Oslo. 'Intriguing,' said Ted Honderich, at the end of the affair on seeing a photo when I came to him to seek consolation.

I could of course have seen it from her perspective: the embarrassment of introducing someone so much older to *her* friends. This was something I doubtless tried to keep under covers. As salient facts were only very slowly presented to me, I was placed in the position of anxious doubter. There was much she kept to herself and, etched with my growing suspicion, the gaps in my knowledge created an anxiety at odds with the confidentiality called for in this or any genuine relationship. I think I could see later that we were exploiting each other in the cause of some fatally foreshortened vision of fulfilment, a vision that mirrored for each an emptiness that neither of us felt like facing.

Her own void was left by a divorce not unconnected with the decision to pursue an academic career. The marriage itself had been, at a guess, her attempt to establish herself outside a family that for several reasons required her constant care. My own voids were due to actually pursuing such a career. There was the additional emptiness of separation after a twenty years' partnership. Interest in another in such a 'perfect' vacuum tends to be prolonged where there is uncertainty and doubt, the doubt easily becomes obsessive, and the uncertainty drags out the time. It would be three years before this flimsy liaison fell apart.

I could in retrospect re-conceive my attachment to this young woman by placing it in the same category as those items in the past that I had reached for with a kleptomaniac's compulsion. They included the irresistible model-tyre ashtray I pocketed on visiting my future headmaster as an eight-year-old; as a late teenager in Edinburgh there was that gleaming two-cylinder Norton motorcycle on display in McAndrews' window on Lothian Road, and more recently a golden yellow Volvo parked outside Los Angeles airport. All left an inexpungible eidetic stain on an acquisitive mind. Now, in Oslo at the age of sixty-four my longing was to fill the eternal empty space with this collector's specimen of decorative femininity. As for what I meant to her, in the heat of the moment I once told her she had booked me as an escort and, not finding satisfaction, had flipped the pages of the catalogue to find another. Or was it that another had found her? I began to think so. 'If only it wasn't for those f——— twenty-seven years', she sighed. Her friends must have been worried about her taste for older men.

Visits to California and Italy failed to compensate for my full-time dedication to Kierkegaard's life, which she must have seen as a threat to my interest in hers. During this later time, as she was later to admit, she had been 'seeing' another. I had no idea of this at the time and it was some months before I extracted the facts. Christmas was celebrated with her family where she made her antipathy obvious. We attended a millennium party given by her ex-husband and where we feasted on oysters provided by myself while he set off fireworks and arranged games for the children. Everything here seemed normal. In the interval between these two occasions she had been receiving exploratory e-mails from the 'other'.

What author is unfamiliar with the rapidity with which the void filled by writing a book reappears once the pages are on their way? Having to the best of my ability put Kierkegaard's life together with his works in over five hundred pages, I wrapped up the result in what seemed a depressingly small bundle. The departmental secretary had sent for the euphemistically named 'overnight' mailing service. It was just before office closing time. I waited for two hours hoping I wouldn't have to hold onto that bundle for a whole day longer. For some reason I couldn't get rid of it fast enough, all notions of proofs, copy-editor's questions and a last-minute index were pushed into an indefinite future. Finally, just before 7:00 p.m., having looked in vain for a 'physical' department, the courier rang the office and with my mobile I guided him to 'philosophy' then signing a form saying 'express plus'. He was still in the parking lot when I left, loading parcels, much bigger ones. The product of two-and-a-half years obsessive hard labour disappeared in the pile. I watched the tail-lights of the van disappearing down the road as I walked home and returned to an empty flat. A pub full of friends would have been useful. Or even a new pile of thoughts impatient to be put down in yet another volume with a sigh of relief that this one was finally out of the way.

On Friday the 13th of February, without negotiation or previous complaint, the lady arrived with a carefully prepared list of grievances openly drummed up for the occasion, and in agreement as it proved later with the 'other' who went to his wife with a similar mission. Whatever crumbs of existential comfort that remained in the emptiness already created were now swept away and I could only reply with shocked protest. But nothing was to be negotiated or even debated. For me it was a cataclysm far greater than the situation realistically called for. I had seen it coming but that it should happen just then was unexpected and for me badly timed. Had I simply failed to live up to her expectations? Since these had never been stated, I wondered whether I was part of a secret test, a research project even, or as suggested, a customer of an escort service whose client was now putting in a complaint.

Further mystery followed. Although she seemed to favour total severance, the evenings were still filled with long telephone conversations. As colleagues it was in any case impossible not to run into each other. We seemed through some freak of fate to arrive at the car park in the morning at exactly the same time and place and several days in a row. As often as not whenever I was waiting for the lift she stepped out of it. So consistently did this occur that she accused me of stalking. Having no hand in it whatever, I could only attribute the coincidences to an accusatory spirit intent on making things difficult for her. She had herself claimed some kind of psychic contact, often remarking on my arrival at her doorstep that she had heard my voice just minutes beforehand. She often told of dreaming what later proved to have happened as she dreamt. Was her genie now reprimanding her for not telling the truth?

Oslo became a desert. From May to early July I visited my younger sister in Hamburg twice and older sister in Banchory. On the way back to Edinburgh I phoned Norma, my first son Tim's mother, to ask if we could meet. She said yes and when I rang her doorbell there she stood with an axe in hand but a friendly smile. We had tea and cakes. I don't quite remember when, but I also met up with my son in Edinburgh, where he was working on his doctorate at my old university. We drove over the 'Rest and be Thankful' to Loch Fyne and met several old friends at a regatta, among them Michael Pollett and Kenneth Gumley, both fellow mariners on that first voyage to Norway back in 1957.

Returning to Norway and Oslo on these trips 'back home' felt like a pointless exercise but one to which there was no realistic alternative. In what sounded like an unselfish suggestion from the lady herself, saying a spell of wind and sea air in California would bring me back refreshed, I took her at her word and booked a condo at Solana Beach. I spent most of March there but it only meant facing the void full on, a mood captured exactly by a CD I had taken with me. It had two pieces, Mahler's orchestrated version of Beethoven's opus 95 quartet in F minor, a private piece that Beethoven called 'quartetto serioso' and apparently never wanted performed, and Arnold Schoenberg's exotic orchestral version of Brahms' G minor piano quartet. The former is at the best of times an eerie piece, its themes vanishing into thin air before becoming properly stated, and quite the opposite with Schoenberg's Tivoli-like redecoration of Brahms, glockenspiel and all, iced with a modernist irony well suited to the occasion to the blues that lurk in all Brahms. Just then Mozart's perfection would have driven me up the wall. Marianne being in 'Europe', as Americans say, I was sustained by almost daily hour-long telephone conversations with Arthur Cody at home in Santa Cruz. The usual hospitality offered by friends and colleagues served only to sharpen the sense of loss – not of the lady herself but of the liaison role she had been playing as a friendly native in a land I felt increasingly was not mine.

What *was* the truth? In May I managed to wrest it from her. Yes, as much as circumstances allowed she and a near neighbour were 'seeing' each other. The neighbour had a wife whose working days were in Bergen. He, too, had been in Trondheim but we hadn't met. I recalled her once dropping his name and asking if I knew him. There being no further mention should have sounded a warning. They met at a seminar, in Norway a setting well known for its role in extra-mural regrouping. A more direct expression is attached to them: 'seminar sex'.

All this being unknown to me at the time, the truth would be revealed by yet another of life's coincidences. As once before long ago, a letter in the mail would play its part. On that occasion, on seeing my sister's handwriting I had opened the envelope, but a quick glance at the contents showed it was intended for another. This time the name on the envelope was my own.

Chapter Twenty: Squared away

Squared away: square-riggers were 'squared away' when with the prevailing wind from aft and the yardarms at right angles to the deck.

I picked up the envelope as I was about to leave for the USA. In it I found a typed letter that began mysteriously saying 'our paths had crossed' and 'in a surprising way'. It was signed with a name I vaguely recalled from some meetings on women's involvement in research, seven years earlier as I later found out. The writer said she was coming to Oslo and if I had time she would appreciate an opportunity to talk. There was a phone number. Noting that this was the date given for her Oslo visit, I called. She answered. It was my successor's wife.

Friends in the United States had invited me over for a five-week transcontinental recreational tour. I had found the letter in the mail three days before departure. It had a University of Bergen imprint and was addressed to the apartment I had shared with Bente. The month was July and from there it had been forwarded to her summer cabin on the coast. Bente then readdressed it to me. From the date, July 1st, it had taken almost two weeks to reach me. Given its path, the time of year and the infrequency with which holiday mailboxes are opened, it was not improbable I should never have received it.

Both pressed for time, we agreed to meet straightaway in town. With no memory of her looks, I waited at a corner by the National Theatre for whosoever she might be to turn up. A number of candidates came by, several of whom I thought it fortunate not to be her. When she did appear, it seemed obvious that she should be the one. She appeared to recognize me too. We walked down to the fjord-side area where we could get some refreshment.

Her business with me? Her husband was no chicken and she was anxious to learn more about this twenty-or-so-years younger woman. Some kind of bimbo? Seeing her alliance with me had been temporary, the same might be true with this new *entente cordiale*. A tardy outbreak of spring fever? Her husband was just twelve years younger than me.

Subjected to unexpected behaviour in those close, people begin to wonder if they really know them. Talking over beers on a sunny evening by the harbour, we warmed to each other and before long the question of how long that liaison might last slipped into the background. After refining each other's knowledge of recent events, our talk turned to ourselves, conspiratorially even, and about what to do next. We walked over to my apartment to fetch a bottle of wine and took the metro to her home where, having recently sent her husband packing, she was now alone. He now lived with my former friend just down the road, a move that I was led to understand had been earlier than he intended. His preference had been to stay at home in separate rooms while cultivating his nearby neighbourly relationship. It seemed that Brit, her name, was to be kept on as a guarantee against failure. 'You are the one I really want' had been his theme song on similar occasions.

Ironically, during these months I had been receiving running reports from a Polish lady who came once a week to clean my apartment. She was a friend of the girl's mother and a trained lawyer who came to Oslo every summer to help with the large garden. It was in a row of new houses at the foot of that garden, erected under the supervision of her ex-husband, that the young lady now lived. My informant had already told me of those exploratory e-mails at the turn of the year, and from her upper storey room overlooking those houses she could now tell me of the night in April when my successor appeared with two suitcases. He had stood outside arguing for some time before she finally let him in.

I could now understand this. Under pressure of conscience or family or both, she was facing the choice of a final solution, no sharing or sideshows, preferably a decent marriage. Leaving his wife would be something the family liked less, but if the present marriage was on the rocks, well such things happen all the time, don't they?

Other things became clear. The day the grievances were presented was one they had chosen to make the necessary break. The only difference was that on that same day Brit's husband had admitted his infatuation with 'another', while to me the midweek assignations were kept secret. As Brit began explaining her plans to divide the house into three, making it possible for her to keep it for herself and harbour tenants or some friends, it occurred to me, with no conscious thought of moving in myself, that I might help her out by buying her husband's share even if it meant taking out a loan. The idea surprised her but seemed not distasteful. She was keen to resist being kept out of the way in Bergen, while I was equally happy to enjoy the sweet taste of revenge in preventing that happening. As for the rest, we agreed that we would return to these matters when my five weeks of recuperation in the USA were over. During that time, we kept almost daily e-mail contact filling in details of our pasts.

It was a vacation the like of which I had never before experienced. I made use of Bruce Kirmmse's open invitation to visit him in his New Hampshire holiday home at Randolph, close by Mount Washington. We met in Boston and he drove me there in his pickup. Margaret and Bruce, together with Margaret's mother Millie, provided a hospitality extended also to visiting friends. We scoured the countryside, followed a trail linking three waterfalls and drove to the Canadian border in a vain search of moose. On another day we visited an expatriate Norwegian, Herman Venheim, his cluttered home full of old newspapers and souvenirs conspicuously betraying his roots. Photographs on the wall showed him driving local couples to their weddings in a horse-drawn wedding-carriage with traditional Scandinavian trappings.

Trudging back from a long trek in the woods to a remote lake called Cherry Pond, we came upon a small airstrip. It was the official regional airport for Mount Washington. Some grey-heads were servicing the engine of one of several small aircraft. 'Can someone of my age learn to fly', I asked, and they chorused 'Of course'. 'Can I go up', I asked. 'Yes, but not today', said Florian, slightly younger and seemingly in charge. We must wait for the weather, he would call on Monday. He did. I sat beside 'Flo' in a Cessna 150, a quite small plane with a flimsy door with a small catch all that divides you from nothingness. I was allowed to fly it and even to steer it towards Mount Washington and back to the airstrip before Florian took over for the landing. Bruce and Margaret meanwhile sat – they said anxiously – as the plane disappeared towards the hills, and no less so when it returned swaying towards the strip.

As mentioned, Bruce had been planning to write his own biography of Kierkegaard. That no one was better qualified was a reason I hesitated to take on the project. But Bruce knew I had completed mine and I had copied it onto several floppy disks in case he wanted to inspect it. He took a printout back with him to Boston, where I was deposited at Logan Airport just in time to make my flight on the next stage of my journey. Later, Bruce admitted that he dreaded reading the printout. It would have been the same with me had he written a biography before mine. I doubt, however, whether I pre-empted much that he as a historian might choose to write. With acknowledgements and Bruce's earlier consent I had made much use of the quoted letters, reminiscences etc. in his own indispensable *Encounters with Kierkegaard*. This was no doubt material he would have thought of using as a resource, just as I had thought of my selection from the journals and papers. Bruce's collection was a gift to his colleagues. He now stands as the excellent translator of that other more anecdotal Kierkegaard biography by Joakim Garff, a literary event beyond anything I could hope for, although I am happy to see my biography of the radical Protestant translated into Spanish for Catholics and, yes, Turkish for Muslims.

From Boston I flew to San Francisco where Arthur Cody picked me up. We drove to his home in the Bonny Doon area, in the hills above Santa Cruz where he and Linda were preparing to move north to Point Arena. I was allowed to spend several days driving an enormous excavator clearing scrub from his fields in preparation for the sale. I saw no reason at all why Arthur should want to move from such an idyllic property with its nearby forest and the wonderful clear and generally cool air, and not least from a house to which he had just added a second-floor office for himself. But Arthur is restive. Linda made excellent meals, which were enjoyed sometimes on a long table under the shade of a large tree with neighbours. It seemed too good a place for anyone to leave.

An unusual philosopher in the good sense that he has little time for passing academic fads or their current heroes, Arthur has a wider than usual catchment area regarding both ideas and friends. One afternoon, after the longish drive that for Americans is the equivalent of a normal stroll elsewhere, we visited a restaurant and, in the bar, met what movies lead us to recognize as an archetypal mountain man – except that in this case his habitat was a large forest. After lunch, we visited him in his caravan home in the middle of the forest. It was his and he told of pointing a gun at those who came too near and of how the Hollywood celebrity Woody Harrelson wanted to buy it. As part of Silicon Valley, the price would be high but he was not selling. I have pondered many times since over Big John, his force and his meaning. I would hesitate to visit him uninvited. The White House, too, is a kind of caravan in the middle of its own forest, its instruments of death ready to hand to eliminate intruders threatening the American way of life, even in foreign lands, and without consultation.

After Santa Cruz it was San Diego, again with a typically hospitable reception by Marianne. I was offered the apartment her son Brian occupied when visiting. By now she and the South African playwright Athol Fugard were going steady. We dined together, but mostly I was left to myself and I used the opportunity to visit old friends. The atmosphere and my head had both cleared considerably since my recent visit in March. Heading back for Norway refreshed, I flew first to Gatwick to visit my son Tim and his family at the military airbase where he was in charge of helicopter maintenance. I planned to combine this with a call at Abingdon the next day. 'My' journal was now with Taylor & Francis, but my friend and colleague George Drennan was still its copy editor and he worked there. Heading first for Oxford, jet lag amplifying confusion, I crashed into another car at a roundabout. It was one its owner had just bought, but he was remarkably civil. It cost me five hundred pounds and I was embarrassed to arrive at an impeccable airbase with my rental in such a battered state. Feeling a little out of place (a regulation haircut might also have improved my appearance), I spent a pleasant evening and part of the next day with the family before setting off for Heathrow and Oslo.

Just back from a jazz festival in Kongsberg, Brit was to drive me to my apartment. But our accumulated e-mail contact over these five weeks gave us much to discuss and we ended up driving directly to her home. It became also mine. I bought out the husband's share and they got a separation. Selling my own apartment with a decent profit, some of which I handed over to my son Jo to help him to buy his own house, we settled down to a stable pattern of life in which I more often than not accompanied Brit to Bergen, where she had a small apartment close to the university. The Oslo house overlooked the city from heights inhabited by its wealthier citizens and was situated in a pleasant garden beside equally pleasant neighbours. A jarring note was the proximity of our two former partners and the fact that my former friend's mother, with whom I had been on good enough terms, chose our peaceful road for the frequent exercising of her dogs. We grew tired of thinking up trite words to hide our mutual embarrassment.

The next few years provided plenty opportunities to be elsewhere. It was a time when the stress of forging a path in a difficult terrain had given way to habitual rehearsals of what were once eagerly grasped opportunities. Once offering escape, California now offered breaks inside a normal routine. An invitation to give a talk at the 2001 Claremont Conference on the Philosophy of Religion sent us on our way to San Diego. We stayed a while in a house owned by Marianne's elder son, now located in Ireland. It was at Olivenhain, on the edge of the residential area in San Diego North County with nearby trails and small roads leading, it seemed aimlessly, into sheer wilderness.

In April 2001 we visited Greece, where Brit had already spent five years in her involvement in the founding the Norwegian Institute in Athens. In the following years we returned there four times. With the Scandinavian library close by I began work on translating Kierkegaard's journals, as part of a team that was to complete the twelve volumes this very year of writing. It was the Greek Easter and my long-standing friend Maria was spending a weekend at her holiday house near Chalcis. She asked us along. Now a widow for the second time, and using her time to chair the Society of Euboean Studies, she was still her good-humoured, teasing self, but the deeper unhappiness was not hard to see. Together we prepared traditional Easter fare, Mayeritsa soup made from the entrails of the Pascal Lamb, and Kokoretsi, which is a kebab with lamb's liver, lungs, heart and intestines – not unlike haggis – and we celebrated Easter with Maria's nephew Alexis, his Scottish wife and their children. Later in the evening, Maria insisted on driving to greet the family that had helped her parents and their daughter who was her help in the Athens apartment. Having imbibed a fair amount of whisky, she insisted that the safest way to drive in the dark was to keep the left side wheel as near as possible to the centre marking on the road. We prayed that no one else would come in the opposite direction with the same idea. Brit said I should have tried to take the wheel, but knowing Maria's obstinacy even when sober, I thought not. Responding to my tentative expressions of anxiety, Maria said that God would see us through.

Later, the shooting, fireworks and general hubbub accompanying the Greek Easter celebrations were too much for Brit. She ran off down a side street and I had to go and look for her before we continued home. The background? On the night of the 23rd to 24th of February 1944, as the official report has it, '[s]eventy-three Lancasters and ten Mosquito light bombers carried out an accurate attack on a possible U-boat base at Horten on the Oslo fjord. 1 Lancaster was lost'. Brit, not yet four years old, had taken refuge with her mother in their cellar close by the dockyard.

The Fourth International Kierkegaard Conference was held in June that same year at St. Olaf's College in Northfield, Minnesota. I had been asked by Gordon Marino to give the opening address and could hardly refuse although set-piece orations are decidedly not my forte. It was a fiasco. The audience at this Mecca wanted to hear words justifying their celebration of the dissident Dane, but at this juncture in my own research I had begun to feel bloody-minded about the way Americans took to Kierkegaard without any suspicion that he might not have welcomed their embrace. Taking up two concepts fashionably associated with Kierkegaard I claimed that neither was his concern. One of these, 'hermeneutics', was a fancy word for interpretation that, through an influential German philosopher and former student of Heidegger, had become current jargon. But everything Gadamer had said about it seemed contrary to what Kierkegaard wanted us to understand. The other concept was 'communication', the Danish word being 'Meddelelse', which may mean simply a message or, as in Kierkegaard, the sharing with, or imparting to, another of something you feel is important but know the recipient may find hard to accept. I had worked too hard on the talk and large segments of it must have bored the audience stiff. Afterwards, an American colleague I'd met in Oslo came up to me and angrily ticked me off for not talking more accessibly. I myself had, in other words, failed to 'communicate'.

In the volume that came out later in which the talks were collected the editors spoke of my 'polemical' rejection of hermeneutics and communication as 'relevant topics and concerns in Kierkegaard's authorship'. I was happy that at least some found it interesting. Recently, the current president of the American Philosophical Association said she had based her doctoral dissertation on it. For myself, this chance to meet Gordon and his family again and to eat pancakes in the street where a Jesse James bank robbery famously failed made it all worthwhile.

Yet another visit to the States in 2001 ended abruptly on our receiving word that Brit's mother had suffered a stroke. It was December and we were staying in Solana Beach, near Del Mar. Brit returned to Norway while I stayed out the rental time. I drove her to Los Angeles Airport and just as we were about to climb the steps to 'departure', Magda and Lara, my brother's wife and daughter, appeared from 'arrivals'. Having said goodbye to Brit, I drove them to their destination and discovered that Ian would himself arrive on the day of my own departure. When that day came, making sure to get there early, I could use that second happy coincidence to have an all-too-rare mutual update.

On another outing we were able to visit my elder sister Mariot at her farm in Banchory. It was in the following spring and before driving north we stayed in Vincent and Annette's Edinburgh flat while they visited in the Borders. It was to be my last meeting with Mariot. She had already developed leukemia and died in May 2003 at the early though once regulation family age of seventy-two. I joined the other mourners at her funeral in June.

Life's ups and down had now become part of life's normal rhythm. The vicissitudes were those to be expected when things seem at last to have ironed themselves out. Before boarding the plane in Edinburgh after that visit to Banchory, I found I'd lost my passport. Brit flew home alone while with an increasingly painful hip I spent two days acquiring a new one in Glasgow. The next month, reaching seventy, I was lying in hospital with a new hip too. The screws holding the original together had blocked circulation, causing the bone to crumble. For rehabilitation I was driven to a centre far south of Oslo, close to the Swedish border. Surrounded by normal natives, I was struck full force by the realization that I had lived in their land for almost forty years with no real appreciation of the surroundings.

Immobilized in a very small room in stifling heat and some pain, the only relief was the kindly company of three ladies of my age with whom I shared a table at meals and one of whom took me for Jesus Christ. In a moment of despair, not to be compared with a spell in the wilderness facing the temptations of the devil, I sent a postcard to Joan Frøstrup only half humorously asking why the hell they had brought me to this hole. Joan told me later that she and Mariella had thought of coming over to fetch me back, but it would have been several decades too late. Instead, I asked a doctor if I could get back to Oslo and was driven there by the local taxi driver. Having several errands of his own to carry out before depositing me at my new home, it seemed that his ferrying arrangement with the health authority had clear advantages.

There was further to-ing and fro-ing. In July 2002 a group of colleagues met under Bert Dreyfus's aegis at Asilomar on the Monterey Peninsula, I joined them and from there called on Arthur Cody still at Santa Cruz. There was also a short visit to Cambridge for one of two vivas that I took part in there. Brit and I then drove to Greece. Two good stretches were covered by ferries, to Kiel and from Ancona to Patras. We stopped in Germany at picturesque Fulda, and Mezzovico in Switzerland on the Italian border. The stretch to Ancona being longer than anticipated, we arrived as the overnight ferry was due to depart. Arriving in Patras the next morning, we toured the Peloponnese, visiting Olympia, Kalamata, Mani. Sparta, Nafplion and Mycenae. In Athens we stayed some nights at the Herodion Hotel and again met Maria, together with the knowledgeable and engaging musicologist Markos Dragoumis. The return voyage was from Patras to Trieste. From there we planned a visit to another of Brit's colleagues. Eugenie Hanreich lived in the Schloss Walchen in Upper Austria, its severe exterior and unrelentingly chilly as well as gloomy interior offset by the attendant 'Welt der Kinder' museum.

By a strange coincidence Eugenie was the daughter of a Viennese family with whom my German brother-in-law Jens had lodged while studying in Vienna. Brit and Eugenie had met doing research work at Lund University in Southern Sweden. We rang the bell and knocked on the door. It was some time before there was a response. When the door opened, Eugenie stood there with a scarf round her head. We learned as we spoke to her, of the house and of this and that, that she was undergoing cancer therapy. Clearly tired, she gave us a tour of the building and spoke of plans for a Beethoven sonata concert in the summer. We had coffee and said our farewells, which proved to be final. When asking after Eugenie some time later, we learned that she had died.

We drove on to Wörth, on the Danube, for the night and along the way climbed the ceremonial steps to the Walhalla temple, a neo-classical hall of fame built near Regensburg in the late mid-nineteenth century by Bavaria's Ludwig I. It overlooks the Danube just east of the city. Apart from two gardeners idly shuffling autumn leaves and two receptionists it was deserted and the fame encapsulated there seemed oddly shuffled aside.

In 2003, Brit's mother now in care, we resumed our interest in California and were once again housed at Olivenhain. It was in conclusion of a longer journey from Seattle, where we had flown to visit Brit's cousin, a war bride at nineteen whose former GI and latterly Boeing executive husband had recently died. With more than a year's study period previously at the University of Washington, Brit had a good grip on local Indian culture. To refresh her experience, and enlighten me, we drove through Tacoma and up and around the Olympic National Park to Port Angeles. Through the rain forest to Neah Bay with its Indian history still much alive, we went spent a night in rain-drenched Forks before heading south through Oregon to visit Arthur and Linda Cody in their new Point Arena property. I got a speeding ticket on the way, a fine that I later didn't pay since the wrongly addressed demand came after the deadline beyond which it would be doubled. I have so far avoided being arrested on returning to the States. I suspect a local pickup driver, who disliked being passed by a car with Californian registration, had notified the nearby Highway Patrolman. It was no secret that Oregonians take Californians to be invaders. We stopped to be astounded at the enormous Redwood trees, drove through countercultural Humboldt County, and with some guidance from Arthur finally arrived at Point Arena, a small settlement with a lighthouse addressing the Pacific.

There, Arthur and Linda introduced us to their neighbour Bill Hay, a potent blend of Italian mother and Scottish father with a fleet of impeccably painted trucks, a caravan full of stuffed prey from Africa, and a private airfield with his own aircraft. Arthur suggested to me once that Bill Hay's life and work were the American equivalent of Shakespeare, or did he mean of one of Shakespeare's flawed heroes? A man of tireless energy, with a correspondingly exhausted wife, Bill showed us the workings of the Point Arena water supply that he owned and ran. His main business was bedrock and he took us to a quarry where he told us that every day at one-o-clock a faint rustle can be heard as the San Andreas fault, to ease some of the strain, also takes a lunch break. Linda would have us stay longer, but we had a schedule to keep to and drove on. Overnighting at San Luis Obispo, we reached Rancho Santa Fe the next day and were shown our pleasant quarters.

President Bush was just then going to war in Iraq with Tony Blair cheering from the sideline. As the invasion got under way, so did my short book *On the Public,* already contracted by Routledge for their Thinking in Action series. At the time the contents were only very vaguely sketched and I was supposed to bring Kierkegaard into the picture. But the focus turned on the reactions of the American public to the war. Olivenhain was a perfect place to start. On the way we had seen banners and posters on isolated houses saying money should be spent on want not war. Among colleagues from the campus there was some support for the war. Since the French opposed it, those who saw Paris or the south of France as a second home risked reprisals if planning as usual to take their vacation there, while friends of Italy had no such problem. Car dealers put small flags on the wings of every automobile in their lot and truck drivers displayed large ones. So easy is it to mobilize national feeling when the enemy is far away. Being close to Fort Pendleton, where the invincible US war machine had one of its main training centres, all this fed into my thoughts on the public and of course the media, knee-bending to the government in matters of national security. In such dramatic situations an unthinking public is putty in their hands. The farce was epitomized in the response of a Fox news commentator who in his starry and striped excitement at the discovery of some rusty cans in the Iraqi desert exclaimed triumphantly 'Game, set and match!'

The trip produced a long-sought-after new editor for *Inquiry*. A junior faculty's questions after my talk back in 1994 had sounded endearingly as though he knew what I was trying to say. Now, nine years on, I asked Wayne Martin to lunch at the UCSD Faculty Club to sound him out on this matter. He seemed not uninterested and to my relief wrote some weeks later to state the terms on which he could accept the offer. These I forwarded to the publishers, who were forthcoming. The UCSD department provided what for me would have been undreamed of benefits and in the ten years of his editorship, latterly based in the University of Essex, the journal I had worked on alone for more than forty years came into its professional own. It was a satisfactory outcome of a history that began haltingly in 1958 in a sordid Earls Court basement in the early 'sixties after Peter Frøstrup had sent me some proofs that he doubted would arouse much interest.

Memorable on a more personal plane during that same visit was a dinner given by Malcolm Wiener, historian of Mediterranean culture, former investment banker and, not unconnectedly, philanthropist. I had met him earlier at a dinner given by Marianne, where my intellectually better schooled but ill-mannered colleagues did little to hide their sense of superiority. Being rich, Wiener must be an amateur; being essentially that myself, I was on his side. A GI in the Pacific, he had worked his way up. I discovered he was also a good friend of Brit's Greek colleague Nanno Marinatos. Wiener's elegant, fragile and highly educated New York wife was there too, as also in amusing contrast an affable and easy-going Gerald Edelmann. He had shared a Nobel prize in 1972 for work on the immune system but was also author of a widely read book on consciousness, *Bright Air, Brilliant Fire: On the Matter of the Mind*. Marianne's former chef Michael prepared the meal, a matter neither of treason nor theft she assured me. Michael's demands for his services didn't always fit in with Marianne's plans and he had left with something close to her blessing.

Autumn 2004 took me to a meeting of the American Academy of Religion in San Antonio, Texas. The invitation was occasioned by two recently published Kierkegaard biographies, my own and Joakim Garff's. Both of us were panellists at a session called 'Kierkegaard: A Life of Writing'. Although there was refreshment in the new surroundings, amenities and meeting with colleagues, with little enthusiasm for the discussion, with my own biography mentally archived, I had little to offer. With his usual elegance, Joakim offered a presentation that far outshone mine., while a discerning paper by Ed Mooney, comparing or rather contrasting our biographies, outshone both.

February 2005 saw the sale of the house in Oslo. Its replacement was to be an apartment in Sandefjord at the head of a fjord just outside the Oslofjord itself, but it wouldn't be ready until the end of March. With nowhere to stay we made yet another trip to Greece. From Kiel we looked for a route that would take us more directly to Trieste, so we drove via Potsdam to Dresden. Then via Prague to Trieste in time, we thought, to book on the ferry, only to discover that it departed now from Venice. We raced to Venice, arriving at the quayside just as they were completing loading. The ship's first officer took charge of our passports and, in the typically innovative and effective Greek *ad hoc* manner, the car was slotted into the last available space. We bought tickets, retrieved our passports, and settled down for a voyage that began with a view of the Piazza San Marco from the Canal Grande, possible only from the elevation of a sizable ship and disembarked the next morning at Igoumenitsa on the Adriatic coast. From there we drove through Byron country, admiring *en route* his statue at Missolonghi, or Mesolongi, where he died in 1824 it is said of blood poisoning. We reached the British School in Athens in the evening and there, in its stately house within a walled garden, were provided with a comfortably spacious room.

Although her good humour failed to conceal that she was drinking and smoking too much, living just a short distance away Maria gallantly walked up the steep hill to join us at a restaurant of her own choosing. I escorted her to a Maria Callas Song Competition. The tobacco on her breath was overpowering, but in soul and spirit this was still the Maria I first met in 1951 and whose embrace had made me hungry for other places. In 1997 she had sent me a copy of a book she had written on her father's life, with the message: 'To my life-time friend ...'.

On the road to the ferry in Patras there was a phone call. Brit's mother had died. We had celebrated her ninetieth birthday at a care home eighteen months earlier. On disembarking in Venice we drove to the airport and found a flight to Oslo for Brit. Overnighting first in Salzburg I continued on to Hamburg, reaching there by late afternoon to have dinner with Jane and Jens. On the following evening I was on the way to Oslo by overnight ferry from Kiel. From there I dashed to the Boat Show at nearby Lillestrøm to see a boat on display. It was mine. In Horten, down the fjord, I found Brit the same day preparing for her mother's funeral. Just before that we moved into our apartment on a pier in Sandefjord's inner harbour. There was a berth there for the boat.

It had been in late summer the year before, the 5th of September 2004 to be exact, a Sunday and before the Oslo house was sold. Brit and I chose to fill the day with an outing to a boat show nearby Sandvika. Among the gleaming white fibreglass yachts over which potential buyers with their children and lonely dreamers swarmed was an almost deserted jetty with just a small wooden dinghy on show. I got talking with the two in attendance and mentioned that in my youth I had once daydreamed of owning a Nordic Folkboat. One of the two said he owned one. Within twenty minutes the discussion had ended with a contract. Ole Jacob Broch, owner of Risør Trebåtbyggeri AS, would be happy to build one ready to sail the next season. He gave me his card, also appropriately wooden. After successive winter telephone calls in which we agreed to a series of refinements, teak decks, inboard engine and more, the boat was duly completed. *Amaryllis* may have become the most expensive Nordic Folkboat ever built.

Building Amaryllis, Risør Trebåtbyggeri, 2005. Photo Ole-Jacob Broch.

There is symbolism here. These chapters have been framed in the imagery of a ship with its keel already laid. The lives of those on board were coloured and even shaped by what the keel itself decreed before they came on deck. But here was a keel being laid to specifications of my own choice. Was this just a geriatric version of all those dreams that periodically offered unreal alternatives to dispiriting corners that a ready-made keel had once led me to? Well, here was one that at least was going to be tested, the dream put to the test, not, though, as an alternative way or walk of life. What a spell at sea offers is a chance to live very close to nature. True, it is a temporary escape from what the disillusioned raconteur in Tolstoy's *The Kreutzer Sonata*[12] calls the 'hollow sham' of a life filled too willingly with social commitments. But then any idea of escaping the social tsunami by making a life on your own either at sea, in the woods, or on a desert island would be an equally hollow sham, an exercise in loneliness at best and at worst a self-centred test of one's survival skills.

The start of Amaryllis's maiden voyage, Risør, July 2005.
Photo Ole-Jacob Broch

That fair nymph Amaryllis was named after the savage flowering plant which according to the myth, when it sprang from her heart, secured her a shepherd's love. The flower's own name comes from the Greek to 'sparkle'. Her fresh varnish sparkling brightly in the sun, and with Brit performing the champagne ceremony, *Amaryllis* was launched at Risør on July the 3rd 2005 at around one-o'clock in the afternoon. Strawberries and more champagne followed for all responsible and friends. Some days later, retrieving what maritime abilities were still to be called upon, I took *Amaryllis* on her maiden voyage to the new homeport Sandefjord. In the variable winds it took eleven hours and it was after midnight that we finally berthed. In the warm summer twilight neighbours were still sitting on their balconies and could greet our arrival. Unfamiliar then with the intricacies of the fjord, I had followed the large ferry from Sweden into the inner harbour, confident that where it went, we could too.

The same might be said of *Amaryllis*. The last verse of a song by the Swedish poet and songwriter Carl Michael Bellman begins: 'Get up, *Amaryllis*, wake up my darling' and suitably mistranslated continues:

> Step on board then, both we sing!
> With love in command of our quest.
> Let Zephyr bestir,
> Yet should storm occur,
>   in your hull secure,
>   lies my trust.
> Happily over the angry brine
>   in your quiet embrace I can but opine
>   how in death my heart will follow thine.
> Sing, sirens, be my ventriloquist!

Chapter Twenty-one: Signing off

Signing off: '[t]he days leading up to sign off consist of sleepless nights, relentless packing and a constant state of euphoria! After all, only a seaman can understand what it is to be going home after a long and tedious stint at sea.'
Shilavadra Bhattacharjee, Marine Safety.

It is soon sixty years since I arrived in Norway for a short spell abroad to complete a doctoral dissertation. That bane of so many lives was for mine a cancerous growth that took over the steering and led to a career in philosophy – an episodic interest that afflicted me one dull and lonely weekend in Bradford back in 1956 and became cemented through the unresolved ambiguity of my father's silence when, just an hour before he died, I told him of my plan. From then on, the least I could do was see what job I could make of it.

Then already twenty-four and now approaching eighty-eight, the question 'Why philosophy?' still lacks a clear answer. My mind-stretching grandmother's reservations about Reason have stayed with me. I tend to think Kant was right in seeing Reason best employed in arriving at rational conclusions on its own limits. As for what can interest us beyond these, and that can be much or little, the rational as well as moral and not least democratic thing to do is tread carefully, and that means honestly and, in the interests of others, on one's own account. As Kierkegaard would say, there is no other 'authority'.

Once seriously occupied with Kierkegaard, I welcomed the chance to become better acquainted with a writer responsive to questions arising inside the front door. It would be nice to believe that translating that extraordinary writer is to make him available for others to raise his questions for themselves but, if not entirely selfish, the actual motives are more self-centred. Having in recent years published several articles and translations, as well as a new and shorter biography, I feel it has been more to prove to *myself* that I am still alive than to broadcast that fact to others. Keeping failing faculties busy is a kind of therapy with clear pathological undertones. When looking at yourself in the face a respectable *curriculum vitae* means nothing more than work done that might have been done better or, in other circumstances, better not done at all. I have never felt at home in academia, but whether gate-crasher, infiltrator or stowaway I have nevertheless found my way about. Some blurb writers describe me as a 'Kierkegaard scholar'. I have even read that I am the 'doyen' among these scholars. Not a few Americans and several Danes will shake their heads at that, even their fists. Comments of editors and reviewers have made their doubts clear. An editor responding to one submission wrote of my 'freewheeling interpretations' and complained that instead of providing arguments to 'hammered' conclusions, my writing led only to 'points of view'. Having accepted previous submissions with only tentative comments, that same editor now felt compelled to inform me that his advisory readers had made 'this sort of criticism' of my style all along. The detailed comments he now passed on to me followed, so he assured me, a 'close, serious and friendly read' by some of my 'most trusted colleagues'. I looked through them but, preoccupied as I was with a biography at the time, chose to withdraw the paper, not out of pique I hope, but realizing I was a misfit in Bob Perkins' excellent and thoroughly scholarly *Kierkegaard International Commentary*.

It is perhaps no accident that my closest associates and shorter term or lasting friends have been outsiders. Their reputations are due as much to conspicuous eccentricity as to their reputations as thinkers. Whether or not they would like to be remembered in this way I can hardly avoid mentioning Ted Honderich, who arrived challengingly on the London scene in the late 1950s just as I was getting started, and Timothy Sprigge whose unfashionable views presented with professional articulacy encouraged me to keep going. Arthur Cody needled me as he did most other philosophers by showing what they left out or took for granted. Also in California, there were encouraging chats with the anarchistic Paul Feyerabend. The Berkeley chair tried hard to fire him for giving all his students straight A's and occasionally letting them give his lectures. Early on in Norway, I had the advantage of close encounters with two unusual philosophers at constant loggerheads, Hans Skjervheim and Arne Naess.

Kierkegaard, too, came as an accidental saviour. He sounded like a radical whose startling titles might be read alongside the currently fashionable French philosophers. Or Nietzsche? John Macmurray in his Junior Honours course in modern philosophy classified Kierkegaard as 'dialectical', bracketing him in this way with Hegel and Marx. These were presented as an interrelated trio that seemed straightaway to invite some higher-level dialectical thought. By putting historical legs onto Hegel's 'idea', Marx was already said to have turned Hegel on his head. Why not add that Kierkegaard's moral psychology turned the thoughts of both these thinkers outside-in? Here, too, and even in the USA, I found collegial support and friendship. There was Gordon Marino with his journalistic flair and personal sense of Kierkegaard's worries, and Bruce Kirmmse whose historical perspective brought them back to base. All this may explain the 'freewheeling interpretations' and why scholarly attention to detail has taken second place to 'points of view'.

Actual translation nevertheless brings you face to face with quite a lot of detail. On a late and brief visit to Athens I tried my hand at a large new dose. We had rented a coastal apartment from Brit's friend Nanno, now teaching in Chicago. With no deadlines in sight I tried a few of the five-hundred-and-seventy-pages of Kierkegaard's *Avsluttende uvidenskabelig Efterskrift* or *Concluding Unscientific Postscript*. The thought was that a revision of the original Swenson and Lowrie translation might capture the work's sparkle and wit better than the academically correct Hong version, now the preferred scholarly reference. When the more ambitious idea of a whole new translation took over, I asked Penguin if they might consider adding it to their list. When the new Classics editor proved unenthusiastic (the last effort, *A Literary Review*, was a relative flop), I sent a proposal to Cambridge and was offered a contract subject to acceptance of the completion by the editors of the Texts in the History of Philosophy series. They did accept it, but not before there was a reminder of those reservations about my work. A reviewer of my translation for the Press proved to be one of those 'most trusted colleagues' who a few years earlier had complained of my style. Here he told the editor that although I was a good enough translator, as a philosopher my thinking was unclear, implying that a better one should be entrusted with the editing and introduction. The hint that he himself would be happy to help was not hard to catch. The same reviewer had previously stepped in to edit an earlier Kierkegaard translation when their original choice had died. Whether through a slip or by friendly intent, the editor passed on his comment. When I remarked on it, she said this was not how *they* saw me.

Time is getting short and there are other authors to read as well as other ways to write and topics to write about. I recall my father's insistence that people find or be found the occupations that help them best to develop their constructive abilities. With a keen eye for inefficiency due to personal frustration and discomfiture, he himself persuaded employees where necessary and possible to change jobs. In my case, it took a long time as well as an unlikely chain of accidents to find an activity that suited the shape of my mind. Given another few years I may try my hand at something else. I have in fact just published a novella. Beatrix Potter, the first author known to me by name, is quoted as saying that to write a book is to start with a sentence without knowing where it will lead. In real life it can take a lifetime to find that sentence.

History and biography have much in common. The Hegelian-Marxist view is that history is a time of conflict that ends when harmony is reached. Paradise Regained. Others see history as beginning when the struggle is over and humanity has a fair chance of making its own. To revert to the vanishingly parochial and 'selfish' viewpoint of the single person we all individually share, my own history could be seen in either way. If in the latter, then the story proper is little more than as in the preceding chapters: a record of these further itineraries, meetings, some not unwelcome recognition here and there, before it all fades, not into history of course – except in the statistically microscopic role of shaker and mover the individual escapes its radar – but into that great impersonal and impenetrable container that makes up the real past. By dint of stories memorable enough to be shared through generations, history in the grand sense supervenes superficially on the reality that is every individual's struggle, great or small, to live a life, a contest that develops and dies with each.

My guess is that most have neither the opportunity nor the desire to go over it again. It would require a touch of masochism, unless of course the past is approached as a place of refuge from a rapidly diminishing future. But given the opportunity to recover things that mattered when there was too little time for what really mattered to register, writing a memoir can be one way of doing better justice to the past. Re-inserting one's presence into a past can be an opportunity to cook the books. That is a chance one takes, but a measured because less engaged assessment of the part one has played in the lives of others is also made possible.

In a life's long run gains and losses should be measured not by achievement or even legacy but by the way others have been treated. Has a life led together with others, especially closely, helped them at all or been too much in their way? Recollections of the kind gathered here and which have occupied me a good part of the last years are a kind of accountancy that tries to do better than just cook the books in the writer's favour. Sometimes I have wondered, am I a bad lot? At others I have asked, just how bad? When the answer threatens to be unwelcome, I may be tempted to reach towards my friend and colleague Ted Honderich's determinism: there are no might-have-beens. Envisaging alternative outcomes works only if you think you have made a mistake or missed an opportunity. But what if there were such alternatives? What opportunities have been missed for making some sacrifice? Has this been ego-tripping all along?

Chaos theory talks of widely diverging outcomes of small initial differences. Life may appear to go in the opposite direction: things at first apparently forever disconnected come together in the end. From as far back as I can remember accidents of place and time have at least framed my own life. Here are some.

When I was thirteen in Carlisle, to local chagrin a young Norwegian naval officer had gone off with a more than pretty young woman whose home was just a hundred yards from our own. In the mid-1970s I was living in Oslo divorced from my first wife and renting the apartment of the lady I would later marry. At the corner of the same building, where Bygdøy Allée and Erling Skjalgssonsgate meet was a small mini-market run by a friendly Dane called not unusually 'Hansen'. I went down to Hansen every day to buy what I needed. A refined grey-haired man who also seemed alone did likewise. The shop being very small we sometimes literally bumped into each other. After several near encounters, we got chatting. He too was divorced and lived by himself in an apartment opposite. Retired from the navy he had been director of the famous *Christian Radich*, a training ship that has won cups in the Tall Ships and was the star of *Windjammer*, the only film shot in widescreen Cinemiracle. He introduced himself. Not long after, I was celebrating a first night with my wife-to-be, together with some of her colleagues one of whom spoke such good English that I asked him if he'd ever been in the UK. He said, 'You've probably never been there', he said, 'but I used to visit a small town in the north of England called Carlisle'. He was a well-known actor and it dawned on me that the man I had bumped into was the now retired Commander whose wife had been that pretty young woman. Later still I found out that the actor's grandmother was born in the very house we lived in just after the war.

Such coincidences, even when unlooked for, are little more than curiosities. I recently discovered that the surrender of German forces in Norway in May 1945 was signed in the large mansion near Edinburgh where I had spent my first unremembered year. These historical accidents don't mean much, but by drawing the many more or less random sub-plots of a seemingly messy life into a novelistic whole they can provide a kind of frame. A year ago, the gods sent me another of their whimsies. I was asked by the editor of a Catholic periodical to write a review of a new biography of Kierkegaard. The author's surname was Carlisle and on further correspondence it turned out that, like mine, the editor's school days had been in the city of that name.

The tramp steamer image appeals because it allows that what may start badly can take a turn or twist for the better. Shortcomings may even become one's saving grace and, given a chance, the deficiency turned to advantage. When there is no set course, the bets are open and the result subject more than otherwise to the whimsies of fate. If it turns out well you should thank the gods as much as yourself. I mentioned the lucky chance that provided me with an academic career, that handwritten paper my teacher in Edinburgh slipped to me at a party he gave to his class. If it hadn't provided the end and the means of my dissertation, who knows what the outcome would have been?

However much or little good or bad luck have had a hand in the outcome, I share a world with those who at one time or another became part of mine. An irony of the situation, an anomaly that deserves investigation, is that two of those who I unthinkingly thought of as friends ceased in the one case to act like one and in the other twice gave me formal notice that he was no longer my friend. Both were men and we ended up friends again though not quite the same ones.

Despite such entrances and exits, there is a strong sense of having been aboard the same ship all along, fate and failure appropriately logged as these variations were recorded in the biographical equivalent of the ship's barometer. There is even a sense of having been set on course, occasionally even of being a stowaway, or even shanghaied, with attendant discomforts and only a rough notion of a ship with compass course already set.

Though understandable at the time, and I am fairly sure owing to a form of alienation that was itself the result of a combination of circumstance, upbringing and native disposition, choosing philosophy was very likely a mistake. For me, that is to say. With no natural facility in its ways, I had to learn by imitation: 'hear, mark, learn and inwardly digest' was my motto. The student advisor's 'Are You mad?' when I said I planned to 'do' philosophy still rings in my ears. Himself a philosopher and not long back from the war, I can see why he should find peace of mind in searching the minds of an Aristotle and a Kant. I won't go so far as to say being crazy helps, though some of philosophy's superstars might make you thinks so. Maybe philosophy should be practiced nearer the market place and not in the catacombs of the past, or confined to campuses where it morphs so easily into a kind of superior career option. In any case, staying with it in my case required effort and some hardship. But, as suggested, such persistence may also, at a deeper level, be a sign of weakness of character, pretending the time hasn't come to stop.

Of this I am not the best judge, but signs of an unusually weak ego are hard to explain away, such as it requiring effort on my part not to walk in step with others even when, as so often, they themselves are quite a lot shorter than myself. Movies have always had a strong influence: the hero or tragic victim on screen can take possession of me as of a vacant lot. But I am soon back to vacancy. A friend and colleague once chided me for being too conciliatory, something he most decidedly is not. If he thinks it is a matter of not standing firm on my opinions, or even lacking any firm enough to stand on, I see it differently as a form of on-course impatience. I say 'right' just to let things ride while continuing on my way. A lady friend featured earlier once said that Bente had warned her that I was a workaholic, hated children, and liked to be alone. She would agree with the last of these but says the conversation never took place. The case for the prosecution rests.

Long ago another friend, close at the time and still both clear and dear in memory, and with her powers of observation supplemented by Eastern wisdom, compared me to cotton wool: easily plucked apart in its natural state but tight as a rope when twisted. When it comes to touchiness and less than admirable reactions to insult, even faint criticism, the justice of the analogy will be evident in my case as in that of many others. Philosophers, who should be wise, tend paradoxically to be among the least immune. Perhaps it is because outside the protective netting of logic there is less to be collectively agreed upon. Where there are no standard indices of success in what you aim to achieve and anything worthwhile in the endeavour requires long-term concentration and focus, resistance to ego-threatening pressure is essential. Conciliation must stop and some noise-cancelling device activated to ensure that behind the scenes something like a voyage is being undertaken and that the ship is still on course.

But now the tramping is over and the vessel is at anchor. Its stowaway has become a homesteading landlubber with some stories to tell. Or an eighty-eight-year-old ship has been hauled up on dryland with its cargo of memories still largely intact.

La Lydia, since *1967* a deliberately stranded casino and tourist attraction at Le Barcarés in the Pyrenées-Orientales (Northern Catalonia): originally MV Moonta, built Denmark *1931*, fairly close to my own origin.

Epi-log: 'When the long trick's over'

Trick: A period of time spent at the wheel.

Sea Fever, John Masefield.

The pier in Sandefjord's inner harbour became home for a decade. An added rural anchorage was acquired in the form of a small cabin half an hour's drive inland. It was Brit's answer to my *Amaryllis*. Here I was crew and woodchopper. There could be storms on dryland too and Brit knew better than I how to cope with them. One spot of weather stands out: Lacking any alternative in town, skateboarders found the stretch of pier outside my working space excellently suited to their noisy acrobatics. Having spoken to their leaders in vain and opting for a non-violent solution, I proposed lying in their path, a provocation that would be just another form of violence. Brit had a better idea: she invited them in for tea and cakes. With some friendly chat, high fives, and some routine runs to show it was their own choice, the skaters left and negotiations with the town led soon to a professional skating park out of earshot.

Hvitsten today, our former house now painted white half visible in the foreground.

For nine summers *Amaryllis*, berthed just below our balcony, was ready for short recreational spells out into the Skagerrak and back. No weekends to islands. But for five of those years the winter lay-up was forty-eight nautical miles down the coast. She plied that distance nine times., the third of which is recorded in our pro-log. As on three other occasions that was a single-handed venture. I was joined on two by Brit and once each by my son Jo and the boat's builder Ole Jacob with Alice his partner.

Seven years ago we bought a small apartment at Cap Coudalère on the coast just north of Perpignan with the easterly Pyrenees forming a backcloth and the Mediterranean a ten-minutes bike-ride away. The expansive Étang de Leucate, a saltwater inland lake with connections to the sea, was at the backdoor. Here were wind and waves enough to remind us of how it is to be afloat, but the time had come to put the sea in a frame. Much has happened in the last fifteen years, some of it regrettable, most of it inevitable. There was a heart attack and also a perilous drive from the south of France on a bleeding stomach ulcer with 'two days to go' on arrival according to the doctor. There were disabilities due to several falls on the winter ice. Brit picked up a serious illness visiting Naples. Both of us are showing signs of wear. I have been awarded a pacemaker (it goes roughly where you might pin a medal).

Otherwise history as conflict seems to have ended. Life is being lived normally towards its end. As confirmation, the last two decades have encompassed the fifteen-year life span of Dennis, a companionable cat who came our way. After looking at the furniture and sampling the refrigerator, he chose us as the solution to his own history. On two summers we joined a group of Brit's ethnological friends aboard *Solrik*, a schooner skippered by a proper sailor, Ben Brynhildsen. *Amaryllis*, in exchange for a Norwegian crown and a bottle of aquavit, is now in his caring and capable hands. Wooden boats uncared for go rapidly to ruin, but if cared for can last forever. A photo showing Ben's grandson at the tiller prompts the thought that good memories are as good a legacy to pass on as a well-kept boat, in some ways better. Leaves break down into mould and contribute to the next year of growth, which is some kind of legacy, but for us the continuity in generations is in minds and selves, and the latter are secured if at all by those vulnerable links called 'parents', something we all have and most of us are. Given the conditions of human survival, life's problems largely centre on that link.

Disturbing thoughts of this kind occupied me on my last voyage. It began on at 15.30 hours on 27 May, 2015, on a sunny afternoon at Framnaes Maritime Senter, Sandefjord.

*

> *Amaryllis* and I are presently bound for a berth at an old heritage-protected boatyard. Holmen Yachtvaerft lies in the inner Oslo fjord about seventy-five land or sixty-five nautical miles north of Sandefjord though as the crow flies ten

shorter. The two of us set out last week once the mast had been stepped and the rigging set up. A fresh southerly was blowing with waves of one and half metre. There was just enough west in the wind to take us to the southern end of the fjord on one tack. Turning north, with the wind more comfortably aft, there were small islands with exotic geology to take in. At 14.40 we were off Tønsberg Tønne, an ancient seamark at the southern tip of Østerøya at the mouth of Tønsberg fjord. It warns of shallows and sometimes dangerously steep seas. Today wave and wind are going amiably in our direction. At 18.00 we are at a safe anchorage at Engø, a secluded bay only ten minutes' drive from Sandefjord. The fjords cut deep into the land and make the sea passage much longer. That night, secured to the seabed by anchor, free of nail-biting shore attachments and with the natural sedative of water rippling gently against the sound-box of a wooden hull, a sense of some stable point having at last been reached begins to take hold.

But no, you sleep well but there comes another day, in this case one in which a mutiny in the skipper's inner arrangements would lead him to postpone the final lap to that new home.

At 05.00 it is overcast and darker than usual for this time of year. But after early breakfast we are away, or is it (anchors) 'a weigh'? At seven the light southerly begins to freshen. There are narrow passages to navigate before entering the broad outer Oslofjord. After five hours at sea, the last two in excessive rain, I am cold and wet and unable to relieve myself of a surfeit of Coca-Cola. Sailing through a line of tankers waiting to unload at the refinery feeding Oslo's faraway airport, then heading inside Bastøy, an island prison described by Michael Moore on television as laughably unlike Alcatraz, at 10.30 I check in at Horten's guest harbour. It is Brit's hometown, and until 1963 Norway's naval base on the west side about halfway up the Oslofjord. I phone her, and then her nearby physician daughter to arrange an appointment at the local Emergency. After some anxious and increasingly unpleasant waiting, I am efficiently fixed up with a catheter by a nurse and a young lady doctor, both very sympathetic to my plight. I breathe several deep sighs of relief. The doctor tells me I was stupid to be sailing alone.

I was and the thought of this trip had been troubling me for some time. I would wake up at four in the morning thinking of what increasingly impossible physical feats might be called for. Three weeks ago, going down on my knees at an Oslo supermarket to pick up a dropped coin, I had to be helped up again by two kind old ladies. Selling the boat or having it transported by road suddenly seemed better ideas – or, yes, well, having someone lend a hand. But no, whatever weakness of character lies behind such obstinacy, it's too late now.

A night's rest in Horten's Best Western might have been enough and a catheter can be quite useful for the solo sailor. How do professional cyclists manage? But frailty and good sense took the upper hand: the final stage was postponed until bodily functions returned to normal.

A week later they did. I was at sea again and 'enjoying' a fresh southwester. With the course close to due north, that was convenient. Chilly for June, but on this early summer morning we were again on course, and what a privilege to have the wide expanse of the outer Oslo Fjord to oneself at this time of day! Well, not quite to oneself, two widely separated fishing boats are exploiting the midfjord shallows. Their drift is however so slow that they tend to blend with the seascape. Otherwise, seen from the solipsistic eye of a small wooden sailing boat, it is a large surround of sea, not a seascape exactly when you are part of it. A true landscape frames the expanse on three sides. To starboard the low Østfold [East and West Fjord. 'Fold' or 'Foldin' in old Norwegian is used in giving the name of a fjord.] coastline tapers down southward to the Swedish coast, to the east Sweden is just a short distance inland. Ahead to port I can see Vestfold's more dramatic profile. A string of islands to the south disappears into the Skagerrak. Skagen on Denmark's northern tip is a good day's sailing away.

Yesterday the Horten Harbour Authority phoned to say a savage wind had broken the boom and there had been 'material damage'. On rounding the corner from the bus station and looking down towards the harbour, I looked anxiously to see how much. The boom and awning were resting on deck like a bird's broken wing, but it was the boom crutch that had succumbed to the wind's battering against the awning. I fixed things, unwound the extra warps that had been expertly provided by the crew's cousin while the storm raged, and reported the boat's departure to the harbour office. The wind still fresh, it had taken me an hour to arrange warps that could be slipped from the cockpit once the engine was started.

Normally, when the task is to take a boat where you are bound, or more truthfully have it take you, the view takes second place. It changes as you go; most often you would rather it changed more quickly. Those headlands seem interminably distant until, having resigned yourself to the slowness of sea travel, they are suddenly there. When new to you, and weather permitting, you may pause to take it all in, but through the years the many glimpses of these coasts from the upper decks of large ferries to Copenhagen and Kiel have made it all familiar. Yet it is quite different when close to the surface as when, back in 1957, five sailing friends from Scotland headed towards an unknown Oslo on a three-weeks' adventure. The unfamiliar coast and a hinterland then invoked romantic pictures of a legendary country of mountains and fjords beyond. Today, the skyline on the port side shadows a coast-wise railway that the skipper had travelled many times between Sandefjord and Oslo. Today he got off the train at Holmestrand before catching a bus.

Just an hour after casting off he was back in the past. Below the lower end of the narrow neck dividing the outer and inner Oslo fjords is Son, once the port of call for goods to Oslo. Further up the fjord there tended to be too little wind. Bente now has a summerhouse there. There is promise of a visit when that season returns. In the channel above the narrow neck lies Hvitsten. Joanne made a home there and it is where Jo spent his early childhood. With two spells abroad the small family lived there for seven years. It was where either an endemic obstinacy or existential panic, or both, finally helped the immigrant to finish the dissertation whose projected existence had brought him to Norway eight years earlier.

Close by 'White Rock City' it seems that the new owners have replaced with three old-style, many-paned windows the two large modern ones I bought in Oslo and were installed by our carpenter neighbour. They may be more in keeping with the character of the house but the big windows had offered a fine view over the fjord to the opposite shore. Instead of rustic red, the house is now regulation white. Let it go, it looks good. Another hour of peaceful sailing up the sheltered strait takes us to Drøbak (Steep Hill), the shore-side town where one wintry day Jo, now 54, was born. The building no longer a maternity home is still there.

The wind whips up and changes direction. Memories fond and otherwise are brushed aside; navigation, always critical at this narrowest part of the fjord, becomes a matter of focus and detail. There is little traffic, nor does the German heavy cruiser *Blücher* pose a threat. That once pride of Hitler's fleet lies several fathoms deep, sunk on April the 9th 1940 by a primitive gun from a nearby island battery. Two buoys mark the bow and stern. There is at least some traffic. An ultra-modern, round-the-world Volvo-trophy-type sailing boat, or machine, the kind with a deep fin keel, a large steering wheel, even two side by side, and multi-coloured Dacron sails, and a large crew sitting up as if sailing a dinghy, it speeds towards Oslo. She heels elegantly in the squalls, accelerating like a sports car, while we plod on under foresail and motor. In a small boat like this, lowering and stowing the mainsail in a wind is difficult enough even with assistance. As the elegant state-of-the-art sailing machine swiftly disappears into the open fjord ahead, *Amaryllis* holds a steady course past the long group of islands that lead into the wide-open space that is inner Oslo Fjord.

Spray is blowing off the waves, the surface is messy and along with it the sense of well-being. With the sun occasionally relieving the chill, I try to concentrate on finding the destination behind the hard-to-separate cluster of islands hugging the northwest shore. The chart has to be held firmly in hand as well as the tiller. The coast looks too uniform from this distance to be able to pick out the inlet I know only from the shore. Where is the GPS? It was below to pick up when needed, but in this wind, and with other boats in the vicinity, I can hardly spend time rummaging around in the cabin. In a moment of desperation, I bind the tiller and try a couple of times but still cannot find it. Tiring, I begin to sense prophecy in those early morning nerves. Sipping coke every five minutes helps and a small can of mackerel in tomato sauce, but with no cutlery or plate to hand there is enough mackerel left on my jacket to make it look as if I'd been sick. To avoid the disgrace should someone see it, I wipe off as much as I can.

Food works wonders. I furl the foresail and find a gap between two islands. There in the distance is a recognizable civic building not far from the where the yard should lie. I motor into a lagoon formed by the meeting of three islands and, exploiting the shelter, stop the engine to make one more attempt at finding the GPS. There it is, hiding in a corner. Consultation tells me I am on the east side of an island that should be lying east of me. I call the land-based crew waiting to receive me, saying I should make port within half an hour. The chart shows two short cuts to the other side of the island, one on the north side, the other on the south. I try the first and nearest, only to run gently aground just after catching sight of an overhead warp marking that the channel is blocked. Breaking free in full reverse, with much relief, I look for the southern channel. It turns out to be a famous creek visited by numerous boats on midsummer night. It is navigable.

But there is more. Wrongly locating the boatyard on the chart in spite of it looking exactly as it should, he sails on past. The mind is suffering or 'softening' is perhaps the better word. On the wrong side of yet another island, an exceedingly small one in the middle of the channel, he again runs aground. A man polishing a plastic motorboat at a pier at the end of his garden looks on in disregard or more likely plain disgust. He says something the skipper is glad not to hear and keeps on polishing. Two younger men of a more Samaritan turn see the skipper's plight and try towing *Amaryllis* off by the stern. Their motor is too weak, their boat too small. They suggest calling the sea rescue service. What shame when so near home! No sir! Instead, the skipper calls the crew, who finds help in the shape of an Italian and a Lithuanian, aliens like himself, yard employees who smile and are happy to be of assistance. As they near, and without their help, with engine in gentle reverse, the skipper's weight heeling the boat from a shroud, *Amaryllis* slides gracefully off. Within five minutes she is moored at the appointed berth.

May 2015

Many mistakes, some worrying moments, a portion of luck – or is there providence? Now five years on, it is a year since my brother Ian, a far more seasoned sailor than I, went on his final voyage. He had not been aboard a year earlier when his schooner hit a reef off Guernsey and sank within minutes. With no time to don lifebelts, the Polish crew of four were swept out by the fierce tide. Three were picked up a mile away by a rescue boat that happened to be on exercise. Alerted by someone on the shore, an off-duty lifeboatman who happened to be tending his boat went out and picked up the fourth.

In July last year my younger sister died. We had good contact. The question now is not 'why am I here?' but 'why am *I* here?'

The trick's over. Time to go below.

6 May 2020

Below deck recovery

Once upon a time, with my brother and two sisters, we could all be collected in a barrow. But not unusually we went our ways and the next generation went theirs. In a world that makes dispersion a norm the reverse process is no great problem. There has been one-by-one re-uniting over the years, but funerals are a special kind of reversal, a resurrection of sorts. My elder sister Mariot Lothian's death in 2003 brought together cousins, nieces and nephews from all corners of the UK. When my brother Ian died a year ago, the catchment area included Germany, Japan, Norway, Poland, Scotland and the USA. They were to meet just two months later in Hamburg. After ten years with Parkinson's disease, Jane Wiebel, my younger sister by six years, died there in July. Both occasions saw a family resurrected in celebration of the lives of those gone but one that also returned them to the context of their living origins.

Inevitably, any memoir, not least this one, can look like an exercise in gross egocentricity. But as was made clear at the beginning, the aim here has been the quite personal one of charting the details of a route that led me to Norway and the circumstances that kept me there. It has allowed me to freeze in order to re-live moments that were swamped too quickly by what came next. Any interest it has for others is not my concern, except perhaps as an attempt to reassure my

Hamburg, Jo with his cousin Tessa Wulff Lothian

... and with his uncle, Jens Wiebel

relatives and some friends on several points. Apart from the therapy of writing itself, which fills time when duty no longer calls, there is the satisfaction of fixing in memory all those who have played a part in my life, big and small. They are very many, whatever they might think or recall of my part in theirs. Many are no longer here, but they too would have had their stories to tell — with all due egocentricity. Those most closely bereaved have their own stories of a sorrow only briefly relieved in these moments of collective remembrance. But especially when a life has been allowed to run its full course, these moments too are occasions worth coming back to in a spirit of good cheer.

References

1 The Rev. W. T. Cairns, D.D., quoted in R. L. Mackie (ed.), *The Letters of James the Fourth 1505-1513*, Calendered by Robert Kerr Hannay, LLD, Edinburgh: T. and A. Constable, 1953, p. xi.
2 Janet Teissier du Cros, *Cross Currents: A Childhood in Scotland*, Tuckwell, 1977, pp. 120 and 124.
3 Ted Honderich, *Philosopher: A Kind of Life,* London: Routledge, 2000, p. 92.
4 Peter Cave, https.://www.ucl.ac.uk/philosophy/alumni/john-watling-obituary.
5 John E. Costello, *John Macmurray: A Biography*, Edinburgh: Floris Books, 2002, p. 308.
6 Cf., e.g., (Sir) Charles Sherrington, *Goethe on Nature and Science*, Cambridge: Cambridge University Press, 2nd ed. 1949, p. 12.
7 *Daily Telegraph*, 18 Sept. 2007.
8 Leicester: Matador, 2010.
9 London: Gollancz, 1966 .
10 J. Heywood Thomas and Richard Summers, 'British Kierkegaard Research: A Historical Survey', *Kierkegaardiana 15*, Copenhagen: C. A. Reitzel, p. 126.
11 George Pattison, ' "From Prophet of the Now" to Postmodern Ironist (and after)', in *Kierkegaard's International Reception*, Vol. 8, Tome 1, ed. Jon Stewart, Farnham/Burlington: Ashgate, 2009, p. 258.
12 Count Tolstoy, *The Kreutzer Sonata*, rev. trans. Ivan Lepinski, London: Greening & Co., no date, p. 140. From my grandmother's collection.

Father's and

Thomas Hannay[1] (1841-1916) m. (1865?) Elizabeth MacDowall[2] (1840-1921)
(Prof.) Robert Kerr Hannay (1867-1940)
Ann Morris Hannay (1869-1938) (m. Loam)
Peter MacDowall Hannay (1870-1943)
Dr. Mary Baird Hannay[3] (1871-1944)
John MacDowall Hannay (1872-1945)
Thomas Hannay Jr.[4] (1873-1914)
Niven Hannay (1876-1880)

(Rev.)James Stewart Wilson (1833-1910) m. (1963) Jane Ewing Brown[5] (1836-1894)
(Sir) Charles Stewart Wilson[6] (1864-1950)
Margaret ('Maggie')Wilson (1865-1950)
Jane Ewing Wilson (1868-1938) (m. Hannay)
Mary Stewart Wilson (1872-1958) (m. Brown)
Isabella Bertha Wilson (1876-1960) (m. Cullum)

Robert Kerr Hannay m. (1899) Jane Ewing Wilson

Robert Stewart Erskine Hannay (1900-1956) m. (1930) Helen O'Hagan Morton
Beatrice Mariot Hannay. (1931-2002) (m. Lothian)
Robert Alastair Hannay (b. 1932)
Ian Morton Hannay (1935-2019)
Margaret Jean (Jane) Hannay (1938-2019) (m. Wiebel)

---

1. Thomas Hannay's origins are in Galloway (Stranraer). The family's wealth had been acquired through slave-grown sugar in the West Indies and, in Thomas Hannay's time, steel at Barrow-in-Furness.
2. Elizabeth MacDowall was the third daughter of Rev. Peter MacDowall (1800-1878), once Moderator of the United Free Church of Scotland, and Mary Baird (d. 1847).
3. Mary Baird Hannay was one of the first women to graduate in medicine (MB and CM) (1886) from Glasgow University.
4. Thomas Hannay Jr. was a mining engineer and preacher in California. He died shortly after moving to West Africa. He has been claimed as the model for John Buchan's hero Richard Hannay.
5. Jane Brown was a half-sister of Dr John Brown, Scottish physician, essayist and correspondent.
6. Jane Ewing Wilson's brother (Sir) Charles Stewart Wilson was a public official in charge of postage in the Punjab.

Mother's Genealogies

Alexander Morton[7] (29 September 1844 - 28 December 1923)
    m. (7 August 1863) Jane 'Jeanie' Wiseman (21 April 1845 - 26 November 1924)
Helen 'Ellen', 'Nellie' Morton (8 May 1864-10 September 1934)
    m. (1 June 1890) Alexander Steel (18 July 1862 - 9 January 1942)
Gavin Morton (4 August 1865-1916) m. (1882) Jane Wilson
(Sir) James ('Jamie') Morton (24 March 1867-1943)
Agnes Morton (29 July 1869-1944) m. (1889) Thomas Richmond
Jane 'Jean' Morton (29 August 1871-1953)
Alexander Morton (1878-1947)
Margaret 'Maggie' Morton (1880-1940)
    m. (1910) David Shedden Service (10 January 1872-1947)
William Morton (1882-1955)
Mary Morton (1882-1956)

William Turton Fagan[8] (1831-1890) m. (1862) Emily Rowe Livermore (1836-1897)
(Sir) Patrick James Fagan[9] (1865-1942)
Brian Noel Fagan (1869-1938)
Hugh Wm. Farquharson Fagan (1872-1952)
Frank Albert Christopher Fagan (1873-1910)
Beatrice Emily Fagan (1878-1958) (m. Morton)
Theodora Mary Fagan (1878-1957)

James Morton (1867-1943) m. (1901) Beatrice Emily Fagan (1878-1958)
Guenevere (Gwennie) Fagan Morton (1903-1990)
Jean O'Hagan Morton (1905-1968) (m. Hill)
Beatrice (Bea) Fagan Morton (1908-1987) (m. Hamilton)
Helen O'Hagan Morton (1908-1995) (m. Hannay)
Alastair James Fagan Morton (1910-1963)
Jocelyn Wiseman Fagan Morton (1912-1987)

---

7. *Leaving school at nine to work as a herdsman, Alexander Morton (later known as 'Big San') was encouraged by his widowed mother to learn the weaving trade. He established factories in Darvel, Ayrshire, and later Carlisle and Donegal.*
8. *William Turton Fagan was an Anglo-Irish Major-General in the Indian Army.*
9. *(Sir) Patrick James Fagan, KCIE, CSL, FRAS was born in Bengal and worked in the Indian Civil Service, as had several generations of his Dublin-based family.*

*With Jane, Banchory, **1996** Photo source unknown*

... and with Ian, Gatehouse-of-Fleet, 2011 Photo Brit Berggreen

www.ingramcontent.com/pod-product-compliance
Lightning Source LLC
Chambersburg PA
CBHW052043220426
43663CB00012B/2426